It was truly edifying, enlightening, and a witness to my spirit to read the manuscript written by Tilly Steward. As I read through several chapters Tilly had asked me to review, I found myself praying in the spirit that the Lord would guide me to the truth of what Tilly was bringing across. As I continued to read, the Lord spoke to me, "Tilly has the faith of a child and believes everything I have written as truth. If only My church would believe as she does."

"Present truth" is what the Holy Spirit is doing right now and what the Lord is saying today. Many books today refer to Jesus as the great I WAS, whereas Tilly Steward's book reveals Jesus as the great I AM.

Thank you, Tilly Steward, for pouring your heart and spirit into your writing. I was so touched by the Lord as I read that my faith exploded. I believe many will come to the Lord because of this writing.

—Fred Palmer
President of Full Gospel Businessmen's
Fellowship International,
Gig Harbor Chapter

REVIVAL IN THE LAND

Revival in the Land

TILLY STEWARD

CREATION HOUSE
A STRANG COMPANY

Revival in the Land: Are You Ready for It? by Tilly Steward
Published by Creation House
A Strang Company
600 Rinehart Road
Lake Mary, Florida 32746
www.creationhouse.com

Unless otherwise noted, all Scripture quotations are from the King James Version of the Bible.

Scripture quotations marked NIV are from the Holy Bible, New International Version of the Bible. Copyright © 1973, 1978, 1984, International Bible Society. Used by permission.

Scripture quotations marked NKJV are from the New King James Version of the Bible. Copyright © 1979, 1980, 1982 by Thomas Nelson, Inc., publishers. Used by permission.

Scripture quotations marked The Message are from *The Message: The Bible in Contemporary English*, copyright © 1993, 1994, 1995, 1996, 2000, 2001, 2002. Used by permission of NavPress Publishing Group.

Scripture quotations marked ASV are from the American Standard Bible. Copyright © 1960, 1962, 1968, 1971, 1972, 1973, 1975, by the Lockman Foundation. Used by permission.

Scripture quotations marked TLB are from The Living Bible. Copyright © 1971. Used by permission of Tyndale House Publishers, Inc., Wheaton, IL 60189. All rights reserved.

Unless otherwise noted, all English definitions are from Victoria Neufeldt and Andrew N. Sparks, eds., *Webster's New World Dictionary, 3rd edition* (Australia: Warner Books, 1990).

The author and publisher have attempted to find every source quoted in this book. Any information found after this printing will be included during the first reprint.

Publisher's Note: The views expressed in this book are not necessarily the views held by the publisher.

Design Director: Bill Johnson
Cover design by Amanda Potter

Library of Congress Control Number: 2008939236
International Standard Book Number: 978-1-59979-533-1

First Edition

08 09 10 11 12 — 987654321
Printed in the United States of America

Contents

FOREWORD

JESUS CHRIST IS COMING soon. Christian men and women of all races must rally around the truth. God's honor is at stake. He has raised Tilly Steward up for such a time as this.

In any sport, every good signal caller understands the instructions of the head coach. He perceives, anticipates, and reacts with great precision and daring. As for the body of Christ, Tilly is that woman.

I have fellowshiped with her over many years and have watched her move by the leadership of the Holy Spirit in life's difficulties, maintaining her loyalty to her Lord and Savior with true passion and total commitment. Her message crosses all racial and cultural barriers. She has a unique way of bringing different races together for reconciliation and restoration to unity in the body of Christ. With her insight in the spirit realm, she has an eternal perspective. Tilly delivers God's vision of freedom from the slavery of false religions and denominations.

I support and trust her in the vision that God has given her to change the world of false teachings. Her love for God's Word and His people has caused her heart to burn with a godly desire that this generation would know Jesus Christ. To understand her, you will need to read and study her work carefully.

Several years ago, Tilly and I were talking about the calling that God has given her to write this spiritual masterpiece. Some time later, the Holy Spirit revealed to me that I was to tell Tilly that this book would be used in colleges and universities as a reference book to teach and enlighten the world of false religions. John 8:32 says, "And ye shall know the truth, and the truth shall make you free." Also Matthew 24:11, "And many false prophets shall rise, and shall deceive many." I admire this woman of God for being bold enough to obey God. Tilly is attuned to the Holy Spirit; her mind and heart are sensitive to the spiritual needs of humanity.

I am always moved and fascinated as I observe how she focuses on the piercing truth of God's remarkable consistency. Tilly is a strong woman of God. She will look you in the eye and point to the Word of God and its divine purpose.

I am standing with her to bring the truth to this generation. This book will set you free and fill you with vision, faith, and courageous insights that will elevate your faith to the next level in your walk with God.

—Arthur D. Harvey, DD
Senior Pastor
New Restoration Christian Ministries
Tacoma, Washington

INTRODUCTION

IN 1991 GOD REVEALED to me the following: "I have sent you two to be the leaders of your revival, but both of them have flunked. Therefore I want you to write a book, and this book will cause your revival." The "two" He spoke to me about were both from Ghana, West Africa. They stayed with me individually at different times from 1987–1991.

It was not the first time that the Holy Spirit quickened a message to my spirit and gave me a calling to fulfill it. I also knew that I had to wait for His precise timing and anointing before I could write and print this book, since I didn't have any idea what all it would contain. I said, "Whatever You want written in it, You have to bring it across my path," because I had absolutely no training. In the meantime, He allowed me numerous experiences, which I was directed to share with you in writing. When I was born again many years ago, as I was standing at the altar in church one day, I said, "Lord, use me." Since I made myself available to serve Him thirty years ago, I have never known in advance what my next assignment was. I say from experience: never fear, if God calls you, He also equips you.

In several of these chapters you will find out the exact Bible truth about some denominational beliefs, as God anointed me to bring to your understanding the requirements of our upcoming nationwide revival. It has already started in a few churches around the country, where the pastors and congregation members are open to the leading of the Holy Spirit.

A friend wanted to borrow some of my videotapes. I told her that this was an opportunity for me to visit her church and that I would bring them to the service. She mentioned that their service started at ten o'clock in the morning but that at nine o'clock a number of them would meet for intercessory prayer. I decided to go early and was surprised to see twenty-seven people praying heaven down to Earth. In the very anointed service, the pastor preached about the work of the Holy Spirit, a topic he had already been speaking on for a number of weeks. Toward the end of the service, a young lady came forward and gave a prophecy. She said that the revival in their church was beginning. I said quietly, "Lord, You told me that the revival will start in our church, and that I would be the leader of it with my book when it is finished. You said it would then go nationwide." He replied, "In the churches in which there is no hindrance to the Holy Spirit's movement, revival can and will break out now! The revival I called you to will be to the denominational churches where the Holy Spirit is not welcomed now. Although they received Him at the time of their salvation, there is no power evidenced. He lies dormant. After they read this book, you will be invited to come and teach them what the Bible says about the Holy Spirit, not their denominational doctrine, since many are deceived by Satan. Some are not even born-again; they only practice religious rituals. You will experience a worldwide revival like you've never seen before."

During the following years, God allowed me to be a so-called guinea pig, to endure many trials and situations in order to share them with you. Some of them were very painful and completely changed my life. A number of times, I had to totally trust God as my faith was tested over and over again.

Yes, God's Word, the Bible, is the absolute truth for any situation in our life from those long ago until today, as you will read in the upcoming chapters. As God spoke in the Old Testament through His prophets, so also will He use willing vessels today.

> I form the light, and create darkness: I make peace, and create evil: I the LORD do all these things.
>
> —ISAIAH 45:7

> Shall a trumpet be blown in the city, and the people not be afraid? shall there be evil in a city, and the LORD hath not done it? Surely the LORD GOD will do nothing, but he revealeth his secret unto his servants the prophets. The lion hath roared, who will not fear? the LORD GOD hath spoken, who can but prophesy?
>
> —AMOS 3:6–8

You will read of the consequences several people had to experience by being disobedient and not receiving what the Holy Spirit had me tell them. Because of it, they missed God's calling for their lives. For my total submission to the Lord, He provided a five-week trip to Israel and eleven days in Egypt in 1985 for me and eventually gave me the calling of an international evangelist, which I will describe to you later.

I firmly believe that as you read each chapter, even the wisest of you can glean some worthwhile advice.

CHAPTER 1

FACING THE FACTS

> You call Me Master and obey Me not. You call Me Light and see Me not. You call Me the Way and walk Me not. You call Me Eternal and seek Me not. You call Me Gracious and trust Me not. If I condemn you, blame Me not.[1]

EXAMINE YOURSELF AND SEE whether this applies to you. The above quote is taken from an inscription found outside a cathedral in Lubeck, Germany. It was mentioned as part of a New Year's Eve sermon preached on Christian TV several years ago. It left quite an impression on me. Some time later I discovered the following Scriptures in the Bible:

> And why call ye me, Lord, Lord, and do not the things which I say?
>
> —LUKE 6:46

> Examine yourselves, whether ye be in the faith; prove your own selves. Know ye not your own selves, how that Jesus Christ is in you, except ye be reprobates?
>
> —2 Corinthians 13:5

Yes, the day will come when we all will have to give an account of ourselves in front of Jesus individually. Will He say, "Away from Me, I never knew you," or, "Enter in"? Which will it be? His answer will depend on our daily lifestyle and obedience to Him, a commitment to Him now while we're here on Earth. It will determine where we spend eternity, which, by the way, is forever. The question is, Will it be in heaven or in hell? How will you answer it? We don't just die and rot in the ground. Our spirit lives on forever.

Paul wrote this to the Corinthian church, as they demonstrated their carnality from time to time. After mentioning certain sins that the unsaved would commit, he said, "And such were some of you: but ye are washed, but ye are sanctified, but ye are justified in the name of the Lord Jesus, and by the Spirit of our God" (1 Cor. 6:11). This does not mean that Christians are perfect; we still sin from time to time. But God has provided us a way to confess our sins so that He can forgive them if we ask. We read in 1 John 1:8–9, "If we say that we have no sin, we deceive ourselves, and the truth is not in us. If we confess our sins, he is faithful and just to forgive us our sins, and to cleanse us from all unrighteousness." If we do that as soon as we are aware of a sin that we have committed, we can apply 1 John 2:28: "When He shall appear, we may have confidence, and not be ashamed before Him at His coming." Will you be among them that return with Jesus and rule the world from Jerusalem after the seven-year Marriage Supper of the Lamb?

Do you remember ever accepting Jesus into your heart? Or maybe you've gotten cold toward God and are a backslider, only going through the motions. Maybe you don't know Him at all. If so, I'll write a sinner's prayer for you later in this chapter.

Jesus looks at our heart to see if it is pure. God allowed the apostle John to see in a vision what the future would hold for us. He tells us in the Book of Revelation what he saw and heard in his vision. I'm sure you also want to take part in it. He describes it in Revelation 21:1–8:

> And I saw a new heaven and a new earth: for the first heaven and the first earth were passed away; and there was no more sea. And I John saw the holy city, new Jerusalem, coming down from God out of heaven, prepared as a bride adorned for her husband. And I heard a great voice out of heaven saying, Behold, the tabernacle of God is with men, and he will dwell with them, and they shall be his people, and God himself shall be with them, and be their God. And God shall wipe away all tears from their eyes; and there shall be no more death, neither sorrow, nor crying, neither shall there be any more pain: for the former things are passed away. And he that sat upon the throne said, Behold, I make all things new. And he said unto me, Write: for these words are true and faithful. And he said unto me, It is done. I am Alpha and Omega, the beginning and the end. I will give unto him that is athirst of the fountain of the water of life freely. He that overcometh shall inherit all things; and I will be his God, and he shall be my son. But the fearful, and unbelieving, and the abominable, and murderers, and whoremongers, and sorcerers, and idolaters, and all liars, shall have their part in the lake which burneth with fire and brimstone: which is the second death.

I sincerely hope you will take part in the New Jerusalem! John describes the New Jerusalem in verses 9–21:

> And there came unto me one of the seven angels which had the seven vials full of the seven last plagues, and talked with me, saying, Come hither, I will shew thee the bride, the Lamb's wife. And he carried me away in the spirit to a great and high mountain, and shewed me that great city, the holy Jerusalem, descending out of heaven from God, Having the glory of God: and her light was like unto a stone most precious, even like a jasper stone, clear as crystal; And had a wall great and high, and had twelve gates, and at the gates twelve angels, and names written thereon, which are the names of the twelve tribes of the children of Israel: On the east three gates; on the north three gates; on the south three gates; and on the west three gates. And the wall of the city had twelve foundations, and in them the names of the twelve apostles of the Lamb. And he that talked with me had a golden reed to measure the city, and the gates thereof, and the wall thereof. And the city lieth foursquare, and the length is as large as the breadth: and he measured the city with the reed, twelve thousand furlongs. The length and the breadth and the height of it are equal. And he measured the wall thereof, an hundred and forty and four cubits, according to the measure of a man, that is, of the angel. And the building of the wall of it was of jasper: and the city was pure gold, like unto clear glass. And the foundations of the wall of the city were garnished with all manner of precious stones. The first foundation was jasper; the second, sapphire; the third, a chalcedony; the fourth, an emerald; The fifth, sardonyx; the sixth, sardius; the seventh, chrysolyte; the eighth, beryl; the ninth, a topaz; the tenth, a chrysoprasus; the eleventh, a jacinth; the twelfth, an amethyst. And the twelve gates were

> twelve pearls: every several gate was of one pearl: and the street of the city was pure gold, as it were transparent glass.

Why would anyone trade this for hell? As I was debating if I should write these lengthy scriptures, the Holy Spirit prompted me to do so, because many people have never read the Bible and don't know of what all it contains.

Then John describes the glory of the New Jerusalem in verses 22–27:

> And I saw no temple therein: for the Lord God Almighty and the Lamb are the temple of it. And the city had no need of the sun, neither of the moon, to shine in it: for the glory of God did lighten it, and the Lamb is the light thereof. And the nations of them which are saved shall walk in the light of it: and the kings of the earth do bring their glory and honour into it. And the gates of it shall not be shut at all by day: for there shall be no night there. And they shall bring the glory and honour of the nations into it. And there shall in no wise enter into it any thing that defileth, neither whatsoever worketh abomination, or maketh a lie: but they which are written in the Lamb's book of life.

He continues to tell us in Revelation 22:14–16:

> Blessed are they that do his commandments, that they may have right to the tree of life, and may enter in through the gates into the city. For without are dogs, and sorcerers, and whoremongers, and murderers, and idolaters, and whosoever loveth and maketh a lie. I Jesus have sent mine angel to testify unto you these things in the churches.

All of us better take a good look at ourselves, turning the searchlight on us individually, and take inventory to make sure that our name is written in the Lamb's Book of Life. Then John gave a warning in verses 18–19: "For I testify unto every man that heareth the words of the prophecy of this book, If any man shall add unto these things, God shall add unto him the plagues that are written in this book: And if any man shall take away from the words of the book of this prophecy, God shall take away his part out of the book of life, and out of the holy city, and from the things which are written in this book."

Yet in many churches they add and subtract to these teachings. In fact, whole denominations teach only part of the Bible, as I will prove to you in some of the following chapters. God called me to expose the errors taught in many churches today, as they, along with their man-made denominational doctrines and interpretations, preach only a partial gospel instead of being a full gospel church. Preachers, please teach only the contents of the Bible, not your opinion of it! You will see that man-made doctrines can lead to false religions. I beg you; turn from your self-imposed Bible beliefs. Lay down your religious beliefs and trust in the Bible—all of it; it is God's Word—in order to be counted worthy to enter heaven's gates. One more request: stop screaming. The people, including God, can hear very well. I promptly turn the TV channel so I don't have to hear you yell, no matter how popular you are.

According to recent surveys, Americans remain some of the most religious people in the world. Ninety-two percent of adults say they believe in the existence of God; 60 percent agree that "God is a person with whom they can have a relationship;"[2] and

88 percent say they believe Jesus was also a real person.[3] However, 41 percent believe that Jesus committed sins while He lived on Earth, and only 60 percent maintain that the Bible is "totally accurate in all of its teachings."[4] My questions are: do you have a personal relationship with Him, and have you accepted Jesus as your Savior and made Him your Lord? The behavior of many tells a different story from how they would respond to those questions. When it comes to such things as dishonesty, charitable giving, cheating, prayer, Bible reading, divorce, sexual activity outside of marriage, pornography, abortion, and physical and sexual abuse, polls show a widening gap between what we say we believe and what we are actually practicing. The problem is not that what we believe is unimportant; rather, it is that over the years we have seen a widening gap develop between what we were taught early on and what we actually do at any given moment. A Barna survey found that two out of every three professing Christian adults were born again before they turned eighteen.[5] That is why the Bible tells us in Hebrews 10:25, "Not forsaking the assembling of ourselves together, as the manner of some is; but exhorting one another: and so much the more, as ye see the day approaching."

As adults go their own way and stray away from God, our children and young people feel the effect and have to pay the price. I heard these horrifying figures: four out of ten children live in broken homes; sixty-five out of one thousand kids between the ages of seven and eleven are under psychiatric care; 1 million girls aged twelve to seventeen will get pregnant each year and deliver their baby. This figure does not even mention all the abortions. The number of abortions by teenage girls is staggering. Yet, a mother's womb should be the safest place for a baby to be. Millions of teenagers are infected with venereal diseases, and between ten to fifteen percent of American children will contemplate suicide.[6] I ask myself what their home life is like. Many mothers work, therefore the kids are by themselves a lot and model their behavior according to peer pressure and what they see on TV, where sex and murder is the norm. An epidemic seems to have broken out, forcing our children to go through metal detectors at school that check them for knives and guns, as some kill their classmates or whoever comes across their path in cold blood. I say, if forbidden drugs and guns can enter the schools, why not Bibles?

Something is drastically wrong with our society. It all started when prayer was taken out of the schools. It was the work of only one person that got prayer out of our schools over twenty years ago. Afterward, our morals fell apart drastically. America was the first country that put a man on the moon nearly forty years ago. Now we are known for being number one in murder, drug abuse, single parenting, pregnancy, and abortion. Many preachers are afraid to call it what it is: sin. Drunkenness is now called a disease, *adultery* has been changed to "having an affair," and abortion is polished up and renamed "choice." A woman is said to be master over her own body.

Unless God is merciful and changes the hearts of many by having the Holy Spirit convict us of our sins and cause us to repent, there is no revival in sight. God cannot condone sin; therefore, we are no better than Sodom and Gomorrah, whom He destroyed. They seem to have been totally erased from the face of the earth. The only few He saved then was Lot's family, because of Abraham's intervention. Spiritually, we are in deep trouble in this country.

Several years ago the pastor's wife of the church I attended asked if some of us were interested in volunteering to gather signatures for Initiative 694 to stop partial-birth infanticide. A nurse's testimony and a description with five pictures of how the procedure was performed were included. If you have a weak stomach, you might want to skip the next several lines and continue on the next paragraph. This is what she experienced:

> In September 1993 Mary (not her real name) a registered nurse with thirteen years' experience, was assigned by her nursing agency to an abortion clinic. Since she considered herself "very pro-choice," she didn't think this would be a problem. She was wrong. She said, "I stood at the doctor's side and watched him perform a partial-birth infanticide on a woman who was six months pregnant. The baby's heartbeat was clearly visible on the ultrasound screen. The doctor delivered the baby's body and arms, everything but his little head. The baby's body was moving. His little fingers were clasping together. He was kicking his feet. Then the doctor took a pair of scissors and inserted them into the back of the baby's head. His little arms jerked out in a flinch reaction, a startled reaction like a baby does when he thinks he might fall. The doctor opened the scissors up. He stuck a high-powered suction tube in the hole and sucked the baby's brain out, which caused the baby to go completely limp. I never went back to that clinic. But I am still haunted by the face of that little boy. It was the most perfect, angelic face I have ever seen."[7]

It is when good people do nothing that these laws will pass allowing procedures like this. Thankfully, I had several petitions filled with signatures from registered voters. Can you be counted on to defend our stand in the Lord Jesus Christ?

One bumper sticker reads, "Abortion doesn't make you unpregnant. It makes you the murderer of a baby."

THE BABY'S CRY BY TANYA LEBLANC

Dear Mommy,
It's early now, the month is one.
You can't see me yet; I've just begun.
I'm so small I have to hide.
I'm just a seed growing inside.
Four weeks later, the month is two.
I'm still small but a part of you.
Mommy, you will love me, just wait and see.
I'll be sure to make you a part of me.
Time has passed now, the month is three,
Now I am someone you can see:
My hair is brown, my eyes are brown,
I'm sure you'll love having me around.
As for today, the month is four.
Now I'm growing even more.
I hope and pray that here I'll stay
Beside my Mommy 'til the month is five.
Mommy killed me,
I'm no longer alive.
Abortion is the name they give it.
Take your life before you live it.
I wanted to be born; the month is six,
It's already done, it can't be fixed.
She will never forget it,
She will never forget.
I'll always say, for her there was no other way.
I've got a new home, the month is seven,

> Mommy has killed me and I am in heaven.
> I was beautiful, but now I'm gone,
> I've left my Mommy to carry on.
> If I were around, the month would be eight.
> I know she loved me, but now it's too late.
> Murdered by my own Mommy's hands,
> I guess I'm too young to understand.
> Goodbye, Mommy! The month is nine,
> If I could have lived I would be fine.
> Although I'm in heaven, I have to cry.
> Because of my Mommy, I had to die![8]

I consider myself personally responsible for the life of a young boy. I sold this yet-unmarried couple a home. At the showing we talked about different things, but I usually probe about their stand with the Lord. During our lengthy conversation, she told me that she was going to abort the baby she was carrying. Of course, I objected, and we actually argued. To top it off, she was a nurse in the delivery room of one of our local hospitals. The next day, I packed her up a bunch of books, including one by a pastor from Oregon who wrote about abortion. He gave me a copy when I ministered in his church in 1985. She told me later that she fought with herself for weeks before she returned my books and agreed to deliver the baby. I located a church for them and stayed in contact. When I held the eight-month-old boy at their wedding, I had a vision of him with a Bible in his hand, dressed in a white tuxedo at about ten years old preaching. The last time I saw him, he was eight years old and attending a Christian school. I call him "preacher man"! His mom said that he has been telling the kids in the neighborhood about Jesus since he was five years old. The miracle is that the Lord totally removed from her memory that she was going to abort him. When I tried to talk about it with her, she had absolutely no recollection of it.

January 2008 marked thirty-five years since our nation's moral collapse, in that the U.S. Supreme Court made abortion on demand legal in all fifty states. Since the Court's 1973 *Roe v. Wade* decision, over 14 million African-American babies have been aborted. In fact, 35 percent of all abortions are performed on African-American women.[9] In many states, a school nurse cannot give your child an aspirin without contacting the parents, but she can take your daughter out of class to have an abortion without notifying the parents.

Many women would not abort their baby if they got to see its features and heartbeat. They even can tell now which parents the baby looks like. Has it come to the point where we are killing people who are made in God's image and trying to clone people made in our image? The blood of the innocent cries to heaven.

> And I heard a great voice out of heaven saying, Behold, the tabernacle of God is with men, and he will dwell with them, and they shall be his people, and God himself shall be with them, and be their God.
>
> —REVELATION 21:3

As I read the above verse, Holy Spirit brought to my mind a prophecy given to me in 1987 by a friend who later became a pastor. At an intercessors prayer meeting in my home, he said that I have the anointing of tabernacles on me and asked me to read chapter 40 in the Book of Exodus. Then he continued, saying that I will establish the body of Christ. The footnotes of Revelation 21:3

in my Bible explain that God's glory filled the tabernacle. Without His glory and presence, the work was not finished and the tabernacle was useless. The repeated message of Exodus is that God was personally present in their midst.

At the time it was given, this prophecy had absolutely no meaning to me, although I knew that it was very powerful. Not even when the Holy Spirit revealed to me in 1991 that this book would cause our revival did I connect the two. Later, it occurred to me that if I was to establish the body of Christ, something had to be out of order with the present one.

I read about a poll conducted by Jeffrey Hadden in 1998 in which 7,441 Protestant ministers were asked if the resurrection of Christ actually happened. The percentages of those who do *not* believe in the resurrection as a historical event, by denominations, are:

American Lutherans—13 percent
The Presbyterian Church (U.S.A.)—30 percent
American Baptist—33 percent
Episcopalians—35 percent
Methodists—51 percent[10]

Are these men and women denouncing their salvation? If they believe that Jesus was not resurrected, then He did not die for them, and neither are their sins forgiven. If they don't believe the following Scriptures, they should throw their Bibles away!

The apostle Paul wrote:

> But God commendeth his love toward us, in that, while we were yet sinners, Christ died for us. Much more then, being now justified by his blood, we shall be saved from wrath

through him. For if, when we were enemies, we were reconciled to God by the death of his Son, much more, being reconciled, we shall be saved by his life. And not only so, but we also joy in God through our Lord Jesus Christ, by whom we have now received the atonement.

—Romans 5:8–11

Who is he that condemneth? It is Christ that died, yea rather, that is risen again, who is even at the right hand of God, who also maketh intercession for us.

—Romans 8:34

For to this end Christ both died, and rose, and revived, that he might be Lord both of the dead and living.... For it is written, As I live, saith the Lord, every knee shall bow to me, and every tongue shall confess to God.

—Romans 14:9, 11

For I delivered unto you first of all that which I also received, how that Christ died for our sins according to the scriptures; And that he was buried, and that he rose again the third day according to the scriptures: And that he was seen of Cephas, then of the twelve: After that, he was seen of above five hundred brethren at once; of whom the greater part remain unto this present, but some are fallen asleep. After that, he was seen of James; then of all the apostles. And last of all he was seen of me also, as of one born out of due time.

—1 Corinthians 15:3–8

And that he died for all, that they which live should not henceforth live unto themselves, but unto him which died for them, and rose again.

—2 Corinthians 5:15

Are they going to stop taking communion next? Did not Paul tell us the following in 1 Corinthians 11:23–31?

> For I have received of the Lord that which also I delivered unto you, that the Lord Jesus the same night in which he was betrayed took bread: And when he had given thanks, he brake it, and said, Take, eat: this is my body, which is broken for you: this do in remembrance of me. After the same manner also he took the cup, when he had supped, saying, this cup is the new testament in my blood: this do ye, as oft as ye drink it, in remembrance of me. For as often as ye eat this bread, and drink this cup, ye do shew the Lord's death till he come. Wherefore whosoever shall eat this bread, and drink this cup of the Lord, unworthily, shall be guilty of the body and blood of the Lord. But let a man examine himself, and so let him eat of that bread, and drink of that cup. For he that eateth and drinketh unworthily, eateth and drinketh damnation to himself, not discerning the Lord's body. For this cause many are weak and sickly among you, and many sleep. For if we would judge ourselves, we should not be judged.

Do you expect to go up in the Rapture? Paul writes in 1 Thessalonians 4:13–18:

> But I would not have you to be ignorant, brethren, concerning them which are asleep, that ye sorrow not, even as others which have no hope. For if we believe that Jesus died and rose again, even so them also which sleep in Jesus will God bring with him. For this we say unto you by the word of the Lord, that we which are alive and remain unto the coming of the Lord shall not prevent them which are asleep. For the Lord himself shall descend from heaven with a shout, with the voice of the archangel, and with the trump of God: and

> the dead in Christ shall rise first: Then we which are alive and remain shall be caught up together with them in the clouds, to meet the Lord in the air: and so shall we ever be with the Lord. Wherefore comfort one another with these words.

Are those men being groomed already for the Antichrist? As Paul explains to us in 2 Thessalonians 2:3–4:

> Let no man deceive you by any means: for that day shall not come, except there come a falling away first, and that man of sin be revealed, the son of perdition; Who opposeth and exalteth himself above all that is called God, or that is worshipped; so that he as God sitteth in the temple of God, shewing himself that he is God.

As time went on and I recognized my calling, God revealed some awesome truths to me, which, if obeyed, will make us the bride of Christ clothed in the white garment without spot and wrinkle that He is coming for. Are you willing to undergo the necessary changes? From the time God gave me my calling to the time I could begin to write this book, He had to do a lot of work in me in order to prepare me for this enormous task. The Lord led me to read Exodus 40 again and made me to understand that as the cloud of the Lord's presence covered the tent of the congregation, His glory filled the tabernacle. God told Moses to start on the first day of the first month to put the tabernacle together. The whole process took exactly one year as he followed the precise instructions, placing in it the ark containing the Ten Commandments, installing the veil to enclose the ark within the holy of holies, and everything else required. When Moses was finished, the cloud covered the tabernacle and the glory of the Lord filled it. Whenever the cloud lifted and moved, the people journeyed onward, following it. But if it stopped, so did the Israelites until it moved again. During the day, the cloud rested upon the tabernacle, but at night there was fire in the cloud so that all the people could see it, which continued throughout their whole journey. Just as He was personally present with them then, so also is it His desire now to personally know us and have the Holy Spirit guide us, instead of us only knowing religious practices?

Stop and talk to Him. He answers. He will make Himself real to you if you are not too busy. Take time and listen to Him. Isaiah says it so beautifully in verse 40:31: "But they that wait upon the LORD shall renew their strength; they shall mount up with wings as eagles; they shall run, and not be weary; and they shall walk, and not faint." But you need to know Him first and become a part of the family of God. If you were to die within a few minutes after reading this book, do you know beyond any shadow of a doubt that you would go to heaven? Although we are born physically alive, we are still then spiritually dead, and it is up to each individual to invite Jesus into his or her heart. God gives us a choice. The bridge between God and man is the Cross. This new birth is called being born again. This gives us spiritual life.

Jesus is the gap between sinful man and God, as we read in John 3:1–3: "There was a man of the Pharisees, named Nicodemus, a ruler of the Jews: The same came to Jesus by night, and said unto him, Rabbi, we know that thou art a teacher come from God: for no man can do these miracles that thou doest, except God be with him. Jesus answered and said unto him, Verily, verily, I say unto thee, Except a man be born again, he cannot see the kingdom of God." Why? He explained it in John 3:16–17: "For God so loved the world, that he gave his only begotten Son, that whosoever believeth in him should not perish, but have everlasting life. For God sent not his Son into the world to condemn the world; but that the world through him might be saved." Jesus continues in John 14:6 "I am the way, the truth, and the life: no man cometh unto the Father, but by Me."

A man may go to heaven without health, wealth, fame, a great name, big earnings, culture, beauty, and friends, yes, without ten thousand other things; but he can never go to heaven without accepting Jesus Christ.

The Bible says that there are four things a person must know to go to heaven:

1. We read in Romans 3:10, 23, "As it is written, there is none righteous, no, not one.... For all have sinned, and come short of the glory of God." And in Ecclesiastes 7:20, "For there is not a just man upon earth, that doeth good, and sinneth not." Both verses mean no matter how hard we try, we will come short of the glory of God, the Lord Jesus Christ.
2. The Bible says in Romans 6:23, "For the wages of sin is death," being in hell forever, a total separation from the love of God.
3. We also read in Romans 6:23,"But the gift of God is eternal life through Jesus Christ our Lord." Ephesians 2:8 emphasizes this point: "For by

grace are ye saved through faith; and that not of yourselves: it is the gift of God."

4. The Bible tells us in Romans 10:9–10, "That if thou shalt confess with thy mouth the Lord Jesus, and shalt believe in thine heart that God hath raised him from the dead, thou shalt be saved. For with the heart man believeth unto righteousness; and with the mouth confession is made unto salvation." God's promise is complete to us in Romans 10:13, "For whosoever shall call upon the name of the Lord shall be saved."

The Bible makes it clear that not everyone is a child of God. We read in John 1:12, "But as many as received Him, to them gave he the power to become sons of God, even to them that believe on his name." Jesus said to those who did not trust Him in John 8:44, "Ye are of your father the devil." You see, my friend, our first birth does not make us children of God, but the second one does. That is why Jesus said in John 3:7, "Ye must be born again."

Dear God, I believe that Jesus Christ is the living Son of God. I believe He was born of a virgin, died on the cross for my sins, and that God raised Him three days later according to the Bible. He is coming again one day soon to take us to glory. Now, Lord Jesus, I ask You to please forgive me of all my sins. I am truly sorry for the things I've done. I repent of them and open my heart right now to invite You in and receive You as my personal Lord and Savior

> *to use me any way You see fit for Your honor and glory. Thank You for saving me. And now I ask You to please fill me with all the fullness and power of the Holy Ghost of God, that I might live to be all You saved me to be. In Jesus' name I pray, amen.*

Now that you have received Jesus, you know that you are saved, because God has given you His Word in Romans 8:16:"The Spirit Himself beareth witness with our spirit, that we are children of God." Congratulations! If you prayed this prayer, you are now my brother or sister in the Lord. Now do the following:

- *Pray daily.* As 1 Thessalonians 5:17 says, "Pray without ceasing."

  > And he spake a parable unto them to this end, that men ought always to pray, and not to faint."
  >
  > —Luke 18:1

- *Read the Bible daily.* We are encouraged in Acts 17:11, "These were more noble…in that they received the word with all readiness of mind, and searched the scriptures daily, whether those things were so." Psalm 119:11, 89, and 165 also say, "Thy word have I hid in mine heart, that I might not sin against thee.…For ever, O Lord, thy word is settled in heaven.…Great peace have they which love thy law: and nothing shall offend them."
- *Witness for Jesus daily.* Acts 1:8 tells us this: "But ye shall receive power, after that the Holy Ghost

is come upon you: and ye shall be witnesses unto me both in Jerusalem, and in all Judaea, and in Samaria, and unto the uttermost part of the earth." In Acts 5:42 we learn that the early followers of Christ "daily in the temple, and in every house…ceased not to teach and preach Jesus Christ."

- *Confess Jesus openly and be baptized by immersion.* We read in Matthew 10:32, "Whosoever therefore shall confess me before men, him will I confess also before my Father which is in heaven." Also, Matthew 28:19–20 says, "Go ye therefore, and teach all nations, baptizing them in the name of the Father, and of the Son, and of the Holy Ghost: Teaching them to observe all things whatsoever I have commanded you: and, lo, I am with you always, even unto the end of the world."
- *Attend church.* Participate in a church where the whole Bible is preached and Jesus is honored and praised and glorified, as recommended in Hebrews 10:25: "Not forsaking the assembling of ourselves together, as the manner of some is; but exhorting one another: and so much the more, as ye see the day approaching."
- *Keep Jesus' commandments.* He told us in John 14:15, "If ye love me, keep my commandments."
- *Pray for the baptism with the Holy Spirit as soon as you accept Jesus as your Savior.* The Scriptures

> promise that it will be given to believers who ask for it. You need it in order to live a powerful Christian life, as described in Acts 2:4, 39: "And they were all filled with the Holy Ghost, and began to speak with other tongues, as the Spirit gave them utterance.... For the promise is unto you, and to your children, and to all that are afar off, even as many as the LORD our God shall call."

You just read that you can't get to heaven by works, and religious practices are not the answer. *It is your personal relationship with Jesus*, not how often you attend church or fast, not baptism, and not anything else. Would it not be a shame if you were doing these rituals all your life and yet missed God completely, not being able to enter heaven? You could even be a choir director in your church and go to hell if you have not made Jesus your personal Savior.

Our intimacy with God is described in Psalm 26:1–8:

> Judge me, O Lord; for I have walked in mine integrity: I have trusted also in the Lord; therefore I shall not slide. Examine me, O Lord, and prove me; try my reins and my heart. For thy lovingkindness is before mine eyes: and I have walked in thy truth. I have not sat with vain persons, neither will I go in with dissemblers. I have hated the congregation of evil doers; and will not sit with the wicked. I will wash mine hands in innocency: so will I compass thine altar, O Lord: That I may publish with the voice of thanksgiving, and tell of all thy wondrous works. Lord, I have loved the habitation of thy house, and the place where thine honour dwelleth.

If we allow it, He will shake everything off of us, so that we stand steadfast in the Lord.

> Whose voice then shook the earth: but now he hath promised, saying, Yet once more I shake not the earth only, but also heaven. And this word, Yet once more, signifieth the removing of those things that are shaken, as of things that are made, that those things which cannot be shaken may remain.
>
> —HEBREWS 12:26–27

As He purifies us, He will produce in us consistency, simply speaking, and a Christlikeness! Holiness and judgment begins in the house of God.

> Hear, ye that are far off, what I have done; and, ye that are near, acknowledge my might. The sinners in Zion are afraid; fearfulness hath surprised the hypocrites. Who among us shall dwell with the devouring fire? who among us shall dwell with everlasting burnings? He that walketh righteously, and speaketh uprightly; he that despiseth the gain of oppressions, that shaketh his hands from holding of bribes, that stoppeth his ears from hearing of blood, and shutteth his eyes from seeing evil; He shall dwell on high: his place of defence shall be the munitions of rocks: bread shall be given him; his waters shall be sure.
>
> —ISAIAH 33:13–16

I realize now why this anointing of tabernacles is upon me. I am to invite you to open your spiritual eyes. The anointing of tabernacles means God's glory is upon me, which I am to offer to each individual. *Strong's Exhaustive Concordance* describes *glory* as follows: "weightiness; that which is substantial or heavy, glory, honor, splendor, power, wealth, authority, magnificence, fame, dignity, riches and excellency."[11] It sounds overwhelming to me. Moses asked God in Exodus 33:18–19, "And he said, I beseech thee, shew me thy glory. And he said, I will make all my goodness pass before thee." Are you ready for His goodness to pass before you? Isn't He an awesome God?

Then I heard a preacher teach that the anointing destroys the yoke and removes our burdens. Listen to Isaiah 10:27: "And it shall come to pass in that day, that his burden shall be taken away from off thy shoulder, and his yoke from off thy neck, and his yoke shall be destroyed because of the anointing." This burden and yoke is that of Satan, who has many people muzzled and burdened down.

Read Habakkuk 2:14: "For the earth shall be filled with the knowledge of the glory of the Lord, as the waters cover the sea." So what is the knowledge that fills the whole earth with the glory of God? Earlier I wrote that the glory is the promises of God manifested. Let's continue in Isaiah 60:1–3: "Arise, shine; for thy light is come, and the glory of the Lord is risen upon thee. For, behold, the darkness shall cover the earth, and gross darkness the people: but the Lord shall arise upon thee, and his glory shall be seen upon thee. And the Gentiles shall come to thy light, and kings to the brightness of thy rising." It means that the Gentiles, as the non-Jews were called in the Old Testament, will come to know the Lord. Also read 2 Corinthians 4:3–4: "But if our gospel be hid, it is hid to them that are lost: In whom the god of this world hath blinded the minds of them which believe not, lest the light of the glorious gospel of Christ, who is the image of God, should shine unto them." So that they are able to say, as described in Colossians

1:13–14, "Who hath delivered us from the power of darkness, and hath translated us into the kingdom of his dear Son: In whom we have redemption through his blood, even the forgiveness of sins." Yes, we are His blood-bought church. Are you ready and committed to bring God's glory to the rest of the world, starting with your own family and neighborhood? If you or I were the only ones alive then, Jesus still would have died on the cross just for you and me. I thank You, Jesus!

The apostle Paul wrote the following encouraging Scriptures to the Ephesian church. His epistle to them is intended to exhort those believers to live a holy life and bring conviction to those that were living together before marriage.

> Blessed be the God and Father of our Lord Jesus Christ, who hath blessed us with all spiritual blessings in heavenly places in Christ: According as he hath chosen us in him before the foundation of the world, that we should be holy and without blame before him in love: Having predestinated us unto the adoption of children by Jesus Christ to himself, according to the good pleasure of his will, To the praise of the glory of his grace, wherein he hath made us accepted in the beloved. In whom we have redemption through his blood, the forgiveness of sins, according to the riches of his grace; Wherein he hath abounded toward us in all wisdom and prudence; Having made known unto us the mystery of his will, according to his good pleasure which he hath purposed in himself: That in the dispensation of the fulness of times he might gather together in one all things in Christ, both which are in heaven, and which are on earth; even in him: In whom also we have obtained an inheritance, being predestinated according to the purpose of him who worketh all things after the counsel of

his own will: That we should be to the praise of his glory, who first trusted in Christ. In whom ye also trusted, after that ye heard the word of truth, the gospel of your salvation: in whom also after that ye believed, ye were sealed with that holy Spirit of promise, Which is the earnest of our inheritance until the redemption of the purchased possession, unto the praise of his glory.... That the God of our Lord Jesus Christ, the Father of glory, may give unto you the spirit of wisdom and revelation in the knowledge of him: The eyes of your understanding being enlightened; that ye may know what is the hope of his calling, and what the riches of the glory of his inheritance in the saints, And what is the exceeding greatness of his power to us-ward who believe, according to the working of his mighty power, Which he wrought in Christ, when he raised him from the dead, and set him at his own right hand in the heavenly places, Far above all principality, and power, and might, and dominion, and every name that is named, not only in this world, but also in that which is to come: And hath put all things under his feet, and gave him to be the head over all things to the church, Which is his body, the fulness of him that filleth all in all.... And you hath he quickened, who were dead in trespasses and sins; Wherein in time past ye walked according to the course of this world, according to the prince of the power of the air, the spirit that now worketh in the children of disobedience: Among whom also we all had our conversation in times past in the lusts of our flesh, fulfilling the desires of the flesh and of the mind; and were by nature the children of wrath, even as others. But God, who is rich in mercy, for his great love wherewith he loved us, Even when we were dead in sins, hath quickened us together with Christ, (by grace ye are saved;) And hath raised us up together, and made us sit together in heavenly places in Christ Jesus: That in the ages to come he might shew the exceeding riches of his

> grace in his kindness toward us through Christ Jesus. For by grace are ye saved through faith; and that not of yourselves: it is the gift of God: Not of works, lest any man should boast. For we are his workmanship, created in Christ Jesus unto good works, which God hath before ordained that we should walk in them.... But now in Christ Jesus ye who sometimes were far off are made nigh by the blood of Christ.... For through him we both have access by one Spirit unto the Father. Now therefore ye are no more strangers and foreigners, but fellow-citizens with the saints, and of the household of God.
>
> —EPHESIANS 1:3–14, 17–23; 2:1–10, 13, 18–19

As people around the world mourned the death of Princess Diana of Great Britain after an accident in the Pont de l'Alma tunnel in Paris, France, on August 31, 1997, I felt compelled to write a few lines about this situation. Was her death necessary? Was it not premature? Could it not have been prevented? As people brought one bouquet of flowers after another and some shed tears as they paid their last respects, thanking her for all she did, they expressed their sense of loss. There is no way for us to know whether or not she made a decision to make Christ her Savior in her lifetime, but many people assume that when you close your eyes and breathe your last breath, you automatically go to heaven. How wrong! I blame their ignorance from false or insufficient teaching about that subject first of all on their parents, who do not take their children to church to hear the good news. Secondly, it is the fault of preachers and teachers who do not teach it to them. Princess Diana deserved better, yet she died while enjoying a happy time in her private life.

We read in James 5:19–20, "Brethren, if any of you do err from the truth, and one convert him; Let him know, that he which converteth the sinner from the error of his way shall save a soul from death, and shall hide a multitude of sins." Also, Psalm 91:1–2, 11–12 says, "He that dwelleth in the secret place of the most High shall abide under the shadow of the Almighty. I will say of the Lord, He is my refuge and my fortress: my God; in him will I trust.... For he shall give his angels charge over thee, to keep thee in all thy ways. They shall bear thee up in their hands, lest thou dash thy foot against a stone."

As the family members of the two men who also died in the car crash were mourning their deaths, I was wondering what consequences a marriage—if Diana and Dodi Al Fayed really were to be married—could have brought for her and Great Britain. Would she have been allowed to continue to be an ambassador for humanity? Would she have been persuaded to convert to Islam, and what effect might that have had on the spiritual condition in Great Britain? What about her children? These are concerns from a spiritual point of view.

Our great revival can begin if you take the following scriptures to heart and practice them so that you know without a doubt where you will spend eternity. Can you see the urgent need of the restoration of the five-fold ministry in our churches? Regarding this ministry, the apostle Paul explained in Ephesians 4:11–32 and 5:1–21:

> And he gave some, apostles; and some, prophets; and some, evangelists; and some, pastors and teachers; For the perfecting of the saints, for the work of the ministry, for the edifying of the body of Christ: Till we all come in the unity

of the faith, and of the knowledge of the Son of God, unto a perfect man, unto the measure of the stature of the fulness of Christ: That we henceforth be no more children, tossed to and fro, and carried about with every wind of doctrine, by the sleight of men, and cunning craftiness, whereby they lie in wait to deceive; But speaking the truth in love, may grow up into him in all things, which is the head, even Christ: From whom the whole body fitly joined together and compacted by that which every joint supplieth, according to the effectual working in the measure of every part, maketh increase of the body unto the edifying of itself in love. This I say therefore, and testify in the Lord, that ye henceforth walk not as other Gentiles walk, in the vanity of their mind, Having the understanding darkened, being alienated from the life of God through the ignorance that is in them, because of the blindness of their heart: Who being past feeling have given themselves over unto lasciviousness, to work all uncleanness with greediness. But ye have not so learned Christ; If so be that ye have heard him, and have been taught by him, as the truth is in Jesus: That ye put off concerning the former conversation the old man, which is corrupt according to the deceitful lusts; And be renewed in the spirit of your mind; And that ye put on the new man, which after God is created in righteousness and true holiness. Wherefore putting away lying, speak every man truth with his neighbour: for we are members one of another. Be ye angry, and sin not: let not the sun go down upon your wrath: Neither give place to the devil. Let him that stole steal no more: but rather let him labour, working with his hands the thing which is good, that he may have to give to him that needeth. Let no corrupt communication proceed out of your mouth, but that which is good to the use of edifying, that it may minister grace unto the hearers. And grieve not the holy Spirit of God, whereby ye are sealed unto the day of redemption. Let all bitterness, and wrath, and anger, and clamour, and evil speaking, be put away from you, with all malice: And be ye kind one to another, tenderhearted, forgiving one another, even as God for Christ's sake hath forgiven you.... Be ye therefore followers of God, as dear children; And walk in love, as Christ also hath loved us, and hath given himself for us an offering and a sacrifice to God for a sweetsmelling savour. But fornication, and all uncleanness, or covetousness, let it not be once named among you, as becometh saints; Neither filthiness, nor foolish talking, nor jesting, which are not convenient: but rather giving of thanks. For this ye know, that no whoremonger, nor unclean person, nor covetous man, who is an idolater, hath any inheritance in the kingdom of Christ and of God. Let no man deceive you with vain words: for because of these things cometh the wrath of God upon the children of disobedience. Be not ye therefore partakers with them. For ye were sometimes darkness, but now are ye light in the Lord: walk as children of light: (For the fruit of the Spirit is in all goodness and righteousness and truth;) Proving what is acceptable unto the Lord. And have no fellowship with the unfruitful works of darkness, but rather reprove them. For it is a shame even to speak of those things which are done of them in secret. But all things that are reproved are made manifest by the light: for whatsoever doth make manifest is light. Wherefore he saith, Awake thou that sleepest, and arise from the dead, and Christ shall give thee light. See then that ye walk circumspectly, not as fools, but as wise, Redeeming the time, because the days are evil. Wherefore be ye not unwise, but understanding what the will of the Lord is. And be not drunk with wine, wherein is excess; but be filled with the Spirit; Speaking to yourselves in psalms and hymns and spiritual songs, singing and making melody in your heart to the Lord; Giving thanks always for all things

> unto God and the Father in the name of our Lord Jesus Christ; Submitting yourselves one to another in the fear of God.

Jesus paid the penalty for our sin with His death on the cross. He became the substitution for our sin by the shedding of His blood, described in both the Old Testament and the New Testament. One becomes a Christian by knowing God through Jesus Christ. As soon as we repent, He forgives us our sins, and the sinful nature that once separated us from God is therefore removed. Many people are misled to believe that because they were born in this country or have been a good person, they are automatically qualified to be a Christian. How awful to be so greatly mistaken. You become one only through Jesus Christ, not by birth. We are God's creation through whom He works. We serve Him by helping others; being His hands extended to the needy; by feeding and comforting them to help make their lives more bearable; by praying for them when they are in need of finances and healing in sicknesses and pain; helping them to come to know God by witnessing to them; and by leading them in a sinner's prayer so that they can live a victorious life in Jesus Christ. Jesus' sympathy for the physical suffering of humanity and His teaching of morality was not all that He did. He also devoted Himself to the spiritually lost sheep of the house of Israel.

Take the following scripture to heart.

> Let this mind be in you, which was also in Christ Jesus: Who, being in the form of God, thought it not robbery to be equal with God: But made himself of no reputation, and took upon him the form of a servant, and was made in the likeness of men: And being found in fashion as a man, he humbled

> himself, and became obedient unto death, even the death of the cross. Wherefore God also hath highly exalted him, and given him a name which is above every name: That at the name of Jesus every knee should bow, of things in heaven, and things in earth, and things under the earth [in Hell]; And that every tongue should confess that Jesus Christ is Lord, to the glory of God the Father.
>
> —Philippians 2:5–11

To follow and practice the principles of the Bible, we must recognize that we are no longer sinners saved by grace, as some people believe. Instead, we are a new creation, as Paul described us in 2 Corinthians 5:17: "Therefore if any man be in Christ, he is a new creature: old things are passed away; behold, all things are become new."

While preparations were being made to lay the thirty-six-year-old princess to rest, the sad news of the death of Mother Teresa from Calcutta, India, was announced. The two knew each other from their work with the poor, sick, and dying. It was said that she was not sick; her eighty-seven-year-old heart just gave out. She did good works of unselfish love for many years. It has been said that the dying asked to receive Jesus after experiencing such great love from her and her helpers. This may serve as a reminder of 2 Peter 3:9: "The Lord is not slack concerning his promise, as some men count slackness; but is longsuffering to us-ward, not willing that any should perish, but that all should come to repentance."

Could the tragic, premature death of Princess Diana serve as a wake-up call for you to receive Jesus Christ as Lord and Savior, because we don't know when we breathe our last breath? How many of you make yourself available to continue her good works in whatever capacity God would have you function? One never knows when our time will come and our life will be snuffed out. That is why we must be ready and absolutely know our destination. We read in 1 Corinthians 6:20, "For ye are bought with a price: therefore glorify God in your body, and in your spirit, which are God's." John 15:8 says, "Herein is my Father glorified, that ye bear much fruit; so shall ye be my disciples." Can you join the saints in singing "The King Is Coming" as we are waiting for Jesus Christ to appear in the clouds to rapture us?

Someday, each one of us will stand before the judgment seat of Christ described in 2 Corinthians 5:10, 14–21; 6:1–2:

> For we must all appear before the judgment seat of Christ; that every one may receive the things done in his body, according to that he hath done, whether it be good or bad.... For the love of Christ constraineth us; because we thus judge, that if one died for all, then were all dead: And that he died for all, that they which live should not henceforth live unto themselves, but unto him which died for them, and rose again. Wherefore henceforth know we no man after the flesh: yea, though we have known Christ after the flesh, yet now henceforth know we him no more. Therefore if any man be in Christ, he is a new creature: old things are passed away; behold, all things are become new. And all things are of God, who hath reconciled us to himself by Jesus Christ, and hath given to us the ministry of reconciliation; To wit, that God was in Christ, reconciling the world unto himself, not imputing their trespasses unto them; and hath committed unto us the word of reconciliation. Now then we are ambassadors for Christ, as though God did beseech you by us: we pray you in Christ's stead, be ye reconciled to God. For he hath made him to be

> sin for us, who knew no sin; that we might be made the righteousness of God in him.... We then, as workers together with him, beseech you also that ye receive not the grace of God in vain. (For he saith, I have heard thee in a time accepted, and in the day of salvation have I succoured thee: behold, now is the accepted time; behold, now is the day of salvation.)

I invite you to join the army of God's ambassadors to make a difference around the world. Your past is unimportant. As you read, we are a new creation once we repent of our sins. It is the Holy Spirit's job to clean you up if you're willing to bring forth much fruit. Listen to the voice of the Holy Spirit and obey it. No matter how small the task is in the beginning, He will graduate you to a greater calling if He can depend on you, but first He will test you. As you continue to read the other chapters, you will find that I am living proof of it.

The Holy Spirit prompted me to include the following prophetic words, which were given to me about twenty years ago. They were given in three parts.

PART 1

> Will you sing the chorus, "Will you be poured out as wine on the altar for Me?"... Will you be broken as bread to feed the hungry? Would you be so one with Me that I might do just as I will to make you "life" and "light" and "love," My Word fulfilled?
>
> You see the work He has to do in us to make that a reality? You say, "But I only did good to that person and they turned and they ran. I did everything I could to show the love." But

you see, Jesus fed the hungry. He fed the multitudes, and they turned and railed on Him. He was poured out as wine. His blood was poured out for their sins and transgressions, and they cried, "If Thou be the Son of God, then deliver Yourself." It's a thankless price; it's a thankless position. It's not a glorious position to be used of God for the masses, because they demanded and they demanded and demanded. And if you don't perform, they hate you. In your time of suffering—when you're required to be nailed there, and they want food, they want healing, they want a kind, comforting word, and you don't respond—they rail on you. They hate you. But the Lord wants many, and that's what He's calling us to. The time of the showmanship is over. The time of all the theatricalism is over. The time of the pomp and the glory and bright lights is over. The time to move and live and have our being in Him has begun. It's not a time of glory. It's a time of humiliation. It's a time of humbling. It's a time of brokenness. It's a time of putting yourself aside, that He might be glorified. It's a time of becoming a laughingstock...so that they can make their decision to be against or for the Lord; so that He can pour out His vials of wrath...or....pour out His vials of mercy; so that He can reach out and redeem them....or their hearts can be seared and His wrath can be poured out and cleanse and purge the earth. It's not an easy time. It's a time of one or another, but nothing in between. It's a commitment. It's a sold-out, completely-yielded vessel. It's no longer what I want; it's "Master, what do You want?" It's "Master, what will You have?" [It is] not what I desire. It's no longer, "Master, I want to do this, I want to do that." It's, "What would You do through me?" It's not a time to be exalted. It's a time to be humiliated. The kings of the earth have set themselves in array against the Lord and against His anointed. They have said, "We have the prison of earth locked in our quarters. You

Christians have nothing to penetrate our barriers. We have shut you out. You cannot permeate or penetrate anymore. If you do, we will kill you."

And many of us that God is calling, we know full well that our lives mean nothing in that enemy camp. But we know that the Spirit of God is saying, "Enter, will you be willing? Will you be willing to go forward?" The Lord is dropping the plumb line on His body. He's saying, "Those that have sung the songs; I want you to consider what you've sung: 'I'll go where You want me to go; I'll do what You want me to do; I'll say what You want me to say on land or mountain or sea. I'll be what You want me to be, dear Lord.'" He's saying: "OK, if you really mean it, come over on this side. But I want you to understand that you're not coming to it by what you have seen in the world of evangelists. You're coming to the realm of dying on the cross. You're coming out of the gardens to weeping and agonizing. You're coming before the kings of the earth, and you won't be allowed to speak a word. You'll have to go, as a lamb before its shearers is dumb.

"Can you do this? Are you willing? If you're willing, I'll make you able; but it will cost you everything you are and everything you have. Yes, it will cost you everything you hold dear. It's going to cost you dearly. Are you willing? Yes, I'll go with you. I'll never leave you or forsake you; but do you really believe Me that I'll never leave you nor forsake you when your body has been beaten and torn and battered and bruised and thrown in that old, dark dungeon? Will you believe that I'll be the blanket that covers you? Will you believe that I'll be the resurrection and the life? Will you believe that I'll be your healer? Will you believe that I'll restore? Will you believe I'll set your feet again in high places? Are you willing? I'm not calling you to stand before the masses in great honor. I'm standing, asking you to walk with Me into the lands of great humiliation. I'm asking you to only do and speak what I speak and do, what you see Me doing. Will you do this? Will you only do that which you hear the Father speak? Will you say it? Don't say in your heart, 'I do not know the Lord well enough.' Don't say in your heart, 'I haven't walked with You long enough.' For if you be willing and obedient, I will teach you. If you just be willing to go, I will be the voice that speaks behind you when you know not what way to turn; and I will say, 'This is the way; walk ye in it. This is the word to speak; speak it.' You will speak the words of My mouth. You will take the steps that I have trodden; even knowing full well that it could be your final steps on this earth, you will take them in My name, laying down your life for My sake.

"My people, I have called many this night and this day. I am dealing in the same way on the side of the earth where the shadows have lengthened, where the moon is shining. Many have wept in My presence this very hour on that side, and many are weeping on this side. I am calling My people to come forth. I have called them, and I am calling them to come forth in great humility. For you see, My children, if I brought forth My glory before I bring forth the enmity; my children, if I brought forth My glory first, you would bond yourselves and be puffed up. You would carelessly use and abuse My presence. You would trample under feet the sons of man, and My glory would be turned into churning and shadows. But if you are willing to suffer with Me; if you're willing to go with Me to the masses that are dying; if you're willing to walk in My footsteps to those that are in the prisons, to suffer where they suffer, and to be thrown in the dungeons where there are those that have already been thrown and are weary; if you're willing to be tossed about on the waves of the sea and be joined with those that are weary of being tossed about, to suffer where they suffer, I know that you'll be ready to reign with Me.

"Are you willing? You say, 'I don't know. I've never learned of You that way.' I'm beckoning you this day to follow Me. I'm beckoning you to cling to Me as your only source and as your only life, as your only sustenance. It's time, My children. There is no other time; it's past. I am calling forth My people all across the earth. I am beckoning you.

"The perils are about to begin. The falling away is about to begin. The name 'Christian' is about to be unheard of among those that are so-called in My name. Will you be one? Are you willing? If you'll be willing and if you'll be obedient, you'll reap the great abilities. But first you must be abased. First you must be humiliated. You must be as the grain that is crushed under [the] foot of the beasts of the earth. You must first be as the grain that is cast to the wind and brought back down and trodden. You must be, My children, for I must first break loose the chaff from off of thee. They are the shackles that have thee bound. They are the leaven that causeth thee to stumble and err perpetually. But as the beasts of the earth trample thee underfoot, thou wilt not be destroyed. But yea, thou shalt be brought in between the rocks and thou shalt be ground as fine, as fine, as fine as can be. Thou shalt lose thy identity. Thou shalt be put together with the rest of the grain. As the kernels begin to lose their identity, they shall be kneaded together in Me. They shall come forth as a loaf to feed the hungry. Yes, thy body shall be weary, for many shall break from thee and pull from thee to be fed. And as they thronged upon Me, they shall throng upon thee. As thy body is weary, I was weary; but I will bring thee through. When thou hast felt that thou canst go no more, I will strengthen thee. Yea, I will sustain thee; I will be a covering over thee. I will bring thee forth. When thou hast felt that thou hath given to the uttermost and hath no more to give, I will charge thee again and I will charge thee again; and I will enlarge thy borders, and thou shall give and give and give. When thou hast felt that thou hath died and died... and there is no more that can die, it is the final death, I shall begin in thee to live and live and live, and thy life shall be My life. Are you willing? Can you trust Me? Can you say yes? Can you lay it down? I plead with you this day.

"Gross darkness has covered the face of the earth. I hear the cries. I hear the moans of the masses. I hear the cries of the multitudes. Millions are dying. Millions are marked for death by the kings of the earth. You think you have heard of the bloodsheds of the Hitlers, the Mussolinis and Maos; but I say unto thee, they are drops in the bucket. For the winepress is full and ready to run over. And the wrath of thy God is soon to come upon all of those that hold the truth in unrighteousness. But first I must know of those who choose to walk with Me. First I must send down My holy angels to mark thee and to seal thee. For if I cannot seal thee, My children, thou wilt be trampled. Thou wilt be destroyed. And the leaven that is within thee will exalt itself and will literally cause thee to curse Me, for thou wilt believe that I am not the God of love. And, thou wilt despair of the little faith that has been in you. Can you lay it down? Can you begin the humiliation? My children, if you will begin to move in the humiliation and choose the abasement, I will cause thee to be sealed, and then nothing shall take you out of My hands. But yet I say unto thee, My children, you can still be plucked out of My hand, for I have yet to seal thee. I have yet to prove thee in the furnace of My affliction.

"For I am beginning to turn the fires up, and thy spirit and thy being and thy emotion are beginning to cry. Oh, will you turn it loose? Will you let go? Will you linger with Me? Will you get to know Me as the One who thoroughly purges this world? Will you let Me be the purger in thee? Will you let Me purge you with hyssop? Will you let your blood be cleansed and purified that your blood may be mingled with Mine? Until your blood is mingled so…as to be one with Me…your blood is no different. You have suffered to the measure you have ceased to sin, and your blood has been made pure, and My blood has flowed through thy veins. 'Till it is My blood that has poured from thee and not thy own, 'till it is holiness and purity, 'till it's royalty that flows from thy veins. Will you walk with Me? Will you go into the valley of the shadow with no guarantees that you will ever come back and see your family again on this side? Are you willing? Can you relinquish [it]? Can you lay down your life and love not your life, even unto death? This is My calling. This is My plea—that you lay down your life for Me. Amen."

Part 2

My little children, will you follow after Me? I say, My little children, will you choose to follow Me this day? I have wept on the mountainsides over the valleys. I have wept before My Father, hearing the cries of the destitute below. I have watched as cruel men have come and trampled the frozen. I watched as cruel men have come and kicked and abused their bodies and still curse them when they die. They, with Me, were crucified. They were not worthy to even stand by My side before they died. But they now, with Me, were crucified. Their cross lays beside them. Their bodies, bruised and broken. They've given, they've given, they've given. The earth cries and languishes. Their innocent blood has been poured out, My children.

My children, the earth is still thirsty, for the cup of iniquity is not yet full, My children. It's not yet full, My children. Can you be poured out as wine upon their altars? Can you be smitten and allow your bodies to be burned, oh, My children? Oh, My children, are you willing?…

You have said in your heart, you have children that have gone away, to depart. If only they would give You their heart. If only they would be one with You. I would give them to You and I would be willing to lay them down for You. I say unto you, My little ones, I will call them back from afar. I will raise them out of their dung heaps and valleys of despair. I will call them back to join you there if you're willing to lay them down, knowing full well that I have for them a crown only if you're willing to lay them down after you see the tenderness of My presence moving over them, after you have seen their spirits so sweet and gentle once again, after your eyes behold them as a child again, after you weep and rejoice with them. Will you not cling to them, but let them go to the jungles and into the cities to die? Will you not cling to them, but let them go? Will you turn them loose? Are you willing for Me to bring them back, only to send them away to die? Are you willing? Will you release them to Me this day?

I would say to thee, I will make a covenant with thee—a covenant to bring them back to thy side. A covenant I hear spoken this day will become a reality only if you are willing to let them go with Me, only if you are willing to love Me when before your eyes they die. Are you willing to keep that covenant? Are you willing for them to die? Are you willing to let go of them? You have clung to them, and they have despised you. You have sought to rule them and force them into Me; but they have fled and run from thee. But if you are willing to stand in humility, if you are willing to be broken, then with you and Me I will restore them. I'll send the spirit of Elijah into your family, and they'll be joined with thee. They will be joined with their Father if you are willing to let them be joined in this way in Me to thee.

Part 3

Yea, the Lord would sing a word to thee. You would express the plan in eternity. The Lord would cause thine eyes to see that which He has determined for thee. The Lord would lift thine heart and thine face up to see all men have taken everything I've created, and he sought to rule and reign in it.

"And yes, I, the Lord, gave him the authority for the fish of the sea and the fowl of the air to dress and to keep it. But man has sought to rule and reign, and man has sought for foolish gain, and man has taken upon himself that which I did not give. He hath taken all that I gave to live. He has sought to transform it in a way that pleases him, that he could say, 'Look what I have created.' And if he could, he'd say to his own son, 'Look at the things that I have done.'

"But I would say to My people, look around and see what he hath done. He tread upon the grass that I have made and says, 'Is this not beautiful, this grass that I have laid?' He taketh all the fruit of the trees, then he says, 'You may take all that you please, but I want you to see that this is what I have done...I have taken that and have brought forth after my kind.' But the fruit cry to Me...for I am not free...I am not free. They've taken of the stones of the ground and they've built all their idols all around. They've raised them up to the sky. They've sent them up to soar around and come back down, and [they] said, 'We did not see any Deity. Therefore, we will place ourselves as gods, you see.' And this shall increase and increase more and more unto the day that they say, 'You see? There is no deity—but me.'

> "But, My little ones, I would lift you up to see and join with Me in the heavenlies. What a difference there is! The difference is there is no despair. If you would come and pick the fruit of a tree, it would smile and say unto thee, 'Thank you for partaking of me!' For that is what I am, you see. The grass comes forth, you see. Every blade radiates the love and glow from Me. The waters, they flow free. There is nothing to hinder me. They say, 'Come and bathe freely. Come and wash freely, for there is nothing to pollute. There is nothing to take away my purity.' Think about the heavenlies; for they all radiate Me. They all show forth My glory, for that is My delight, you see. I desire you to be that way right up until your final day. For those that have built and those that have commanded believe that they can rule you as well, but I will show them that they have not the command. I will show them that you are in My hand, and I will show them a bit of heaven in you, for you will cry and laugh and sing. You will rejoice and dance in Me. You will delight yourself in My glory on your way to your Calvary. And they will not understand. They will either flee or join thee in Me."

Could God be communicating a requirement for us to reign with Him in eternity? Is this the preparation for our upcoming worldwide revival? Only He knows. If He would tell us everything up front, we could not handle it. God is asking all of us to be completely sold out to Him, even unto death, so that we become as one with Him, allowing the Holy Spirit to flow through us. You can see that our commitment to serve God depends on our own will to the degree we make ourselves available, holding nothing back, saying, "Here am I; use me." Whom and what do you stand for? Can He count on you?

Chapter 2

What Is Revival?

Since I started this book, my time with the Lord has increased. I often spend several hours with Him—as many as eight—without having breakfast in the morning. These times sometimes go late into the night. He has so much to reveal to me. I'm writing certain chapters about topics I had no knowledge of before.

On one particular morning I could not get enthused about reading my Bible. I had no idea where or what to read. Finally, I just let my Bible fall open, which I did so many times when I wrote my first book. I was always guided to the exact Scriptures by the Holy Spirit. That day, my Bible opened to the first chapter in the book of John. My eyes focused on verse 14: "And the Word was made flesh, and dwelt among us." As I read a few more verses, the Holy Spirit revealed to me the following: just as John the Baptist was that voice in the wilderness that foretold Jesus' coming, which was already prophesied in Isaiah 40:3, and as he told the people of their need to repent and to be baptized, so I was being called to tell our present generation to receive the baptism in the Holy Spirit and to get ready for His outpouring.

This revival will come not by might, nor by power, but by His Spirit. It is birthed through prayer and will only start when we Christians—not the unbelievers—confess our sins and truly repent, emptying ourselves from all that would hold us back, completely cleansing and cleaning up our own lives, so that there will be Holy Spirit power in our prayer once we are truly humble. Remember, God is looking for a pure heart. People, I plead with you: repent and let the Holy Spirit fill you to overflowing. Receive the baptism in the Holy Spirit and all His gifts, so you, too, will be operating in His power and have your spiritual eyes opened, believing that it is God's power that flows through many anointed vessels, young and old. Stop badmouthing them, as many of you do now in your spiritual ignorance.

Let me give you a firsthand account of the Holy Spirit's power in some of these anointed men. As I watched Christian TV in December 1994, a pastor announced his upcoming crusade in Hawaii in January 1995. At that moment, a strong surge came out of the TV toward me, like I was caught in the suction of a vacuum cleaner. I never experienced anything like that before, but I knew in my spirit that it was supernatural and that God wanted me to attend. Neither time-wise nor financially did this trip fit in my plan, but I obeyed. I talked a friend into coming along so we could share the hotel bill.

Since we left a few days before the crusade, we had time to witness wherever we went. On the airplane over to Hawaii we shared with a young Mormon man while his wife was asleep. We invited him to the crusade, but when she woke up she was furious and threatened to leave him if he came to the crusade. He really wanted to go and was in tears. In our hotel, we witnessed to the night clerk. On the beach we met vacationers from different countries. We experienced quite a language barrier with a Jehovah's Witness family from South America until we shared about the Lord; then we understood the lady much better. I told her to look up all the Scriptures about hell for herself in her Bible, because Jehovah's Witnesses don't believe in a literal hell. Another evening, we talked for hours in a restaurant to two Catholic ladies from Germany and told them to share our conversation when they got home. They will never be the same. On a tour through a jewelry factory, which was included in our trip, we witnessed to a Russian couple. I called them aside and shared with them their need for the baptism in the Holy Spirit after they told me that they were believers. After meeting a man from Spain who needed a physical healing, we confronted a local demoniac on the beach. These are only a sample of the testimonies.

Hawaii would make a great mission field for someone called there by the Holy Spirit. Remember, I said *called there*, not operating in the flesh; otherwise, the anointing would be missing. We also made two trips across town, where my friend practiced with the crusade choir. It was glorious to hear them sing. In one service, the pastor called all the ministers up on the platform to get anointed. The Holy Spirit prompted me to go up there also. As the pastor swung his arm toward me like he did to everyone, calling God's anointing upon me, I felt as if a truck hit me going fifty miles per hour, even with several feet of distance between us.

It was impossible for me to stand on my own. That is why they have a catcher behind each person to prevent him or her from hitting the floor. The crusade was awesome. Besides, numerous miracles and healings were taking place. I saw with my own eyes as a man got out of a wheelchair with wobbly knees, learning to walk with the assistance of a crusade attendant. He shared later on the platform that his wife had dressed and fed him for a couple of years because he couldn't do it himself. It is the power of God that flows through different individuals who are called and anointed by Him.

Ten months later when we had a crusade in our city, I was able to lay hands on an eight or nine-year-old girl from Yakima. Her name was Orchid. She was sitting in front of me with her family. I noticed her being restless, so I asked her what was wrong with her. She told me that her eyes were burning and feeling hot. After telling her mother who I was and getting her permission, I had the girl take her thick glasses off. As I prayed for her, I touched her eyes. She was instantly healed and shared her healing the next evening with the pastor on the platform. Did God plant her in front of me on purpose? She told the announcer that since her healing things are blurry if she reads with her glasses on. If I was looking for recognition, I could have joined her on the platform, acknowledging that I prayed with her, but I know that the time will come when God will elevate me Himself. She told him that she felt someone touch her and that she almost fell back a couple of times as she felt the power of the Holy Spirit. In her childlike way, she explained it the best she could, being put on the spot. The pastor tested her eyes by having her read from his own Bible without her glasses. She read fluently, like an adult. I recorded it when it was shown on TV to prove it to any skeptic.

I told Orchid's mother to find a different church when they got home. Being at the crusade was Orchid's first experience with the Holy Spirit. She did not know about the power of the Holy Spirit, nor, as the mother admitted, the baptism in the Holy Spirit.

Several friends of mine also experienced different healings during the crusade.

I prayed with a young boy, too, for deliverance of a generational curse that attacked the males of his family. It had also afflicted his father, who was not with him.

Iniquity is passed down from generation to generation. As we read in Lamentations 5:7, "Our fathers have sinned, and are not; and we have borne their iniquities." Also, in Psalm 51:5 it says, "Behold, I was shapen in iniquity; and in sin did my mother conceive me." As each seed reproduces and multiplies after its own kind, so are we. Paul tells us in Galatians 6:7–8, "Be not deceived; God is not mocked: for whatsoever a man soweth, that shall he also reap. For he that soweth to the flesh shall of the flesh reap corruption; but he that soweth to the Spirit shall of the Spirit reap life everlasting." It is just that cut and dry with God. Then after we are born again, we are not automatically free; we need to be delivered from the curse of our forefathers. Be it a reoccurring pregnancy out of wedlock, drug addiction, alcoholism, numerous divorces, molestation—you name it, it passes from generation to generation. We are told by God in Exodus 20:5–6 "For I the LORD thy God am a jealous God, visiting the iniquity of the father upon the children unto the third and fourth generation of them that hate Me; And shewing mercy unto thousands of them that love Me, and keep My commandments." Now you see that we cannot do it in our own strength.

Some of the older, well-known healing evangelists shared on Christian TV that they each individually held crusades in over seventy nations of the world. Even at their ripe age of seventy-plus, they continued to go oversees. You see, if you are completely sold out to God, there is no retirement. One evangelist told of a man coming to a particular crusade in Uganda. As a child the Ugandan man had polio, and he could not use his legs because he had no hips. When he heard of the upcoming crusade, he went. Never being witnessed to before, he thought that the evangelist was Jesus. He believed in a healing for himself. Sure enough, God touched him and even gave him new hips where there were none before. This man had total faith and believed in the supernatural. Let me tell you, absolutely nothing happens unless God's anointing is upon evangelists like those on the TV program, or otherwise they would be guilty of operating in the flesh without results. The difference is that they accepted their calling from God and totally submitted their lives to Him, making many sacrifices. They allowed themselves to be guided by the Holy Spirit Himself instead of their denominational doctrine, which in many cases is no more than a religious spirit that keeps people from the full-gospel truth of the Bible. But God will change that.

By the time you finish reading this book, you will agree. They believed in 2 Peter 3:9: "The Lord is not slack concerning his promise, as some men count slackness; but is longsuffering to us-ward, not willing that any should perish, but that all should come to repentance."

Reinhard Bonnke, a German evangelist with a great ministry in Africa shared that as he ministered in Nigeria to over nine million people in six crusades, several million received Jesus as their Savior and many experienced some awesome miracles and healings. Filmed on location with the nationals as interpreters, the lame walked and the blind could see. Several years later, the number increased drastically. As a guest on Christian TV in the middle of February 2006, he announced that through his ministry alone over 100 million souls were saved in the last decade, with over 44 million documented decisions already. He is confident that by the end of this decade, that number will also reach 100 million.[1] Yes, with faith in God, nothing is impossible.

Would you like to know why we don't see the same miracles in this country? Many people are ignorant of God's promises or have an alternative, or both. Why should they have a strong faith and believe in healing? If God will drop it down from heaven on their lap, they will take it. Otherwise, some people's medical coverage allows a hospital bed, a wheelchair, or even a motorized van. Maybe because of these things they are not desperate enough to turn to serious prayer and fasting. I'm not making a blanket statement. Many people don't even know that they can pray for themselves instead of waiting for an evangelist to come to town, call some ministry, or wait until Sunday and have the pastor or the elders of their church lay hands on them. Why don't they know? Because they were never taught. The church as a whole has been lulled to sleep and the anointing that should be upon them is missing. Get ready and enter into the power of the Holy Spirit. Read it for yourself in the Bible.

Many unkind words have been spoken against great evangelists of God by ignorant people who have a religious spirit and deny the Holy Spirit's power. It seems as if we, the body of Christ, are in different camps. We don't read a different Bible, and we believe in the same Jesus, but evidently to a different degree. Is their Jesus still hanging on the cross? Did they stay in kindergarten and never advanced spiritually? They confess to be Christians, yet at the same time they deny the supernatural power of God. At least these days we seem to be able to worship together, which minimizes the wedge inflicted from prior years.

I have heard numerous ministers testify to the profound transformation that took place in their lives when they received the baptism in the Holy Spirit and were freed from the bondage they were under. Is this the reason many of the members in our churches don't watch Christian TV? Are they afraid of the truth? A former Baptist pastor told on Christian TV how he used to preach against the baptism in the Holy Spirit until he received it himself. He explained how he learned the hard way. He was a speaker overseas among other ministers but was there without the anointing from the Holy Spirit. As he cried in desperation to the Lord all night, recognizing what was missing, he received the baptism in the Holy Spirit and preached a powerful sermon like the others the next day.

If we are told the truth and still refuse it, is this not a type of blasphemy against the Holy Spirit? A spirit-filled pastor friend of mine agreed with me when I asked him one day. This is what it is all about, but many denominations simply deny the Holy Spirit's power. It is He that is the force behind our revival. You all want and pray for revival, but you will not allow Him into your church doors. You are unbelieving believers. Did not Jesus say that He is leaving to go sit at the right hand of the Father and that He will send the Holy Spirit, who will guide us in to all truth? (See John 16:13.) This very same Holy Spirit, the third one of the Trinity—the triune God—is the one you refuse in your spiritual ignorance. How do you expect revival to come without Him? What do you think revival is?

This is why many pastors don't preach anointed sermons. They read their text and some even have to read their prayers. Their head knowledge in many churches puts the people to sleep or even drives them away. When pastors realize that it is not their doctorate degree but rather the Holy Spirit's anointing through the baptism of the Holy Spirit that empowers them, we will have revival. Only when we humbly open our hearts and allow Him to make the necessary change in us—from head knowledge to heart knowledge—will we have revival. It will only come when the pastors turn the control of their churches over to the Holy Spirit and let Him reign that the people will follow. In many congregations the people are ready for more of God, but the pastor has no way to give it to them and is not even aware of his spiritual lacking.

Many of us know Joel 2:28: "And it shall come to pass afterward, that I will pour out my spirit upon all flesh; and your sons and your daughters shall prophesy, your old men shall dream dreams, your young men shall see visions." God must be at work in me concerning this book even while I'm asleep, because this is the scripture that was on my mind when I opened my eyes at five-thirty one morning before I began writing. I got up, and with the help of the Holy Spirit, I wrote part of this chapter.

Before the prophet Joel wrote the above Scripture, he warned that the day of the Lord is coming soon. He called for the blowing of a trumpet made from a ram's horn, often known as a *shofar*, to warn of the impending danger. He gave a call to repentance in order to avoid the consequences we would otherwise suffer because of our sins. He wrote:

> Blow ye the trumpet in Zion, and sound an alarm in my holy mountain: let all the inhabitants of the land tremble: for the day of the Lord cometh, for it is nigh at hand.... Therefore also now, saith the Lord, turn ye even to me with all your heart, and with fasting, and with weeping, and with mourning: And rend your heart, and not your garments, and turn unto the Lord your God: for he is gracious and merciful, slow to anger, and of great kindness, and repenteth him of the evil.... Blow the trumpet in Zion, sanctify a fast, call a solemn assembly: Gather the people, sanctify the congregation, assemble the elders, gather the children, and those that suck the breasts: let the bridegroom go forth of his chamber, and the bride out of her closet. Let the priests, the ministers of the Lord, weep between the porch and the altar.
>
> —Joel 2:1, 12–13, 15–17

It occurred to me that I am called to blow the trumpet to you with this book.

The prophet Obadiah confirmed Joel's message with the following verse: "For the day of the Lord is near upon all the heathen: as thou hast done, it shall be done unto thee: thy reward shall return upon thine own head" (Obad. 1:15). The Old Testament prophets used this term—*the day of the Lord*—to signify a time in the history of mankind when God would directly intervene to bring salvation to His people and punishment to the rebellious. By doing so, God would restore His righteous order in the earth.

Joel told us that God does not want our garments to be torn with grief, as was customary then; rather He wants our heart, as we confess our sins (2:13). Why would He give Joel this prophecy so many years ago if it were not so—and of great importance? God wants a true confession and repentance from our heart, a sense of brokenness, so that He can revive us. That means that we were once "vived," alive. What happened to us? We need to return to our first love. The Holy Spirit can and will not do what is described in Joel 2:28 unless we repent first and hold nothing, absolutely nothing back.

The main hindrance is our pride in our denominational doctrines, which are based on man's beliefs and create these different denominations instead of a unified church led by the Holy Spirit. Obadiah tells us in verse 3, "The pride of thine heart hath deceived thee." According to this verse, pride has been around for a long time and is very deceptive. Allow God to do it His way.

None of us lived during the Azusa Street revival, so who knows how God has our revival planned? Let's not dictate to Him in which wrapping it has to appear in order for us to accept it. In Jesus' time it was the scribes and Pharisees that came against Him as He told them in Matthew 23:13, 15: "But woe unto you, scribes and Pharisees, hypocrites! for ye shut up the kingdom of heaven against men: for ye neither go in yourselves, neither suffer ye them that are entering to go in.... Woe unto you, scribes and Pharisees, hypocrites! for ye compass sea and land to make one proselyte, and when he is made, ye make him twofold more the child of hell than yourselves." Not only did they themselves refuse the truth, but also, by their legalism, they erected barriers before those who were seeking the truth. Yes, they were zealous missionaries of evil.

If we're not familiar with it, we want to throw it out. Did not the Scripture say that God is doing a new thing—new to us? (See Isaiah 43:19.) The Book of Ecclesiastes reminds us over and over that there is nothing new under the sun; it just repeats itself. If we are familiar with it, it is no longer a new thing. Can you see my point: how man, with his carnal wisdom, is trying to control and manipulate the Holy Spirit? Forget it! Let me remind you that He is in charge. Will you let Him be the boss of your life?

You see, there are many other people depending on us. It is my firm belief that our American money, largely, will spread the revival to many other nations, especially to third world countries that cannot finance it themselves and have to rely on outsiders to bring it to them free. As people here are converted and let go of the money in their billfold, we can bring them the good news. Remember, Jesus will not return until all have heard the gospel. And how will they hear it if someone does not tell them? It might be via satellite, radio, TV, books, or going in person to these countries. Can you see our great responsibility? God blessed America financially so we in turn can bless others.

I gave a videotape about the Toronto Blessing called *Decently and in Order* to my then-pastor. A pastor friend of his whom I also know and who has the baptism in the Holy Spirit, shared in our church that he visited Toronto and told us of its validity. My pastor was satisfied that his friend approved the happenings there. When I asked my pastor for his response after viewing my video, he said that it was all right if God was using Canada in that way. Was he implying, "...but not here in my church?" You see, God knew the pastor's heart, therefore He wouldn't allow the Holy Spirit's outpouring in our church. The Holy Spirit only goes where He is welcomed without restrictions.

Most of the amazing testimonies on the video I shared with him about the Toronto Blessing were from pastors all around the world who needed a fresh anointing from the Lord. On it, they share about their changed lives after being prayed for. Most of them are seen falling under the power, slain in the Spirit. During their time on the floor, the Holy Spirit did spiritual surgery in them. One pastor from Norway testified that he told his son a couple of weeks before attending the Blessing service of his decision to move out of their home. He said that there was like a wall of demons between him and his wife. On his way to Mexico he heard of the Toronto Blessing and told his wife that they should experience this together. With tears flowing down his face and their arms around each other, he shared that he and his wife are like newlyweds again. He was a man of about fifty years of age. I would like to ask all you critics if you can produce that. No, only the power of the Holy Spirit can accomplish such instant deliverance. It is easy to criticize if you have not been walking in their shoes.

I found that many denominations don't even believe in healing. They say they do, but they are not empowered by the Holy Spirit. Yet, healing is one of the nine gifts described in 1 Corinthians 12. You simply don't believe in one and refuse all the others. Speaking in tongues is one of them that many people will not accept and have been refusing for so long. The devil did a good job on many denominations by keeping them powerless, although they go through the motions. Why don't you tear the pages out of the Bible that you don't believe in? Can you show me proof in the Bible that the gifts went away when the disciples died? No, instead Jesus Himself tells us in Mark 16:17–18, "And these signs shall follow them that believe; In my name shall they cast out devils; they shall speak with new tongues; They shall take up serpents; and if they drink any deadly thing, it shall not hurt them; they shall lay hands on the sick, and they shall recover."

While these people lay on the floor slain in the Spirit, as seen in the video, some of them moan and groan. I assume it depends on the severity of their deliverance. Many pastors, full of the anointing, started their own revival meetings upon returning home. According to testimonies from England, it caused quite a revival there. If it is from God, it will last. Only the one experiencing the transformation can explain what happened to him or her.

A senior pastor from Sydney, Australia, was sent to Toronto by his own congregation because his ministry was no longer effective. After he got prayed for, he shared that he was adopted when he was two years old. All his pain and hurts were swept under the carpet before and never dealt with. He had never confronted his pain and problems. As he would counsel his church members, he lacked compassion and would simply tell them to repent before going on to the next case. While being prayed for in Toronto and lying on the floor for quite some time, he said that God gave him a new heart. As he expounded on the change in him, he also told them that God held him on His lap as if he were a two year old being loved by Him. Was this the love he never had experienced growing up and therefore was not able to give to others? Evidently God filled him up, because he said the first thing he was going to do when he got home was love on his little boy. God must have erased many years of bad experiences and memories as he lay on the floor.

Seeing on the video the pain some endure during their deliverance made me think of Isaiah 43:18–19: "Remember ye not the former things, neither consider the things of old. Behold, I will do a new thing; now it shall spring forth; shall ye not know it? I will even make a way in the wilderness, and rivers in the desert." We see that with God nothing is impossible. So, what is this new thing God is able to do that Isaiah talks about? If He can make a road in the wilderness and rivers in the desert, don't you think that He is able to bring our revival about the way He sees fit? It is those that resist the Holy Spirit's power in their life that cause the delay. Ecclesiastes 1:9–10 reminds us, "There is no new thing under the sun. Is there any thing whereof it may be said, See, this is new? it hath been already of old time, which was before us." Just because we have not experienced something does not mean that it has not been around for a long time. It may have lain dormant for a while. If you were with Moses at the Red Sea, would you have told him that it was impossible to part the waters? Get your brain out of the way instead of playing God! My pastor from the conservative Baptist church told me that he had to go to Argentina a number of years ago to see that it was proper for believers to raise their hands in worship! He reasoned that since they were people he ministered and fellowshiped with, it must have been all right, whereas at home he probably only heard that Pentecostals behaved like that. You see how bound one can be by trusting that only their denomination has the truth?

Let me give you an eye opener. If you read your Bible as a Lutheran, you totally ignore Matthew 3:16, which says, "And Jesus, when He was baptized, went up straightway out of the water." The same is true of Jesus' own words in Mark 16:16: "He that believeth and is baptized shall be saved." According to the Bible, sprinkling at birth is not correct and therefore not acceptable. If Jesus was dunked, who are you to change the procedure? Babies are only dedicated to the Lord. When they are old enough and are ready to understand, then they may accept Jesus as their Savior. In my case, in third grade my whole class in school received first communion. It was only head knowledge, if even that, because we were told what to do. With Jesus, it is a very personal relationship, not mass production. Furthermore, a baby cannot make a confession of faith. Jesus said in the above Scripture that after you believe you get baptized, and then you're saved. Is it not time that we return to the truth of the Bible, instead of our denominational habits?

Now, the Baptist believer knows that the Lutherans and Catholics practice the wrong form of baptism, yet when most of them read the Bible, they totally disbelieve tongues, which is one of the nine gifts mentioned in 1 Corinthians 12. You can't pick and choose; either you believe in the entire Bible or none of it. If you don't believe in tongues, does that mean that you also don't believe in the gift of healing? It looks like you are being found out! When people who never believed in healing are diagnosed with a terminal illness and have only a few months to live, they show up. When a certain Baptist lady who attended a Benny Hinn crusade got healed of a terminal illness was asked why she came, she said that she had been desperate. She even worked in a Baptist college. Since receiving her healing, she travels and testifies all over the country. In seconds, God changed her from almost dead to a healthy, happy, traveling Baptist lady who gives God all the glory for her healing.

The Lutherans don't believe in tongues, either; that makes them twice wrong. The Catholics have even some additional chapters added to their Bible called The Apocrypha in which praying to the dead and the existence of purgatory are taught. Let's look at the difference between the Catholic and Coptic Orthodox Church's belief systems, with which I became acquainted in Egypt. Coptic is one of the oldest religions in the world. The Catholic priest cannot be married, yet the Coptic priest must be married. (In another chapter I will explain more on this subject.) How does God feel about that? If they would let the Catholic priests get married, we would not hear about all these molestation cases that are so devastating to the victims. It is a disgrace and should be punished.

We read in 2 Peter 1:20–21, "Knowing this first, that no prophecy of the scripture is of any private interpretation. For the prophecy came not in old time by the will of man: but holy men of God spake as they were moved by the Holy Ghost." Anyone teaching that we need another book to explain the Bible is in error and belongs to a cult. God's Word is not in that extra book. If it's anything other than the Bible, it contains man-made doctrine that corrupts the truth of the Bible, and it is from the pit of hell. There is only one Word of God, which should be easy to understand.

When I try to explain the truth to different individuals, the majority of them don't even want to hear it, because their belief is so shallow that they cannot discern for themselves. If Jesus is the Head and we are His body, don't you think it is high time that we believe in His teaching—He, the Living Word and the Bread of Life—and not our man-made denominational doctrines? If you don't believe in everything written in the Bible, Jesus won't have any part of you; because if He is the Head and we are His body, He will not allow any partial believer with man-made doctrines to be attached to Him. By not believing in the full message of the gospel, which includes the Holy Spirit the way He is described in the Bible, many of you are no different from the many other religions, with or without a second book, because your denomination dictates to you what to believe, instead of the Holy Spirit's revelation. Do you want to go to heaven or not? Make sure that you allow the following Scripture to sink in to your understanding:

> For I testify unto every man that heareth the words of the prophecy of this book, If any man shall add unto these things, God shall add unto him the plagues that are written in this book: And if any man shall take away from the words of the book of this prophecy, God shall take away his part out of the book of life, and out of the holy city, and from the things which are written in this book.
>
> —Revelation 22:18–19

This means that the names of those who add to or take away from the Bible are not even written in the Book of Life, which means that heaven is off-limits for them. This is described in Revelation 20:15: "And whosoever was not found written in the book of life was cast into the lake of fire."

Even Dr. John G. Lake said that eight people in his family had to die before he heard and believed in God's healing power. He called it a great new light that had dawned in his soul. Instead of his wife being victim number nine, she was instantly healed in 1898 under the ministry of John Alexander Dowie. Lake said that their own church had diligently taught them that the days of miracles had past, but he came to understand that such teaching was a lie from the devil that had infiltrated the church and was slowly stealing mankind's inheritance through Christ. In 1908, Dr. Lake went to South Africa as a missionary, where his work attracted worldwide attention. He returned after five years. Some time afterwards he moved to Spokane, Washington. His ministry there demonstrated the power of God, which resulted in over one hundred thousand healings over a period of five years. In 1920, Dr. John G. Lake moved to Portland, Oregon, where he founded a similar work. He died in Spokane on September 16, 1935, at the age of sixty-five. He credited his outstanding healing ministry to receiving the Holy Spirit baptism.[2]

Let me remind you that this was over one hundred years ago, and yet it has not changed to this day. Can you see the urgent need for establishing the body of Christ? Get ready, because the time is short. God will pour out His Spirit. The Word says that He will pour it out "on all flesh," which means on all classes of people, whatever their status. It means on the young and old, both men and women, but it does not mean on every individual. The person not willing to empty themselves of all prior judgments and hang-ups—like racism, discrimination, pride, religious doctrines, and the like—will simply miss out, because they are not allowed to attach themselves to Jesus' headship. They are part of the body of someone else's head. Whose head, do you think?

The Holy Spirit will not penetrate a hard heart that is not willing to repent. The Bible tells us in 2 Samuel 6:14–23 that King David danced before the Lord with all his might, but because Michal, his wife, criticized him for it, she could bare no children until her death. We need to be very careful when we appoint ourselves as judge over others. By doing so, Michal paid the consequences by being barren all her life. What will God allow to happen to you if you appoint yourself judge over other peoples circumstances? Has He given you the consent to do so, or is your critical mind in control? All too often, we blame the devil for a negative happening in our life when in reality God allowed us the experience, as He grooms us to His liking. Remember Job's experience. God gave the devil permission to take everything away from Job except his life. Afterward God restored it all to him, and more. Another person cannot judge for us what circumstances the Lord allows in our life.

We read in Hebrews 12:5–7, "And ye have forgotten the exhortation which speaketh unto you as unto children, My son, despise not thou the chastening of the Lord, nor faint when thou art rebuked of him: For whom the Lord loveth he chasteneth, and scourgeth every son whom he receiveth. If ye endure chastening, God dealeth with you as with sons; for what son is he whom the father chasteneth not?" Why is this true? Because of 1 Peter 1:7:

"That the trail of your faith, being much more precious than gold that perisheth, though it be tried with fire, might be found unto praise and honour and glory at the appearing of Jesus Christ." We don't hear that preached from our pulpits anymore, yet the Bible is full of passages like these. All we hear is that God is love, love.

Just because we are not familiar with something does not mean that it is from the devil. If we are truly Spirit-filled, we can ask the Holy Spirit for discernment, which is another one of the nine gifts, and then stand our ground instead of bowing down to the pressures of others to conform. Some people are not fulfilling what God called them to do because they allow themselves to be influenced by others, which puts them totally out of the will of God. If I listened to my friends and certain pastors, I would have given up a long time ago. I hope you understand by now and allow revival to take place in you personally, as well as in your church!

Yes, sin is the culprit for the delay in our long-awaited revival. It blocks the work of the Holy Spirit and prevents revival among God's people. There is no alternative and there can be no compromise, because God will not work as long as sin is covered up and swept under the carpet. We simply cannot hold on to sin anymore. Our heart must be broken with sorrow over our sinful condition, which results in full confession and the forsaking of sin. Nothing less than repentance will satisfy God. David wrote in Psalm 66:18, "If I regard iniquity in my heart, the Lord will not hear me." Isaiah 59:2 reads, "But your iniquities have separated between you and your God, and your sins have hid his face from you, that he will not hear."

Sin must be utterly forsaken before God will manifest a revival. For some, it may mean lying prostrate on the floor before God. The following Scripture describes the conditions.

> If my people, which are called by my name, shall humble themselves, and pray, and seek my face, and turn from their wicked ways; then will I hear from heaven, and will forgive their sin, and will heal their land.
>
> —2 CHRONICLES 7:14

We simply must die completely to our flesh. Only after we have turned from our wicked ways will He hear from heaven and forgive our sins. We must get right with God and also with each other, as we read in 1 John 4:20–21: "If a man say, I love God, and hateth his brother, he is a liar: for he that loveth not his brother whom he hath seen, how can he love God whom he hath not seen? And this commandment have we from him, That he who loveth God love his brother also."

There are three kinds of confessions:

- *Private:* A sin committed against God only needs to be confessed to no one but Him. As we read in 1 John 1:9, "If we confess our sins, he is faithful and just to forgive us our sins, and to cleanse us from all unrighteousness." Psalm 32:5 says, "I acknowledge my sin unto thee, and mine iniquity have I not hid. I said, I will confess my transgressions unto the LORD; and thou forgavest the iniquity of my sin. Selah."

- *Personal:* A sin committed against another person must be confessed both to God and to the one wronged. There will be no peace until confession has been made and forgiveness sought. This can be a tough one; our pride often gets in the way, especially if some time has passed since. As we read in the following scripture, don't delay; do it quickly. "Therefore if thou bring thy gift to the altar, and there rememberest that thy brother hath ought against thee; Leave there thy gift before the altar, and go thy way; first be reconciled to thy brother, and then come and offer thy gift" (Matt. 5:23–24).
- *Public:* Whenever a sin has been committed against a group of people, the confession must be as public as the transgression. The apostle Paul wrote in 2 Corinthians 2:10–11, "To whom ye forgive any thing, I forgive also: for if I forgave any thing, to whom I forgave it, for your sakes forgave I it in the person of Christ; Lest Satan should get an advantage of us: for we are not ignorant of his devices."

Sometimes groups gather for several nights of prayer asking for revival to come to their church, but God does not answer their prayers. "Why?" one would ask. Remember, we read earlier in Isaiah 59:2, "But your iniquities have separated between you and your God, and your sins have hid his face from you, that he will not hear."

We cannot expect showers of blessings until we deal with our sins, until we have a clean slate. The communication between God and us is broken off and our prayers don't go through to heaven. Allow the Holy Spirit to convict you now by asking yourself the following questions:

- Have I forgiven those who have offended me?
- Is there malice in my heart toward anyone?
- Am I holding grudges?
- Do I refuse to be reconciled?
- Do I get angry?
- Do I lose my temper?
- Do I allow wrath to get the best of me?
- Do I have feelings of jealousy when another is preferred before me?
- Do I become envious of those who can do things better than I can? (Focusing on my own gifts eliminates envy.)
- Am I impatient?
- Do I get easily irritated?
- Do little things annoy me?
- Am I easily offended?
- Do I get hurt when people overlook me?
- If I am neglected, do I engage in self-pity?
- Is there pride in my heart?
- Do I think more highly of myself than I ought to think?
- Am I too proud to seek forgiveness?
- Have I been dishonest?

- Am I above reproach in all my transactions?
- Do I give a day's work for a day's pay?
- Do I gossip?
- Do I slander the character of others?
- Am I a talebearer and busybody?
- Am I a faultfinder?
- Am I worldly?
- Am I taken up with the glitter and show of this life?
- Am I stealing?
- Do I take even little things that do not belong to me?
- Am I bitter towards others?
- Is there any hatred deep within my heart?
- Am I worried or anxious?
- Do I fail to trust God for my temporal and spiritual needs?
- Am I continually fretting over the future?
- Am I guilty of lustful thoughts?
- Do I allow my mind to be taken up with impure and unholy thoughts?
- Do I lie?
- Do I exaggerate and convey false impressions?
- Am I afraid to confess Christ openly?
- Am I ashamed of Jesus?
- Do I hide my relationship with Christ when surrounded by the world's people?

These are some things that hinder the work of God in the midst of His people, but let's call them what God calls them—sins! The sooner we admit that we have sinned and confess and forsake those sins, the sooner we can expect God to open the channels of communication and blessing to hear us and to work His mighty power through us. We cannot deceive God. Why deceive ourselves? Let's remove the obstacle before we take another step. First Corinthians 11:31 tells us, "For if we would judge ourselves, we should not be judged."

Throughout the centuries, man has attempted to produce revival, and night after night the Word of God has been ministered—but it will be without results until someone bursts out in open confession, begging forgiveness from the one wronged. Another may break down in tears, confessing a root of bitterness or hard feelings or even jealousy. Once confession and restitution take place, once our sins are uncovered and acknowledged, then—and not until then—will the Spirit of God bring revival in our midst.

It is my prayer that as you read some of the chapters in this book, sincere repentance will take place so that God can fill us with His reviving power and bring our long-awaited revival. Teenagers from many different denominations are on their knees repenting and promising God to live a pure life. The adults must wake up like our young people. Many are committed and sold out to God. Instead of calling the psychic hotlines, they want to see the supernatural power of God. We will see cancers healed, organs recreated, and demons cast out.

Search me, O God, and know my heart: try me, and know my thoughts: And see if there be any wicked way in me, and lead me in the way everlasting.

—Psalm 139:23–24

Chapter 3

When Will He Return?

God gives us all a chance to get our act together, as we read in 2 Peter 3:9: "The Lord is not slack concerning his promise, as some men count slackness; but is long-suffering to us-ward, not willing that any should perish, but that all should come to repentance." He loves us so much that He tells us the truth about ourselves through His Word. If we choose not to obey, He gets our attention through circumstances He allows or even sends someone to confront us.

Only by His grace toward us has He not yet appeared in the clouds for us, as described in 1 Thessalonians 4:16–17: "For the Lord himself shall descend from heaven with a shout, with the voice of the archangel, and with the trump of God: and the dead in Christ shall rise first: Then we which are alive and remain shall be caught up together with them in the clouds, to meet the Lord in the air: and so shall we ever be with the Lord." First Corinthians

15:51–52 tells us, "Behold, I shew you a mystery; We shall not all sleep, but we shall all be changed, In a moment, in the twinkling of an eye, at the last trump: for the trumpet shall sound, and the dead shall be raised incorruptible, and we shall be changed." This is the reason why we need to be ready and prepared and live as if it could happen any second. Remember the story of the ten virgins in Matthew 25. Only five of them were ready.

Are you watching for Jesus' appearing? These are Jesus' words in Matthew 7:21–23: "Not every one that saith unto me, Lord, Lord, shall enter into the kingdom of heaven; but he that doeth the will of my Father which is in heaven. Many will say to me in that day, Lord, Lord, have we not prophesied in thy name? and in thy name have cast out devils? and in thy name done many wonderful works? And then will I profess unto them, I never knew you: depart from me, ye that work iniquity."

I firmly believe that we prolong Jesus' return by our denominational prejudices. The unity is missing, and Satan has plotted our division by deception, causing our separation, because we are no longer of one mind. Believe me, no confusion will enter heaven. Satan's old tricks have worked, deceiving many denominations by letting them be influenced by him, that, for example, tongues could be of the devil. By instilling such a thought, who would be interested in tongues? Very few; therefore, he has won. His gain is your loss as you conduct your affairs without the power of the Holy Spirit. It is just a matter of time until you admit it.

Jesus warns against self-deception. He tells us in Matthew 15:7–9, "Ye hypocrites, well did Esaias prophesy of you, saying, This people draweth nigh unto me with their mouth, and honoureth me with their lips; but their heart is far from me. But in vain they do worship me, teaching for doctrines the commandments of men." Even today, people move their lips, but in their heart they are way off. We need to be walking in genuine obedience and believe in all of God's Word. It is written in our Bible, which is for us to read so we have no excuse later. Yet many today don't even drive out demons. Why? The reason is simple: many don't believe in them.

You say deliverance couldn't happen in our day because you believe that these signs went away with the disciples when they died. Therefore, you don't even believe the entire sayings of Jesus. How can you claim to be His if you don't believe in all of His teaching? The words of Jesus were not just for the disciples. The Bible was written for all of us. Study it and believe all of it to make sure that you are not going to miss the Rapture and that you can avoid the seven years of Tribulation. Are there a few of you pastors who keep your spirituality a secret? Are you afraid of losing your monthly retirement check when they kick you out of their denomination if you declare to them that you speak in tongues? Don't worry; if you're committed to God, He'll find another church for you. But if you don't believe in the full gospel, then someone has to tell you that your man-made denominational doctrine, which came from the pit of hell, is a total deception

The Holy Spirit warns us prophetically through the writers of the Bible. The term *Latter Times* refers to the period of time between the first coming of Christ and His second coming. Let's back it up with God's Word:

> Now the Spirit speaketh expressly, that in the latter times some shall depart from the faith, giving head to seducing spirits, and doctrines of devils.
>
> —1 TIMOTHY 4:1

Just as Eve listened to Satan, so have some of your teachers in the past and made up their own doctrine. Yet Jesus said not everyone that calls Him Lord will enter heaven, only he who does the will of His Father. Do you think it is the Father's will that we have so many different doctrines? The Baptists have one way and the Catholics, for instance, have another way. Unless you line up with God's Word, you can expect Jesus to say, "Away from Me; I never knew you!" Why not? You had your own belief; each denomination does how they see fit. Our commitment should be to God alone, not to the church or organization's doctrine.

If there are disagreements within a denomination, they have a church split and start their own congregation, adding another man-made doctrine to the previous one. Why are there over fifty different kinds of Baptist affiliations alone? There are the Southern Baptists, the conservative Baptists, and the list goes on. Just open your phone book and see for yourself.

This is the reason for this book: God does not want that any should perish. So you decide; each person for himself. It is a decision from your own heart. When you turn away from your man-made doctrines, a phenomenal revival is going to break out as the Holy Spirit is allowed to rule in His fullness. Our churches will be alive and overflowing when the people are filled with the power and the glory of the Lord. Unbelievers come to get converted, as they hear and see the changed lives and are amazed of the healings people are experiencing from God.

Watch out, devil! I compare many of today's churches with Israel. They walk where Jesus walked, yet they are too blind spiritually to realize that He was here once already. As many of our churches made up their own rules over the years to govern themselves, their revelations come from their head knowledge instead of divine revelation, which comes from the Spirit of God. Jesus said in Matthew 16:18, "I will build my church; and the gates of hell shall not prevail against it." He did not say *churches*. He also said that He is praying to the Father that they be one. (See John 17:20–21.) Will you be a part of His unified body?

During the first meeting I had with the pastor of a conservative Baptist church before I attended there, he told me that their church was Jesus' church when I expressed concern about whether or not I was even welcome there because of my Pentecostal beliefs. It sounded so nice to have him say that it was Jesus' church. But was it true? As the Holy Spirit gave me a message for the pastor at different times—which he rejected each time—I realized quickly that it was not so. Jesus was not in control; he was. So, too, is it with many churches today. There can be no Holy Spirit anointing upon the pastor if the church is controlled by the carnal mind. All we have to do is go to the Bible. It has an answer for everything. As time went on, there was no money left at the conservative Baptist church to support both pastors, and he, the senior pastor, was asked to leave. We read in 1 Corinthians 2:14, "But the natural man receiveth not the things of the Spirit of God: for they are foolishness unto him: neither can he know them, because they are spiritually discerned."

This is why the baptism in the Holy Spirit is of great importance, a fact which many pastors deny. As long as they rule in their flesh, which is man's opinion, they have no revelation from the Holy Spirit. It is so easy to spot them. One pastor gave himself away in his preaching, as he forever quoted what other people wrote or said instead of getting a fresh *rhema* word himself from the Lord. One Sunday morning he preached that if God speaks and says, "Go now," we don't need to pray about it. He said that when God spoke in the past, no one ever questioned it. He continued that it was crucial for our revival and asked us if there was a famine in our spirit that keeps us from hearing God and if our unbelief is stifling our experience in Him. Evidently he did not know that God is also speaking through people.

A few months later, he shared the following from the pulpit. It will show you how insensitive he is to the Holy Spirit. He was at a hamburger place before the Sunday morning service. When he got ready to leave, the Holy Spirit prompted him to talk to a young man and told him what to say, but he ignored it and went out to his car. There, the Holy Spirit revealed to him that he would not be preaching that day if he disobeyed, which startled him enough to return and talk to the young man. Why didn't he obey right away? I was shocked that he was not too embarrassed to tell that story.

Jesus said in Matthew 16:19, "And I will give unto thee the keys of the kingdom of heaven: and whatsoever thou shalt bind on earth shall be bound in heaven: and whatsoever thou shalt loose on earth shall be loosed in heaven." Jesus rules the kingdom of God, which is different from religion. When I attended the first weekly prayer meeting for revival in our church, I soon recognized that the meeting was being conducted in the flesh. A lady complained to God in prayer about the awful treatment she was receiving from her husband. She went on and on. Being an evangelist, I came to pray for revival, not what I saw. The Holy Spirit showed me that their prayers would not go past the ceiling. Needless to say, I did not return the next week. It grieved my spirit because they would not listen.

In most churches the pastor is in charge of everything. What he says goes. He is the spiritual leader as well as the businessman. When whole denominations turn to the truth of the Bible, another change will occur. I knew in my spirit for several years that we would have masses getting baptized in the Holy Spirit, but I was at a loss for how God was going to bring it to pass. I knew it had to happen before Jesus would return, simply because it was written in the Bible.

When people get sensitive to the Holy Spirit, He will raise apostles, prophets, and evangelists in the churches for the perfecting of the saints. How? "Not by might, nor by power, but by my spirit, saith the Lord" (Zech. 4:6). Then the five-fold ministry implemented by Jesus will come into operation again, as described in Ephesians 4:11–16:

> And he gave some, apostles; and some, prophets; and some, evangelists; and some, pastors and teachers; For the perfecting of the saints, for the work of the ministry, for the edifying of the body of Christ: Till we all come in the unity of the faith, and of the knowledge of the Son of God, unto a

> perfect man, unto the measure of the stature of the fulness of Christ: That we henceforth be no more children, tossed to and fro, and carried about with every wind of doctrine, by the sleight of men, and cunning craftiness, whereby they lie in wait to deceive; But speaking the truth in love, may grow up into him in all things, which is the head, even Christ: From whom the whole body fitly joined together and compacted by that which every joint supplieth, according to the effectual working in the measure of every part, maketh increase of the body unto the edifying of itself in love.

The pastor then will only tend to his sheep, which will keep him plenty busy and fulfilled.

If Jesus said, as we just read, that it takes five ministries to effectively govern His church, then that is what He meant—five ministries, although in many churches only two of them are in operation, the pastor and the teacher. The other three are simply denied because the elders or deacons, who are voted on by the congregation, cannot replace them. Sometime the voting process is not even led by the Holy Spirit.

Being an evangelist is different from assisting in the support of missionaries in foreign lands. My burden is for the conversion of as many souls as possible. The apostle and prophet can only function in a Holy Spirit-filled church because their revelations for the church body are divine; it comes straight from the Holy Spirit, not your brain. As I evangelize, I ask different people if they are Spirit-filled. They all always say yes. When you accept Jesus into your heart, you are indwelt by the Spirit, but afterward He will lie dormant unless you let Him empower you.

It seems as if God is using that conservative Baptist church as an example to open your eyes to spiritual understanding. I surely did not have it planned like that. The pastor believes that he is Spirit-filled. His denominational doctrine teaches it. When we added two new deacons some time ago, I asked them if they were Spirit-filled. The first one said yes. When I asked the second one more directly if he spoke in tongues, he replied that God told him not to.

Are we not exhorted in 1 Timothy 6:1, "That the name of God and his doctrine be not blasphemed." The restoration of the apostles, prophets, and evangelists is necessary in order to bring the church into the fullness of Christ and prepare the people for the Lord, as described by the angel of the Lord to Zechariah when he made the birth announcement of John the Baptist in Luke 1:15–17: "And he shall be filled with the Holy Ghost, even from his mother's womb. And many of the children of Israel shall he turn to the Lord their God. And he shall go before him in the spirit and power of Elias, to turn the hearts of the fathers to the children, and the disobedient to the wisdom of the just; to make ready a people prepared for the Lord." The office of the apostle, prophet, and evangelist is not a church-appointed one; it is a special calling from the Lord. I know that I am called to be an evangelist. God gave me a heavy burden for souls. At the prompting of the Holy Spirit, He will also give me a prophetic message from time to time for a specific individual or the church as a whole.

Let me share these powerful words with you from a poem by Henry Crocker:

EVANGELIZE

Give us a watchword for the hour,
A thrilling word, a word of power;
A battle cry, a flaming breath,
A call to conquest or to death;
A word to rouse the church from rest,
To heed her Master's high behest [command],
The call is given, ye hosts arise,
The watchword is Evangelize!

To dying men, a fallen race,
Make known the gift of gospel grace.
The world that now in darkness lies,
Evangelize, evangelize![1]

As I go about my business, the Holy Spirit brings different people across my path that I then witness and minister to. An apostle, prophet, or evangelist is an office in the church appointed and anointed by God, not by man. The result is evident. The Holy Spirit is cleaning house to prepare us for the Rapture. As Jesus Himself told the scribes and Pharisees, so it is still with us today: "Thus have ye made the commandment of God of none effect by your tradition" (Matt. 15:6). Then He reminded them of Isaiah's prophecy, saying, "This people draweth nigh unto me with their mouth, and honoureth me with their lips; but their heart is far from me. But in vain they do worship me, teaching for doctrines the commandments of men" (Matt. 15:8–9).

Listen to what Paul told the Corinthian church in 2 Corinthians 11:3–4, 14–15:

> But I fear, lest by any means, as the serpent beguiled Eve through his subtilty, so your minds should be corrupted from the simplicity that is in Christ. For if he that cometh preacheth another Jesus, whom we have not preached, or if ye receive another spirit, which ye have not received, or another gospel, which ye have not accepted, ye might well bear with him.... And no marvel; for Satan himself is transformed into an angel of light. Therefore it is no great thing if his ministers also be transformed as the ministers of righteousness; whose end shall be according to their works.

Another time, Paul tells them in 1 Corinthians 4:15, "For though ye have ten thousand instructers in Christ, yet have ye not many fathers: for in Christ Jesus I have begotten you through the gospel." He writes also, "For our gospel came not unto you in word only, but also in power, and in the Holy Ghost." It involves signs, wonders, and miracles that demonstrate the power of God—which are not evident in most churches today. There is no excuse because Jesus Himself said when He gave the Great Commission in Mark 16:17–18, "And these signs shall follow them that believe; In my name shall they cast out devils; they shall speak with new tongues; They shall take up serpents; and if they drink any deadly thing, it shall not hurt them; they shall lay hands on the sick, and they shall recover." What is keeping you from practicing it in your church? Jesus began by saying, "And these signs shall follow those who believe." It is a matter of fact, not *if* or *maybe*. Can your faith stretch far enough to believe it?

Again, Paul the apostle writes in 1 Corinthians 4:14–21:

> I write not these things to shame you, but as my beloved sons I warn you. For though ye have ten thousand instructers in Christ, yet have ye not many fathers: for in Christ Jesus I have begotten you through the gospel. Wherefore I beseech you, be ye followers of me. For this cause have I sent unto you Timotheus, who is my beloved son, and faithful in the Lord, who shall bring you into remembrance of my ways which be in Christ, as I teach every where in every church. Now some are puffed up, as though I would not come to you. But I will come to you shortly, if the Lord will, and will know, not the speech of them which are puffed up, but the power. For the kingdom of God is not in word, but in power. What will ye? shall I come unto you with a rod, or in love, and in the spirit of meekness?

As their spiritual father, he asks them if he should come with a stick for a spanking or in love, with a gentle spirit? Evidently, they went astray if he had to warn them and bring correction.

God allowed Malachi to see into the future. His prophetic utterance closes the Old Testament as he views Christ's second advent, the final judgment of the wicked, and the ultimate salvation of those who fear His name: "Behold, I will send you Elijah the prophet before the coming of the great and dreadful day of the Lord: And he shall turn the heart of the fathers to the children, and the heart of the children to their fathers, lest I come and smite the earth with a curse" (Mal. 4:5–6).

As I typed these words on the keyboard, my heart was palpitating and I started to weep as the Holy Spirit gave me this awesome revelation: I will be coming in the spirit of Elijah. He reminded me of what He had told me two days prior, that I have the same calling as John the Baptist, who turned many of the children of Israel to the Lord their God. John the Baptist also went before Christ in the spirit and power of Elijah, to turn the heart of the fathers to the children, and the disobedient to the wisdom of the just, to make ready a people prepared for the Lord.

As rampant as crime, shootings, and AIDS are amongst our young people, it shows me that God will turn our rebellious children around, and there will be repentance by the multitudes. I firmly believe that our young people will be the leaders of our revival. As they get turned on to the Lord and understand the Scriptures, they won't want anyone left behind to experience the floods, storms, fires, severe winters, extreme heat, hurricanes, earthquakes, and famine that will be experienced in those days. Even these examples are only a sample of what is to come after the church is snatched away (raptured). Malachi begins, "Behold, I will send you Elijah the prophet," who was translated about five hundred years before the time of Malachi and whom the Lord will send back to Earth in the midst of the coming Great Tribulation. Revelation 11:3 tells us, "And I will give power unto my two witnesses, and they shall prophesy a thousand two hundred and threescore days, clothed in sackcloth." No Scripture mentions the names of both these men, so we cannot be sure if it will be Moses or Enoch, or someone else who will minister with Elijah. A prophet is a messenger who foretells of things to come and warns the people of God's wrath and the consequence of hell if they don't repent from their evil deeds.

John the Baptist prepared the way for the first advent of Christ. The two witnesses will prepare the way for the second coming of

Christ. As John the Baptist came in the spirit of Elijah, so also, I believe, will it be before we experience the Rapture. Another one sent by the Lord will awaken the people in our day and age from their spiritual slumber. Is the content of this book the instrument God is using? He told me so in 1991 when He asked me to write this book, saying that it would cause our revival! John walked with a stick in the wilderness. We put messages in print or broadcast them on TV for maximum exposure and allow the Holy Spirit bring conviction and repentance. If men have flunked, He will use women or anyone else He can depend upon.

According to the Scriptures, Elijah was led by the Lord to a widow who was to feed him. As we read in 1 Kings 17:9–24, Elijah performed his first miracle in Zarephath, a city on the Mediterranean coast. He asked a widow, almost out of food herself, to fix him a meal. She told him that she was going to prepare it for herself and her son as their last meal before they died from starvation. The Lord inspired Elijah to tell her to fix a meal for him first and that He would multiply her flour and oil to overflowing. We read that even after preparing the meal, the flour in her bin was not used up, nor did the jar of oil run dry. In the same chapter, a second miracle took place. As Elijah lodged with the woman, her son died. Elijah took the boy upstairs and laid him on his bed, stretched himself three times out over his body, and cried out to the Lord. Then he brought the child back down and gave him to his mother saying, "See, your son lives!" In response, the woman said to him, "Now by this I know that you are a man of God, and that the Word of the Lord in your mouth is the truth" (author's paraphrase). In chapter 18 it says that Elijah overthrew the prophets of

Baal and called fire and rain down from heaven. In chapter 19, he received a revelation from God to anoint Hazael as king of Syria, Jehu as king over Israel, and Elisha as a prophet in his place.

This tells me that I will be doing great and mighty exploits for the Lord, which different people have prophesied over me already in times past. A prophetess from Seattle with a proven ministry of more than thirty years told me on several different occasions that I was going to be the leader of our revival. A few years ago she prophesied to me that God is teaching me to hear His voice and that God was "giving me His insignia ring," a symbol of the authority I will have in Him. Another time, she said that God would do great things through me that if I were told, I would not believe. I have all these prophecies on tape and have copied most of them in a separate chapter. It all seems to be slowly falling into place, but let me tell you, there is a price to pay to be groomed by the Lord for such a calling. I will explain my training process in a later chapter. Moses was forty years in training in the wilderness before he started his ministry.

Later, the Holy Spirit gave me another awesome revelation that came from deep down in my spirit: the one coming in the spirit of Elijah was meant to be a friend of mine who was on fire for the Lord and who spent many hours in my home several years ago. He had this calling upon him. I remember how he used to talk about Elijah, and I believe that he knew he was chosen by the Lord. Once, a whole group of us attended a Passover Seder put on by a messianic Jewish congregation. It is a Jewish tradition to put an extra place setting out, including a chair. This is so that if Elijah returns, there will be room for him to sit at the table with them.

I remember how my friend reacted when this was announced and Elijah's name was mentioned. He literally flew about a foot up in the air in his chair. He had a great desire to go to Israel and minister to the Jewish people.

Only one thing has changed: he is living in sin now. He has left his wife and children and is living with a woman who has left her husband and children for him. I loved this man as a brother and there was no doubt in our mind that we would minister together one day. I tried many times to convince him that his lifestyle was wrong and have also ministered to his now ex-wife, to the extent she would allow me. He always carried a little Bible with him and knew the Scriptures well. But when it came to himself, he could not break the bond with this woman. I visited him several times at his job. He even showed me where the Holy Spirit pointed out certain Scriptures to him in the Bible that said he was to go home to his family.

Living in sin will cause us to lose our anointing if we don't repent and turn from our wicked ways. King David sinned greatly, but he repented. Because of it, God described him as a man after His own heart. It is God who calls individuals to His work, and only God can remove His anointing. We simply cannot live in sin and expect God's approval and anointing upon us. His wife finally went through with the divorce after several years of this mess. Every time the divorce was going to be final, he came home, but he always left again soon afterward.

God replaced him and gave me the calling that was once upon him. Whenever I hear the song "Days of Elijah," my spirit gets so touched that I weep. I believe that I now have upon me the calling of four individuals who God could not trust to be involved in our revival. I did nothing to acquire it from them. They are:

1. The self-appointed prophet from Ghana, West Africa, who lived with me three different times for, all together, six months over a period of two years. He had women, included married ones, call him from all over any time of day and night. Some also supplied him with money, which he could not hang on to. He still ministers today.
2. The pastor from the conservative Baptist church I attended.
3. My friend with the Elijah calling.
4. The Methodist pastor from Ghana who bought himself a new home with the over one hundred thousand dollars I sent him to help build a school for children with mental and physical defects.

It kind of puzzled me why God even allowed me to get acquainted with these men. Was He trying to teach me something through these experiences? Or did He know that He could depend on me? God will use whoever makes himself available. As Galatians 3:28 explains, "There is neither Jew nor Greek, there is neither bond nor free, there is neither male nor female: for ye are all one in Christ Jesus." All He is looking for are faithful servants who are totally sold out to Him and are willing to lay down their life for His cause. I remember the Holy Spirit revealing to me in 1991, "I have sent you two [men] to be the leaders of your revival, but both of them have flunked. Therefore, I want you to write a book, which will cause your revival." These were the two men from Ghana.

While I was still attending the conservative Baptist church, some of the ladies in the congregation went on an overnight outing. We prayed collectively and individually for each other. One of them asked me to pray for her so that she could conceive a baby. She already had some older children and had wanted another baby for some time. As soon as she got home, she got pregnant and nine months later gave birth to a healthy girl. I constantly have opportunities to pray for different individuals for deliverance and healing, from a simple headache to whatever else they need to be set free from.

As these things continued to happen, the prophecy spoken over me in 1987 made more sense: That I will establish the body of Christ, and that I have the anointing of tabernacles upon me (which I described in the first chapter). I am confident that many people will accept Jesus as their Savior when they read this book.

A great revival will break out when we obey, so God won't have to strike the earth with a curse, as the prophet Malachi warned. Our self-rule with man-made committees, which is an unbiblical form of government, must stop. As we restore the five-fold ministry and say, "Lord, not mine, but Your will be done," we will see blind eyes opening, the lame walk, limbs grow out, and yes, even the dead will rise. I do believe it—with all my heart.

As soon as we conform to all of God's Word, repent from our secret sins, and realize that some of us had false teachers and therefore must denounce every kind of doctrine taught by the trickery of men in cunning craftiness of deceitful plotting, God will be pleased with us. And after spreading the revival to other countries that He calls us to, we will be ready for the Rapture, which I believe is coming very soon. Jesus will appear in the clouds and rapture us to celebrate the seven-year Marriage Supper of the Lamb. The apostle Paul wrote to the Ephesians as to what kind of a church Jesus would come back for. He said in Ephesians 5:27, "That He might present it to himself a glorious church, not having spot, or wrinkle, or any such thing; but that it should be holy and without blemish." We are exhorted in 1 Peter 1:15–16, "But as He which hath called you is holy, so be ye holy in all manner of conversation; Because it is written, Be ye holy; for I am holy." Also note Revelation 19:5–9:

> And a voice came out of the throne, saying, Praise our God, all ye his servants, and ye that fear him, both small and great. And I heard as it were the voice of a great multitude, and as the voice of many waters, and as the voice of mighty thunderings, saying, Alleluia: for the Lord God omnipotent reigneth. Let us be glad and rejoice, and give honour to him: for the marriage of the Lamb is come, and his wife hath made herself ready. And to her was granted that she should be arrayed in fine linen, clean and white: for the fine linen is the righteousness of saints. And he saith unto me, Write, Blessed are they which are called unto the marriage supper of the Lamb. And he saith unto me, These are the true sayings of God.

How many people have yet to get rid of their spots, wrinkles, and blemishes on their white robes in order for them to be holy and qualify for the Rapture? Are you ready?

Chapter 4

The Holy Spirit and His Gifts

In the beginning, from the creation of the world, the Holy Spirit was present and active. As we read in Genesis 1:2, "The earth was without form, and void; and darkness was upon the face of the deep. And the Spirit of God moved upon the face of the waters." Let's continue in Genesis 1:1 and 2:7, "In the beginning God created the heaven and the earth.... And the Lord God formed man of the dust of the ground, and breathed into his nostrils the breath of life; and man became a living soul." Just as the Holy Spirit was breathing breath into the first physical man, Adam, so He also breathes into the spiritual life of a born-again person. In the Old Testament, God spoke through His prophets to the people. In the New Testament we read that after Jesus ascended to heaven, we may get our instructions directly from the Holy Spirit. Nonetheless, the work of the prophet is a part of the five-fold ministry, and He still appoints prophets to declare a word for the people on behalf of the Lord. Let us examine the Holy Spirit, His power, and His works.

Jesus Himself told us, as it is recorded in the Bible in John 14:15–17, 26:

> And I will pray the Father, and he shall give you another Comforter, that he may abide with you for ever; Even the Spirit of truth; whom the world cannot receive, because it seeth him not, neither knoweth him: but ye know him; for he dwelleth with you, and shall be in you.... But the Comforter, which is the Holy Ghost, whom the Father will send in my name, he shall teach you all things, and bring all things to your remembrance, whatsoever I have said unto you.

Here you see that the Holy Spirit is with us and also dwells in us to teach us all things. Jesus explains that the Comforter, who is the Holy Ghost, shall teach you all things and bring all things to your remembrance. In order for us to be teachable by Him, we must first know Him by receiving the baptism in the Holy Spirit. John the Baptist said in Matthew 3:11, "I indeed baptize you with water unto repentance: but he that cometh after me is mightier than I, whose shoes I am not worthy to bear: he shall baptize you with the Holy Ghost, and with fire." Many denominations have not only the Holy Ghost absent in their life, but what about the fire? Do they even know what on fire for the Lord means? Most likely not; they are just waiting for Jesus to come and rapture them.

I heard a certain person with a daily radio ministry tell a caller the other day that the baptism of fire is Jesus' wrath towards us. How can Jesus baptize you with the Holy Ghost and wrath at the same time? The fire purifies us; it literally makes us pure by burning up what is undesirable in us and sets us free to be anointed for a great work for His kingdom. For example, we lay hands on the sick and see them healed through the power of the Holy Spirit. Only an ignorant person who refuses the truth of what the Bible teaches about the Holy Spirit would tell such a lie. That pastor considers himself an authority on the Bible, yet he is a Holy Spirit basher and cuts down certain TV ministers who are full of the Holy Ghost on the air. Why? Because he will not know what he is talking about until he has had this experience himself.

A reader board at a church says, cars aren't the only thing to be recalled by their maker. Yes, He is in control of our very next breath. He sits on the throne and will not be unseated by false teachers.

> Then Peter said unto them, Repent, and be baptized every one of you in the name of Jesus Christ for the remission of sins, and ye shall receive the gift of the Holy Ghost.
>
> —ACTS 2:38

> Now he which stablisheth us with you in Christ, and hath anointed us, is God; Who hath also sealed us, and given the earnest of the Spirit in our hearts.
>
> —2 CORINTHIANS 1:21–22

> Who also hath made us able ministers of the new testament; not of the letter, but of the spirit: for the letter killeth, but the spirit giveth life.
>
> —2 CORINTHIANS 3:6

Yes, water baptism and Holy Spirit baptism are two separate experiences, as confirmed in Acts 19:1–6, 11–12:

> And it came to pass, that, while Apollos was at Corinth, Paul having passed through the upper coasts came to Ephesus: and finding certain disciples, He said unto them, Have ye received the Holy Ghost since ye believed? And they said unto him, We have not so much as heard whether there be any Holy Ghost. And he said unto them, Unto what then were ye baptized? And they said, Unto John's baptism. Then said Paul, John verily baptized with the baptism of repentance, saying unto the people, that they should believe on him which should come after him, that is, on Christ Jesus. When they heard this, they were baptized in the name of the Lord Jesus. And when Paul had laid his hands upon them, the Holy Ghost came on them; and they spake with tongues, and prophesied.... And God wrought special miracles by the hands of Paul: So that from his body were brought unto the sick handkerchiefs or aprons, and the diseases departed from them, and the evil spirits went out of them. And God wrought special miracles by the hands of Paul: So that from his body were brought unto the sick handkerchiefs or aprons, and the diseases departed from them, and the evil spirits went out of them.

You see that the people were not only healed from their diseases, but also evil spirits (demons) left them.

We depend on the Holy Spirit's guidance for our life. He certainly is not an "it," as some people try to call Him. In fact, He is the third one of the Trinity. Paul, in his second epistle to the Corinthians, wrote, "The grace of the Lord Jesus Christ, and the love of God, and the communion of the Holy Ghost, be with you all" (2 Cor. 13:14). How do we have communion with the Holy Ghost? If we want to have fellowship with the Holy Ghost or Holy Spirit, we first need to know Him and speak His language, which is speaking in other tongues. The Trinity is one of the great theological mysteries that we will understand clearly one day. We know that the Bible teaches that the Godhead consists of three divine persons—Father, Son, and Holy Spirit—each fully God, each showing fully the divine nature. Jesus Himself revealed it, and the Christian church from the beginning has confessed and safeguarded this precious truth given us.

Upon the occasion of Jesus' baptism, all three persons in the Trinity were present and active. The Father spoke from heaven, the Son was fulfilling all righteousness, and the Spirit descended upon the Son like a dove.

> Now when all the people were baptized, it came to pass, that Jesus also being baptized, and praying, the heaven was opened, And the Holy Ghost descended in a bodily shape like a dove upon him, and a voice came from heaven, which said, Thou art my beloved Son; in thee I am well pleased.
>
> —LUKE 3:21–22

The Holy Spirit, the third person of the Trinity, inspired the writing of the Scriptures, empowers God's people, and convicts "the world of sin, and of righteousness, and of judgment," as Jesus explains to us in John 16:7–8: "Nevertheless I tell you the truth; It is expedient for you that I go away: for if I go not away, the Comforter will not come unto you; but if I depart, I will send him unto you. And when he is come, he will reprove the world of sin, and of righteousness, and of judgment."

When we first accept Jesus into our heart—being born again—we receive the indwelling of the Holy Spirit. Through Jesus' death on the cross, we get forgiveness of our sins, which cleanses us, and we become temples for the Holy Spirit to dwell in, as described in 2 Corinthians 5:17: "Therefore if any man be in Christ, he is a new creature: old things are passed away; behold, all things are become new."

It is up to each individual how much we choose to yield to the Holy Spirit and His will. He is the divine Paraclete, or Comforter, called alongside to help us supernaturally. He is the one who brings to our remembrance whatever our Savior has said. He is the Spirit of life, God Himself within us. Do you agree that we need the Holy Spirit to be inside of us? The baptism in the Holy Spirit is a gift for every believer. Receiving the Holy Spirit empowers us. Jesus instructed His disciples in Luke 24:49, "And, behold, I send the promise of my Father upon you: but tarry ye in the city of Jerusalem, until ye be endued with power from on high." We call this power in us the baptism in the Holy Spirit, which was unleashed for the first time in the Upper Room on the day of Pentecost and has brought the most far-reaching changes ever in history. The impact from this initial outpouring of the Holy Spirit is still being felt today around the world.

This power has been given to us for a specific purpose. Jesus told His disciples in Acts 1:8, "But ye shall receive power, after that the Holy Ghost is come upon you: and ye shall be witnesses unto me both in Jerusalem, and in all Judaea, and in Samaria, and unto the uttermost part of the earth." Now that you are the temple of the Holy Spirit, He is both in you and upon you, but you must first submit to Jesus' instruction and receive this baptism in the Holy Spirit. Many denominations believe that they receive this baptism in the Holy Spirit at the time they get water baptized. However, you can clearly see from the Scriptures that you must first accept Jesus, be water baptized, and then you may receive the baptism in the Holy Spirit. We read in Acts 8:14–17, "Now when the apostles which were at Jerusalem heard that Samaria had received the word of God, they sent unto them Peter and John: Who, when they were come down, prayed for them, that they might receive the Holy Ghost: (For as yet he was fallen upon none of them: only they were baptized in the name of the Lord Jesus.) Then laid they their hands on them, and they received the Holy Ghost."

Jesus was very clear about the reason for this outpouring of the Holy Spirit's power upon us believers. Then and now, the purpose of the Holy Spirit's outpouring is to help believers be effective in building the kingdom of God. This awesome gift is to equip believers with power and authority in fulfilling the Great Commission. After Jesus had risen from the dead, He appeared to His disciples and said:

> And he said unto them, Go ye into all the world, and preach the gospel to every creature. He that believeth and is baptized shall be saved; but he that believeth not shall be damned. And these signs shall follow them that believe; In my name shall they cast out devils; they shall speak with new tongues; They shall take up serpents; and if they drink any deadly thing, it shall not hurt them; they shall lay hands on the sick, and they shall recover.
>
> —MARK 16:15–18

First He sent His twelve disciples out, then the seventy, and eventually the whole body of Christ was spreading this good news all over the world, converting unbelievers into Christians.

It is vital that we understand more about this power. More importantly, we must seek to be endowed with it and have it upon us. It begins by us yielding to the Holy Spirit, how He wants to do things through us, not the way we think it should happen or in what package or wrapping it should come. As long as we are in command and control, revival cannot and will not come. God's work of restoration is a work of the Holy Spirit in and through the lives of those who have been born from above. This was explained by Jesus Himself in John 3:3: "Verily, verily, I say unto thee, Except a man be born again, he cannot see the kingdom of God." Our upcoming revival was already prophesied long ago in Joel 2:28–29, which says, "And it shall come to pass afterward, that I will pour out my spirit upon all flesh; and your sons and your daughters shall prophesy, your old men shall dream dreams, your young men shall see visions: And also upon the servants and upon the handmaids in those days will I pour out my spirit." This power is not limited to certain individuals only. It will be shared with all His people who choose to accept the Holy Spirit to come and live within them. By receiving the baptism in the Holy Spirit, given by Jesus and yielding to Him, He can and will totally transform you.

John the Baptist questioned Jesus in Matthew 11:3, asking, "Art thou he that should come, or do we look for another?" Jesus replied, "The blind receive their sight, and the lame walk, the lepers are cleansed, and the deaf hear, the dead are raised up, and the poor have the gospel preached to them" (v. 5). Yet in many churches we only hear the gospel preached. What happened to the rest of the Scripture? Why is it ignored? Did we not just read that miracles are part of the gospel of Jesus Christ? He tells us Himself in John

14:12–14, "Verily, verily, I say unto you, He that believeth on me, the works that I do shall he do also; and greater works than these shall he do; because I go unto my Father. And whatsoever ye shall ask in my name, that will I do, that the Father may be glorified in the Son. If ye shall ask any thing in my name, I will do it." But it must be His will that we pray for, not that of Satan.

If some of you want to receive the baptism in the Holy Spirit and don't know how, here are some Scriptures.

> Then Peter said unto them, Repent, and be baptized every one of you in the name of Jesus Christ for the remission of sins, and ye shall receive the gift of the Holy Ghost. For the promise is unto you, and to your children, and to all that are afar off, even as many as the LORD our God shall call.
>
> —Acts 2:38–39

In order to receive this blessing you need to do a number of things.

First, you need to be born again. The person who is going to be filled with the Holy Spirit must have the indwelling of the Spirit and must belong to Jesus.

> So then they that are in the flesh cannot please God. But ye are not in the flesh, but in the Spirit, if so be that the Spirit of God dwell in you. Now if any man have not the Spirit of Christ, he is none of his. And if Christ be in you, the body is dead because of sin; but the Spirit is life because of righteousness. But if the Spirit of him that raised up Jesus from the dead dwell in you, he that raised up Christ from the dead shall also quicken your mortal bodies by his Spirit that dwelleth in you. Therefore, brethren, we are debtors, not to the flesh, to

> live after the flesh. For if ye live after the flesh, ye shall die: but if ye through the Spirit do mortify the deeds of the body, ye shall live. For as many as are led by the Spirit of God, they are the sons of God. For ye have not received the spirit of bondage again to fear; but ye have received the Spirit of adoption, whereby we cry, Abba, Father. The Spirit itself beareth witness with our spirit, that we are the children of God.
>
> —Romans 8:8–16

The second thing you have to do is ask. The Bible says if we ask for the Holy Spirit, that prayer will be answered. Luke records that Jesus said in Luke 11:9: "And I say unto you, Ask, and it shall be given you; seek, and ye shall find; knock, and it shall be opened unto you."

The third thing you have to do is surrender. The apostle Paul made this need clear when he said in Romans 12:1, "I beseech you therefore, brethren, by the mercies of God, that ye present your bodies a living sacrifice, holy, acceptable unto God, which is your reasonable service."

Fourth, you must be willing to obey the Spirit. God does not give this power to someone and then say, "You can take the part you like and leave the part you do not like." If you want to be immersed in the Holy Spirit, you need to be prepared to obey the Spirit, as it says in Acts 5:32: "We are his witnesses of these things; and so is also the Holy Ghost, whom God hath given to them that obey him."

Fifth, you need to believe. The apostle Paul said in Galatians 3:2, "This only would I learn of you, Received ye the Spirit by the works of the law, or by the hearing of faith?" The answer, obviously, is by faith. You have to believe that if you ask you will receive.

Finally, you have to exercise what God has given you. Having asked, having received, having been willing to obey, and having believed, you need to respond in a biblical fashion. Speak the words out loud that you receive from the Holy Spirit. For some, it is only one syllable or two, yet others take off speaking this new language right away. Whatever the Holy Spirit gives you, speak it out loud, because you are the one that needs to hear it. It will give you courage to go on for more. For some it starts slow, but keep practicing until you get fluent in your new heavenly language. When you speak in tongues, you bypass Satan. He cannot understand what you are saying, because your prayers go straight up into the throne room of God.

Acts 2:4 says those that were baptized in the Holy Spirit on the Day of Pentecost spoke the words that the Spirit gave them: "And they were all filled with the Holy Ghost, and began to speak with other tongues, as the Spirit gave them utterance." The Holy Spirit gave the words, but the apostles and disciples voluntarily responded. There was action based on faith, not merely passive acceptance of the blessing. That is the way it is with God; you must be teachable. God is offering the baptism in the Holy Spirit to people who need only to reach out and take it and then enjoy the blessing. Just as it was in the days of the apostles, so is it still today with us. The gifts did not go away when the disciples died, as some pastors tried to tell me. Because I could not and would not agree with them, one pastor accused me of having false teaching.

The Gifts of the Holy Spirit

In order to give you an overall view of the gifts of the Holy Spirit, we will address first the whole chapter, and afterward I will come back to each individual gift.

> Now concerning spiritual gifts, brethren, I would not have you ignorant. Ye know that ye were Gentiles, carried away unto these dumb idols, even as ye were led. Wherefore I give you to understand, that no man speaking by the Spirit of God calleth Jesus accursed: and that no man can say that Jesus is the Lord, but by the Holy Ghost. Now there are diversities of gifts, but the same Spirit. And there are differences of administrations, but the same Lord. And there are diversities of operations, but it is the same God which worketh all in all. But the manifestation of the Spirit is given to every man to profit withal. For to one is given by the Spirit the word of wisdom; to another the word of knowledge by the same Spirit; To another faith by the same Spirit; to another the gifts of healing by the same Spirit; To another the working of miracles; to another prophecy; to another discerning of spirits; to another divers kinds of tongues; to another the interpretation of tongues: But all these worketh that one and the selfsame Spirit, dividing to every man severally as he will. For as the body is one, and hath many members, and all the members of that one body, being many, are one body: so also is Christ. For by one Spirit are we all baptized into one body, whether we be Jews or Gentiles, whether we be bond or free; and have been all made to drink into one Spirit. For the body is not one member, but many. If the foot shall say, Because I am not the hand, I am not of the body; is it therefore not of the body? And if the ear shall say, Because I am not the eye, I am not of the body; is it therefore not of the body? If

> the whole body were an eye, where were the hearing? If the whole were hearing, where were the smelling? But now hath God set the members every one of them in the body, as it hath pleased him. And if they were all one member, where were the body? But now are they many members, yet but one body. And the eye cannot say unto the hand, I have no need of thee: nor again the head to the feet, I have no need of you. Nay, much more those members of the body, which seem to be more feeble, are necessary: And those members of the body, which we think to be less honourable, upon these we bestow more abundant honour; and our uncomely parts have more abundant comeliness. For our comely parts have no need: but God hath tempered the body together, having given more abundant honour to that part which lacked. That there should be no schism in the body; but that the members should have the same care one for another. And whether one member suffer, all the members suffer with it; or one member be honoured, all the members rejoice with it. Now ye are the body of Christ, and members in particular. And God hath set some in the church, first apostles, secondarily prophets, thirdly teachers, after that miracles, then gifts of healings, helps, governments, diversities of tongues. Are all apostles? are all prophets? are all teachers? are all workers of miracles? Have all the gifts of healing? do all speak with tongues? do all interpret? But covet earnestly the best gifts: and yet shew I unto you a more excellent way.
>
> —1 Corinthians 12

These Scriptures talk about nine gifts: wisdom, knowledge, faith, healing, the working of miracles, prophecy, discerning of spirits, diverse kind of tongues, and the interpretation of tongues.

Let me give you some samples from Scripture of what a Spirit-filled believer can expect and is privileged to experience.

Being Slain in the Spirit

> It came even to pass, as the trumpeters and singers were as one, to make one sound to be heard in praising and thanking the LORD; and when they lifted up their voice with the trumpets and cymbals and instruments of music, and praised the LORD, saying, For he is good; for his mercy endureth for ever: that then the house was filled with a cloud, even the house of the LORD; So that the priests could not stand to minister by reason of the cloud: for the glory of the LORD had filled the house of God.
>
> —2 CHRONICLES 5:13–14

> And for fear of him the keepers did shake, and became as dead men.
>
> —MATTHEW 28:4

> As soon then as he had said unto them, I am he, they went backward, and fell to the ground.
>
> —JOHN 18:6

> And he fell to the earth, and heard a voice saying unto him, Saul, Saul, why persecutest thou me?
>
> —ACTS 9:4

> And when I saw him, I fell at his feet as dead. And he laid his right hand upon me, saying unto me, Fear not; I am the first and the last.
>
> —REVELATION 1:17

Lifting Up Holy Hands

Thus will I bless thee while I live: I will lift up my hands in thy name.

—Psalm 63:4

Lift up your hands in the sanctuary, and bless the Lord.

—Psalm 134:2

Arise, cry out in the night: in the beginning of the watches pour out thine heart like water before the face of the Lord: lift up thy hands toward him for the life of thy young children, that faint for hunger in the top of every street

—Lamentations 2:19

I will therefore that men pray every where, lifting up holy hands, without wrath and doubting.

—1 Timothy 2:8

Healing, the Laying on of Hands, Anointing with Oil

They shall take up serpents; and if they drink any deadly thing, it shall not hurt them; they shall lay hands on the sick, and they shall recover.

—Mark 16:18

And Ananias went his way, and entered into the house; and putting his hands on him said, Brother Saul, the Lord, even Jesus, that appeared unto thee in the way as thou camest, hath sent me, that thou mightest receive thy sight, and be filled with the Holy Ghost.

—Acts 9:17

> And they cast out many devils, and anointed with oil many that were sick, and healed them.
>
> —MARK 6:13

> And it came to pass, that the father of Publius lay sick of a fever and of a bloody flux: to whom Paul entered in, and prayed, and laid his hands on him, and healed him.
>
> —ACTS 28:8

> Is any sick among you? let him call for the elders of the church; and let them pray over him, anointing him with oil in the name of the Lord.
>
> —JAMES 5:14

> And Jesus answered and said, Suffer ye thus far. And he touched his ear, and healed him.
>
> —LUKE 22:51

> Verily, verily, I say unto you, He that believeth on me, the works that I do shall he do also; and greater works than these shall he do; because I go unto my Father.
>
> —JOHN 14:12

Speaking in Tongues

> And they were all filled with the Holy Ghost, and began to speak with other tongues, as the Spirit gave them utterance.
>
> —ACTS 2:4

> To another the working of miracles; to another prophecy; to another discerning of spirits; to another divers kinds of tongues; to another the interpretation of tongues.
>
> —1 CORINTHIANS 12:10

> For they heard them speak with tongues, and magnify God.
>
> —ACTS 10:46

> For he that speaketh in an unknown tongue speaketh not unto men, but unto God: for no man understandeth him; howbeit in the spirit he speaketh mysteries.... He that speaketh in an unknown tongue edifieth himself; but he that prophesieth edifieth the church. I would that ye all spake with tongues but rather that ye prophesied: for greater is he that prophesieth than he that speaketh with tongues, except he interpret, that the church may receive edifying.... Wherefore let him that speaketh in an unknown tongue pray that he may interpret. For if I pray in an unknown tongue, my spirit prayeth, but my understanding is unfruitful.... I thank my God, I speak with tongues more than ye all.... Wherefore tongues are for a sign, not to them that believe, but to them that believe not: but prophesying serveth not for them that believe not, but for them which believe.... Wherefore, brethren, covet to prophesy, and forbid not to speak with tongues.
>
> —1 CORINTHIANS 14:2, 4–5, 13–14, 18, 22, 39

We just read that if we pray in an unknown tongue, our spirit prays through us and our understanding (brain) does not. That is why it is so hard to convince certain people, because they can only reason with their mind and are not able to distinguish one from another. Yet, there is a world of difference in praying in the spirit (in tongues)—where you edify yourself—and prophesying. If you prophesy in a meeting or congregation, you either need to do it in your own language so that the people present can understand it, or, if you prophesy in tongues, there must be an interpretation. You must understand this. Satan does not want you to comprehend the truth, and therefore keeps you from understanding these very simple scriptures. He keeps your head full of cobwebs so that you argue continually because you have not yet had this Spirit-filled experience, in which rivers of living water flow out of you. Paul wrote that he thanked God that he spoke with tongues more than the church to which he was writing.

The Scriptures tell us that speaking in tongues is for the unbeliever and prophesy is for the believer. What about those denominations that don't believe in either one? Do they get hung up on 1 Corinthians 13:8–10?

> Charity never faileth: but whether there be prophecies, they shall fail; whether there be tongues, they shall cease; whether there be knowledge, it shall vanish away. For we know in part, and we prophesy in part. But when that which is perfect is come, then that which is in part shall be done away.

You see, the gifts are only temporary, compared to His eternal love. Though we are waiting for Jesus' return now, when "that which is perfect is come" we will no longer need the gifts of the Holy Spirit to preach and confirm the Word. Was not the Word—Jesus—made flesh, and did He not dwell among us? (See John 1:14.) Then He went to be with the Father and sent us the Holy Spirit to guide us into all truth. Then when He, the perfect One, comes back again, we will no longer see through a glass darkly, as described 1 Corinthians 13:11–12:

> When I was a child, I spake as a child, I understood as a child, I thought as a child: but when I became a man, I put away childish things. For now we see through a glass, darkly; but then face to face: now I know in part; but then shall I know even as also I am known.

How much longer will it be before you believe in the whole Bible? If the gifts had gone away or were to go away at any certain time in the future, I'm sure that our Lord would have made provision for it in His Word to let us know in writing.

Singing in the Spirit

> Sing unto him a new song; play skilfully with a loud noise.
>
> —PSALM 33:3

> And he hath put a new song in my mouth, even praise unto our God: many shall see it, and fear, and shall trust in the LORD.
>
> —PSALM 40:3

> What is it then? I will pray with the spirit, and I will pray with the understanding also: I will sing with the spirit, and I will sing with the understanding also.
>
> —1 CORINTHIANS 14:15

Word of Knowledge

> For to one is given by the Spirit the word of wisdom; to another the word of knowledge by the same Spirit.
>
> —1 CORINTHIANS 12:8

> The woman answered and said, I have no husband. Jesus said unto her, Thou hast well said, I have no husband: For thou hast had five husbands; and he whom thou now hast is not thy husband: in that saidst thou truly.
>
> —JOHN 4:17–18

> For what man knoweth the things of a man, save the spirit of man which is in him? even so the things of God knoweth no man, but the Spirit of God. Now we have received, not the spirit of the world, but the spirit which is of God; that we might know the things that are freely given to us of God.... For who hath known the mind of the Lord, that he may instruct him? but we have the mind of Christ.
>
> —1 Corinthians 2:11–12, 16

> But Peter said, Ananias, why hath Satan filled thine heart to lie to the Holy Ghost, and to keep back part of the price of the land?
>
> —Acts 5:3

Interpretation of Tongues, Prophecy

> To another the working of miracles; to another prophecy; to another discerning of spirits; to another divers kinds of tongues; to another the interpretation of tongues.
>
> —1 Corinthians 12:10

> The woman saith unto him, Sir, I perceive that thou art a prophet.
>
> —John 4:19

> Follow after charity, and desire spiritual gifts, but rather that ye may prophesy....But he that prophesieth speaketh unto men to edification, and exhortation, and comfort....I would that ye all spake with tongues but rather that ye prophesied: for greater is he that prophesieth than he that speaketh with tongues, except he interpret, that the church may receive edifying.... Wherefore let him that speaketh in an unknown tongue pray that he may interpret.... Wherefore

> tongues are for a sign, not to them that believe, but to them that believe not: but prophesying serveth not for them that believe not, but for them which believe.... But if all prophesy, and there come in one that believeth not, or one unlearned, he is convinced of all, he is judged of all: And thus are the secrets of his heart made manifest; and so falling down on his face he will worship God, and report that God is in you of a truth.... For ye may all prophesy one by one, that all may learn, and all may be comforted. Wherefore, brethren, covet to prophesy, and forbid not to speak with tongues.
>
> —1 CORINTHIANS 14:1, 3, 5, 13, 22, 24–25, 31, 39

WHAT IS PROPHECY?

Prophecy is a supernatural message given by a man or woman, inspired by the Holy Spirit. It is your responsibility to judge any prophecy that is spoken over you. If you find it not to be true, it is your responsibility to reject it, since there are some self-proclaimed prophets without God's anointing who operate in the flesh. We are warned, as it is written in 1 John 4:1, "Beloved, believe not every spirit, but try the spirits whether they are of God: because many false prophets are gone out into the world."

A prophecy may be for a future event unknown to you yet. Don't try to bring it to pass by force. Sometimes a prophecy may take years to be fulfilled and you need confirmation from another person or the Word of God written in the Bible. Wait on the Lord; He will open the door for it, if it is of Him. Allow Him to bring it to pass. Don't make your decision based on what some prophet told you would happen. Just because a person is popular does not mean that he or she is correct. I have firsthand experience to back it up. This is one of the reasons why we are in need of the baptism in the Holy Spirit—to operate in the gifts and be able to discern for ourselves. I had many prophesies given to me over the years; often they told exactly what was going on in my life, yet the person giving them knew absolutely nothing about me. (You can read a number of them in chapter 10.) Prophecy must build a person up, not tear them down. We read in 1 Thessalonians 5:20–21, "Despise not prophesyings. Prove all things; hold fast that which is good."

Someone once said that a prophet of God must: be anointed of the Lord; ordained for service of God; enduring to the end; filled with the Spirit of God; able to withstand the chastisements of the Almighty; have the wisdom of Isaiah; the endurance of Daniel; the heart of Jeremiah; the visions of Ezekiel; the staff of Moses; the feet and faith of Abraham; the mantle of Elijah; the speech of Zechariah; the witness of Malachi; the psalms and sling of David; the mentality of Job; the stubbornness of Jonah; the stillness of a still wind, yet destroying the works of sin while saving the soul of the sinner; the voice of thunder, yet the appearance of a dove; and the character of his Messiah, continually bearing the cross. The prophet of God must walk diligently, not commercially but quietly. The prophet of God must not be a profit-prophet, but only one who speaks God's Word and speaks it faithfully, for which he will be hated among men in this wicked generation.

The Word of Knowledge

> I have already written, that the secrets of the heart are revealed.
>
> —1 Corinthians 14:25

Let me give you an example what happened in the Old Testament as far as telling things to happen in the future.

> Then Samuel took a vial of oil, and poured it upon his head, and kissed him, and said, Is it not because the Lord hath anointed thee to be captain over his inheritance? When thou art departed from me to day, then thou shalt find two men by Rachel's sepulchre in the border of Benjamin at Zelzah; and they will say unto thee, The asses which thou wentest to seek are found: and, lo, thy father hath left the care of the asses, and sorroweth for you, saying, What shall I do for my son? Then shalt thou go on forward from thence, and thou shalt come to the plain of Tabor, and there shall meet thee three men going up to God to Bethel, one carrying three kids, and another carrying three loaves of bread, and another carrying a bottle of wine: And they will salute thee, and give thee two loaves of bread; which thou shalt receive of their hands. After that thou shalt come to the hill of God, where is the garrison of the Philistines: and it shall come to pass, when thou art come thither to the city, that thou shalt meet a company of prophets coming down from the high place with a psaltery, and a tabret, and a pipe, and a harp, before them; and they shall prophesy: And the Spirit of the Lord will come upon thee, and thou shalt prophesy with them, and shalt be turned into another man. And let it be, when these signs are come unto thee, that thou do as occasion serve thee; for God is with thee. And thou shalt go down before me to Gilgal; and, behold, I will come down unto thee, to offer burnt offerings, and to sacrifice sacrifices of peace offerings: seven days shalt thou tarry, till I come to thee, and shew thee what thou shalt do. And it was so, that when he had turned his back to go from Samuel, God gave him another heart: and all those signs came to pass that day. And when they came thither to the

> hill, behold, a company of prophets met him; and the Spirit of God came upon him, and he prophesied among them. And it came to pass, when all that knew him beforetime saw that, behold, he prophesied among the prophets, then the people said one to another, What is this that is come unto the son of Kish? Is Saul also among the prophets?
>
> —1 Samuel 10:1–11

As you have just read, the Holy Spirit was present and powerfully at work in the Old Testament. This very same Holy Spirit is just as powerful at work today in those who will allow Him to work in them. As a matter of fact, Jesus Himself said in John 14:26, "But the Comforter, which is the Holy Ghost, whom the Father will send in my name, he shall teach you all things, and bring all things to your remembrance, whatsoever I have said unto you." This word was confirmed in John 14:12: "Verily, verily, I say unto you, He that believeth on me, the works that I do shall he do also; and greater works than these shall he do; because I go unto my Father." Were it not so, we would no longer call them the Trinity—Father, Son, and Holy Spirit.

I mentioned earlier that a certain pastor wanted to retrain me. He said that I had false teaching and tried to convince me that the Holy Spirit ceased to work when the disciples died. He evidently did not know that the Holy Spirit is just as powerfully at work today as He was in the Old Testament and in Jesus' time. This is another example of how Satan works through people, even in the church. Satan has come up with all kinds of lies to confuse and cause a misinterpretation of the truth of the Scriptures. Do not be deceived; remember, Satan is a counterfeit specialist from way back. He is a liar and the father of all lies. Jesus Himself told the Jews in John 8:43–45, "Why do ye not understand my speech? even because ye cannot hear my word. Ye are of your father the devil, and the lusts of your father ye will do. He was a murderer from the beginning, and abode not in the truth, because there is no truth in him. When he speaketh a lie, he speaketh of his own: for he is a liar, and the father of it. And because I tell you the truth, ye believe me not."

Paul wrote to the Corinthians in 2 Corinthians 11:13–15, "For such are false apostles, deceitful workers, transforming themselves into the apostles of Christ. And no marvel; for Satan himself is transformed into an angel of light. Therefore it is no great thing if his ministers also be transformed as the ministers of righteousness; whose end shall be according to their works." Peter warns us to be aware and vigilant in 1 Peter 5:8: "Be sober, be vigilant; because your adversary the devil, as a roaring lion, walketh about, seeking whom he may devour." We read in Exodus 20:5–6, "Thou shalt not bow down thyself to them, nor serve them: for I the Lord thy God am a jealous God, visiting the iniquity of the fathers upon the children unto the third and fourth generation of them that hate me; And shewing mercy unto thousands of them that love me, and keep my commandments." It is mentioned again in Deuteronomy 7:9–10: "Know therefore that the LORD thy God, he is God, the faithful God, which keepeth covenant and mercy with them that love him and keep his commandments to a thousand generations; And repayeth them that hate him to their face, to destroy them: he will not be slack to him that hateth him, he will repay him to his face."

These are strong words.

THE WORD OF WISDOM

The Lord Himself gives us wisdom and guidance.

> For the LORD giveth wisdom: out of his mouth cometh knowledge and understanding. He layeth up sound wisdom for the righteous: he is a buckler to them that walk uprightly. . . . When wisdom entereth into thine heart, and knowledge is pleasant unto thy soul; Discretion shall preserve thee, understanding shall keep thee.
>
> —PROVERBS 2:6–7, 10–11

> Happy is the man that findeth wisdom, and the man that getteth understanding.
>
> —PROVERBS 3:13

THE FRUIT OF THE SPIRIT

> But the fruit of the Spirit is love, joy, peace, longsuffering, gentleness, goodness, faith, Meekness, temperance: against such there is no law.
>
> —GALATIANS 5:22–23

These nine manifestations of the fruit of the Holy Spirit enable us to eliminate spiritual barrenness, become fruitful, escape the corruption of the world, and become a partaker of the divine nature of God.

Should we not take the next few verses to heart and live accordingly?

> And they that are Christ's have crucified the flesh with the affections and lusts. If we live in the Spirit, let us also walk in

> the Spirit. Let us not be desirous of vain glory, provoking one another, envying one another.
>
> —Galatians 5:24–26

> Brethren, if a man be overtaken in a fault, ye which are spiritual, restore such an one in the spirit of meekness; considering thyself, lest thou also be tempted. Bear ye one another's burdens, and so fulfil the law of Christ.
>
> —Galatians 6:1–2

Love

The Holy Spirit places a supernatural love in our heart as a sign of the fruit being evident.

> And hope maketh not ashamed; because the love of God is shed abroad in our hearts by the Holy Ghost which is given unto us.
>
> —Romans 5:5

I couldn't pass up the following Scriptures, although they are lengthy.

> And to make all men see what is the fellowship of the mystery, which from the beginning of the world hath been hid in God, who created all things by Jesus Christ: To the intent that now unto the principalities and powers in heavenly places might be known by the church the manifold wisdom of God, According to the eternal purpose which he purposed in Christ Jesus our Lord: In whom we have boldness and access with confidence by the faith of him. Wherefore I desire that ye faint not at my tribulations for you, which is your glory. For this cause I bow my knees unto the Father of our Lord Jesus Christ, Of whom the whole family in heaven and earth is named, That

> he would grant you, according to the riches of his glory, to be strengthened with might by his Spirit in the inner man; That Christ may dwell in your hearts by faith; that ye, being rooted and grounded in love, May be able to comprehend with all saints what is the breadth, and length, and depth, and height; And to know the love of Christ, which passeth knowledge, that ye might be filled with all the fulness of God. Now unto him that is able to do exceeding abundantly above all that we ask or think, according to the power that worketh in us, Unto him be glory in the church by Christ Jesus throughout all ages, world without end. Amen.
>
> —Ephesians 3:9–21

Some people are chosen by God to accomplish special tasks and are marked to serve Him before they are in their mother's womb. But none of this can be accomplished without totally yielding to the Holy Spirit. You can't keep one foot in the world. If Jesus told us in the Bible that the Holy Spirit will guide us into all truth, why do certain people then refuse His guidance and let their religions dictate to them what to believe? Jesus tells us in Mark 3:28–29, "Verily I say unto you, All sins shall be forgiven unto the sons of men, and blasphemies wherewith soever they shall blaspheme: But he that shall blaspheme against the Holy Ghost hath never forgiveness, but is in danger of eternal damnation."

Joy

Joy results in strength, as we read in Nehemiah 8:10, "For the joy of the Lord is your strength." We even sing it as a song in church. This supernatural joy has nothing to do with our emotions. It is manifested in the spiritual realm. When the Holy Spirit joins

Himself with our spirit at the time of salvation, the result is instant joy. It can also produce the spirit of laughter in some people. It is a divine joy that comes from God's Word in us. Jesus said in John 15:11, "These things have I spoken unto you, that my joy might remain in you, and that your joy might be full."

Peace

This is a supernatural peace given to us by our Lord, so that even in the midst of turmoil we can have peace. Jesus told us in John 14:27, "Peace I leave with you, my peace I give unto you: not as the world giveth, give I unto you. Let not your heart be troubled, neither let it be afraid."

Longsuffering

Longsuffering enables us to forgive others and be patient.

> That ye might walk worthy of the Lord unto all pleasing, being fruitful in every good work, and increasing in the knowledge of God; Strengthened with all might, according to his glorious power, unto all patience and longsuffering with joyfulness.
>
> —Colossians 1:10–11

> Forbearing one another, and forgiving one another, if any man have a quarrel against any: even as Christ forgave you, so also do ye.
>
> —Colossians 3:13

Gentleness

Gentleness is a quality that pleases God and makes you great in His sight.

> Thou hast also given me the shield of thy salvation: and thy gentleness hath made me great.
>
> —2 Samuel 22:36

> But we were gentle among you, even as a nurse cherisheth her children.
>
> — 1 Thessalonians 2:7

Goodness

We are to do good, even to the ones that hate us. Once you're grounded in the Lord, the Holy Spirit will convict you to do so from within.

> And I myself also am persuaded of you, my brethren, that ye also are full of goodness, filled with all knowledge, able also to admonish one another.
>
> —Romans 15:14

> But I say unto you which hear, Love your enemies, do good to them which hate you.
>
> —Luke 6:27

> As we have therefore opportunity, let us do good unto all men, especially unto them who are of the household of faith.
>
> —Galatians 6:10

> Therefore to him that knoweth to do good, and doeth it not, to him it is sin.
>
> —James 4:17

Faith

The gift of faith is that of a special faith. It is the supernatural ability of the Holy Spirit to believe what seems impossible and wait expectantly for its results.

> By whom also we have access by faith into this grace wherein we stand, and rejoice in hope of the glory of God.
>
> —ROMANS 5:2

> But without faith it is impossible to please him: for he that cometh to God must believe that he is, and that he is a rewarder of them that diligently seek him.
>
> —HEBREWS 11:6

> And though I have the gift of prophecy, and understand all mysteries, and all knowledge; and though I have all faith, so that I could remove mountains, and have not charity, I am nothing.
>
> —1 CORINTHIANS 13:2

Meekness

Meekness does not mean weakness. Meekness knows no pride and is free from rebellion. Jesus taught, "Blessed are the meek: for they shall inherit the earth" (Matt. 5:5).

> The meek will he guide in judgment: and the meek will he teach his way.
>
> —PSALM 25:9

> For the LORD taketh pleasure in his people: he will beautify the meek with salvation.
>
> —PSALM 149:4

> But let it be the hidden man of the heart, in that which is not corruptible, even the ornament of a meek and quiet spirit, which is in the sight of God of great price.
>
> —1 Peter 3:4

Temperance

Temperance is self-control over the whole person: body, soul, and spirit.

> And every man that striveth for the mastery is temperate in all things. Now they do it to obtain a corruptible crown; but we an incorruptible
>
> —1 Corinthians 9:25

> And beside this, giving all diligence, add to your faith virtue; and to virtue knowledge; And to knowledge temperance; and to temperance patience; and to patience godliness; And to godliness brotherly kindness; and to brotherly kindness charity. For if these things be in you, and abound, they make you that ye shall neither be barren nor unfruitful in the knowledge of our Lord Jesus Christ.
>
> —2 Peter 1:5–8

It is my desire that you study these Scriptures very carefully so that you grow even more in the love and knowledge of our Lord Jesus Christ and receive and practice the gifts of the Holy Spirit.

Following is a chart that lets you chose how you will react:

Holy Spirit Thoughts	Demon Thoughts	Demon Habits	Demon Control
Holy Spirit Fruit	**Rulers**	**Powers**	**Principalities**
Love	Unforgiveness Resentment Bitterness Jealousy Hurts	Hatred	Murder
Joy	Depression Despair Discouragement Disillusionment	Hopelessness	Suicide
Peace	Nerves, Tension Worry, Fretting Confusion Restlessness	Fear	Nervous breakdown
Longsuffering	Impatience Selfishness Disharmony Annoyance Temper	Wrath	Violence
Gentleness	Harshness Cruelty Inconsideration Arguing Jealousy	Unreasonableness	Insanity
Goodness	Filthy thoughts Evil imagination Pornography Flirting, Seduction Masturbation	Immortality Fornication	Perversity

Holy Spirit Thoughts	Demon Thoughts	Demon Habits	Demon Control
Holy Spirit Fruit	**Rulers**	**Powers**	**Principalities**
Faith	Doubt, Hesitation Anxiety Indecision Negative faith Backsliding	Agnosticism Atheism	Blasphemy against the Holy Spirit
Meekness	Pride, self-ego Self-exaltation Dissension Disunity Unteachable spirit	Domination	Witchcraft
Self-control (Temperance)	Drunkenness Drugs Gluttony Gossip, Slander Manic depression Compulsive behavior Hypnosis	Emotional instability	Mania

(See Psalm 34:6–7; Proverbs 23:7; 1 Corinthians 6:19–20; 10:13; 2 Corinthians 10:4–5; Galatians 5:22–23; Ephesians 6:11–12; Philippians 4:8–9; Hebrews 4:13–15; 1 Peter 5:8–9; and 1 John 1:7–9.)

Will you apply these Scriptures to you personally and practice and obey them in order to be that powerful, Christlike follower of Jesus?

Chapter 5

The Baptism of Suffering

The word *suffering* sounds awful and cruel. One could ask why a loving God would even allow such a thing. But if we expect to reign with Him, we should also be prepared to suffer with Him. The Bible tells us how much some of His disciples had to suffer.

> They said unto him, Grant unto us that we may sit, one on thy right hand, and the other on thy left hand, in thy glory. But Jesus said unto them, Ye know not what ye ask: can ye drink of the cup that I drink of? and be baptized with the baptism that I am baptized with? And they said unto him, We can. And Jesus said unto them, Ye shall indeed drink of the cup that I drink of; and with the baptism that I am baptized withal shall ye be baptized: But to sit on my right hand and on my left hand is not mine to give; but it shall be given to them for whom it is prepared.
>
> —Mark 10:37–40

What is the baptism of suffering? John the Baptist got his name because he baptized people in water. In other words, he dunked them, or immersed them. He said, "I indeed baptize you with water unto repentance. but he that cometh after me is mightier than I, whose shoes I am not worthy to bear: he shall baptize you with the Holy Ghost, and with fire: Whose fan is in his hand, and he will thoroughly purge his floor, and gather his wheat into the garner; but he will burn up the chaff with unquenchable fire" (Matt. 3:11–12).

Many preachers say that God is love and any adversity comes from the devil. Here are some scriptures that contradict that statement.

> For what glory is it, if, when ye be buffeted for your faults, ye shall take it patiently? but if, when ye do well, and suffer for it, ye take it patiently, this is acceptable with God. For even hereunto were ye called: because Christ also suffered for us, leaving us an example, that ye should follow his steps.
>
> —1 Peter 2:20–21

The next four verses explain why we should follow in Christ's steps.

> Forasmuch then as Christ hath suffered for us in the flesh arm yourselves likewise with the same mind: for he that hath suffered in the flesh hath ceased from sin; that he no longer should live the rest of his time in the flesh to the lust of men, but to the will of God.... Yet if any man suffer as a Christian, let him not be ashamed; but let him glorify God on this behalf.... Wherefore let them that suffer according to the will of God commit the keeping of their souls to him in well doing, as unto a faithful Creator.
>
> —1 Peter 4:1–2, 16, 19

Now you can see that it is even scriptural. Let's get to the point.

I will give you an explanation through relating a personal experience. In my case it was an immersion into suffering, suffering for the cause of Jesus Christ. Yes, I endured a lot of pain. It all started when the Lord called me to attend a Baptist church in October 1992. When I first began to attend the church, the Holy Spirit would have me talk to the pastor every so often about his need to receive the baptism of the Holy Spirit, that it was God's will for him. I probably got on his nerves so that he wanted to take off running every time he saw me coming. In January 1993 two Sunday school classes started, one about the Book of Revelation and the other one about the Holy Spirit. Since I had already had several conversations with the pastor by then about the baptism in the Holy Spirit, I wanted to find out what their interpretation was. Sure enough, I disagreed a number of times with the teacher and continued to correct his teaching, so the Lord had to get me out of there before they would possibly ask me to leave the church. Because of the vast difference in their belief, mainly concerning the Holy Spirit, I was not allowed by the Lord to be a member of this church. Since He sent me there to do a job, He had to temporarily remove me in order to see it fulfilled down the road. At this time I was not totally aware of my function there and had no idea that it would take a number of years to see it all completed.

That winter I stayed home from work for a few days in order to avoid having an accident on the icy roads. When the snow melted and the roads were clear again, I decided to pick up some pictures for my office in the late morning before going on to work to relieve another employee for a couple hours. As I was driving along, I prayed, "Lord, I want to be completely in Your will, even if it is uncomfortable what I have to endure." As I write this chapter, I'm amazed that I even remember the words of the prayer. The Holy Spirit must have given me these words to say, because He knew ahead of time what I was going to have to endure. I, myself, would have never prayed like that, but my flesh was not in charge. The Holy Spirit prayed through me. He knew why He gave me such specific words.

I continued communicating with the Lord, when I suddenly hit a patch of black ice on the road, which was shaded by some tall trees. My car spun around several times on the black ice and then came to rest hanging down a small embankment with the front of the car facing the road. A passerby stopped and helped me out of my car. There was nothing wrong with me, nor my car, except that I had to call a wrecker to pull me out on to the road again. I walked around my car to the passenger side in order to get the tow truck's phone number out of the glove compartment. As I was standing behind the open passenger door, suddenly a car with two ladies in it had the same experience I had. Within a split second of hitting the black ice, their car was traveling at a high speed toward my car. It was as if our cars had an appointment with each other to collide, because the other car was heading straight at me. Everything happened so fast. Both our vehicles hit head-on with me standing sideways at my open passenger door. The enormous impact pushed my car even further downhill and threw me down. My open door could have easily decapitated me. Instead, it caused me several painful injuries.

The two ladies must have panicked after their car came to a stop about fifteen feet from mine because they got out and ran, maybe to a phone; I don't know. The same man that had just offered to help me before the collision got a blanket out of his car and laid me on it while we waited for the ambulance to arrive. It all happened so fast that he had not left yet. The two ladies never came to check how bad I was hurt, which really disappointed me.

The ambulance came within minutes. After checking the extent of my injuries, they lifted me carefully on a stretcher with a neck brace and took me to the nearby hospital for X-rays. On the way to the hospital, I had the ambulance attendant call my office from my cell phone, so they could find a replacement for me. I also had him call my hairdresser to cancel my appointment for that day. He was amazed that I would be concerned about that after just being injured.

I had to wait a long time at the hospital because many hurt people came in that morning from having their own experience with black ice. My left arm was broken close to the shoulder, my left knee hurt, and my feet felt as if they were broken in two. My left side was pretty much banged up, so that I could only use my right hand. Since the break was so high up, they could not put a cast on it; therefore, I had to hold my arm in a sling close to my body for seven weeks. From not being moved for such a long time, my shoulder froze. You can't imagine the pain I endured from the months of physical therapy to loosen my shoulder again. It was pure torture. In order to move my little finger one-quarter of an inch, the pain shot all the way to my elbow. I never dreamed that I would be able to reach my back with my left hand again. After the doctor performed arthroscopy surgery on my knee, I needed physical therapy again. I lived in a muumuu for several months. Through my insurance coverage, until it run out, someone came five days a week for a few hours to fix my meals and give me a shower, tidy up the place, and take me grocery shopping and to my doctor appointments. But on the weekends I was alone to fend for myself.

Everything stops when you live alone and can't get around. Unless you have gone through such an ordeal, it is hard to imagine how one gets around with only one arm functioning. The ladies from my church brought me one meal a day for three weeks. It sure helped, and I was very grateful. You might consider it, unless you're doing it already in your circle or church. One of the ladies picked me up for church—even in my muumuu—once I could get around a little better. I was literally at the mercy of someone else, not being able to wash and dry myself, nor even dress myself without the help of another person. A couple of times I had to settle for a young man, because all the ladies were already booked for other homes. When you're desperate, you don't care; your pride quickly goes out the window.

On the weekends when I was alone I was often cold. In the beginning I needed to be literally pulled out of bed. I had to lie in the same position all night the way I fell into the bed. What an ordeal. I learned what pain was. When it got so bad that I could hardly stand it time and time again, I reminded the Lord that I was suffering for Him, which made it bearable. The podiatrist that examined and x-rayed my feet said that my feet would turn inward. From the enormous impact, my body shifted. My feet bothered me a lot. The bottoms hurt, and my toes had bumps and are arthritic, which limited me for a while to wearing only certain shoes. Sometimes I could not lift my feet from the pain, so I shuffled along.

I'm amazed how well I get around now. I also needed the help of a chiropractor for my back for a long time. In the meantime, I suffered quietly. When I look at the pictures I had one lady caretaker snap of my black-and-blue body, I'm in awe how wonderful God made our bodies and how well the body can heal itself. The large bone on my upper arm, for instance—which the doctor let me see in the X-ray—was completely broken in two. By holding it still, it mended itself. Believe me, God had it all figured out before He created us. But my car did not mend itself and had to be totaled. Since the driver of the other car had the same insurance company, it took longer to settle the claim. I thought we could just get together and settle the matter, but instead I was forced to hire an attorney as time went on. It was worse that we had the same company; yet, one would think it be less complicated. They called the weather condition an act of God.

In time my body healed itself, and I returned to the church. God sometimes allows us to experience all sorts of pain in serving His purpose. For example, if the apostles Paul and John had not been imprisoned for such a lengthy time, could they or would they have taken the time to write the many beautiful chapters in the New Testament for us? So, be careful when you judge someone for suffering or wonder why they are not healed. Yes, it can be and often is due to unforgiveness, but they might just be experiencing the baptism of suffering. I would assume that if the individual has a close relationship with God, he or she knows if their suffering for such a cause, but you have no idea. An intercessor, for instance, may even be bedridden, set aside in order to pray all day long in the spirit (in tongues), often not knowing for which person, country, cause, or battle they are commissioned by the Holy Spirit. What if the prayers of this very same person, which you don't even know, just saved you from having a disastrous experience? You may never know what you escaped.

God loves us so much, and through our prayers, the angels are stationed around us for protection. Don't forget to thank Him afterward for all He has done for you and brought you through. Numerous wonderful, anointed hymns have been written by a very contented blind lady named Ms. Fanny Crosby. She kept a positive attitude and said on a number of occasions that she saw her "disability" as a blessing, not an obstacle.

Let me share the following Scriptures with you.

> He that dwelleth in the secret place of the most High shall abide under the shadow of the Almighty.... For he shall give his angels charge over thee, to keep thee in all thy ways. They shall bear thee up in their hands, lest thou dash thy foot against a stone.
>
> —PSALM 91:1, 11–12

How about that? So be careful what you say. Your brain might not understand it. We serve a big God who knows the end before the beginning, who has it all under control.

I already wrote in the first chapter that we must accept joyously whatever it takes to make us pliable and become one with Him. But many in this day and age don't believe that people of faith should have to suffer anymore, that this only took place in Bible times. No, instead, suffering for our Lord Jesus Christ is a part of following Him. As we live for Him and proclaim His sacrifice for us to a lost and sin-sick world, we will experience suffering. When the disciples were falsely imprisoned, they didn't write in the Bible that they were depressed. Instead, they sang at midnight so that the prison gate opened, which is described in Acts 16:25–26: "And at midnight Paul and Silas prayed, and sang praises unto God: and the prisoners heard them. And suddenly there was a great earthquake, so that the foundations of the prison were shaken: and immediately all the doors were opened, and every one's bands were loosed." Not even a shipwreck and being in danger of dying could keep them from joyfully suffering for Jesus Christ, as they were being a blessing to many others by bringing them the good news of salvation.

Let me leave you with these encouraging Scriptures from the apostle Paul in 2 Corinthians 6:4–10:

> But in all things approving ourselves as the ministers of God, in much patience, in afflictions, in necessities, in distresses, In stripes, in imprisonments, in tumults, in labours, in watchings, in fastings; By pureness, by knowledge, by long suffering, by kindness, by the Holy Ghost, by love unfeigned, By the word of truth, by the power of God, by the armour of righteousness on the right hand and on the left, By honour and dishonour, by evil report and good report: as deceivers, and yet true; As unknown, and yet well known; as dying, and, behold, we live; as chastened, and not killed; As sorrowful, yet alway rejoicing; as poor, yet making many rich; as having nothing, and yet possessing all things.

Chapter 6

Water Baptism

New Testament Christianity is not a ritualistic religion, but rather it is based on a personal relationship with God through Jesus Christ. Yet, our Lord divinely ordered water baptism. It is the public confession of entrance into the Christian church, or the body of Christ, and symbolizes the spiritual life that has begun in the believer. We read in Romans 6:3–4, "Know ye not, that so many of us as were baptized into Jesus Christ were baptized into his death? Therefore we are buried with him by baptism into death: that like as Christ was raised up from the dead by the glory of the Father, even so we also should walk in newness of life."

As washing with water cleanses the body, so God, in connection with the death of Christ and through the Holy Spirit, cleanses the soul. Water baptism illustrates this cleansing.

> Arise, and be baptized, and wash away thy sins, calling on the name of the Lord.
>
> —Acts 22:16

Water baptism also signifies that the convert, by faith, has put on Christ and is now a part of the kingdom, as Galatians 3:27 tells us: "For as many of you as have been baptized into Christ have put on Christ."

In Catholic Germany, where I was raised, it was the custom to take a baby to church to be baptized. Even after I grew up, I never heard of or saw an adult getting baptized. Certain denominations here in this country also only sprinkle the baby or adult, but that is not what the Bible teaches us.

A few years ago I made the acquaintance of a very influential person of such a denomination. We conversed at different times, and I inquired about his standing with the Lord. As I ministered to him several times, he expressed an interest in the baptism in the Holy Spirit. Since we were close to the end of our time together that day, I told him the next time we met I would pray for him to receive it. After we parted that day, the Holy Spirit revealed to me that he never was properly baptized. At our next meeting I confronted him with my revelation from the Holy Spirit and we searched the Scriptures for the truth in the Bible. I had already done a study on it at home and provided him with the following Scriptures:

> And were baptized of him in Jordan, confessing their sins.... And Jesus, when He was baptized, went up straightway out of the water.
>
> —MATTHEW 3:6, 16

This tells me that the people that John the Baptist baptized were immersed in water and repented of their sins. How can an infant do that? According to the Bible, which is the Word of God, baptizing by sprinkling is not a valid baptism, because the participant is not able as a baby to confess his or her sins. It is only a religious ritual in certain denominations. John the Baptist said, "I indeed baptize you with water unto repentance: but He that cometh after me is mightier than I, whose shoes I am not worthy to bear: he shall baptize you with the Holy Ghost, and with fire." Some people—although this is rare—speak in tongues immediately, as soon as they come up from under the water.

Jesus gave His disciples the Great Commission in Mark 16:15–16: "And he said unto them, Go ye into all the world, and preach the gospel to every creature. He that believeth and is baptized shall be saved; but he that believeth not shall be damned." He that believes and is baptized evidently must be of the age of accountability, capable of thinking, in order to make the decision.

Then, we read about the conversion of Simon the sorcerer in Acts 8:12–13: "But when they believed Philip preaching the things concerning the kingdom of God, and the name of Jesus Christ, they were baptized, both men and women. Then Simon himself believed also: and when he was baptized, he continued with Philip, and wondered, beholding the miracles and signs which were done."

Philip also baptized the Ethiopian eunuch: "And as they went on their way, they came unto a certain water: and the eunuch said, See, here is water; what doth hinder me to be baptized? And Philip said, If thou believest with all thine heart, thou mayest. And he answered and said, I believe that Jesus Christ is the Son of God. And he commanded the chariot to stand still: and they went down both into the water, both Philip and the eunuch; and he baptized him" (Acts 8:36–38).

In Acts 18:8 we read that "Crispus, the chief ruler of the synagogue, believed on the Lord with all his house; and many of the Corinthians hearing believed, and were baptized." You see, babies cannot make a confession of their faith. Many denominations have parents bring their babies to the church to be dedicated to the Lord by having the pastor pray over them. Then when they are old enough, they make a confession of faith and get properly baptized by immersion.

By the way, my friend was not baptized by immersion. He recognized the error he was taught.

Any denomination that baptizes other than by immersion is in disagreement with the Bible and acts on its own behalf. If it was the correct way for Jesus, as we read already, why would it not be the proper way for us? Maybe it is high time that we stop being rebellious, doing our own denominational thing as we please, and return to doing it God's way, obeying how He commanded us to be baptized in the Bible.

Here are some key points, which are a privilege to remember:

1. Satan and sin have no power over a dead person. We read in Romans 6:7 that "he that is dead is freed from sin."

2. Satan cannot remind you of your past. You do not have one, because you don't live; Christ lives in you.

> I am crucified with Christ: nevertheless I live; yet not I, but Christ liveth in me: and the life which I now live in the flesh I live by the faith of the Son of God, who loved me, and gave himself for me.
>
> —GALATIANS 2:20

3. You are no longer bound by Adamic or natural life, because you become one with Christ in spirit.

> But he that is joined unto the Lord is one spirit.
>
> —1 CORINTHIANS 6:17

4. In this death, you renounce Satan's stronghold in your soul. This is a death to the independent, rebellious "I."

> Likewise reckon ye also yourselves to be dead indeed unto sin, but alive unto God through Jesus Christ our Lord.
>
> —ROMANS 6:11

5. The soul—the mind, will, and emotions—is at this point swept clean. On the other hand, salvation is of the spirit.

> Jesus answered, Verily, verily, I say unto thee, Except a man be born of water and of the Spirit, he cannot enter into the kingdom of God.
>
> —JOHN 3:5

6. This death is very important as a statement to Satan, the accuser of our past, and the old sinful, carnal—Adamic—nature. Revelation 12:11 tells us, "And they overcame him by the blood of the Lamb, and by the word of their testimony; and they loved not their lives unto the death."

Galatians 3:26–27 tells us, "For ye are all children of God by faith in Christ Jesus. For as many of you as have been baptized into Christ have put on Christ."

We know that when Jesus our Lord had concluded His ministry on Earth, just prior to His ascension into heaven, He instructed us, "Go ye, therefore, and teach all nations, baptizing them in the name of the Father, and of the Son, and of the Holy Spirit" (Matt. 28:19).

Chapter 7

Different Holidays

As soon as we finish our Thanksgiving dinner toward the end of November, we are bombarded by the news media telling us how many shopping days are left until Christmas.

Christmas

The merchants expect to make a big profit and advertise their products early. It all seems so secular and has absolutely nothing to do with the actual reason we celebrate Christmas. Several of the larger department stores have a man dressed up in a red suit and beard as Santa Claus so that the smaller children can have their picture taken with him. As they sit on his lap, he asks them what they want from Santa for Christmas. I heard on the news that children make an additional sixty thousand requests yearly to Santa through the mail. Yet, the whole purpose of this joyous event is to celebrate the birth of Jesus Christ, the Savior of the world, although in many homes His name is never mentioned. To many, it is strictly a secular celebration of getting gifts. The children don't know it any other way unless they are taught differently. Some call it "X-mas." The schools call the Christmas vacation "Winter Fest."

When I grew up in Germany, St. Nikolaus, as we called him, came on December 6. In my home he announced himself by rattling a chain outside on the street. When we were small, it scared us. We had to say a prayer in front of him. He brought us nuts and apples, and in later years, after the war, also oranges.

The story about him is totally distorted and is a corruption of the tale of the real St. Nikolaus, who was a great Christian man from Turkey. Early on in his ministry, he brought souls to Christ and helped orphans and poor children. Around Christmastime he got a donkey and loaded it up with fruit and sweets as an act of generosity. He gave everything away and lived a life of complete selflessness. He was so powerful in his conversions that the emperor of Rome hated him and came to Constantinople, Turkey, to stop him. He had his soldiers arrest and imprison him for ten years, where he was tortured and suffered, but he would never deny Jesus Christ.

Later, when Constantine conquered the Roman Empire and became a believer, he released St. Nikolaus and began to honor him. Constantine wanted to go to Israel, the Holy Land, and on his way, they encountered a violent storm. One of the sailors washed overboard. They fished his body out of the sea, and as St. Nikolaus prayed over the sailor, God raised him back to life. He did cast out devils and worked over hundred miracles. Later he became a cardinal, and as such he would have worn red, blue, or black clothing all the time. In each picture that was taken of him, he had a white beard and even once went down a chimney to help some children because the wicked man of the house would not let him in the front door. Yes, he was a great giver of gifts.

Why Do We Celebrate Christmas on December 25?

Most people you ask could not even tell you why we celebrate Christmas on December 25. Some will say that it was a pagan holiday on that date way back. But this is not the reason why. My friend Ruth Mills Grant, who went to be with the Lord several years ago, gave me the following study she did on the history of Christmas Day:

> The last prophet in the Old Testament was Malachi, who prophesied about four hundred years before the birth of Jesus. Our Bible does not give us a record of those years, although Daniel gives us some prophecy concerning those times. We must turn to history and other sources to find a record of those years. Many of the Jews had returned to their homeland after the Babylonian captivity and were under the rule of other nations. Palestine suffered much from the constant wars between Persia and Egypt. In 333 B.C. Syria fell under the power of the third of the world empires, the Greco-Macedonian empire of Alexander the Great, who had swept across the then-known world very swiftly. But His victory was short-lived, as he died in his early thirties. His empire was then divided between four of his generals. It is described in Daniel 2:36–45 and 7:1–28. In this breakup, Judea came under the power of Syria and later under Egypt. Then in 198 B.C. Judea was conquered by Antiochus the Great and annexed to Syria.

The younger son of Antiochus the Great, known as Antiochus Epiphanes in 170 B.C. caused much interference in Jerusalem, the temple, and the priesthood. He plundered Jerusalem and profaned the temple. On December 25 in 168 B.C., the Jewish month of Kislev, he offered swine upon the altar of sacrifice and erected an altar to Jupiter. He took the golden altar of incense, the lampstand, table of shewbread, along with all the utensils and censer, curtains, crowns, etc.; stripped them of all the gold; and took them to his own land…He was known as "the Madman," who forbade Jews, under penalty of death, to practice circumcision and observe their sabbath or feast days of the Jewish year…It was one of the darkest times in their history up until that time. They were flogged to death if they refused to eat swine meat, which was strictly against their laws. Many did refuse and lost their lives. Then Mattathias, an aged priest, refused to sacrifice on the pagan altar, and with his five sons started the Maccabean revolt, consisting of guerrilla warfare. But soon after the beginning of the revolt, Mattathias died. His third son, Judas, known as the Maccabee, carried on the revolt, and many Jews rallied to the cause, which caused them three years of suffering. Judas and his army finally were able to enter Jerusalem and take the temple. They entered, removed all signs of paganism, and threw out the altar dedicated to Jupiter. The statue of Zeus-Antiochus was ground to dust, and a new altar was built for temple sacrifices.

In the month of Kislev—which is our December—on the twenty-fifth day, they observed eight days of feasting, known as Hanukkah. This was three years to the day from the day Antiochus had offered swine on the altar. (Antiochus was the "little horn" of Daniel 8:9–14, a type of the abomination of desolation of Matthew 24:15 and a type of the Beast in Revelation.) The Jews had regained their temple, but their struggles did not end. Much of this history is given in first and second Maccabees [in the Apocrypha], especially 1 Maccabees 1:10, 33–40, 54–62.... The books of the Apocrypha are not in our Bible because they were rejected by the religious leaders who formed the canon of our Bible as not being inspired. But they are a good source of historical information relating to the four hundred silent years.

Quoting here from 2 Maccabees 10:5–8: "It happened that on the same day which the sanctuary had been profaned by the foreigners, the purification of the sanctuary took place, that is, on the twenty-fifth day of the same month, which is Kislev. And they celebrated it for eight days with rejoicing, in the manner of the Feast of Booths, remembering how not long before, during the Feast of Booths, they had been wandering in the mountains and caves like wild animals. While bearing palm branches, they offered hymns of thanksgiving to Him who had given success to the purifying of His own holy place. They decreed by public ordinance and vote that the whole nation of Jews should observe these days every year."

We might ask the question many other people wonder about: was Christ born on December 25? Many people answer with an emphatic no. And some refuse to celebrate the birth of Christ because we do not know for sure when He was born. If we search the Scriptures and study history we come to the conclusion that these people may be wrong. From the evidence one can find, it seems possible that Christ was born on December 25. Let's examine some of the evidence that can be found. We must admit that absolute certainty of Christ's nativity is not possible as to the month and day, but enough Scripture and history can be incorporated to give us data to invest it with probability and almost certainty of the exact year. The date of Herod's death is known, and Christ was born before that. Herod died shortly before Passover [in] 750 A.U.C., in a specific year from the founding of Rome. This date corresponds to about April 4 B.C. It is thought Herod's death occurred between March 12 and April 12. Considering that the murder of the children of Bethlehem occurred before Herod's death, as described in Matthew 2:16–18...the birth of Christ could not possibly have occurred after the beginning of February 4 B.C. and most likely [took place] several weeks earlier, allowing time for the following events before that, such as Mary's purification and the stories of Simeon and Anna in the temple, the visit of the wise men, etc. This would bring us close to the ecclesiastical date of December 25.

Among the reasons some give for not holding to December 25 as the date of Jesus' birth is that [the Scriptures say the] shepherds were watching their flocks by night. They say that this could not have happened in December. Why not? This theory can be dismissed because by checking on a globe we find in what latitude the Holy Land lays. It is approximately the same as northern Florida and southern Georgia. December is generally not cold in that latitude.

Besides, there are two other factors to consider: I'm told that December in that locale is not a rainy month, and secondly, that the shepherds were watching their flocks by night, which is written in the Bible in Luke 2:8. These were not ordinary shepherds; instead they were special shepherds who were caring for the sheep raised for the purpose of being sold for the temple sacrifices and were in the fields near Bethlehem and Jerusalem the year around.... We should understand that if the sheep were being raised for temple sacrifice, they certainly would be kept nearby the whole year, because the Jews sacrificed all year long.

Let us get a better understanding of our subject by considering Scriptures along with some historical facts. Starting with the biblical history of John the Baptist, we find that during the time of King David, there were twenty-four courses of the priesthood formed, each designated to serve in the temple at certain times. (You can read it in 1 Chronicles 24:1, 10.) Then we find in Luke 1:5–10 that a certain Priest, Zacharias of the course of ABIA, had a wife, Elizabeth, who was of the daughters of Aaron and also of the priesthood. Zacharias officiated in the temple in the course of ABIA. History says this course was on duty from October 2 to 9 of 748 A.U.C. Each course served twice yearly. This was the year before Christ's birth. During this term of service, Zacharias encountered the angel who foretold of the birth of his son, John the Baptist, described in Luke 1:11–24. Let us look at this time on a Jewish calendar. October of our time would be the month Tishri—the first month of their civil calendar or the seventh of their sacred calendar. Elizabeth conceived soon afterward. Add nine months, and the birth of John would have occurred in the third month; using the sacred calendar, the month is Sivan. Luke 1:26–38 tells us that in Elizabeth's sixth month was when the angel appeared to Mary telling her that she would have a Son. Counting nine months from Vedar, we come to the month Kislev, which is our December.

...We also know that Jesus was in Jerusalem to celebrate that feast, as [it says] in John 10:22. And consider that in this chapter Jesus is asserting His deity, telling us that He is the Good Shepherd recorded in Psalm 23; Hebrews 13:20; 1 Peter 5:4; John 14:9; John 20:28–29. Then we read in John 10:22, "And it was at Jerusalem the feast of the dedication, and it was winter." This was when and where He spoke of His sheep and being the Good Shepherd. Jesus also said of Himself in John 8:12, "I am the light of the world: he that followeth me shall not walk in darkness, but shall have the light of life."

...In each reference, Jesus refers to Himself as the Light of the world. (See Matthew 4:16; John 1:1–14.) Even in the Old Testament where we read of the promise of the coming Messiah in Isaiah 9:2, "The people that walked in darkness have seen a great light: they that dwell in the land of the shadow of death, upon them hath the light shined." To sum up this point: at Hanukkah, at the temple, Jesus said He is the Light of the world. Jesus and the temple had something of great magnitude in common. The temple, built by Solomon...had housed the Glory of God. We read in 1 Kings 8:10–11 "And it came to pass, when the priests were come out of the holy place, that the cloud filled the house of the Lord, So that the priests could not stand to minister because of the cloud: for the glory of the Lord had filled the house of the Lord." So also is Jesus now housing the glory of God—the Light of the world in us.

Following the death, burial, and resurrection of Jesus, the Hebrew Christians began to identify *light* with Christ and the temple at Hanukkah. We read in John 1:9: "That was the true Light, which lighteth every man that cometh into the world." The lights of Hanukkah pointed to the One who alone is the Light of the world...

The Jewish historian Hayyim Schause made the statement that the Hanukkah lights played an important role in the lives of the early Christians before the destruction of the temple, which occurred in 70 A.D. We must remember that many of those early Christians were the disciples themselves, like James and John, the sons of Zebedee; and Salome, the sister of Mary, mother of Jesus; and His own brothers; and even Mary herself; plus several more. They all could have known exactly when Jesus was born. Certainly His mother did, since she made this trip from Nazareth to Bethlehem with Joseph to register in order to vote! Remember also that John was still alive in 90 A.D., which was long after the destruction of the temple. So, if the early Christians connected the Feast of Lights—Hanukkah—with the birthday of Jesus Christ before the destruction of the temple, certainly John would have known the date in 90 A.D. Why should we have a lot of doubt about it now?

And Luke, who so beautifully wrote about the events of Jesus' birth, could have got the facts directly from Mary. According to this information, the early Christians were already observing the birth of Jesus at the same time as other Jews were observing the Feast of Lights. Even though God did not give the Jews Hanukkah as a day commemorating the coming of the Lamb of God, I believe the date is very symbolic, and could be the exact date of Jesus' birth. Some of Jesus' disciples who were with Him during His earthly ministry were alive at that time. Luke certainly could verify the record by obtaining Jesus' correct birth date from His mother Mary. Instead, it seems, more likely than not, that it occurred on the same day as the Feast of Dedication.

We know Jesus, the Messiah, did come, and in commemoration of His coming, the December 25 was chosen to celebrate and give thanks to God for His unspeakable gift, as written in 2 Corinthians 9:15: "Thanks be unto God for his unspeakable gift;" and in John 3:16: "For God so loved the world, that he gave his only begotten Son, that whosoever believeth in him should not perish, but have everlasting life." God loved us enough to send His only begotten Son down from the glories of heaven to be the Lamb of God. Jesus humbled Himself to be born—deity clothed in human flesh—into the fallen human race so that we of Adam's race could be redeemed from the power of Satan.

Although His birth did occur in a most lowly way, in a smelly barn on a pile of straw and hay, nevertheless He is the

Savior of the world, recorded in Isaiah 9:6–7: "For unto us a child is born, unto us a son is given: and the government shall be upon his shoulder: and his name shall be called Wonderful, Counsellor, The mighty God, The everlasting Father, The Prince of Peace. Of the increase of his government and peace there shall be no end, upon the throne of David, and upon his kingdom, to order it, and to establish it with judgment and with justice from henceforth even for ever. The zeal of the Lord of hosts will perform this."

I'm so thankful to God the Father and God the Son for loving us enough to provide such wonderful salvation for fallen mankind—for me and for you.

Kwanzaa

Kwanzaa is a week-long Pan-African festival celebrated primarily in the United States, honoring African American heritage. It is observed from December 26 to January 1 each year. Kwanzaa consists of seven days of celebration, featuring activities such as candle-lighting and pouring of libations, and culminating in a feast and gift giving. It was created by Ron Karenga, and first celebrated from December 26, 1966, to January 1, 1967. Karenga calls Kwanzaa the African American branch of "first fruits" celebrations of classical African cultures.[1]

Kwanzaa is a festivity that has its roots in the black nationalist movement of the 1960s, and was established as a means to help African Americans reconnect with their African cultural and historical heritage by uniting in meditation and study of "African traditions" and "common humanist principles."[2]

Kwanzaa derives from the Swahili phrase *matunda ya kwanza,* which means "first fruits." Karenga created Kwanzaa while living in California, and explained that his goal was "to give a Black alternative to the existing holiday and give Blacks an opportunity to celebrate themselves and history, rather than simply imitate the practice of the dominant society." He changed his position in 1997. Now the official Kwanzaa Web site explains, "Kwanzaa was not created to give people an alternative to their own religion or religious holiday. And it is not an alternative to people's religion or faith but a common ground of African culture."[3]

Can Kwanzaa get you in to heaven? Jesus Christ belongs to all people. He is the Savior of the world.

EASTER—RESURRECTION DAY

It was on Resurrection Day that the crucified Son of God—Jesus Christ, the Savior of the world who died on the cross—rose from the dead. God the Father Himself sent Him to the cross to keep us out of hell. This event changed the calendar. We refer to the years after Jesus' death as A.D. (*Anno Domini,* "in the year of the Lord") and B.C. ("before Christ").

The world celebrates Easter with its Easter bonnets, Easter bunnies, Easter lilies, and Easter eggs.

> In ancient times, eggs were used in the religious rites of the Egyptians and the Greeks. They were hung up for mystic purposes in their temples. These sacred eggs can be distinctly traced from Egypt to the banks of the Euphrates. An egg of wondrous size is said to have fallen from heaven into the

> Euphrates River. Fish rolled it to the bank, were doves settled upon it and hatched it. Out came Venus, who afterwards was called the Syrian Goddess—that is, Astarte. The egg became one of the symbols of Astarte, or Easter. In some languages also known as Ishtar, held in the month of Nisan, equivalent to April.[4]

Baby chickens, rabbits, and hot cross buns all lend their ornamentation to the day when Christendom celebrates the resurrection of Christ.

The Easter lily has long been associated with fertility and reproduction, as have the rabbit and the egg.[5] Symbolic of the season, churches worldwide decorate their altars with these beautiful flowers.

The hot cross bun goes back to the ancient pagan custom of worshiping the queen of heaven with offerings and cakes marked with her image. In earlier times, people offered them to her; now they eat them. Egyptians supposedly made buns with two horns on them to offer to the moon goddess. The Greeks changed the symbol to a cross in order to divide it more easily.[6] We read in Jeremiah 7:18, "The children gather wood, and the fathers kindle the fire, and the women knead their dough, to make cakes to the queen of heaven, and to pour out drink offerings unto other gods, that they may provoke me to anger." This queen of heaven's name is Ishtar, or Easter. Hot cross buns are a veiled ascription of worship to her. By consuming them, we participate in pagan Babylonianism. No wonder the Bible tells us in Revelation 18:4, "Come out of her, my people, that ye be not partakers of her sins, and that ye receive not of her plagues."

Easter is believed to be a celebration of the arrival of spring—the resurrection of life from the dead of winter. What seems to be the connection? The name *Easter* and an element of its celebration, the "Ishtar egg" may be traced to Babylon, which predates the resurrection of Jesus Christ by more than two thousand years. Therefore, there cannot be any connection among eggs, Easter, and Jesus. Babylonian paganism spread worldwide during these two thousand years and became the diabolical substitute for biblical truth. Paul wrote about this heathen religious system in Romans 1:21–23: "Because that, when they knew God, they glorified him not as God, neither were thankful; but became vain in their imaginations, and their foolish heart was darkened. Professing themselves to be wise, they became fools, And changed the glory of the uncorruptible God into an image made like to corruptible man, and to birds, and fourfooted beasts, and creeping things."

Easter is not a Christian term and can be traced to the goddess Astarte, who in Nineveh was worshiped as Ishtar. The resemblance of Easter and Ishtar worship is easily recognized. It is said that the ancient Druids introduced into the British Isles the worship of pagan gods such as Bel and Astarte, who is the Ishtar of the Assyrians. Others have pointed out that the term *Easter* originated in the British Isles.[7]

Many of the practices that accompany the celebration of Easter attest to the fact that it had a Babylonian origin. The hot cross buns of Good Friday and the dyed eggs of Pasch on Easter Sunday related to ancient Chaldaic ceremonies. The buns were known by that very name and were used in the worship of the queen of heaven, the goddess Ishtar, around 1500 B.C.[8]

The origin of Easter eggs is just as clear. Ancient Druids used the egg as the sacred emblem of their order. The worship of the Greek deities in Athens consisted in part of the consecration of an egg, while the Hindus, Japanese, and Chinese all dyed or painted eggs to be used in sacred festivals. Egyptians and Greeks hung eggs in their temples for the very same purpose.[9]

The term *Easter* and some of the practices connected with its observation are totally pagan. Is God trying to open our spiritual eyes to these ancient pagan traditions now in order to reveal to us the truth? Let's focus on the celebration of the resurrection of our Lord. The death, burial, and resurrection of Jesus Christ represent the singular, most important event in history: the atonement for sin and the beginning of the age of grace.

Just as He reconciled Himself with us, so also gave He us the ministry of reconciliation, as we read in 2 Corinthians 5:17–21:

> Therefore if any man be in Christ, he is a new creature: old things are passed away; behold, all things are become new. And all things are of God, who hath reconciled us to himself by Jesus Christ, and hath given to us the ministry of reconciliation; To wit, that God was in Christ, reconciling the world unto himself, not imputing their trespasses unto them; and hath committed unto us the word of reconciliation. Now then we are ambassadors for Christ, as though God did beseech you by us: we pray you in Christ's stead, be ye reconciled to God. For he hath made him to be sin for us, who knew no sin; that we might be made the righteousness of God in him.

After I saw the movie *The Passion of the Christ* on February 25, 2004—opening day—the Holy Spirit revealed to me that if there was a resurrection, there first had to be a crucifixion. I had been waiting patiently for several years for the Lord's anointing to write about this subject. I will explain it to you with Scriptures from the Bible, because it describes the whole process.

Jesus existed from the very beginning of the world. We read in John 1:14, "And the Word was made flesh, and dwelt among us," to die later for the sins of all mankind. Yes, as cruel as it sounds, He was born to die. Isaiah prophesied it about seven centuries before Calvary. Therefore, no one should blame a certain people group or point their finger for nailing Him to the cross and is responsible. Several passages relate specifically to the Messiah, the suffering Servant, and the Savior of the World. No one is to blame for Jesus' crucifixion, it was preordained by God before the foundation of the World, as I will confirm to you.

Here are some of the Old Testament Scriptures to prove it:

> We did esteem him stricken, smitten of God, and afflicted. But he was wounded for our transgressions, he was bruised for our iniquities: the chastisement of our peace was upon him; and with his stripes we are healed.... Yet it pleased the LORD to bruise him...by his knowledge shall my righteous servant justify many; for he shall bear their iniquities...because he hath poured out his soul unto death.
>
> —ISAIAH 53:4–5, 10–12

Other messianic psalms are Psalm 2, 16, 21, 22, 69, and 118. Jesus said in Psalm 22:1, 16, 18, "My God, my God, why hast thou forsaken me?...they pierced my hands and my feet....They part my garments among them, and cast lots upon my vesture."

> And one shall say unto him, What are these wounds in thine hands? Then he shall answer, Those with which I was wounded in the house of my friends.
>
> —ZECHARIAH 13:6

Are these Scriptures not enough proof for any doubter? Let's continue with excerpts from the Gospels as we follow along with numerous New Testament scriptures:

> After two days was the feast of the passover, and of unleavened bread: and the chief priests and the scribes sought how they might take him by craft, and put him to death. But they said, Not on the feast day, lest there be an uproar of the people. And being in Bethany in the house of Simon the leper, as he sat at meat, there came a woman having an alabaster box of ointment of spikenard very precious; and she brake the box, and poured it on his head. And there were some that had indignation within themselves, and said, Why was this waste of the ointment made? For it might have been sold for more than three hundred pence, and have been given to the poor. And they murmured against her. And Jesus said, Let her alone; why trouble ye her? she hath wrought a good work on me. For ye have the poor with you always, and whensoever ye will ye may do them good: but me ye have not always. She hath done what she could: she is come aforehand to anoint my body to the burying. Verily I say unto you, Wheresoever this gospel shall be preached throughout the whole world, this also that she hath done shall be spoken of for a memorial of her. And Judas Iscariot, one of the twelve, went unto the chief priests, to betray him unto them. And when they heard it, they were glad, and promised to give him money. And he sought how he might conveniently betray him. And the first day of unleavened bread, when they killed the pass-

> over, his disciples said unto him, Where wilt thou that we go and prepare that thou mayest eat the passover? And he sendeth forth two of his disciples, and saith unto them, Go ye into the city, and there shall meet you a man bearing a pitcher of water: follow him. And wheresoever he shall go in, say ye to the goodman of the house, The Master saith, Where is the guestchamber, where I shall eat the passover with my disciples? And he will shew you a large upper room furnished and prepared: there make ready for us. And his disciples went forth, and came into the city, and found as he had said unto them: and they made ready the passover. And in the evening he cometh with the twelve. And as they sat and did eat, Jesus said, Verily I say unto you, One of you which eateth with me shall betray me.
>
> —MARK 14:1–18

> And he took bread, and gave thanks, and brake it, and gave unto them, saying, This is my body which is given for you: this do in remembrance of me. Likewise also the cup after supper, saying, This cup is the new testament in my blood, which is shed for you. But, behold, the hand of him that betrayeth me is with me on the table. And truly the Son of man goeth, as it was determined: but woe unto that man by whom he is betrayed! And they began to enquire among themselves, which of them it was that should do this thing.
>
> —LUKE 22:19–23

Later we read in 1 Corinthians 10:16–17, "The cup of blessing which we bless, is it not the communion of the blood of Christ? The bread which we break, is it not the communion of the body of Christ? For we being many are one bread, and one body: for we are all partakers of that one bread."

Paul wrote the following Scriptures, which are read to this day when we take communion:

> For I have received of the Lord that which also I delivered unto you, that the Lord Jesus the same night in which he was betrayed took bread: And when he had given thanks, he brake it, and said, Take, eat: this is my body, which is broken for you: this do in remembrance of me. After the same manner also he took the cup, when he had supped, saying, this cup is the new testament in my blood: this do ye, as oft as ye drink it, in remembrance of me. For as often as ye eat this bread, and drink this cup, ye do shew the Lord's death till he come. Wherefore whosoever shall eat this bread, and drink this cup of the Lord, unworthily, shall be guilty of the body and blood of the Lord. But let a man examine himself, and so let him eat of that bread, and drink of that cup. For he that eateth and drinketh unworthily, eateth and drinketh damnation to himself, not discerning the Lord's body. For this cause many are weak and sickly among you, and many sleep. For if we would judge ourselves, we should not be judged.
>
> —1 CORINTHIANS 11:23–31

> And the Lord said, Simon, Simon, behold, Satan hath desired to have you, that he may sift you as wheat: But I have prayed for thee, that thy faith fail not: and when thou art converted, strengthen thy brethren. And he said unto him, Lord, I am ready to go with thee, both into prison, and to death. And he said, I tell thee, Peter, the cock shall not crow this day, before that thou shalt thrice deny that thou knowest me.
>
> —LUKE 22:31–34

> And he came out, and went, as he was wont, to the mount of Olives; and his disciples also followed him. And when he

was at the place, he said unto them, Pray that ye enter not into temptation. And he was withdrawn from them about a stone's cast, and kneeled down, and prayed, Saying, Father, if thou be willing, remove this cup from me: nevertheless not my will, but thine, be done. And there appeared an angel unto him from heaven, strengthening him. And being in an agony he prayed more earnestly: and his sweat was as it were great drops of blood falling down to the ground. And when he rose up from prayer, and was come to his disciples, he found them sleeping for sorrow, And said unto them, Why sleep ye? rise and pray, lest ye enter into temptation. And while he yet spake, behold a multitude, and he that was called Judas, one of the twelve, went before them, and drew near unto Jesus to kiss him. But Jesus said unto him, Judas, betrayest thou the Son of man with a kiss?... Then took they him, and led him, and brought him into the high priest's house. And Peter followed afar off. And when they had kindled a fire in the midst of the hall, and were set down together, Peter sat down among them. But a certain maid beheld him as he sat by the fire, and earnestly looked upon him, and said, This man was also with him. And he denied him, saying, Woman, I know him not. And after a little while another saw him, and said, Thou art also of them. And Peter said, Man, I am not. And about the space of one hour after another confidently affirmed, saying, Of a truth this fellow also was with him: for he is a Galilaean. And Peter said, Man, I know not what thou sayest. And immediately, while he yet spake, the cock crew. And the Lord turned, and looked upon Peter. And Peter remembered the word of the Lord, how he had said unto him, Before the cock crow, thou shalt deny me thrice. And Peter went out, and wept bitterly. And the men that held Jesus mocked him, and smote him. And when they had blindfolded him, they struck him on the face, and asked him, saying, Prophesy, who

> is it that smote thee? And many other things blasphemously spake they against him. And as soon as it was day, the elders of the people and the chief priests and the scribes came together, and led him into their council, saying, Art thou the Christ? tell us. And he said unto them, If I tell you, ye will not believe: And if I also ask you, ye will not answer me, nor let me go. Hereafter shall the Son of man sit on the right hand of the power of God. Then said they all, Art thou then the Son of God? And he said unto them, Ye say that I am. And they said, What need we any further witness? for we ourselves have heard of his own mouth.
>
> —LUKE 22:39–48, 54–71

Let me continue with Matthew's account of the trial of Jesus, the thirty pieces of silver Judas was paid, the crucifixion and resurrection of Jesus, and the Great Commission He gave. Again, the best way to describe it is with the Scriptures themselves.

> When the morning was come, all the chief priests and elders of the people took counsel against Jesus to put him to death: And when they had bound him, they led him away, and delivered him to Pontius Pilate the governor. Then Judas, which had betrayed him, when he saw that he was condemned, repented himself, and brought again the thirty pieces of silver to the chief priests and elders, Saying, I have sinned in that I have betrayed the innocent blood. And they said, What is that to us? see thou to that. And he cast down the pieces of silver in the temple, and departed, and went and hanged himself. And the chief priests took the silver pieces, and said, It is not lawful for to put them into the treasury, because it is the price of blood. And they took counsel, and bought with them the potter's field, to bury strangers in. Wherefore that field was called, The field of blood, unto this day. Then

was fulfilled that which was spoken by Jeremy the prophet, saying, And they took the thirty pieces of silver, the price of him that was valued, whom they of the children of Israel did value; And gave them for the potter's field, as the Lord appointed me. And Jesus stood before the governor: and the governor asked him, saying, Art thou the King of the Jews? And Jesus said unto him, Thou sayest. And when he was accused of the chief priests and elders, he answered nothing. Then said Pilate unto him, Hearest thou not how many things they witness against thee? And he answered him to never a word; insomuch that the governor marvelled greatly. Now at that feast the governor was wont to release unto the people a prisoner, whom they would. And they had then a notable prisoner, called Barabbas. Therefore when they were gathered together, Pilate said unto them, Whom will ye that I release unto you? Barabbas, or Jesus which is called Christ? For he knew that for envy they had delivered him. When he was set down on the judgment seat, his wife sent unto him, saying, Have thou nothing to do with that just man: for I have suffered many things this day in a dream because of him. But the chief priests and elders persuaded the multitude that they should ask Barabbas, and destroy Jesus. The governor answered and said unto them, Whether of the twain will ye that I release unto you? They said, Barabbas. Pilate saith unto them, What shall I do then with Jesus which is called Christ? They all say unto him, Let him be crucified. And the governor said, Why, what evil hath he done? But they cried out the more, saying, Let him be crucified. When Pilate saw that he could prevail nothing, but that rather a tumult was made, he took water, and washed his hands before the multitude, saying, I am innocent of the blood of this just person: see ye to it. Then answered all the people, and said, His blood be on us, and on our children. Then released he Barabbas unto them: and when he had scourged Jesus, he delivered him to be crucified. Then the soldiers of the governor took Jesus into the common hall, and gathered unto him the whole band of soldiers. And they stripped him, and put on him a scarlet robe. And when they had platted a crown of thorns, they put it upon his head, and a reed in his right hand: and they bowed the knee before him, and mocked him, saying, Hail, King of the Jews! And they spit upon him, and took the reed, and smote him on the head. And after that they had mocked him, they took the robe off from him, and put his own raiment on him, and led him away to crucify him. And as they came out, they found a man of Cyrene, Simon by name: him they compelled to bear his cross. And when they were come unto a place called Golgotha, that is to say, a place of a skull, They gave him vinegar to drink mingled with gall: and when he had tasted thereof, he would not drink. And they crucified him, and parted his garments, casting lots: that it might be fulfilled which was spoken by the prophet, They parted my garments among them, and upon my vesture did they cast lots. And sitting down they watched him there; And set up over his head his accusation written, THIS IS JESUS THE KING OF THE JEWS. Then were there two thieves crucified with him, one on the right hand, and another on the left. And they that passed by reviled him, wagging their heads, And saying, Thou that destroyest the temple, and buildest it in three days, save thyself. If thou be the Son of God, come down from the cross. Likewise also the chief priests mocking him, with the scribes and elders, said, He saved others; himself he cannot save. If he be the King of Israel, let him now come down from the cross, and we will believe him. He trusted in God; let him deliver him now, if he will have him: for he said, I am the Son of God. The thieves also, which were crucified with him, cast the same in his teeth. Now from the sixth hour there was darkness over all the land unto the ninth hour. And about the ninth hour Jesus cried with a loud voice, saying, Eli, Eli, lama sabachthani? that is to say, My God, my God, why hast thou forsaken me? Some of them that stood there, when they heard that, said, This man calleth for Elias. And straightway one of them ran, and took a sponge, and filled it with vinegar, and put it on a reed, and gave him to drink. The rest said, Let be, let us see whether Elias will come to save him. Jesus, when he had cried again with a loud voice, yielded up the ghost. And, behold, the veil of the temple was rent in twain from the top to the bottom; and the earth did quake, and the rocks rent; And the graves were opened; and many bodies of the saints which slept arose, And came out of the graves after his resurrection, and went into the holy city, and appeared unto many. Now when the centurion, and they that were with him, watching Jesus, saw the earthquake, and those things that were done, they feared greatly, saying, Truly this was the Son of God. And many women were there beholding afar off, which followed Jesus from Galilee, ministering unto him: Among which was Mary Magdalene, and Mary the mother of James and Joses, and the mother of Zebedee's children. When the even was come, there came a rich man of Arimathaea, named Joseph, who also himself was Jesus' disciple: He went to Pilate, and begged the body of Jesus. Then Pilate commanded the body to be delivered. And when Joseph had taken the body, he wrapped it in a clean linen cloth, And laid it in his own new tomb, which he had hewn out in the rock: and he rolled a great stone to the door of the sepulchre, and departed. And there was Mary Magdalene, and the other Mary, sitting over against the sepulchre. Now the next day, that followed the day of the preparation, the chief priests and Pharisees came together unto Pilate, Saying, Sir, we remember that that deceiver said, while he was yet alive, After three days I will rise again. Command therefore that the sepulchre be made sure until the third day, lest his disciples come by night, and steal him away, and say unto the people, He is risen from the dead: so the last error shall be worse than the first. Pilate said unto them, Ye have a watch: go your way, make it as sure as ye can. So they went, and made the sepulchre sure, sealing the stone, and setting a watch.

—Matthew 27:1–66

In the end of the sabbath, as it began to dawn toward the first day of the week, came Mary Magdalene and the other Mary to see the sepulchre. And, behold, there was a great earthquake: for the angel of the Lord descended from heaven, and came and rolled back the stone from the door, and sat upon it. His countenance was like lightning, and his raiment white as snow: And for fear of him the keepers did shake, and became as dead men. And the angel answered and said unto the women, Fear not ye: for I know that ye seek Jesus, which was crucified. He is not here: for he is risen, as he said. Come, see the place where the Lord lay. And go quickly, and tell his disciples that he is risen from the dead; and, behold, he goeth before you into Galilee; there shall ye see him: lo, I have told you. And they departed quickly from the sepulchre with fear and great joy; and did run to bring his disciples word. And as they went to tell his disciples, behold, Jesus met them, saying, All hail. And they came and held him by the feet, and worshipped him. Then said Jesus unto them, Be not afraid: go tell my brethren that they go into Galilee, and there shall they see me. Now when they were going, behold, some of the watch came into the city, and shewed unto the chief priests all the things that were done. And when they were assembled with the elders, and had taken counsel, they gave large money unto the soldiers, Saying, Say ye, His disciples

> came by night, and stole him away while we slept. And if this come to the governor's ears, we will persuade him, and secure you. So they took the money, and did as they were taught: and this saying is commonly reported among the Jews until this day. Then the eleven disciples went away into Galilee, into a mountain where Jesus had appointed them. And when they saw him, they worshipped him: but some doubted. And Jesus came and spake unto them, saying, All power is given unto me in heaven and in earth. Go ye therefore, and teach all nations, baptizing them in the name of the Father, and of the Son, and of the Holy Ghost: Teaching them to observe all things whatsoever I have commanded you: and, lo, I am with you always, even unto the end of the world. Amen.
>
> —Matthew 28:1–20

During Jesus' three-and-one-half years of ministry on Earth, He performed many miracles, but the Pharisees could not stand that He was that powerful. They felt threatened by Him. We read in Matthew 9:35, "And Jesus went all about the cities and villages, teaching in their synagogues, and preaching the gospel of the kingdom, and healing every sickness and every disease among the people." He raised the dead, healed the lame, drove out demons, opened blind eyes, sat the captives free, and most of all, He forgave their sins. He tells us in John 14:12, "Verily, verily, I say unto you, He that believeth on me, the works that I do shall he do also; and greater works than these shall he do; because I go to my Father." According to this Scripture we will perform mighty miracles. I prayed with the young girl at the crusade and for another child at church with pink eye, and both were healed. The lady I prayed for so that she could conceive gave birth nine months later to a baby girl and had numerous more children.

Here are a few examples of the miracles Jesus performed: Mary, the sister of Lazarus, came to tell Jesus that her brother had died since Jesus was a friend of the family. I visited Mary, Martha, and Lazarus's house on the 1985 trip I took to Israel and Egypt. I also saw the empty tomb were Lazarus once laid.

> Jesus said, Take ye away the stone. Martha, the sister of him that was dead, saith unto him, Lord, by this time he stinketh: for he hath been dead four days. Jesus saith unto her, Said I not unto thee, that, if thou wouldest believe, thou shouldest see the glory of God? Then they took away the stone from the place where the dead was laid. And Jesus lifted up his eyes, and said, Father, I thank thee that thou hast heard me. And I knew that thou hearest me always: but because of the people which stand by I said it, that they may believe that thou hast sent me. And when he thus had spoken, he cried with a loud voice, Lazarus, come forth. And he that was dead came forth, bound hand and foot with graveclothes: and his face was bound about with a napkin. Jesus saith unto them, Loose him, and let him go. Then many of the Jews which came to Mary, and had seen the things which Jesus did, believed on him.
>
> —John 11:39–45

> Now there is at Jerusalem by the sheep market a pool, which is called in the Hebrew tongue Bethesda, having five porches.... And a certain man was there, which had an infirmity thirty and eight years. When Jesus saw him lie, and knew that he had been now a long time in that case, he saith unto him, Wilt thou be made whole?... Jesus saith unto him, Rise, take up thy bed, and walk. And immediately the man was made whole, and took up his bed, and walked.
>
> —John 5:2, 5–6, 8–9

> Therefore said they unto him, How were thine eyes opened? He answered and said, A man that is called Jesus made clay, and anointed mine eyes, and said unto me, Go to the pool of Siloam, and wash: and I went and washed, and I received sight.
>
> —JOHN 9:10–11

Through Jesus' shed blood on the cross, we have forgiveness of our sins. That is why we can sing: "What can wash away my sin? Nothing but the blood of Jesus." He became our:

- Sin offering—Jesus Christ was offered for our sin.
- Firstfruit offering—Jesus died and arose to become the firstfruit of resurrection.
- Blood offering—Jesus shed His blood for the remission of our sins.
- Peace offering—Jesus made peace with God for us by way of His cross.
- Burnt offering—Jesus suffered so that we might escape the judgment of hell.
- Sacrificial offering—Jesus was sacrificed for us.
- Tithe offering—Our Lord of glory became poor so that we might inherit the riches of heaven.

He tells us that He went to hell and took the keys away from the devil in Revelation 1:18: "I am he that liveth, and was dead; and, behold, I am alive for evermore, Amen; and have the keys of hell and of death." But before He ascended to heaven to sit at the right hand of the Father, making intersession for us, He allowed Himself to be seen on numerous occasions.

And the angel answered and said unto the women, Fear not ye: for I know that ye seek Jesus, which was crucified. He is not here: for he is risen, as he said. Come, see the place where the Lord lay. And go quickly, and tell his disciples that he is risen from the dead; and, behold, he goeth before you into Galilee; there shall ye see him: lo, I have told you. And they departed quickly from the sepulchre with fear and great joy; and did run to bring his disciples word. And as they went to tell his disciples, behold, Jesus met them, saying, All hail. And they came and held him by the feet, and worshipped him. Then said Jesus unto them, Be not afraid: go tell my brethren that they go into Galilee, and there shall they see me.

—Matthew 28:5–10

Now when Jesus was risen early the first day of the week, he appeared first to Mary Magdalene, out of whom he had cast seven devils. And she went and told them that had been with him, as they mourned and wept. And they, when they had heard that he was alive, and had been seen of her, believed not. After that he appeared in another form unto two of them, as they walked, and went into the country. And they went and told it unto the residue: neither believed they them. Afterward he appeared unto the eleven as they sat at meat, and upbraided them with their unbelief and hardness of heart, because they believed not them which had seen him after he was risen.

—Mark 16:9–14

But ye shall receive power, after that the Holy Ghost is come upon you: and ye shall be witnesses unto me both in Jerusalem, and in all Judaea, and in Samaria, and unto the uttermost part of the earth. And when he had spoken these things, while they beheld, he was taken up; and a cloud received him out

> of their sight....Then returned they unto Jerusalem from the mount called Olivet, which is from Jerusalem a sabbath day's journey. And when they were come in, they went up into an upper room, where abode both Peter, and James, and John, and Andrew, Philip, and Thomas, Bartholomew, and Matthew, James the son of Alphaeus, and Simon Zelotes, and Judas the brother of James....And in those days Peter stood up in the midst of the disciples, and said, (the number of names together were about an hundred and twenty).
>
> —ACTS 1:8–9, 12–13, 15

Peter said in Acts 5:30–32, "The God of our fathers raised up Jesus, whom ye slew and hanged on a tree. Him hath God exalted with his right hand to be a Prince and a Saviour, for to give repentance to Israel, and forgiveness of sins. And we are his witnesses of these things; and so is also the Holy Ghost, whom God hath given to them that obey him."

Lent

At the time of Jesus Christ and the apostles, no one had ever kept Lent, the forty days of abstinence preceding Easter. It was not ordained by Christ, and it has pagan origin. It was borrowed from the worshipers of the Babylonian goddess and has absolutely no Christian roots. Catholics teach that Lent is closely associated with the transition from winter to spring. The word *Lent*, for example, comes from the Anglo–Saxon word for "springtime," *lencten*. It describes the gradually lengthening of daylight after the winter solstice. Lent therefore, has no spiritual meaning itself.

Easter Sunrise Services

In order to understand why Christians observe an Easter sunrise service, we need to know where it came from. A Catholic encyclopedia explains, "The English term 'Easter' relates to Estre, a Teutonic goddess of the rising light of day and spring."[10] The Babylonian name for this goddess was *Ishtar*. The Phoenician name was *Astarte*. She was said to be the wife of the sun god, Baal, the worship of whom is continually denounced in the Bible as the most abominable of all pagan idolatry.

> For he served Baal, and worshipped him, and provoked to anger the Lord God of Israel, according to all that his father had done.
>
> —1 Kings 22:53

> And they built the high places of Baal, which are in the valley of the son of Hinnom, to cause their sons and their daughters to pass through the fire unto Molech; which I commanded them not, neither came it into my mind, that they should do this abomination, to cause Judah to sin.
>
> —Jeremiah 32:35

Semiramis was the mother and later the wife of Nimrod, the mighty warrior. Nimrod emerged after Noah's flood and built the tower of Babel to serve as an astrological observatory. However, God confused the people's language, which halted construction on the tower and scattered the people to the ends of the earth. He rebelled against God, and we read in Genesis 10:8–9: "And Cush begot Nimrod: he began to be a mighty one in the earth. He was a mighty hunter before the Lord: wherefore it is said, Even as Nimrod the mighty hunter before the Lord." They were the founders and inspiration behind the pagan religion of ancient Babylon. Since she claimed to be the wife of the sun god Baal (after Nimrod's death), Satan's fiercest demon and the second in command, Semiramis became widely known as the queen of heaven.[11]

This brings us to the first scripture relating to Easter observance, Jeremiah 7:17–19: "Seest thou not what they do in the cities of Judah and in the streets of Jerusalem? The children gather wood, and the fathers kindle the fire, and the women knead their dough, to make cakes to the queen of heaven, and to pour out drink offerings unto other gods, that they may provoke me to anger. Do they provoke me to anger? saith the LORD: do they not provoke themselves to the confusion of their own faces?" Easter was originally about worshiping the self-proclaimed queen of heaven! Another relevant scripture is found in Ezekiel 8:16–17: "And he brought me into the inner court of the LORD's house, and, behold, at the door of the temple of the LORD, between the porch and the altar, were about five and twenty men, with their backs toward the temple of the LORD, and their faces toward the east; and they worshipped the sun toward the east. Then he said unto me, Hast thou seen this, O son of man? Is it a light thing to the house of Judah that they commit the abominations which they commit here? for they have filled the land with violence, and have returned to provoke me to anger: and, lo, they put the branch to their nose." Though this Scripture refers to a time centuries before Christ, a little research shows that this is the identical thing that millions of Christians do every Easter Sunday today. As Ezekiel writes, the observance of this service provokes God to anger! It has nothing to do with Christ; rather, it is about worshiping the gods of Babylon.

> Muslims [pray] to the idol Cybele or Allah.... The name of the moon goddess in Arabia was Allah. Satan put his third in command in charge of moon worship. All of Satan's demons are male but the moon god masqueraded as a female divinity or moon goddess. In Egypt her name was Isis. In Pheonicia her name was Asteroth and in Rome her name was Venus. [The] Ziggurat of Nanna the Moon goddess at Ur of the Chaldees was a thing of the past.[12]

Once God led Abraham to the land of Canaan, where He promised Abraham that he would be the father of many nations.

> As for me, behold, my covenant is with thee, and thou shalt be a father of many nations.... And I will establish my covenant between me and thee and thy seed after thee in their generations for an everlasting covenant, to be a God unto thee, and to thy seed after thee. And I will give unto thee, and to thy seed after thee, the land wherein thou art a stranger, all the land of Canaan, for an everlasting possession; and I will be their God. And God said unto Abraham, Thou shalt keep my covenant therefore, thou, and thy seed after thee in their generations.
>
> —Genesis 17:4, 7–9

> The crescent moon also represents Diana of the Ephesians. It represents the filthy fertility cult of the mother goddess who is called Allah, Circe, Venus, Artemis, Aphrodite, Medusa, etc. The pagan trinity consisted of the worship of the sun, moon and stars.[13]

How, then, did Easter become part of traditional Christianity? I hope that many recognize the error we have been taught by observing all these manmade pagan rituals, and return to the roots of true Christianity by observing Resurrection Day for what it stands for, when our Lord Jesus Christ arose from the grave.

Halloween

How did Halloween originate? There are several legends; however, I came up with the following information in my extended study. I want to warn you that Halloween is a point of contact with evil of every sort. Halloween and Christianity are totally incompatible and not an acceptable holiday for Christians to celebrate. Its practices are prohibited by the Bible.

Halloween, the last day of October, is short for All Hallow's Eve. There is nothing holy or hallowed about the activities that happen on this day.

> It's on Halloween or "All Halloween eve," as it's called, that the witch covens have their great annual worship service and offer a blood sacrifice to Satan. All through the year the Satanists sacrifice cats, dogs, and other animals, but on the special day they offer a human being—one of their own children—which they select for this ghoulish murder![14]

Does this shock you? Halloween originally had no religious connections, but after the people of Great Britain converted to Christianity, the celebration became associated with All Holy Day and All Saint's Day—a day to honor all departed martyrs and saints of the church.

Halloween traditionally was designed to conjure up dark, evil, and devilish spirits. The world today still carries on this tradition, as well as the wearing of costumes. The American version of Halloween came from Ireland, where Halloween is still a national holiday.

> Ralph Linton wrote: "The American celebration (of Halloween) rests upon Scottish and Irish folk customs which can be traced in a direct line from pre-Christian times. The earliest celebrations were held by the Druids in honor of Shamhain, Lord of Death, whose festival fell on November 1st."[15]

As Christianity spread through Europe the Roman church designated November 1 as All Hallows Day to eulogize departed saints.

> The Celts called winter the "season of death" and believed it was ruled by Samhain (the devil), the Lord of the Dead and Prince of Darkness, who called together all the dead, wicked souls who had died in the last year and, to pay for their sins, had been condemned to inhabit the bodies of animals. The greater the person's sins, the lower the animal into which his or her soul had been placed. The Festival of Samhain, held on October 31st (the day before winter began), was for the Celts, a "celebration" of death, to honor and "worship" their sun god, the spirits and Samhain. Druids, men who were the Celts' priests and teachers, would lead the fanatical night ceremonies. The Druids, who practiced witchcraft and fortune telling, believed that on Halloween, the ghosts, spirits, fairies, witches, and elves of the dead returned to their former homes and came out to harm crops and trouble the Celtic people.[16]
>
> Pagans believed that on one night of the year the souls of the dead returned to their original homes. These wandering spirits were the habit of haunting the living, but there was a way in which these ghosts might be exorcised. To exorcise

> these ghosts, that is to free yourself from an evil spirit, you would have to set out food (give the demons a treat) and provide shelter for them for the night. If you didn't they would "trick" you by casting a spell on you or hurting you. It was the Celts who chose the date of October 31st as their New Year's Eve and who originally intended it as a celebration of everything wicked, evil and dead. Also during their celebration they would gather around the campfire and offer their animals, their crops and sometimes themselves as a sacrifice. The celebration remained much the same after the Romans conquered the Celts around 43 A.D. The Romans however added a ceremony honoring their goddess of fruit and trees, thus the association with apples. The apparently harmless lid pumpkin face or "Jack-O-Lantern" is an ancient symbol of a damned soul. They were named for a man named Jack, who could not enter Heaven or Hell. As a result he was doomed to wander in darkness with his lantern until Judgment Day. Fearful of spooks, folks began to hollow out turnips and pumpkins and placing lighted candles inside to scare away evil spirits from the house.[17]

After more research, I found that Satanists still celebrate Halloween today. One high priest of the church of Satan commented, "We enjoy the commercial exploitation of the public at Halloween…it's free publicity."[18] Yet, unsuspecting mothers—Christian and otherwise—pour millions of dollars annually into the purchase of Halloween costumes. Many businesses allow their employees to dress in costumes of their imagination. So when you dress your child as a ghost, goblin, imp, or some grotesque, horrible, deformed creature and send your child out into the streets to trick or treat for a little piece of candy, you'll be recreating the ideals of eerie, demonic, destructive spirits that were thought to inhabit the countryside and streets of old. Halloween night is party time for Satanic cults and the celebration of the "witch's new year." Do you really want your children out asking for candy?

We, as Christians, in our ignorance about the real meaning of Halloween, have joined forces with the world in setting aside this night to honor Satan and his party. I have noticed that parents often promote Halloween more than children do; they almost insist that their child has a costume. Some parents even dress up in costumes themselves. Now, since we have come into the light, let us not dress our children up in hideous and grotesque costumes, inviting destruction by allowing them to practice those ideals. If you are practicing Christians, can't you explain to your children that you don't believe in such activity? Parents, you may say that there is no harm in children dressing up in costumes and receiving a little candy. Do you realize what you exposing them to these days—that people are now poisoning candy, putting needles and razor blades into the foods that are passed out to your children? You say that you only take them to the houses where you know the residents. But you are still promoting Halloween. Are we not what we practice? Take a minute and look beyond the costumes and candy, and look at the real meaning and destructive actions that take place on Halloween.

In the Old Testament, the penalty for being a witch was death, as described in Exodus 22:18: "Thou shalt not suffer a witch to live." We are also warned in 1 Peter 5:8, "Be sober, be vigilant; because your adversary the devil, as a roaring lion, walketh about, seeking whom he may devour." We are taught in Philippians 5:8,

"Finally, brethren, whatsoever things are true, whatsoever things are honest, whatsoever things are just, whatsoever things are pure, whatsoever things are lovely, whatsoever things are of good report; if there be any virtue, and if there be any praise, think on these things." We are told in Ephesians 5:11, "And have no fellowship with the unfruitful works of darkness, but rather reprove them."

You say that the kids look so cute in their costumes, although they dress up like the enemy of the souls of mankind. You say on Halloween it is all right to join the fun, even though it means partaking in the celebration of the witch's new year; after all, it's only one night. After reading these verses from the Bible that speak out against this type of holiday celebration, do you really believe that God accepts it as fun? Educate your children. Explain to them the history of Halloween when they are old enough.

As I grew up in Germany, we did not dress up in costumes. Instead of Halloween, we celebrated two church holidays—All Holy Day and All Souls Day. We went to the cemetery and offered up prayers for our departed loved ones at the decorated graves with greenery and a lit candle, followed by several church services.

Occult means "hidden, secret, mysterious, of mystic arts, such as magic, astrology, etc." Included in occult practices are the following: divination, astrology, spiritualism, numerology, yoga, demonology, divining with a rod or pendulum, and numerous other related practices. They are occult because they are hidden, and they are hidden because they thrive on their mysterious nature. In addition, Scripture forbids them, and for centuries the church has limited them to covert practices.

Each October 31 we dabble with the occult and satanic. Witch-hunts continued through 1750 A.D. Hundreds of people were tortured, executed, and their bodies burned and desecrated. But witchcraft continues and grows to this day. In the United States, an organization called Wicca, which means "wise woman," boasts a membership of around 130,000 individuals. (Other pagan religious groups consist of approximately 150,000 individuals.)[19] Halloween, or Samhain, is one of the eight major festivals celebrated annually by wiccans, or witches.

The following Scriptures are directly taken from the Bible to emphasize their connections to Halloween:

> *Enchantment*—the act of influencing by charms and incantations the practice of magical arts
>
> > There shall not be found among you any one that maketh his son or his daughter to pass through the fire, or that useth divination, or an observer of times, or an enchanter, or a witch. Or a charmer, or a consulter with familiar spirits, or a wizard, or a necromancer. For all that do these things are an abomination unto the Lord: and because of these abominations the Lord thy God doth drive them out from before thee.
> >
> > —Deuteronomy 18:10–12
>
> *Witchcraft*—the practice of dealing with evil spirits, the use of sorcery or magic
>
> > Now the works of the flesh are manifest, which are these; Adultery, fornication, uncleanness, lasciviousness, Idolatry, witchcraft, hatred, variance, emulations, wrath, strife, seditions, heresies, Envyings, murders, drunkenness, revellings,

> and such like: of the which I tell you before, as I have also told you in time past, that they which do such things shall not inherit the kingdom of God.
>
> —GALATIANS 5:19–21

Sorcery—the use of power gained from the assistance or control of evil spirits, especially for divining

> But the fearful, and unbelieving, and the abominable, and murderers, and whoremongers, and sorcerers, and idolaters, and all liars, shall have their part in the lake which burneth with fire and brimstone: which is the second death.
>
> —REVELATION 21:8

Divination/fortune-telling

> For thus saith the LORD of hosts, the God of Israel; Let not your prophets and your diviners, that be in the midst of you, deceive you, neither hearken to your dreams which ye cause to be dreamed. For they prophesy falsely unto you in my name: I have not sent them, saith the LORD.
>
> —JEREMIAH 29:8–9

Wizardry—the art of practices of a wizard; sorcery.

Wizard—one skilled in magic; male witch; sorcerer.

> Regard not them that have familiar spirits, neither seek after wizards, to be defiled by them: I am the LORD your God.
>
> —LEVITICUS 19:31

Necromancy—communication with the dead, conjuring up of the spirits of the dead for purposes of magically revealing the future or influencing the course of events.

> And when they shall say unto you, Seek unto them that have familiar spirits, and unto wizards that peep, and that mutter: should not a people seek unto their God? for the living to the dead?
>
> —Isaiah 8:19

Charm—put a spell upon someone; to effect by magic.

> And the spirit of Egypt shall fail in the midst thereof; and I will destroy the counsel thereof: and they shall seek to the idols, and to the charmers, and to them that have familiar spirits, and to the wizards.
>
> —Isaiah 19:3

Stargazing/astrology—the divination of the supposed influence of the stars upon human affairs and terrestrial events by their positions and aspects

> Thus saith the Lord, Learn not the way of the heathen, and be not dismayed at the signs of heaven; for the heathen are dismayed at them.
>
> —Jeremiah 10:2

Soothsaying—the act of foretelling events; prophesying by a spirit other than the Holy Spirit.

> And I will cut off witchcrafts out of thine hand; and thou shalt have no more soothsayers.
>
> —Micah 5:12

Prognostication—to foretell from signs or symptoms; prophesying without the Holy Spirit; soothsaying

> Stand now with thine enchantments, and with the multitude of thy sorceries, wherein thou hast laboured from thy youth; if so be thou shalt be able to profit, if so be thou mayest prevail. Thou art wearied in the multitude of thy counsels. Let now the astrologers, the stargazers, the monthly prognosticators, stand up, and save thee from these things that shall come upon thee. Behold, they shall be as stubble; the fire shall burn them; they shall not deliver themselves from the power of the flame: there shall not be a coal to warm at, nor fire to sit before it. Thus shall they be unto thee with whom thou hast laboured, even thy merchants, from thy youth: they shall wander every one to his quarter; none shall save thee.
>
> —ISAIAH 47:12–15

Observing times/astrology

> And he made his son pass through the fire, and observed times, and used enchantments, and dealt with familiar spirits and wizards: he wrought much wickedness in the sight of the LORD, to provoke him to anger.
>
> —2 KINGS 21:6

Magic/witchcraft

> There shall not be found among you any one that maketh his son or his daughter to pass through the fire, or that useth divination, or an observer of times, or an enchanter, or a witch.
>
> —DEUTERONOMY 18:10

If you're oppressed or possessed with unclean spirits as a result of participating in any of the aforementioned demonic activities, you can be freed from them. Remember, Jesus died for your sins on the cross about two thousand years ago. If you repent of your sins and forsake them, making Jesus Christ your Savior and Lord, you, too, can claim the following Scripture:

> But as many as received him, to them gave he power to become the sons of God, even to them that believe on his name.
>
> —JOHN 1:12

Chapter 8

Religious Versions—What Is the Truth?

You might ask, If there is only one God, why are there then so many different religions? For many people, it is too simple to believe that God sent us His Son, Jesus Christ, who died on the cross for all of our sins. Only by accepting Him as Savior can we enter heaven when we die, yet certain people, influenced by Satan, have interpreted the gospel truth to their own liking and made up their own belief. By denying Jesus, God cannot protect them; therefore they open themselves up to demonic influence.

As you examine the other beliefs I have written about, it is obvious that they have made up their own far-fetched stories. I will expose certain ones by explaining their different origins. But first, What does the Word of God say?

Sin

As it is written, There is none righteous, no, not one.... For all have sinned, and come short of the glory of God.

—Romans 3:10, 23

If we say that we have not sinned, we make him a liar, and his word is not in us.

—1 John 1:10

If we say that we have no sin, we deceive ourselves, and the truth is not in us.

—1 John 1:8

Whosoever committeth sin transgresseth also the law: for sin is the transgression of the law.

—1 John 3:4

All unrighteousness is sin: and there is a sin not unto death.

—1 John 5:17

Whatsoever is not of faith is sin.

—Romans 14:23

Therefore to him that knoweth to do good, and doeth it not, to him it is sin.

—James 4:17

Redemption

We have redemption through his blood, the forgiveness of sins, according to the riches of his grace.

—Ephesians 1:7

You were not redeemed with corruptible things...But with the precious blood of Christ.

—1 Peter 1:18–19

Unto him that loved us, and washed us from our sins in his own blood, And hath made us kings and priests unto God and his Father.

—Revelation 1:5–6

Without shedding of blood [there] is no remission.

—Hebrews 9:22

Made peace through the blood of His cross.

—Colossians 1:20

This man, after he had offered one sacrifice for sins for ever, sat down on the right hand of God....For by one offering he hath perfected for ever them that are sanctified.

—Hebrews 10:12, 14

Salvation

Believe on the Lord Jesus Christ, and thou shalt be saved, and thy house.

—Acts 16:31

But as many as received him, to them gave he power to become the sons of God, even to them that believe on his name.

—John 1:12

He that believeth on him is not condemned: but he that believeth not is condemned already, because he hath not believed in the... only begotten Son of God.

—John 3:18

He that believeth on the Son hath everlasting life: and he that believeth not the Son shall not see life.

—John 3:36

Not by works of righteousness which we have done, but according to his mercy he saved us, by the washing of regeneration, and renewing of the Holy Ghost.

—Titus 3:5

For by grace are ye saved through faith; and that not of yourselves: it is the gift of God: Not of works, lest any man should boast.

—Ephesians 2:8–9

Justified freely by his grace through the redemption that is in Christ Jesus

—Romans 3:24

For Christ is the end of the law for righteousness to every one that believeth.

—Romans 10:4

Retribution

The wages of sin is death.

—Romans 6:23

> And many of them that sleep in the dust of the earth shall awake, some to everlasting life, and some to shame and everlasting contempt.
>
> —Daniel 12:2

> And as it is appointed unto men once to die, but after this the judgment
>
> —Hebrews 9:27

> And I saw the dead, small and great, stand before God... and the dead were judged out of those things which were written in the books, according to their works.
>
> —Revelation 20:12

> The Lord Jesus shall be revealed from heaven... In flaming fire taking vengeance on them that know not God, and that obey not the gospel of our Lord Jesus Christ: Who shall be punished with everlasting destruction.
>
> —2 Thessalonians 1:7–9

> And if thy foot offend thee, cut it off: it is better for thee to enter halt into life, than having two feet to be cast into hell, into the fire that never shall be quenched.
>
> —Mark 9:45

New Age

In the immediate beginnings of the New Age movement in the 1960s we encountered the hippie culture, interest in drugs and mysticism, the destruction of traditional morality, humanistic psychology, Wicca, and secular humanism. In the 1980s, the New Age movement became entwined in every area of society:

Public education became heavily influenced and is getting worse. Executive trainers use its influence. Political and military leaders push it. The United Nations promotes it, and many churches, it is sad to say, teach New Age concepts.

Catholicism

Catholic means "universal church," but the Catholic Church is not the only true one.

> Pope Benedict XVI reasserted the primacy of the Roman Catholic Church, approving a document released [on July 10 2007] that says other Christian communities are either defective or not true churches and Catholicism provides the only true path to salvation.[1]

The commentary repeated church teaching that says the Catholic Church "has the fullness of the means of salvation" and that Christ "established here on earth" only one church. Your eyes will open to the truth as you continue to read.

Being raised in Germany as a Catholic, I would never have believed that there was such a difference from the way we were taught and what I later learned is written in the Bible. We prayed, for instance, "Holy mother of God, plead for us sinners now and in the hour of our death." In German it is translated, "*Heilige Mutter Gottes, bitte fuer uns suender, jetzt und in der stunde unseres todes*." We had no Bible to read in our home, and most likely, there wasn't one in any of the other Catholic homes. In the earlier years of the church, people were told they couldn't understand the Bible, so they didn't need to have one. Since the truth was kept from the people, the church leaders could teach their own religious doctrine; and no one would know the difference, if it was true or false.

On my visit to Germany in 1990 when we buried my father, I visited with an older lady whose daughter and I attended school together. I mentioned my relationship with Jesus to her. Since I had a German Bible with me, she asked me where she could get one. She never had a Bible, although she was past seventy then. Can you imagine? I told her that they sell them in the bookstore in the city three miles away, which was where I had bought mine several years ago. I acquired it in order to minister to the local people whenever I was home.

The writers of the Bible were inspired and anointed by the Holy Spirit to write such an awesome book, but it will remain and read as "just a book" to an unbeliever or a religious person until they have had a touch from the Holy Spirit themselves. It can not happen until they are born-again or "saved," as we also call it, accepting Jesus into their heart instead of having only head knowledge of Him. It means accepting Jesus as Savior and making Him Lord—meaning He is Master over our lives. It means following Him alone, denouncing prayer to Mary and the saints, which can't help you anyway. If you want to buy a loaf of bread, for instance, you don't go to the butcher and expect to receive it. If you do, it is a counterfeit. Likewise, so many Catholics have been deceived by the devil, as they believe that their doctrine it is the real thing.

Yes, Satan has power too, but his is demonic, which leads to destruction and, in the end, to death. But to each born-again Christian individual the Holy Spirit Himself will interpret the

Scriptures. That is why we get a deeper understanding of the Bible as we grow more and more in the Lord. I have read certain Scriptures for years, and all at once when I read them again, it is as if a lightbulb turns on inside of me. At that time the Holy Spirit gives me a revelation and spiritual understanding of the meaning of the passage I'm reading, which is different from head knowledge that I had before. The Scriptures tell us that "rivers of living water will flow out of us" (John 7:38). Yes, once we are filled with the Spirit—which is another separate experience after salvation—we bubble over with the presence of the Holy Spirit.

For some of you this may sound foreign, because it does not happen to a religious person. Can you see how much truth of the Word of God you are missing? Instead of teaching the Bible, some religious leaders keep their congregations in the dark, spiritually speaking. Throughout this chapter I will include verses from the Bible to show you what you may have been missing. We read in 1 Timothy 4:1, "In the latter times some shall depart from the faith, giving heed to seducing spirits, and doctrines of devils." *Latter times* means the period of time between the first and second coming of Jesus Christ—the time we presently live in. You see, it was already foretold when the Bible was written so many years ago. Notice the phrase "seducing spirits" in that verse. They are false teachers influencing the innocent with their own demonic doctrine inspired by Satan. If someone questioned it in earlier years, they were considered a witch and burned at the stake.

I still remember when I heard my priest read the mass in Latin over fifty years ago. On one of my father's visits here to the US, I asked him about Martin Luther. He put his hands on his hips and in a disgusted tone he let me know that he was the greatest enemy of the Catholic Church. Is this the reason that I am compelled by the Holy Spirit to expose this religious system for what it really is? In the following pages I will attempt to show you the difference in Protestant doctrine and that of the Catholic Church, which is in complete defiance of the Scriptures in the Bible, the true Word of God.

Some Catholics in this country say that they are Spirit filled and speak in other tongues; but if they can't break away from their indoctrination of Mary and still pray to her, they are wrong and misled. I saw a reader board in front of a Catholic school that reads "Mary, Queen of peace, pray for us." This contradicts what Jesus told us in John 14:27: "Peace I leave with you, my peace I give unto you: not as the world giveth, give I unto you. Let not your heart be troubled, neither let it be afraid." The Scriptures tell us that we should have no idols nor other gods before Him. These are the first and second commandments, as written in Exodus 20:3–4: "Thou shalt have no other gods before me. Thou shalt not make unto thee any graven image, or any likeness of any thing that is in heaven above, or that is in the earth beneath, or that is in the water under the earth." We also read in the Bible that He is a jealous God.

Let us start exposing this issue from the top. People, I can't be gentle about this topic. If you want to spend eternity in heaven, you need to know the truth. Many of you will be heartbroken—I was, too—when you find out that for generations your family has been led astray while you were dedicated and devoted to the teachings of the Catholic Church, not knowing that you were deceived. That is why you need to know the Scriptures for yourself—in order to discern the truth. But who would ever doubt and question that it is only a religious system instead of true Christianity?

The Catholic Church teaches that the pope is infallible, but is he? He is called "God's representative on Earth," and therefore he is supposedly not accountable to any earthly authority. The Catholic Church says that what he says is final, even if it is contrary to the Bible—which is the Word of God. It seems by doing so, he elevates himself to be equal with God or even above. But the Bible says that God is the ruler of heaven and Earth. Here are the words of Jesus to substantiate the fact:

> But be not ye called Rabbi: for one is your Master, even Christ; and all ye are brethren. And call no man your father upon the earth: for one is your Father, which is in heaven. Neither be ye called masters: for one is your Master, even Christ. But he that is greatest among you shall be your servant. And whosoever shall exalt himself shall be abased; and he that shall humble himself shall be exalted.
>
> —MATTHEW 23:8–12

His title, "Pontiff," stems from ancient Rome.

John Paul II was born Karol Wojtyla in Krakow, Poland. He assumed the papacy in 1978. In the middle of August 2002, the eighty-two year old pope visited his homeland for four days. I read in our local newspaper that he warned Poles of dangers posed when man "puts himself in God's place"—referring to genetic engineering and euthanasia—and by encroachments on traditional church teaching. He said, "When the noisy propaganda of liberalism, of freedom without truth or responsibility, grows stronger in our country, too, the shepherds of the church cannot fail to proclaim the one fail-proof philosophy of freedom, which is the truth of the cross of Christ."[2]

Why is there, then, such an obvious difference? I will point a few of the drastic differences out to you, those which are not acceptable to Christianity. Some of them have the truth removed so far that they deny God's Word completely. They are an abomination to our Lord. Because many Catholics were never taught about the Holy Spirit, the gifts listed in 1 Corinthians 12—wisdom, tongues, interpretation, healing, and discernment—are unfamiliar to them, and the pope remains the unquestionable authority. Judge for yourself!

The differences between Catholicism and what the Bible teaches begins in Jerusalem with the location of the tomb that Jesus was buried in.

The Ten Commandments have been tampered with, as I will prove to you.

Infant baptism, which is practiced by the Catholic Church, is incorrect, as you already read in an earlier chapter.

Confession of your sins to the priest is totally wrong. Only God can forgive us if we ask Him and repent of our sin.

A dead and powerless Jesus still hangs on the cross, instead of the Christ who was buried and resurrected two thousand years ago, as the Bible teaches. Yes, He arose and is alive.

This is not Christian teaching according to the Bible, and it is high time that this ungodly way is exposed. Catholics are entitled to the truth. When they make the sign of the cross before and after a prayer is recited, instead of saying, "In the name of the Father, the Son, and the Holy Spirit," should they not say, "In the name of the pope"? He seems to be in charge in many people's lives, instead of God.

Throughout the centuries, the pope has been the one to elevate a person to sainthood a certain number of years after his or her death. Yet, the Bible tells us differently. We who have accepted Jesus Christ as our Savior and made Him Lord are called saints while we are alive. Here are three Scripture references from the Old Testament as well as the New Testament that demonstrate this point:

> But to the saints that are in the earth, and to the excellent, in whom is all my delight.
>
> —Psalm 16:3

> And he that searcheth the hearts knoweth what is the mind of the Spirit, because he maketh intercession for the saints according to the will of God.
>
> —Romans 8:27

> For God is not the author of confusion, but of peace, as in all churches of the saints.
>
> —1 Corinthians 14:33

Is yours a church of saints? The saints are very much alive and live on the earth, as mentioned in the Scriptures. This proves the Catholic ritual of sainthood is man-made and false. A variety of saints and the Virgin Mary are the main "protectors" of the Catholics, since prayer is regularly offered up to them. If one looses something, he or she prays to St. Anthony to help him find it. When one travels, he prays to St. Paul for protection. There are many other examples, all of which distract us from the true source—Jesus Christ. I obtained two printed pages full of such names of patrons and protectors from a lady who makes and sells prayer bracelets. Many countries add their own traditions. In Mexico, they visit and worship the Virgin Mary at the shrine of Our Lady of Guadalupe. A young couple from Guam showed me the small statue of St. Joseph that they had pinned on the pillow of their baby for protection.

We are supposed to pray to the Father in the name of Jesus. Here are some examples from the Bible.

> And whatsoever ye shall ask in my name, that will I do, that the Father may be glorified in the Son. If ye shall ask any thing in my name, I will do it.
>
> —JOHN 14:13–14

> And all things, whatsoever ye shall ask in prayer, believing, ye shall receive.
>
> —MATTHEW 21:22

> These things have I written unto you that believe on the name of the Son of God; that ye may know that ye have eternal life, and that ye may believe on the name of the Son of God. And this is the confidence that we have in him, that, if we ask any thing according to his will, he heareth us: And if we know that he hear us, whatsoever we ask, we know that we have the petitions that we desired of him.
>
> —1 JOHN 5:13–15

We need to have confidence in Him alone and none other, as we read in Matthew 28:18. Was it not He that died on the cross for our sins, and not Mary? Why then do so many stray away from the truth? I believe that if people were asked, most of them would have to admit that they pray a lot more to Mary than to the Father in the name of Jesus. Satan deceives anyone that believes like that. Instead of praying to God the Father in the name of Jesus as the Scriptures tell us, they plead with Mary. It is Jesus who sits on the right hand of the Father making intercession for us, as described in Hebrews 7:25: "Wherefore he is able also to save them to the uttermost that come unto God by him, seeing he ever liveth to make intercession for them." Mary cannot save you, only Jesus Christ.

After I opened and read parts of the *Catechism of the Catholic Church,* a book that I bought several years ago, I could not believe what great deception it contained. I was so baffled by what I read that I studied it until three o'clock in the morning. It would be unbelievable to any Christian believer, because it displays evidence of the teachings of a cult! The next morning as I engaged in business with a Catholic friend, she asked me why my ankles were so swollen. I told her that I stayed up late studying for my book. She asked me what could be so interesting to miss sleep. I told her what I read and that the claims made were in conflict with the Scriptures. She promptly said, "Maybe the Bible is not correct, then." I did not have to say any more to her; it was obvious that she was in denial of the truth.

Lord, have mercy and open their spiritual eyes.

On Good Friday Catholics carry a cross through town, calling it "the veneration of the cross." Veneration means "to look upon with feelings of deep respect," but they have Jesus Christ still on the cross. He walked the Stations of the Cross two thousand years ago, and by Sunday His tomb was empty. He is risen and alive.

A few years later, a friend asked me to read a book that someone gave her to pass on to her granddaughter. It was the first of the Harry Potter series. I had not read any of these books, which have sold by the millions. She asked me to read it and tell her why her granddaughter shouldn't read it, since I told her earlier that Christians call them demonic. I had only read the first chapter when she borrowed the first two Harry Potter movies from a neighbor. We watched the first one, which was over two hours long. Harry and his classmates rode through the air on brooms, plus a lot more. My friend didn't see anything wrong with it.

My dictionary describes *magic* as "having seemingly supernatural qualities or powers." *Sorcery* means "the use of power gained from the assistance or control of evil spirits."[3] You see, after a while, many people still call themselves Christians, although they believe what the secular world teaches. As time goes by they override God's Word, which gets watered down more and more. I told my friend that I would look up some Scriptures when I got home that related to magic and sorcery, and I gave her several of them over the phone. She told me that she was taking the Scriptures I gave her to her Bible study to present them to the group.

> But there was a certain man, called Simon, which beforetime in the same city used sorcery, and bewitched the people of Samaria, giving out that himself was some great one: To whom they all gave heed, from the least to the greatest, saying, This man is the great power of God. And to him they had regard, because that of long time he had bewitched them with sorceries.
>
> —ACTS 8:9–11

And when they had gone through the isle unto Paphos, they found a certain sorcerer, a false prophet, a Jew, whose name was Barjesus: Which was with the deputy of the country, Sergius Paulus, a prudent man; who called for Barnabas and Saul, and desired to hear the word of God. But Elymas the sorcerer (for so is his name by interpretation) withstood them, seeking to turn away the deputy from the faith. Then Saul, (who also is called Paul,) filled with the Holy Ghost, set his eyes on him. And said, O full of all subtilty and all mischief, thou child of the devil, thou enemy of all righteousness, wilt thou not cease to pervert the right ways of the Lord? And now, behold, the hand of the Lord is upon thee, and thou shalt be blind, not seeing the sun for a season. And immediately there fell on him a mist and a darkness; and he went about seeking some to lead him by the hand. Then the deputy, when he saw what was done, believed, being astonished at the doctrine of the Lord.

—Acts 13:6–12

But the fearful, and unbelieving, and the abominable, and murderers, and whoremongers, and sorcerers, and idolaters, and all liars, shall have their part in the lake which burneth with fire and brimstone: which is the second death.

—Revelation 21:8

And the light of a candle shall shine no more at all in thee; and the voice of the bridegroom and of the bride shall be heard no more at all in thee: for thy merchants were the great men of the earth; for by thy sorceries were all nations deceived.

—Revelation 18:23

Woe to the bloody city! it is all full of lies and robbery.... there is a multitude of slain, and a great number of carcases; and

> there is none end of their corpses; they stumble upon their corpses. Because of the multitude of the whoredoms of the wellfavoured harlot, the mistress of witchcrafts, that selleth nations through her whoredoms, and families through her witchcrafts.
>
> —NAHUM 3:1, 3–4

> Now the works of the flesh are manifest, which are these; Adultery, fornication, uncleanness, lasciviousness, Idolatry, witchcraft, hatred, variance, emulations, wrath, strife, seditions, heresies, Envyings, murders, drunkenness, revellings, and such like: of the which I tell you before, as I have also told you in time past, that they which do such things shall not inherit the kingdom of God.
>
> —GALATIANS 5:19–21

Other scriptures about witchcraft are: Exodus 22:18, 1 Samuel 15:23, 2 Chronicles 33:6, 2 Kings 9:22, and Micah 5:12.

We can only walk in victory and live a holy life if we repent of such sins, because there is only one way of salvation—and that is Jesus Christ, and Him crucified.

Catholics also call Mary the mother of God, which is not true. The very first verse in the Bible substantiates it:

> In the beginning God created the heaven and the earth. And the earth was without form, and void; and darkness was upon the face of the deep. And the Spirit of God moved upon the face of the waters.... And God said, Let us make man in our image, after our likeness... So God created man in his own image, in the image of God created he him; male and *female* created he them.
>
> —GENESIS 1:1–2, 26–27, EMPHASIS ADDED

You can see that Mary was not part of the creation of the earth. How can she, then, be the mother of God when the earth was void? It is pure deception by the Catholic Church. Other denominations know that for a fact, but when you only hear Catholic doctrine and are not familiar with what the Bible says, you naturally receive this false teaching as truth. Mary was the mother only of the earthly Jesus, who is the Word which became flesh.

> In the beginning was the Word, and the Word was with God, and the Word was God.... And the Word was made flesh, and dwelt among us, (and we beheld his glory, the glory as of the only begotten of the Father,) full of grace and truth.
>
> —John 1:1, 14

It seems so clear that a little falsehood is added here and there to the Catholic doctrine. I suppose if you tell a lie long enough, after a while it is believed as truth. By placing so much emphasis on all their rituals, it completely deceives the innocent. We read in Ephesians 4:17–24:

> This I say therefore, and testify in the Lord, that ye henceforth walk not as other Gentiles walk, in the vanity of their mind, Having the understanding darkened, being alienated from the life of God through the ignorance that is in them, because of the blindness of their heart: Who being past feeling have given themselves over unto lasciviousness, to work all uncleanness with greediness. But ye have not so learned Christ; If so be that ye have heard him, and have been taught by him, as the truth is in Jesus: That ye put off concerning the former conversation the old man, which is corrupt according to the deceitful lusts; And be renewed in the spirit of your

> mind; And that ye put on the new man, which after God is created in righteousness and true holiness.

Jesus said in John 4:23–24:

> But the hour cometh, and now is, when the true worshippers shall worship the Father in spirit and in truth: for the Father seeketh such to worship him. God is a Spirit: and they that worship him must worship him in spirit and in truth.

He also declared, "I and My Father are one" (John 10:30). Matthew 17:5 tells of the Transfiguration, which took place while Peter was speaking to Jesus: We read, while Peter spoke to Jesus the transfiguration of Him took place in Matthew 17:5 "While he yet spake, behold, a bright cloud overshadowed them: and behold a voice out of the cloud, which said, This is my beloved Son, in whom I am well pleased; hear ye him."

God, in His mercy, is cleaning house now and offering you the truth of His Word. You have been deceived and misled long enough. We are told in 2 Peter 3:9, "The Lord is not slack concerning his promise, as some men count slackness; but is longsuffering to us-ward, not willing that any should perish, but that all should come to repentance." Devil, watch out! You're being found out. God's Holy Spirit will expose you. Your time is up. You deceived these people long enough.

Let's read Hebrews 4:12:

> For the word of God is quick, and powerful, and sharper than any twoedged sword, piercing even to the dividing asunder of soul and spirit, and of the joints and marrow, and is a discerner of the thoughts and intents of the heart.

Get ready; I feel it so strong in my spirit that as you read this chapter your delivery is about to happen and there will be an upcoming exodus of Catholics into freedom, as the Holy Spirit will open your spiritual eyes to the truth.

Galatians 5:1 tells us, "And be not entangled again with the yoke of bondage." Just as God spoke through Isaiah to the Israelites in the Old Testament, so also is He speaking through me in our day to you. He said in Isaiah 10:27, "And it shall come to pass in that day, that his burden shall be taken away from off thy shoulder, and his yoke from off thy neck, and the yoke shall be destroyed because of the anointing." Yes, dear people, God's anointing is upon me to write this profound chapter to you, which will destroy the spiritual yoke of bondage from Satan with which you are burdened. I praise God for your victory, as described in Romans 8:37: "Nay, in all these things we are more than conquerors through him that loved us." Yes, dear people, Jesus loves you and wants you to be a part of the family of God, not missing the Marriage Supper of the Lamb at the Rapture when He appears in the clouds for us.

A Catholic lady originally from Guam told me that as soon as her divorce is final she'll receive an annulment of her marriage from the local priest. She told me that it will be totally wiped out, as if it never existed. The price tag was three hundred dollars. What a rip-off.

Communion is another sore subject. When I grew up in Germany, our priest took the wafer and drank the wine himself out of the silver chalice, but the rest of the congregation only got the wafer. As he gave the wafer to each person, he said, "The body of Christ." But that was only half of the Communion. By omitting the wine or grape juice, the "sacrament" as the Catholics call it, the ceremony is incomplete—or rather, deliberately perverted. We read in Leviticus 17:11, "For the life of the flesh is in the blood;" and in Hebrews 2:14–15, "Forasmuch then as the children are partakers of flesh and blood, he also himself likewise took part of the same; that through death he might destroy him that had the power of death, that is, the devil; And deliver them who through fear of death were all their lifetime subject to bondage." Let's read what Paul the Apostle wrote in his first epistle to the Corinthians, which includes Jesus' own words. He specifically said to take Communion in remembrance of Him.

> And when he had given thanks, he brake it, and said, Take, eat: this is my body, which is broken for you: this do in remembrance of me. After the same manner also he took the cup, when he had supped, saying, this cup is the new testament in my blood: this do ye, as oft as ye drink it, in remembrance of me. For as often as ye eat this bread, and drink this cup, ye do shew the Lord's death till he come. Wherefore whosoever shall eat this bread, and drink this cup of the Lord, unworthily, shall be guilty of the body and blood of the Lord. But let a man examine himself, and so let him eat of that bread, and drink of that cup. For he that eateth and drinketh unworthily, eateth and drinketh damnation to himself, not discerning the Lord's body. For this cause many are weak and sickly among you, and many sleep.
>
> —1 Corinthians 11:24–30

When the apostle wrote that "many sleep," he was referring to their premature death. Jesus never mentioned that the bread and wine changed into His actual body, which we were made to believe when I was growing up Catholic. They call this the doctrine of transubstantiation. They refer to it as "the sacrifice of the mass" when it is served, and it is one of the seven sacraments, or ways of receiving grace, by which they mistakenly believe to receive forgiveness of their sins and have eternal life. Now that I know better, I ask myself, Who is the magician that does the transforming? This belief is far fetched from the truth and will be totally rejected by Bible believers. Each time the mass is celebrated, on a daily basis, Communion is served in the Catholic Church and Jesus Christ is sacrificed over and over again. You see, your leaders are also deceived, because we read in the Bible in Hebrews 10:10, 12, 14–17:

> By the which will we are sanctified through the offering of the body of Jesus Christ once for all.... But this man, after he had offered one sacrifice for sins for ever, sat down on the right hand of God.... For by one offering he hath perfected for ever them that are sanctified. Whereof the Holy Ghost also is a witness to us: for after that he had said before, This is the covenant that I will make with them after those days, saith the Lord, I will put my laws into their hearts, and in their minds will I write them; And their sins and iniquities will I remember no more.

Are you sure that you are sanctified, or have you only had religious experiences? Being deceived once myself, just as many of you are now, I am able to back my argument up with the Scriptures. Praise God the Holy Spirit pointed me to the truth, but I first had to come to the U.S.A. in order to hear the true gospel. God anointed me to expose the false doctrine of different religions.

Before we partake of Communion, we examine ourselves. If we have sinned, we ask Jesus right then to forgive us for them. We do not have to see a priest and be dependent upon him, a mere man who can't forgive us anyway, as we read in 1 John 1:9: "If we confess our sins, he is faithful and just to forgive us our sins, and to cleanse us from all unrighteousness;" and Hebrews 10:26: "For if we sin wilfully after that we have received the knowledge of the truth, there remaineth no more sacrifice for sins."

Ever since I got born again over thirty years ago, it has bothered me a great deal to remember having to tell the priest my sins. As I studied the Bible for myself, I realized what false teaching I got growing up as a Catholic and that many of their traditions are man made. They hang their belief system on these false doctrines, which lead people into hell instead of heaven. What a deception. The people are defrauded. Why weren't we taught the truth? No wonder the Lord called me to open your eyes. I asked different people over the years, many of whom agreed that the Catholic Church is a cult. It might sound awful, but when the truth of the Bible is changed over and over again, even in serious matters like the Lord's Supper—of which Jesus Himself told us exactly how to partake—then you are being taught lies.

We go straight to Jesus, as it says in the Bible, to have our sins forgiven, not through the priest. Why are the people deprived of the wine? The life is in His blood. The Catholic Church's version of Jesus still has Him hanging on the cross. He is a dead and powerless Jesus, but in the Protestant Church, He died but was resurrected and is alive. He is off the cross, just like the Bible tells us. The doctrine of the Holy Spirit is also perverted. He is not taught because He would open the people's spiritual eyes to the truth, which Catholic leaders want to prevent. Jesus said:

> If ye love me, keep my commandments. And I will pray the Father, and he shall give you another Comforter, that he may abide with you for ever; Even the Spirit of truth; whom the world cannot receive, because it seeth him not, neither knoweth him: but ye know him; for he dwelleth with you, and shall be in you. I will not leave you comfortless: I will come to you. Yet a little while, and the world seeth me no more; but ye see me: because I live, ye shall live also. At that day ye shall know that I am in my Father, and ye in me, and I in you. He that hath my commandments, and keepeth them, he it is that loveth me: and he that loveth me shall be loved of my Father, and I will love him, and will manifest myself to him. Judas saith unto him, not Iscariot, Lord, how is it that thou wilt manifest thyself unto us, and not unto the world? Jesus answered and said unto him, If a man love me, he will keep my words: and my Father will love him, and we will come unto him, and make our abode with him. He that loveth me not keepeth not my sayings: and the word which ye hear is not mine, but the Father's which sent me. These things have I spoken unto you, being yet present with you. But the Comforter, which is the Holy Ghost, whom the Father will send in my name, he shall teach you all things, and bring all things to your remembrance, whatsoever I have said unto you.
>
> —John 14:15–26

> Howbeit when he, the Spirit of truth, is come, he will guide you into all truth: for he shall not speak of himself; but whatsoever he shall hear, that shall he speak: and he will shew you things to come. He shall glorify me: for he shall receive of mine, and shall shew it unto you. All things that the Father

> hath are mine: therefore said I, that he shall take of mine, and shall shew it unto you.
>
> —JOHN 16:13–15

If you are Catholic and love Jesus, turn from your deception and keep His commandments. Right now you're like a baby in the womb that can't help itself; it is trusting to find an exit out of the womb in nine months when it is fully grown. Like that baby, you are trusting in your spiritual leaders to bring you to maturity in our Lord Jesus Christ and someday exit to heaven in the Rapture. Why does the angel bind Satan for a thousand years? Because he deceived many who are like you, not ever finding out for themselves what the Word of God teaches. John, the beloved disciple of Jesus, recorded some of the visions given to him. He described in Revelation 20:1–3, "And I saw an angel come down from heaven, having the key of the bottomless pit and a great chain in his hand. And he laid hold on the dragon, that old serpent, which is the Devil, and Satan, and bound him a thousand years, And cast him into the bottomless pit, and shut him up, and set a seal upon him, that he should deceive the nations no more, till the thousand years should be fulfilled: and after that he must be loosed a little season."

There are a number of other denominations that also rule their congregations by their own man-made doctrines. Some are far off from what the Bible teaches. I'm called by the Lord to expose some of them. Examine the Scriptures to see how your belief lines up with it. If Pope Constantine didn't establish the Roman Catholic Church until A.D. 326, how can Peter have been the first pope, as Catholics say?

Catholicism is a religion all of its own, with eternal consequences described in Revelation 22:14–16, 18–19:

> Blessed are they that do his commandments, that they may have right to the tree of life, and may enter in through the gates into the city. For without are dogs, and sorcerers, and whoremongers, and murderers, and idolaters, and whosoever loveth and maketh a lie. I Jesus have sent mine angel to testify unto you these things in the churches. I am the root and the offspring of David, and the bright and morning star.... For I testify unto every man that heareth the words of the prophecy of this book, If any man shall add unto these things, God shall add unto him the plagues that are written in this book: And if any man shall take away from the words of the book of this prophecy, God shall take away his part out of the book of life, and out of the holy city, and from the things which are written in this book.

Get your Bible out and find out what is written in it. Study it until you understand its meaning. You are responsible on your own for entering heaven. Don't tell Jesus when you stand in front of Him someday that you were not taught properly. He will say, "Away, I never knew you!" There will be severe consequences. As I got more familiar with the Word of God, I could discern that Catholicism is a religious system, which I will expose as we go on. If you continue in this belief system that I have described so far, you will not take part in the Rapture of the church. If you do not start believing in the truth of the Bible, Jesus will not come to snatch you up. He only comes for those that are really looking for Him and believing in His truth.

For the Lord himself shall descend from heaven with a shout, with the voice of the archangel, and with the trump of God: and the dead in Christ shall rise first: Then we which are alive and remain shall be caught up together with them in the clouds, to meet the Lord in the air: and so shall we ever be with the Lord.

—1 Thessalonians 4:16–17

For God hath not appointed us to wrath, but to obtain salvation by our Lord Jesus Christ.

—1 Thessalonians 5:9

Let no man deceive you by any means: for that day shall not come, except there come a falling away first, and that man of sin be revealed, the son of perdition [the Antichrist]; Who opposeth and exalteth himself above all that is called God, or that is worshipped; so that he as God sitteth in the temple of God, shewing himself that he is God. Remember ye not, that, when I was yet with you, I told you these things? And now ye know what withholdeth that he might be revealed in his time. For the mystery of iniquity doth already work: only he who now letteth will let, until he be taken out of the way. And then shall that Wicked be revealed, whom the Lord shall consume with the spirit of his mouth, and shall destroy with the brightness of his coming: Even him, whose coming is after the working of Satan with all power and signs and lying wonders, And with all deceivableness of unrighteousness in them that perish; because they received not the love of the truth, that they might be saved. And for this cause God shall send them strong delusion, that they should believe a lie: That they all might be damned who believed not the truth, but had pleasure in unrighteousness.

—2 Thessalonians 2:2–12

> Wherefore, beloved, seeing that ye look for such things, be diligent that ye may be found of him in peace, without spot, and blameless. And account that the longsuffering of our Lord is salvation; even as our beloved brother Paul also according to the wisdom given unto him hath written unto you; As also in all his epistles, speaking in them of these things; in which are some things hard to be understood, which they that are unlearned and unstable wrest, as they do also the other scriptures, unto their own destruction. Ye therefore, beloved, seeing ye know these things before, beware lest ye also, being led away with the error of the wicked, fall from your own stedfastness.
>
> —2 PETER 3:14–17

Now, once you are told the truth through the Scriptures, you are responsible to get out from under this demonic bondage like I did. John 8:32 says, "And ye shall know the truth, and the truth shall make you free." Romans 1:18–19 tells us, "For the wrath of God is revealed from heaven against all ungodliness and unrighteousness of men, who hold the truth in unrighteousness; Because that which may be known of God is manifest in them; for God hath shewed it unto them." I will further prove to you in the following Scriptures that the priest has no power to forgive sins; therefore those sins remain. It is Jesus alone who can forgive our sins. He died for this reason.

> If we confess our sins, he is faithful and just to forgive us our sins, and to cleanse us from all unrighteousness.
>
> —1 JOHN 1:9

> In whom we have redemption through his blood, the forgiveness of sins, according to the riches of his grace.
>
> —EPHESIANS 1:7

The estimated number of Catholics is also exaggerated. If you're born into a Catholic family, you're automatically counted a member. I am an example. Since there is no way to withdraw your membership, I'm still counted as one to this day. This explains the great number of Catholics. Over the years, it became a rich organization. But many millions have been paid out to settle judgments from lawsuits that have been brought against some of their clergy in which innocent boys, often altar boys who befriended and trusted the priests, were molested by them, some for many years. Here are Jesus' own words in Luke 17:1–2: "Then said he unto the disciples, It is impossible but that offences will come: but woe unto him, through whom they come! It were better for him that a millstone were hanged about his neck, and he cast into the sea, than that he should offend one of these little ones." If these perverted priests were men of God, they would not stoop that low.

Such a case took also place in my home in Germany many years ago. I had met a certain priest on several of my visits. He was very outgoing and sociable. Because of his accomplishments, he got transferred to the city, where he began molesting some of the boys until someone contacted the authorities. Since there was a shortage of priests, they transferred him to another city. Where is the punishment for these men? You never heard where they were sent to prison. They, of all people, should know what the Bible teaches. Someday they will stand before Jesus and have to explain. If the church would let them get married, many of these embarrassing situations could be avoided. Instead, they start to study for the priesthood at an early age before they realize what a commitment it is, unless God gives them the gift of celibacy. I remember over fifty years ago a young man from my hometown got ordained, but he left the priesthood after a few years to get married. This kind of news was the talk of the town. Not letting priests marry is against the Bible. There is nothing taking place under the sun for which the answer can not be found in the Bible. First Timothy 4:1–3 makes this clear:

> Now the Spirit speaketh expressly, that in the latter times some shall depart from the faith, giving heed to seducing spirits, and doctrines of devils; Speaking lies in hypocrisy; having their conscience seared with a hot iron; Forbidding to marry, and commanding to abstain from meats, which God hath created to be received with thanksgiving of them which believe and know the truth.

You see, I'm not just making up stories. The truth can be backed up with the Scriptures. Nearly nine hundred years ago, the Catholic Church started to forbid their priests to marry.[4] Also, the celibacy conflict is one of the leading reasons that priests leave the priesthood. I discovered *Lutherisches Gesangbuch*, a German book dated 1915, on my bookshelf. It tells that historic writings prove that in the early Christian churches priests and deacons had wives. It says in 1 Timothy 3:2, "A bishop then must be blameless, the husband of one wife, vigilant, sober, of good behavior, given to hospitality, apt to teach." Paul wrote in 1 Corinthians 7:2, "Nevertheless, to avoid fornication, let every man have his own wife, and let every woman have her own husband." When the church's stance began to change, they even murdered the innocent priests because they were married. The article included that God Himself instituted marriage to prevent lust.

When I was growing up, we could not eat meat on Fridays. One of our neighbor ladies told me that it was a "dead-sin," as we called it. This meant that you would surely go to hell if you ate meat on Friday. In later years, which was about forty years ago, it was announced that people working outside the home were excused from it. In 1966, Pope Paul VI declared that abstinence from meat on Friday was no longer universally binding. Why must the facts be changed? How can what was once considered truth get reversed? These are all man-made rules to keep the people in bondage.

Remember, I was once one of you, but God in His grace delivered me and set me free to worship Him, the living God, and not traditions. I also know with surety that, being born again, I will enter heaven. Now I can truly say that I'm free in the Lord. It is such a relieved feeling. As I was writing this chapter I realized that God has ordained for you to be set free and know the truth. How about you? Can you be certain after you read this chapter?

When I'm anointed like this I seem to need no sleep. I sensed an urgency to finish this chapter and realized that God wants everyone to know His truth, including the Jews and Muslims. He loves you and wants you to spend eternity with Him in heaven instead of in hell. This is the reason why He is opening your understanding by having me include all these Scriptures so you are able to see the difference in order to compare them with your doctrine. It is not pleasant for me to expose all this, but I have to be obedient to God's calling upon my life. About twenty-five years ago the Lord revealed this to me: "Men will not understand in what measure

I pour My Word into you. I will do to you as I did to Paul." As you see, the devil always gives some truth, but the gospel of Jesus Christ is *all* truth.

The celebration of Jesus' ascension up to heaven (called *Christi Himmelfahrt* in Germany) was a national holiday. But we celebrated not only His ascension, but they also have one for Mary, called *Maria Himmelfahrt.* She supposedly has also ascended to heaven. But that is not true; she died just like you and I will. Otherwise, she would be part of the Trinity—the triune God; Father, Son, and Holy Spirit. A friend of mine told me recently that her priest was telling them from the pulpit that the Catholic Church is trying to declare Mary a coredeemer with Jesus. What a farce. She is honored as being truly the Mother of God and of the Redeemer. That means she was before God was, if she is His mother. They also teach that she was free from original sin and was body and soul taken up to heaven and exalted as queen by the Lord over all things. As the holy mother of God, as they call her, or the new Eve and also the mother of the church, she continues her maternal role in heaven on behalf of the members of Christ. The faithful turn their eyes to Mary because in her the church is already the all-holy. Through Mary the church has already reached that perfection of being without spot or wrinkle.

The Scriptures tell us differently. She herself said that she was in need of a Savior. (See Luke 1:47.) Why? Because she was human like you and me. My blood boils every time I think of the corruption being taught to innocent people who trust in their leadership. I strongly protest the doctrine that makes Mary so powerful. She is being adorned with claims that belong only to Jesus Christ, our Savior.

> That he might present it to himself a glorious church, not having spot, or wrinkle, or any such thing; but that it should be holy and without blemish.
>
> —Ephesians 5:27

> But Christ being come an high priest of good things to come, by a greater and more perfect tabernacle, not made with hands, that is to say, not of this building; Neither by the blood of goats and calves, but by his own blood he entered in once into the holy place, having obtained eternal redemption for us. For if the blood of bulls and of goats, and the ashes of an heifer sprinkling the unclean, sanctifieth to the purifying of the flesh: How much more shall the blood of Christ, who through the eternal Spirit offered himself without spot to God, purge your conscience from dead works to serve the living God? And for this cause he is the mediator of the new testament, that by means of death, for the redemption of the transgressions that were under the first testament, they which are called might receive the promise of eternal inheritance.... So Christ was once offered to bear the sins of many; and unto them that look for him shall he appear the second time without sin unto salvation.
>
> —Hebrews 9:11–15, 28

According to these Scriptures, it is Jesus that presents to Himself this glorious church—which are the believers in Him—without spot and wrinkle, for whom He shed His precious blood. How is anything in these Scriptures referring to Mary? Jesus alone died for our sins. He alone hung on the cross for us.

This deception started way back.

> Nimrod, grandson of Ham and son of Cush, was the founder of a great false religious system that has always opposed the truths of God. Genesis 10:8 says that Nimrod "began to be a mighty one [or tyrant] in the earth." He set out to conquer and exploit other people by forming the first "kingdom" on Earth at Babylon in Shinar (verse 10). Nimrod also built the infamous tower of Babel (Genesis 11:1–9).
>
> ...Nimrod not only wanted to lead his people, he wanted to be worshiped by them. It is said that he married his own mother, Semiramis. She became known as the "queen of heaven" and Nimrod as the "divine son of heaven." He claimed to be the "savior" of all mankind and came to be worshiped as their messiah—their great deliverer. The problem was, he was attempting to save man from God, not from their sins....
>
> ...when he died Semiramis saw to it that he was still worshiped as a divine hero and given the name *Baal,* which means master, or lord....Shortly after Nimrod's untimely death, Semiramis gave birth to an illegitimate child, which she claimed was begotten by a "spirit" as a rebirth of Nimrod. This "mother and child" soon became the chief objects of worship throughout the world. There are many versions of this story, one for each nation and tongue as they were scattered from Babel by God, but whether they worshiped the mother and child under the Egyptian names of Isis and Horus, or the Roman names of Venus and Jupiter, or under the eventual Christian names of the "Virgin Mary" and the "Christ child," it was the same old Babylonian religion. Even in China, Japan and Tibet, the counterpart of the Madonna and child were worshiped long before the birth of Christ.[5]

What do you think when you purchase a stamp at Christmas depicting them? Jesus is not that little baby anymore. He is the Savior of the world. Let's give Him the honor due Him!

There are a number of other traditions and beliefs held by the Catholic Church that are not in the Bible. The first is that of salvation by water baptism. The Lord Himself affirms that baptism is necessary for salvation, but the Catholic Church does not know of any other means. They believe that by baptism all sins are forgiven—original sin and all personal sins, as well as all punishment for sin. However, the Catholic Church cannot save you, and neither will this false doctrine of baptism. Jesus told Nicodemus in John 3:3, 5, "Jesus answered and said unto him, Verily, verily, I say unto thee, Except a man be born again, he cannot see the kingdom of God.... Verily, verily, I say unto thee, Except a man be born of water and of the Spirit, he cannot enter into the kingdom of God." He repeated in Mark 16:16, "He that believeth and is baptized shall be saved; but he that believeth not shall be damned."

November 1 and 2 are All Saints' Day and All Souls Day, in which Catholics remember their deceased relatives, celebrate a mass, and pray at the cemetery.

Would a Catholic believe that their Ten Commandments have been tampered with? They are rearranged, and one of them is literally removed from the Catholic Catechism in order to allow them to continue their worship and the making and displaying of statues and images. As you read this, your eyes will opened to the fact that the second commandment is done away with altogether and the tenth is split in two, creating the ninth and tenth commandments, in order to cover up the deception. Can you believe that? It had to be done on purpose. Why didn't anyone discover it earlier?

Exodus 20:2–14 are the same in the Torah as the King James Version, except that in the Torah's footnotes it states that tradition varies as to the division of the commandments in verses 2–14 and as to the numbering of the verses from 13 on. Here are the Ten Commandments as they appear in Exodus 20:2–17 of the King James Version.

> I am the Lord thy God, which have brought thee out of the land of Egypt, out of the house of bondage. (vv. 2–3)
>
> Thou shalt not make unto thee any graven image, or any likeness of any thing that is in heaven above, or that is in the earth beneath, or that is in the water under the earth. Thou shalt not bow down thyself to them, nor serve them: for I the Lord thy God am a jealous God, visiting the iniquity of the fathers upon the children unto the third and fourth generation of them that hate me; And shewing mercy unto thousands of them that love me, and keep my commandments. (vv. 4–6)
>
> Thou shalt not take the name of the Lord thy God in vain; for the Lord will not hold him guiltless that taketh his name in vain. (v. 7)
>
> Remember the sabbath day, to keep it holy. Six days shalt thou labour, and do all thy work: But the seventh day is the sabbath of the Lord thy God: in it thou shalt not do any work, thou, nor thy son, nor thy daughter, thy manservant, nor thy maidservant, nor thy cattle, nor thy stranger that is within thy gates: For in six days the Lord made heaven and earth, the sea, and all that in them is, and rested the seventh day: wherefore the Lord blessed the sabbath day, and hallowed it. (vv. 8–11)

Honour thy father and thy mother: that thy days may be long upon the land which the Lord thy God giveth thee. (v. 12)
Thou shalt not kill. (v. 13)
Thou shalt not commit adultery. (v. 14)
Thou shalt not steal. (v. 15)
Thou shalt not bear false witness against thy neighbour. (v. 16)
Thou shalt not covet thy neighbour's house, thou shalt not covet thy neighbour's wife, nor his manservant, nor his maidservant, nor his ox, nor his ass, nor any thing that is thy neighbour's. (v. 17)

Following are the Ten Commandments Catholics are taught from *The Catechism of the Catholic Church*:

I am the Lord your God: you shall not have strange Gods before Me.
You shall not take the name of the Lord your God in vain.
Remember to keep holy the Lord's Day.
Honor your father and your mother.
You shall not kill.
You shall not commit adultery.
You shall not steal.
You shall not bear false witness against your neighbor.
You shall not covet your neighbor's wife.
You shall not covet your neighbor's goods.[6]

The second commandment is removed altogether and the ninth split in two in order to establish the tenth one! How slick. God is exposing all these lies so that the people can choose for themselves if they want to believe the truth or keep following this deception.

This is the reason I included the Jewish Scriptures. There should be no doubt in your mind now.

Martin Luther, a German professor with a doctorate in theology, lived from 1483–1546. Risking his life, he divided the Western church into two parts, the Catholic and the Protestant, by the Reformation he led. The main point he was proving was that only God, not the pope or priest, can forgive sins. God forgives our sins freely if we repent; we cannot buy our forgiveness with money, as the Catholic Church said. The Holy Spirit gave Martin Luther this revelation, and the news of it spread throughout Germany. The people were tired of paying out money for indulgences, seeing their German money being sent off to Rome to build the pope's St. Peter's Church. You see, it was big business. On October 31, 1517, Martin Luther nailed the Ninety-five Theses on the Castle Church door (*Schloss Kirche* in German) in Wittenberg. The opening lines read, "Out of love for the truth and the desire to bring it to light, the following propositions will be discussed at Wittenberg, under the presidency of the Reverend Father Martin Luther, Master of Arts and of Sacred Theology, and Lecturer in Ordinary on the same at that place. Wherefore he requests that those who are unable to be present and debate orally with us, may do so by letter. In the Name of Our Lord Jesus Christ. Amen."[7]

The only recently developed printing presses made it possible for Luther's protest to be known throughout Germany within a few weeks, and the church authorities in Rome began to be worried. As attempts were made to stop him, Luther had to defend himself three times. But remember, the Bible tells us, "If God is for us, who can be against us?" (Rom. 8:31). In April 1518, after walking all the way to Heidelberg, he defended himself against his fellow Augustinians who disagreed with his teachings. About the same time, the Dominican order began a campaign against Luther, making a formal charge of heresy against him in Rome. They said in their charges that his views were against the true Christian faith and hoped that he would be declared a heretic, which sentence would call for being burned to death, unless he would change his belief. He walked to Augsburg in October 1518 to be confronted by Cardinal Cajetan, the pope's representative. Luther knew then that his life was in danger and that he could be put to death. It was demanded of him to give up all "errors" and promise never to teach them again. But he refused, and angry shouting continued. His friends, being afraid that he would be arrested, smuggled him out of the city back to Wittenberg.

In June and July 1519 he experienced his third challenge in Leipzig. It developed to the point that he not only was involved in a debate about indulgences but was accused of challenging the power of the pope and the authority of the church itself. Over the next few months, Luther wrote, "Farewell, unhappy, hopeless, blasphemous Rome!...Let us leave her then that she may become the dwelling place of dragons, specters and witches!"[8] Is that what happened?

Amongst the other accomplishments of Martin Luther are that he translated the New Testament from Greek—the language it was first written in—into German. He also translated the Old Testament from the original Hebrew, which took him a long time. When he was asked if he would take back and deny the things he had written in his books his reply was, "Unless I am convinced, by

Scripture or by plain reason . . . I cannot and I will not recant . . . For to go against one's conscience is neither right nor safe. God help me. Amen."[9]

Luther was from then on an outlaw of the Holy Roman Empire as well as excommunicated by the church. His friends kidnapped him as he traveled through a dark forest near Eisenach and carried him off to the Wartburg for safekeeping.

Here are five of Luther's Ninety-five Theses:

1. Our Lord and Master Jesus Christ, when He said Poenitentiam agite ["repent"], willed that the whole life of believers should be repentance.
2. This word cannot be understood to mean sacramental penance, i.e., confession and satisfaction, which is administered by the priests.
20. Therefore by "full remission of all penalties" the pope means not actually "of all," but only of those imposed by himself.
21. Therefore those preachers of indulgences are in error, who say that by the pope's indulgences a man is freed from every penalty, and saved;
27. They preach man who say that so soon as the penny jingles into the money-box, the soul flies out [of purgatory].[10]

The latter accuses the church of selling forgiveness in the form of indulgences. As soon as you pay, your soul was said to fly out of purgatory. People were able to buy themselves out of purgatory while they were still alive. Remember the Bible tells us in

John 10:10 that Satan comes as an angel of light, to steal, kill, and destroy. He influences people to do his dirty work. Through this back-buying process, which is impossible, these greedy church leaders were filling their pockets.

Among the most important documents of the Reformation are the three manifestos Luther wrote in 1520. The first was entitled "Address to the Christian Nobility of the German Nation." It began, "The time for silence is gone and the time to speak has come." Here are a few points he addressed: that all Christians were equal and that bishops, priests, and monks were not—as was generally thought—of a higher or more spiritual state than other people. He stated that the pope did not have the right to interpret the Bible to his liking. He also believed that priests should be allowed to marry, and accused the bishops of not even knowing the gospel.[11]

He referred to the second manifesto as "On the Babylon Captivity of the Church." It mainly dealt with the sacraments. He complained that the church was enslaved by sacramental rules and practices and compared it with Israel's captivity in Babylon. Luther denied the teaching of the seven sacraments of the Catholic Church: baptism, Holy Communion, penance, confirmation, ordination, matrimony, and extreme unction. He believed in only two, baptism and Holy Communion, which were commanded by Jesus.

In his third manifesto, "Concerning Christian Liberty," Luther wrote that Christians are justified by faith alone. He believed that God's forgiveness was imprisoned by the church's power of its laws and politics over the whole western world. People do not have to earn their salvation by doing good deeds, fasting, or keeping described rules.[12]

I felt so free in the Lord after I was born again. It was such a good feeling, as if a heavy load was taken off of my shoulders. Good works will follow automatically with an attitude of servanthood, but they are not a condition. There is no need to pray for someone in purgatory because it does not exist. The Catholic Bible refers to it in one of their added books, the Maccabees, but Second Corinthians 5:8 tells us, "We are confident, I say, and willing rather to be absent from the body, and to be present with the Lord."

A proclamation by the pope from Rome was issued to condemn Luther. He had sixty days in which to give up all his errors or he would be declared a heretic and excommunicated. His response was, "I will do what I believe to be right." Since he saw the pope as an enemy of Jesus Christ, he could no longer obey him. In December, Luther threw his books of the canon law, which described the rules, laws, and practices of the church, into a huge bonfire. Luther was openly defying the pope—a declaration of war.

In June 1525, Martin Luther married Katherine von Bora. He was forty-two; she was twenty-six. Years later, while he was in Eisleben, the town where he has been born sixty-two years prior, Luther caught a chill and died there on February 18, 1546.

The Stations of the Cross are only rituals. Stop reliving the past. Take Jesus off the cross! Let Him be your Savior, instead of keeping Him dead and helpless on the cross. He rose from the dead two thousand years ago. By keeping Jesus on the cross, He cannot send you the Holy Spirit; without the guidance of the Holy Spirit, the people have to listen to the pope for direction. It is evident that Catholicism is a religion of works. What a farce!

According to the *Catechism of the Catholic Church*, Catholics need to adhere to the seven sacraments: baptism, penance, Holy Eucharist, confirmation, holy orders, matrimony, and anointing of the sick. The first two are not biblical. You shouldn't get baptized until you accept Jesus as your Savior. Penance is man made. We pray to God, who alone forgives our sins. The Eucharist is only half of the communion. That means that the whole setup is phony.

Lamplighter magazine reported the following in 2005 about Pope John Paul II's 1999 meeting with leaders in the Middle East:

> During a meeting with Iraqi Muslim leaders at the Vatican in May of 1999 Pope John Paul II is shown kissing the Koran—the Muslim Holy Book. He is also pictured welcoming an African voodoo priest to his conference of world spiritual leaders, held at Assisi, Italy. The bizarre gathering was attended by Confucians, Shintoists, Buddhists, Hindus, Wiccans, African witch doctors, and American Indian chiefs, among many others representing all sorts of pagan beliefs, whom he all welcomed most enthusiastically. John Paul even went so far as to proclaim that the god of Islam is the same as the God of Christianity, when the truth is that they are as different as light is from darkness.[13]

Mary was and is not a coredeemer with Christ. They are aimed at seducing the members and leaders of other groups or denominations to make them join or step in. Only the body is changed; the motor is still the same. Instead of vinegar, honey is being used to catch flies. It's a cunning and diplomatic policy. Will you be able to walk away from this falsehood and believe the truth, or can you not do without the comfortable rituals you have been used to for so long? It is sad to say that numerous Christians, even well-known leaders, allow themselves to be suckered in. Is this already part of the ingathering for the one world religion when the Antichrist comes on the scene?

At the ripe age of eighty-four, Pope John Paul II passed away on April 2, 2005. He faithfully led the 1.1 billion Catholics for four decades. Cardinal Ratzinger performed the service and named many of the saints when he sang the litany: Saint John the Baptist, Saint Cornelius, Saint Johannes, Saint Marin, Saint Clements, and Saint Teresa. I believe he named seventy-three total. Communion was served to a large crowd by two hundred priests in the St. Peter's Cathedral.

On April 18, 2005, 115 cardinals from fifty-two countries went into conclave, where they voted four times a day. A jiminy (smoke-stack) was erected on top of the Sistine Chapel. The people could tell if and when they elected the new pope because when a decision was made, the smoke changed from black to white. This happened on the second day. Cardinal Joseph Ratzinger from Germany was elected the new pontiff. He is the 265th pope at seventy-eight years of age, and he chose the name Pope Benedict XVI. It was announced on Christian TV that he once said that Catholicism is the only true religion. They reported that he is a hardliner, a defender of the Catholic doctrine, and will not give in to certain people wanting a more modern religion in the twenty-first century.

A January–February 2008 Christian magazine published the following:

> In August of last year Pope Benedict issued a proclamation in which he affirmed the divine attributes of Mary, the mother

> of Jesus. Equaling her with Jesus, he said, "Mother and Son appear closely bound in the fight against the infernal enemy until they completely defeat him. This victory is expressed in particular in overcoming sin and death. Therefore, just as Christ's glorious Resurrection was the definitive sign of this victory, so Mary's glorification in her virginal body is the ultimate confirmation of her total solidarity with the Son, both in the conflict and the victory."
>
> The pope then restated the infallible dogma of Pope Pius X from 1950 in which he referred to Mary as the "Mother of God, from all eternity…" The pope closed his statement with these words: "Attracted by the heavenly brightness of the Mother of the Redeemer, let us turn with trust on the One who looks upon us and protects us from on high. May the example and prayers of Mary, Queen of Heaven, inspire and sustain us on our pilgrimage of faith…"[14]

One hundred twenty cardinals congratulated Pope Benedict XVI with a handshake and kiss on the hand where he was wearing the papal ring.

> Now the Spirit speaketh expressly, that in the latter times some shall depart from the faith, giving heed to seducing spirits, and doctrines of devils.
>
> —1 Timothy 4:1

What Do Jehovah's Witnesses Believe?

Arians were the original Jehovah's Witnesses. They were named after Arius, a false teacher who died in A.D. 336. He argued that while Jesus is the mighty God, He is definitely not the Almighty God—and is therefore inferior to God the Father. However, the same Hebrew word used in Isaiah 9:6 to refer to the Child as "the Mighty God" is used with reference to the God of Israel in Isaiah 10:21: "The remnant shall return, even the remnant of Jacob, unto the mighty God." The Bible says that there is only one God.

> Thus saith the Lord the King of Israel, and his redeemer the Lord of hosts; I am the first, and I am the last; and beside me there is no God.... Fear ye not, neither be afraid: have not I told thee from that time, and have declared it? ye are even my witnesses. Is there a God beside me? yea, there is no God; I know not any.
>
> —Isaiah 44:6, 8

> I am the Lord, and there is none else, there is no God beside me: I girded thee, though thou hast not known me
>
> —Isaiah 45:5

Let me open your understanding. In His redemptive relation to man, Jehovah has numerous compound names, which reveal Him as meeting every need of man, from his lost state to the end. *Jehovah* is the transliteration of the Hebrew name of God (the supreme God). The compound names of Jehovah are:

- Jehovah-Jireh: "The Lord will provide" (Gen. 22:1–14).
- Jehovah-Rophe: "The Lord that healeth thee" (Exod. 15:26).
- Jehovah-Nissi: "The Lord our Banner" (Exod. 17:8–15).
- Jehovah-Rohi: "The Lord is my Shepherd" (Ps. 23).

- Jehovah-Shamma: "The Lord is present, or there" (Ezek. 48:35).
- Jehovah-Tsidkenu: "The Lord our Righteousness" (Jer. 23:6).
- Jehovah-Shalom: "The Lord our Peace" (Judg. 6:24).
- Jehovah-M'Kaddesh: "I am the Lord who sanctifies you" (Lev. 20:7–8).

Biblical teaching on the Trinity of God and the deity of Christ are vital issues in understanding the doctrinal errors of the Jehovah Witnesses, which without a doubt theologically divide the cults from biblical Christianity. Christians do not believe that the triune God will ever cease to be anything but triune. In His essential nature Jesus is not inferior to the Father. Because of the requirements of the plan of redemption, without the shedding of blood there is no remission of sins; therefore Christ became subordinate to the Father, even to the point of death on the cross. God's plan required that His Son die on the cross, and that could not have been possible apart from the Incarnation.

This profound truth seems to escape Jehovah's Witnesses and various other cults. That means that they have no forgiveness of their sins and no possibility of eternal life. Why bother to believe anything if your name is not written in the Lamb's Book of Life? The Tri-unity of the Godhead and the deity of Jesus Christ is not a human invention but a precious truth taught in the Bible. Jehovah's Witnesses do not believe in the Trinity doctrine, yet Jesus and the Holy Spirit were already from the very beginning, otherwise the Bible would be in error. We read in Genesis 1:26, "And God said, Let us make man in our image, after our likeness." The word for "God" in the Hebrew is *Elohim,* which is a plural word sometimes used with a singular or plural verb or pronoun. The word can mean more than one person. The great King, the Messiah, the Savior of all is also God! He was joint participant in Creation. If you don't believe that, you better tear the whole New Testament out of your Bible. Genesis 1:27 continues, "So God created man in his own image, in the image of God created He him; male and female created he them."

The New Testament confirms it as well in John 1:1–3: "In the beginning was the Word, and the Word was with God, and the Word was God. The same was in the beginning with God. All things were made by him; and without him was not any thing made that was made." Let's continue with verse 14: "And the Word was made flesh, and dwelt among us, (and we beheld his glory, the glory as of the only begotten of the Father,) full of grace and truth." You see, when God spoke, "In the beginning," He spoke of Himself in the plural. And that "Word" which was from the beginning is Jesus Christ. It can't be any clearer. If you do not understand, is it because you have been taught that the Bible cannot be understood without the guidance and publications of the Watchtower Bible and Tract Society, the organization that produces all the Jehovah's Witness literature? They produce their own translation of the Scriptures and claim that it takes precedence over the truth in the real Bible. It is called the New World Translation, and it was first published in 1950. It contains many changes in the wording of key passages. In 1920 some of their Scriptures were removed. Therefore the true Bible itself, the one

Christians read, is not even used by the Jehovah's Witnesses. The New World Translation is distorted and deviates from the truth, although Jehovah's Witnesses claim that the Bible is their final authority. You have to ask them, which Bible? Also, one will soon find out that the interpretation of their leaders is considered to be the final authority, not the Bible itself.

We read in 2 Timothy 3:16–17, "All scripture is given by inspiration of God, and is profitable for doctrine, for reproof, for correction, for instruction in righteousness: That the man of God may be perfect, thoroughly furnished unto all good works." Unless you are saved, meaning born-again, you are reading the Bible as a book with head knowledge only instead of spiritual discernment.

The apostle Paul explained in 1 Corinthians 2:12–14, "Now we have received, not the spirit of the world, but the spirit which is of God; that we might know the things that are freely given to us of God. Which things also we speak, not in the words which man's wisdom teacheth, but which the Holy Ghost teacheth; comparing spiritual things with spiritual. But the natural man receiveth not the things of the Spirit of God: for they are foolishness unto him: neither can he know them, because they are spiritually discerned." Furthermore, the Holy Spirit is not an "it," as the Jehovah's Witnesses call Him.

Let's check into the doctrine of the Trinity. Christians believe that there is only one God and that this one God is in three persons. The three persons are God the Father; God the Son, who is Jesus Christ; and God the Holy Spirit, who is also called the Holy Ghost. The three persons are distinct. The Father is not the Son. The Son is not the Holy Spirit. The Holy Spirit is not the Father. God is one perfect divine being in three persons. His being is what God is, in relation to the universe He created. The reason we call them persons is that they relate to each other in personal ways.

"One God in three persons" means:

- The Father is God—the first person of the Trinity.
- The Son is God—the second person of the Trinity.
- The Holy Spirit is God—the third person of the Trinity.

The title "Holy Ghost" is an old English expression for "Holy Spirit," and both are acceptable translations of the phrase in the Bible.

Why do Christians believe in the Trinity? Because the Bible clearly teaches that there is only one God, yet all three persons are called God, but have their own function.

There is only one God.

> Hear, O Israel: The LORD our God is one LORD.
>
> —DEUTERONOMY 6:4

> Before me there was no God formed, neither shall there be after me.
>
> —ISAIAH 43:10

The Father is God.

> Grace unto you, and peace, from God our Father and the Lord Jesus Christ.
>
> —2 THESSALONIANS 1:2

The Son is God.

> The Word [Jesus] was God."
>
> —JOHN 1:1

> I and my Father are one.
>
> —JOHN 10:30

In addition to these examples, Jesus' disciple Thomas addressed Jesus as "My Lord and my God" (John 20:28). Jesus did not tell Thomas he was mistaken; instead, Jesus accepted these titles. Yet we read in the Scriptures that other people like Paul and Barnabas refused to accept worship as gods. (See Acts 14:11–15.)

> But unto the Son he saith, Thy throne, O God, is for ever and ever: a sceptre of righteousness is the sceptre of thy kingdom.
>
> —HEBREWS 1:8

> Wherefore God also hath highly exalted him, and given him a name which is above every name: That at the name of Jesus every knee should bow, of things in heaven, and things in earth, and things under the earth; And that every tongue should confess that Jesus Christ is Lord, to the glory of God the Father.
>
> —PHILIPPIANS 2:9–11

The Holy Spirit is God.

> But Peter said, Ananias, why hath Satan filled thine heart to lie to the Holy Ghost...thou hast not lied unto men, but unto God.
>
> —ACTS 5:3–4

> Now the Lord is that Spirit.
>
> —2 CORINTHIANS 3:17

Here are some proofs that the Holy Spirit was already at work in the Old Testament. We read in Genesis 1:2:

> And the earth was without form, and void; and darkness was upon the face of the deep. And the Spirit of God moved upon the face of the waters.

> And Pharaoh said unto his servants, Can we find such a one as this is, a man in whom the Spirit of God is?
>
> —GENESIS 41:38

> See, I have called by name Bezaleel the son of Uri, the son of Hur, of the tribe of Judah: And I have filled him with the spirit of God, in wisdom, and in understanding, and in knowledge, and in all manner of workmanship, To devise cunning works, to work in gold, and in silver, and in brass, And in cutting of stones, to set them, and in carving of timber, to work in all manner of workmanship.
>
> —EXODUS 31:2–5

> And when the children of Israel cried unto the LORD, the LORD raised up a deliverer to the children of Israel, who delivered them, even Othniel the son of Kenaz, Caleb's younger brother. And the Spirit of the LORD came upon him, and he judged Israel, and went out to war: and the LORD delivered Chushanrishathaim king of Mesopotamia into his hand; and his hand prevailed against Chushanrishathaim.
>
> —JUDGES 3:9–10

> And Saul sent messengers to take David: and when they saw the company of the prophets prophesying, and Samuel

> standing as appointed over them, the Spirit of God was upon the messengers of Saul, and they also prophesied.... And he went thither to Naioth in Ramah: and the Spirit of God was upon him also, and he went on, and prophesied, until he came to Naioth in Ramah.
>
> —1 Samuel 19:20, 23

> But truly I am full of power by the spirit of the Lord, and of judgment, and of might, to declare unto Jacob his transgression, and to Israel his sin.
>
> —Micah 3:8

> Then will I sprinkle clean water upon you, and ye shall be clean: from all your filthiness, and from all your idols, will I cleanse you. A new heart also will I give you, and a new spirit will I put within you: and I will take away the stony heart out of your flesh, and I will give you an heart of flesh. And I will put my spirit within you, and cause you to walk in my statutes, and ye shall keep my judgments, and do them. And ye shall dwell in the land that I gave to your fathers; and ye shall be my people, and I will be your God. I will also save you from all your uncleannesses: and I will call for the corn, and will increase it, and lay no famine upon you.
>
> —Ezekiel 36:25–29

In the New Testament we understand the Holy Spirit to be the assurance of the risen Lord Jesus indwelling believers.

More than sixty Bible verses mention the three persons together.

> And Jesus, when he was baptized, went up straightway out of the water: and, lo, the heavens were opened unto him, and

> he saw the Spirit of God descending like a dove, and lighting upon him: And lo a voice from heaven, saying, This is my beloved Son, in whom I am well pleased.
>
> —MATTHEW 3:16–17

> Go ye therefore, and teach all nations, baptizing them in the name of the Father, and of the Son, and of the Holy Ghost.
>
> —MATTHEW 28:19

> The grace of the Lord Jesus Christ, and the love of God, and the communion of the Holy Ghost, be with you all.
>
> —2 CORINTHIANS 13:14

> There is one body, and one Spirit, even as ye are called in one hope of your calling; One Lord, one faith, one baptism, One God and Father of all, who is above all, and through all, and in you all.
>
> —EPHESIANS 4:4–6

> But after that the kindness and love of God our Saviour toward man appeared, Not by works of righteousness which we have done, but according to his mercy he saved us, by the washing of regeneration, and renewing of the Holy Ghost; Which he shed on us abundantly through Jesus Christ our Saviour.
>
> —TITUS 3:4–6

Here are numerous more: Romans 14:17–18; 15:13–17, 30; 1 Corinthians 6:11, 17–19; 12:4–6; 2 Corinthians 1:21–22; 3:4–6; Galatians 2:21–3:2; Ephesians 2:18; 3:11–17; 5:18–20; Philippians 2:1; Colossians 1:6–8; 1 Thessalonians 1:1–5; 4:2, 8; 5:18–19; 2 Thessalonians 3:5; Hebrews 9:14; 1 Peter 1:2; 1 John 3:23–24; and Jude 20–21.

Without the Trinity, the Christian doctrine of salvation cannot stand. The Trinity is a profound doctrine that must be accepted by faith. The Bible tells us that there are some things we cannot understand. Certain religious groups that claim to believe in the God of the Bible but reject the Trinity have an understanding of salvation that is based on good works. The word *Trinity* was used to explain the eternal relationship between the Father, the Son, and the Holy Spirit. Following are some divine attributes of the Father, the Son, and the Holy Spirit.

Creator of all things

- Father: "Know ye that the Lord he is God: it is he that hath made us" (Ps. 100:3).
- Son: "For by Him were all things created" (Col. 1:16).
- Holy Spirit: "Who hath directed the Spirit of the Lord?" (Isa. 40:13).

Omnipresent—capable of being at all places at once

- Father: "Can any hide himself in secret places that I shall not see him? saith the Lord" (Jer. 23:24).
- Son: "I am with you always, even unto the end of the world" (Matt. 28:20).
- Holy Spirit: "Whither shall I go from thy spirit? or whither shall I flee from Thy presence?" (Ps. 139:7).

Eternal

- Father: "According to the commandment of the everlasting God" (Rom. 16:26).
- Son: "Fear not; I am the first and the last" (Rev. 1:17).
- Holy Spirit: "How much more shall the blood of Christ, who through the eternal Spirit offered himself without spot to God, purge your conscience from dead works to serve the living God?" (Heb. 9:14).

Jehovah's Witnesses believe that only the Father is God. His name is Jehovah. They neither believe that God is omniscient (knows everything) nor that He is omnipresent. Also, they profess that Jesus Christ is not God, that He was created as a spirit creature. This creature, Michael the archangel, supposedly gave up His heavenly existence as Michael to become the human man Jesus Christ, in obedience to His Father. Although it is certainly true that there is only one God, we must allow the Bible to define what the Trinity means. From such a study, it is quite clear that the Father, Son, and Holy Spirit are distinct persons.

> And we have seen and do testify that the Father sent the Son to be the Saviour of the world.
>
> —1 John 4:14

> But the Comforter, which is the Holy Ghost, whom the Father will send in my name, he shall teach you all things,

> and bring all things to your remembrance, whatsoever I have said unto you.
>
> —JOHN 14:26

> Then said Jesus unto them, When ye have lifted up the Son of man, then shall ye know that I am he, and that I do nothing of myself; but as my Father hath taught me, I speak these things.
>
> —JOHN 8:28

> Howbeit when he, the Spirit of truth, is come, he will guide you into all truth: for he shall not speak of himself; but whatsoever he shall hear, that shall he speak: and he will shew you things to come. He shall glorify me: for he shall receive of mine, and shall shew it unto you. All things that the Father hath are mine: therefore said I, that he shall take of mine, and shall shew it unto you.
>
> —JOHN 16:13–15

After you read all the previous Scriptures, they surely must have opened your understanding. Ask God if all of them are true and if He is the triune God. If you are sincere, He will not disappoint you. He will reveal the truth to you. Isn't that what you want?

A Jehovah's Witness client of mine gave me a booklet called "Should you believe in the Trinity?" Let me tell you, it is very much distorted. In the back of the booklet it reads, "Live forever in Paradise on Earth." It proceeds, "God promises eternal live to those who honor him." Then it quotes a Scripture from a translation other than the King James version: "The righteous themselves will possess the earth, and they will reside forever upon it" (Ps. 37:29). My King James version reads as follows: "The righteous shall inherit the land, and dwell therein for ever." The pamphlet takes this Scripture totally out of context. First of all, there is no paradise on Earth forever; just think of the seven years of Tribulation here on Earth after Jesus appears in the clouds and raptures the saints. Let me describe it to you by quoting Luke 21:25–28:

> And there shall be signs in the sun, and in the moon, and in the stars; and upon the earth distress of nations, with perplexity; the sea and the waves roaring; Men's hearts failing them for fear, and for looking after those things which are coming on the earth: for the powers of heaven shall be shaken. And then shall they see the Son of man coming in a cloud with power and great glory. And when these things begin to come to pass, then look up, and lift up your heads; for your redemption draweth nigh.

Did you not read it in your Bible? Do you want to experience the Tribulation by your own choosing instead of being raptured with the believers?

The pamphlet also says that God promises eternal life to those who honor Him. His Word assures us of this. The scripture the pamphlet quotes, Psalm 37:29, is a psalm of David. It did not come from the mouth of God as assurance to us. We will be gone to be with Jesus in heaven when He returns for us, His bride. Be careful that you are telling and believing the truth. There are many other false interpretations, and you will be accountable for all the souls you lead astray.

In Matthew 13 Jesus gives many parables as a means of teaching kingdom truth. In some He compares the kingdom of heaven to now; in others they are for a future time. Here are some examples.

Jesus explains the parable of the tares in Matthew 13:36–43:

> Then Jesus sent the multitude away, and went into the house: and his disciples came unto him, saying, Declare unto us the parable of the tares of the field. He answered and said unto them, He that soweth the good seed is the Son of man; The field is the world; the good seed are the children of the kingdom; but the tares are the children of the wicked one; The enemy that sowed them is the devil; the harvest is the end of the world; and the reapers are the angels. As therefore the tares are gathered and burned in the fire; so shall it be in the end of this world. The Son of man shall send forth his angels, and they shall gather out of his kingdom all things that offend, and them which do iniquity; And shall cast them into a furnace of fire: there shall be wailing and gnashing of teeth. Then shall the righteous shine forth as the sun in the kingdom of their Father. Who hath ears to hear, let him hear.

Then Jesus tells them of the parable of the dragnet in verses 47–51:

> Again, the kingdom of heaven is like unto a net, that was cast into the sea, and gathered of every kind: Which, when it was full, they drew to shore, and sat down, and gathered the good into vessels, but cast the bad away. So shall it be at the end of the world: the angels shall come forth, and sever the wicked from among the just, And shall cast them into the furnace of fire: there shall be wailing and gnashing of teeth. Jesus saith unto them, Have ye understood all these things? They say unto him, Yea, Lord.

The apostle Paul wrote this to the Philippians:

> Let this mind be in you, which was also in Christ Jesus: Who, being in the form of God, thought it not robbery to be equal with God: But made himself of no reputation, and took upon him the form of a servant, and was made in the likeness of men: And being found in fashion as a man, he humbled himself, and became obedient unto death, even the death of the cross. Wherefore God also hath highly exalted him, and given him a name which is above every name: That at the name of Jesus every knee should bow, of things in heaven, and things in earth, and things under the earth; And that every tongue should confess that Jesus Christ is Lord, to the glory of God the Father.
>
> —Philippians 2:5–11

Jesus told Thomas in John 14:6, "I am the way, the truth, and the life: no man cometh unto the Father, but by me."

Everyone needs to understand these above verses, repent and believe in the one and only true God, and receive Jesus as his or her Savior; or you will be part of those that will be wailing and gnashing their teeth. First, Jesus will come and gather His saints—the bride of Christ, adorned with the white garment—to Himself in the Rapture, when we celebrate the Marriage Supper of the Lamb for seven years. By believing in an earthly Paradise, Jehovah's Witnesses seem to want to stay down here on Earth. The Bible says that after three and one-half years of the Tribulation have passed, the Antichrist will set himself in the temple to be worshiped as god; those who are left will be persecuted.

The Jehovah believed in by Jehovah's Witnesses is not the Jehovah of the Bible, who would have you believe in His truth and all the Scriptures as they are written in the Bible—not the way a group of people interprets them. Many innocent people are led astray by false doctrine. Yes, Jehovah's Witnesses are very much deceived. The Bible teaches us in Ephesians 2:8, "For by grace are ye saved through faith; and that not of yourselves; it is the gift of God." Jehovah's Witnesses teach that one has to work for his or her salvation, going door-to-door, inviting people to your meetings. They believe that their founder's teachings are the only way to salvation and that his writings are the only way to understand the Bible, but any group who uses other writings and opinions to interpret the Bible is a cult.

The Jehovah's Witnesses started as a Bible study in 1870. Their founder, Charles Taze Russell, was then ordained as pastor by that Bible study group in 1876. Since he was the founder, he could teach anything because he was not accountable to anyone for the truth. In my study, I found that Mr. Russell's integrity was less than admirable. He died in 1916.[15]

Jehovah's Witnesses say that there are two classes of believers. The heavenly class is limited to 144,000, who will be resurrected as spirit creatures and who alone can be born again and live eternally in heaven. The larger earthly class will be resurrected to new human bodies and will live under the rule of Jesus and the 144,000 on a Paradise Earth. They can never be born again. This statement alone tells that your doctrine is from the pit of hell, the devil himself, because Jesus says in the Bible that you must be born again. (See John 3:3.) How did their founder come up with such lies? In the foreword of the New World Translation it explains that it is a very responsible thing to translate the Holy Scriptures from their original language into modern speech. What a lie. God's Word can stand on its own and needs no help from any human to interpret and distort it.

I will disprove their assertions with Scriptures. The 144,000 are the Jewish remnant. Where were the founders of this religion when the Bible was written so long ago? Jehovah's Witness doctrine didn't come along until 1870. We read in Revelation 14:1, "And I looked, and, lo, a Lamb stood on the mount Sion, and with him an hundred forty and four thousand, having his Father's name written in their foreheads." Throughout the Scriptures, the Lamb is Jesus; the 144,000 with Him have His Father's name (that of God the Father) written on their foreheads. Tell me how these could be Jehovah's Witnesses. Impossible!

Next, Jesus told Nicodemus in John 3:3, "Verily, verily, I say unto thee, Except a man be born again, he cannot see the kingdom of God." Since Jehovah's Witnesses don't believe in being born again, this makes them automatic candidates for hell. However, they are taught that hell does not exist. However, once someone is there he or she can't escape. Remember, Jesus came and died on the cross for everyone, including Jehovah's Witnesses, so that we could have eternal life by being born again.

If you are a Jehovah's Witness, receive Christ as your Savior now instead of hell's damnation later. Let me give you some Bible verses that hopefully will open your understanding. The reason Jesus hasn't returned yet is to give everyone a chance to receive Him, including you. We read in 2 Peter 3:9–18:

> The Lord is not slack concerning his promise, as some men count slackness; but is longsuffering to us-ward, not willing

> that any should perish, but that all should come to repentance. But the day of the Lord will come as a thief in the night; in the which the heavens shall pass away with a great noise, and the elements shall melt with fervent heat, the earth also and the works that are therein shall be burned up. Seeing then that all these things shall be dissolved, what manner of persons ought ye to be in all holy conversation and godliness, Looking for and hasting unto the coming of the day of God, wherein the heavens being on fire shall be dissolved, and the elements shall melt with fervent heat? Nevertheless we, according to his promise, look for new heavens and a new earth, wherein dwelleth righteousness. Wherefore, beloved, seeing that ye look for such things, be diligent that ye may be found of him in peace, without spot, and blameless. And account that the longsuffering of our Lord is salvation; even as our beloved brother Paul also according to the wisdom given unto him hath written unto you; As also in all his epistles, speaking in them of these things; in which are some things hard to be understood, which they that are unlearned and unstable wrest, as they do also the other scriptures, unto their own destruction. Ye therefore, beloved, seeing ye know these things before, beware lest ye also, being led away with the error of the wicked, fall from your own stedfastness. But grow in grace, and in the knowledge of our Lord and Saviour Jesus Christ. To him be glory both now and for ever. Amen.

After seven years, Jesus will return with us to rule the world from Jerusalem. It is then that the tares will be removed by His angels. The tares are people that have their own belief system, but it does not line up with the Word of God. Since Jehovah's Witnesses don't believe in a literal hell, they will go there and experience wailing and gnashing of teeth, along with many others. This is not a threat, only the facts as they are stated in the Bible. Don't blame me; I only deliver the message. You need to know this so you can decide where you will spend eternity. Jehovah's Witnesses have many more beliefs that take certain Bible verses totally out of context. I will just mention a few.

They are taught that the Bible prohibits blood transfusions, even in a medical emergency; to do so would mean losing your salvation forever. They arrive at that ridiculous conclusion from the following scripture:

> And God blessed Noah and his sons, and said unto them, Be fruitful, and multiply, and replenish the earth.... Every moving thing that liveth shall be meat for you; even as the green herb have I given you all things. But flesh with the life thereof, which is the blood thereof, shall ye not eat.
>
> —Genesis 9:1, 3–4

> And whatsoever man there be of the children of Israel, or of the strangers that sojourn among you, which hunteth and catcheth any beast or fowl that may be eaten; he shall even pour out the blood thereof, and cover it with dust. For it is the life of all flesh; the blood of it is for the life thereof: therefore I said unto the children of Israel, Ye shall eat the blood of no manner of flesh: for the life of all flesh is the blood thereof: whosoever eateth it shall be cut off.
>
> —Leviticus 17:13–14

These verses are talking about animals that are hunted. People surely don't receive blood transfusions from an animal. By having a blood transfusion from human blood, how is that similar to eating it? This doctrine is way off and in a world of its own. A blood transfusion replenishes the supply of life-sustaining fluid that has, because of an injury possibly, been drained away. Cutting of blood vessels are also reason for loss of blood. Certain diseases can affect those parts of the body that produce blood, and because they are not functioning properly, the individual has an insufficient blood supply. Giving a blood transfusion to such a person may sustain his life—and no one is eating blood.

My own father had a blood disease at age fifty. He was very tired for some time and barely managed to get to the doctor's office that day. He was told that he would have died in a short time if he had not been given blood from a twenty-year-old man in a neighboring town, whom he also met. Because of that transfusion, my father looked better at seventy then he did at fifty and lived to the ripe age of eighty-six.

Does not the Bible explain in Revelation 22:18–19, "For I testify unto every man that heareth the words of the prophecy of this book, If any man shall add unto these things, God shall add unto him the plagues that are written in this book: And if any man shall take away from the words of the book of this prophecy, God shall take away his part out of the book of life, and out of the holy city, and from the things which are written in this book"? This tells Jehovah's Witnesses that the way they interpret the Bible with their own writings, none of them will have their names written in the Book of Life. They are all going to hell, including the 144,000 of the heavenly class, unless they change.

The Watchtower Society is also known as a date-setting organization because they believe that God still gives new revelations through today's prophets and that a false prophet is a person who prophesies something that does not come to pass. This makes them many times false prophets. After the following dates passed without a fulfillment of their predictions, they found ways to reinterpret and explain them away. In 1874 there was supposed to be the invisible second coming of Jesus. Two different times during the twentieth century they predicted the end of the world. They declared that all members of the body of Christ would be changed to heavenly glory in 1925 and that World War II was Armageddon.[16]

Jehovah's Witnesses don't celebrate birthdays nor any holidays. They also don't believe in voting; running for an elected office; and worse yet, they refuse to defend their country by serving in the military or saluting our flag. These are all against their beliefs because they are considered a form of idolatry. Yet, we read in Romans 13:1–4, "Let every soul be subject unto the higher powers. For there is no power but of God: the powers that be are ordained of God. Whosoever therefore resisteth the power, resisteth the ordinance of God: and they that resist shall receive to themselves damnation. For rulers are not a terror to good works, but to the evil. Wilt thou then not be afraid of the power? do that which is good, and thou shalt have praise of the same: For he is the minister of God to thee for good. But if thou do that which is evil, be afraid; for he beareth not the sword in vain: for he is the minister of God, a revenger to execute wrath upon him that doeth evil. " I guess the rest of us have to cover and protect you too, or the terrorists of the September 11, 2001, tragedy would take over. Yet, in the Old Testament we read that on numerous occasions God sent the Israelites into war. True Christians are identified not by a mere profession of piety but by a faith that reflects the beautiful qualities produced by God's Holy Spirit. (See Galatians 5:22–23; James 1:22; 2:26.) Outstanding among these qualities—and the identifying mark of genuine Christianity—is the sublime quality of love. (See John 13:34–35.) Note this crucial point, however: neither Jesus nor his apostles expected the Christian congregation to continue in the form in which it was originally established. They knew that apostasy would develop and that the true religion would be overshadowed for a time.

Jehovah's Witnesses never once said that Jesus told them to repent of their sins and get saved. They deny the fact that He was God in the flesh and had the power to deliver them and therefore keep them from going to hell. True Christians were not identified by their love; instead, they were believers in Jesus Christ. True Christians are first and foremost defined by their belief in the divinity of Jesus Christ and the atonement He made for the sins of the world, but they should also be identifiable by their love. A true Christian is a disciple of Jesus and a follower of Him all of his life.

As I write these lines today, my spirit is in turmoil. These false religions are as sneaky as the serpent himself. May the Jehovah's Witnesses see the light as they read this chapter, and may God have mercy on them and open their spiritually blind eyes.

Are Mormons Christians?

The Church of Jesus Christ of Latter-day Saints

Certain cults have borrowed the name "Christian." They call themselves Christian, yet they don't believe at all what Christianity stands for. Their followers are deceived. Right in the front of the Book of Mormon, below the title, it says in smaller print, "Another Testament of Jesus Christ." It is supposed to recount the story of the tribes of Israel who by divine command migrated to America centuries before Christ.

Just because you admire your neighbor's trees, which shade your yard as well, you can't claim them as your own. Your money has not purchased them. Neither can you claim the name Christian, if you're not following Jesus Christ—the one who gave His life when He shed His blood for the forgiveness of our sins. Unless you repent of your sins and accept Jesus Christ into your heart as your Savior and follow Him by making Him Lord over your life, you have no right to call yourself something that you're not. Satan has slipped this one in, and people have swallowed his bait—hook, line, and sinker. I can't call myself a Mormon if I don't belief in their doctrine; and since Mormons don't believe in the Bible as it is written, they absolutely cannot call themselves Christians. We read in Acts 11:26, "And it came to pass, that a whole year they assembled themselves with the church, and taught much people. And the disciples were called Christians first in Antioch." You see, Christians don't follow the teachings of Joseph Smith but rather those of Jesus Christ. He is the Son of God who is the Messiah, the Anointed One. Mormon doctrine does not compare in the least bit to Christianity, although Jesus Christ is mentioned all the way through their writings. This way the people are made to believe that they are being told the truth.

The Church of Jesus Christ of Latter-day Saints is commonly known as the Mormon Church. They have a following of about 13 million people.[17] It came into being shortly after the publication of the Book of Mormon in 1830 in New York State. It is therefore described as an American religion. Today its headquarters is in Salt Lake City, Utah. Joseph Smith (1805–1844) was the founder of Mormonism. Although they are divided now into two major groups, the other one being The Reorganized Church of Jesus Christ of Latter-day Saints. Their headquarters are in Independence, Missouri.

The Book of Mormon says that the constant warfare between their descendants, the Nephites, and the renegade, red-skinned tribe of Lamanites, continued for about a thousand years, interrupted briefly by the appearance of Christ to the Nephites after His resurrection and their conversion to Christianity. The descendants of the Lamanites were the American Indians. The Book of Ether, which was taken from the twenty-four plates found by the people of Lemhi in the days of King Mosiah, records that Jared and his brother were supposedly spared by God when He confounded the language of the people and swore in His wrath that they should be scattered upon all the face of the earth. We read in Ether 1:33–37:

> Which Jared came forth with his brother and their families, with some others and their families, from the great tower, at the time the Lord confounded the language of the people, and swore in his wrath that they should be scattered upon all the face of the earth; and according to the word of the Lord the people were scattered. And the brother of Jared being a large and mighty man, and a man highly favored of the Lord, Jared, his brother, said unto him: Cry unto the Lord, that he will not confound us that we may not understand our words. And it

> came to pass that the brother of Jared did cry unto the Lord, and the Lord had compassion upon Jared; therefore he did not confound the language of Jared; and Jared and his brother were not confounded. Then Jared said unto his brother: Cry again unto the Lord, that it may be that he will turn away his anger from them who are our friends, that he confound not their language. And it came to pass that the brother of Jared did cry unto the Lord, and the Lord had compassion upon their friends and their families also, that they were not confounded.

The Bible does not mention anything about having spared a certain people group, as they claim. Genesis 11:1, 4–9 tells us:

> And the whole earth was of one language, and of one speech.... And they said, Go to, let us build us a city and a tower, whose top may reach unto heaven; and let us make us a name, lest we be scattered abroad upon the face of the whole earth. And the Lord came down to see the city and the tower, which the children of men builded. And the Lord said, Behold, the people is one, and they have all one language; and this they begin to do: and now nothing will be restrained from them, which they have imagined to do. Go to, let us go down, and there confound their language, that they may not understand one another's speech. So the Lord scattered them abroad from thence upon the face of all the earth: and they left off to build the city. Therefore is the name of it called Babel; because the Lord did there confound the language of all the earth: and from thence did the Lord scatter them abroad upon the face of all the earth.

The following Scriptures mention absolutely nothing about God favoring certain people. In fact, we read that He confound the language of *all* the earth and scattered *all* abroad. Did Joseph Smith make up his story? If it were true, it certainly would have been mentioned first in the Bible. Furthermore, all the strange names listed in the Book of Mormon are not found in the Bible anywhere. Were they invented, then, at the time their religion came into being?

Someday we will stand before Jesus and will have to give an account of our lives. We must remember what He said in Matthew 7:23: "And then will I profess unto them, I never knew you: depart from me, ye that work iniquity." If we do not believe in Him, He will order us to spent eternity in hell. The only problem is that from this point there is no return. We have to accept Jesus while we are alive. I'm sorry, but there is not a nice way to say it. The truth is the truth and you still have a chance now. The Bible tells us this devastating truth in Luke 16:19–31:

> There was a certain rich man, which was clothed in purple and fine linen, and fared sumptuously every day: And there was a certain beggar named Lazarus, which was laid at his gate, full of sores, And desiring to be fed with the crumbs which fell from the rich man's table: moreover the dogs came and licked his sores. And it came to pass, that the beggar died, and was carried by the angels into Abraham's bosom: the rich man also died, and was buried; And in hell he lift up his eyes, being in torments, and seeth Abraham afar off, and Lazarus in his bosom. And he cried and said, Father Abraham, have mercy on me, and send Lazarus, that he may dip the tip of his finger in water, and cool my tongue; for I am tormented in this flame. But Abraham said, Son, remember that thou in thy lifetime receivedst thy good things, and likewise Lazarus evil things: but now he is comforted, and thou

> art tormented. And beside all this, between us and you there is a great gulf fixed: so that they which would pass from hence to you cannot; neither can they pass to us, that would come from thence. Then he said, I pray thee therefore, father, that thou wouldest send him to my father's house: For I have five brethren; that he may testify unto them, lest they also come into this place of torment. Abraham saith unto him, They have Moses and the prophets; let them hear them. And he said, Nay, father Abraham: but if one went unto them from the dead, they will repent. And he said unto him, If they hear not Moses and the prophets, neither will they be persuaded, though one rose from the dead.

God looks at your heart. Ask yourself, Have you been deceived with wrong doctrine?

Some of the ordinances of the church are the baptism of the dead, sealing, and endowment. The baptism ceremony is done in the temple in a secret ceremony. While the living are baptized, Joseph Smith taught that even those who did not believe during their lifetimes might gain eternal life through the prayers of their posterity and baptism by proxy. Endowment and sealing may also take place on behalf of the dead by proxy. *Sealing* is the term for the religious ceremony of marriage, and endowment is the process by which one is ritually bathed and anointed with oil. At that time, the individual receives temple garments, which represent faithfulness and are believed to serve as a type of protection against evil. Due to the nature of these rituals and their secrecy, it is not surprising that Joseph Smith instituted these ordinances as a part of the Mormon Church after he became a part of the Masons.[18]

Romans 12:2 tells us, "And be not conformed to this world: but be ye transformed by the renewing of your mind, that ye may prove what is that good, and acceptable, and perfect, will of God." Otherwise you're deceived by those described in 2 Corinthians 11:13–15: "For such are false apostles, deceitful workers, transforming themselves into the apostles of Christ. And no marvel; for Satan himself is transformed into an angel of light. Therefore it is no great thing if his ministers also be transformed as the ministers of righteousness; whose end shall be according to their works."

At age fourteen, Joseph Smith had a vision of what he believed was the appearing of the Father and Son before him. At age seventeen, in 1823, he saw the angel Moroni appearing before him, telling him of a book written on golden plates. Four years later, Smith dug the plates and translated their Reformed Egyptian writing with the help of two special stones called Urim and Thummim. Around 1830, he started his new religion and translated the Book of Mormon. He taught his followers, "You have got to learn to become Gods yourselves," and "The Lord created you and me for the purpose of becoming Gods like Himself."[19] The Bible, however, clearly teaches us in Isaiah 43:10, "Ye are my witnesses, saith the Lord, and my servant whom I have chosen: that ye may know and believe me, and understand that I am he: before me there was no God formed, neither shall there be after me."

Mormon Belief vs. Christian Doctrine

Mormons dismiss, twist, change, or add to all biblical doctrines, particularly those of revelation, the Trinity, and salvation by grace alone through faith alone. Jesus said in Matthew 28:19, "Go ye therefore, and teach all nations, baptizing them in the name of the Father, and of the Son, and of the Holy Ghost." First Peter 1:5 says that believers are those "who are kept by the power of God through faith unto salvation ready to be revealed in the last time." Ephesians 2:8–9 explains the biblical doctrine of salvation: "For by grace are ye saved through faith; and that not of yourselves: it is the gift of God: Not of works, lest any man should boast."

Mormon doctrine teaches that Jesus and Satan are brothers.

> The Appointment of Jesus to be Savior of the world was contested by one of the other sons of God—Lucifer. This spirit-brother of Jesus desperately tried to become the Savior of mankind."[20]

The Bible teaches that the real Jesus is the only begotten Son of God. Read John 1:1–14:

> In the beginning was the Word, and the Word was with God, and the Word was God. The same was in the beginning with God. All things were made by him; and without him was not any thing made that was made. In him was life; and the life was the light of men. And the light shineth in darkness; and the darkness comprehended it not. There was a man sent from God, whose name was John. The same came for a witness, to bear witness of the Light, that all men through him might believe. He was not that Light, but was sent to bear witness of that Light. That was the true Light, which lighteth every man that cometh into the world. He was in the world, and the world was made by him, and the world knew him not. He came unto his own, and his own received him not. But as many as received him, to them gave he power to become the sons of God, even to them that believe on his name: Which

> were born, not of blood, nor of the will of the flesh, nor of the will of man, but of God. And the Word was made flesh, and dwelt among us, (and we beheld his glory, the glory as of the only begotten of the Father,) full of grace and truth.

Satan was a created angel, not a son of God. This is described in Isaiah 14:12: "How art thou fallen from heaven, O Lucifer, son of the morning! how art thou cut down to the ground, which didst weaken the nations!" Jesus created all things, and in Him the fullness of God dwells! (See Philippians 2:5–11; Colossians 1:15–20; and Hebrews 1:1–13.)

Freemasonry

Prayer of Release for Freemasons and Their Descendants

If you or one of your ancestors was a Mason, you should take the time to pray the following prayer of repentance and renouncement of your (or your family's) ties to that organization. It is also a prayer of protection so that there would be no enduring spiritual effect or curse in your bloodline. If possible, it should be prayed aloud, with another Christian present in agreement with you.

> *Father God, Creator of heaven and earth, I come to you in the name of Jesus Christ your Son.... I honor... all of my ancestors of flesh and blood... but I utterly turn away from and renounce all their sins. I forgive all my ancestors for the effects of their sins on me and my children. I confess and renounce all of my own sins. I renounce and rebuke Satan*

and every spiritual power of his affecting me and my family. I renounce and forsake all involvement in Freemasonry or any other lodge or craft by my ancestors and myself. I renounce Baphomet, the spirit of Antichrist and the curse of the Luciferian doctrine. I renounce the idolatry, blasphemy, secrecy, and deception of Masonry at every level. I specifically renounce the insecurity, the love of position and power, the love of money, avarice or greed, and the pride, which would have led my ancestors into Masonry. I renounce all the fears that held them in Masonry.... I renounce the calling of any man "Master," for Jesus Christ is my only master and Lord...

Now dear Father God, I ask humbly for the blood of Jesus Christ, your Son, to cleanse me from all these sins I have confessed and renounced; to cleanse my spirit, my soul, my mind, my emotions, and every part of my body which has been affected by these sins... I take to myself the whole armor of God in accordance with Ephesians 6, and rejoice in its protection as Jesus surrounds me and fills me with His Holy Spirit. I enthrone you, Lord Jesus, in my heart, for you are my Lord and my Savior, the source of eternal life. Thank you, Father God, for your mercy, your forgiveness, and your love, in the name of Jesus Christ. Amen.[21]

A more detailed prayer may be found in Selwyn Stevens' book *Unmasking Freemasonry: Removing the Hoodwink* or by visiting www.healinghouse.org/pubdownloads/MasonicPrayer.ppt.

Urantia

The Urantia Book is said to be written by celestial beings and communicated by automatic handwriting—an occult practice. Seven spirit beings supposed to delivered it to Dr. Bill Sadler, its founder. It was first printed in 1958. Is this new religion supposed to replace Christianity?

The paragraphs that follow describe the contents of the four parts of The Urantia Book.

Part I

The Central and Superuniverses

These thirty one papers depict the nature of Deity, the reality of Paradise, the organization and working of the central and superuniverses, the personalities of the grand universe, and the high destiny of evolutionary mortals. They were sponsored, formulated, and put into English by a commission of twenty-four spiritual administrators acting in accordance with a mandate issued by high deity authorities (the Ancients of Days) directing that they do this on Urantia in the year A.D. 1934.

Part II

The Local Universe

Our world, Urantia, belongs to a local universe whose sovereign is Michael, the Son of God and the Son of Man, known on this world as Jesus of Nazareth. In the central universe the Universal Father (God) is personally present; in the universes and planets of space our Father is being represented by his Sovereign Sons, while he is intimately present in the minds of his mortal children through his indwelling spirit, The Thought Adjusters. The twenty-five papers comprising Part II tell the story of man's ascension career following his initial life on the evolutionary planet.

Part III

The History of Urantia

The sixty-three papers comprising this section relate the history of our planet, the geologic development, the establishment of life, and the evolution and history of man, evolving civilizations, human institutions and governments.

Part IV

The Life and Teachings of Jesus

Jesus' life and precepts, in their original form, unencumbered by tradition and dogma, are by far the greatest possible help that moral man can have in his age long climb to Paradise. "The great hope of Urantia lies in the possibility of a new revelation of Jesus with a new and enlarged presentation of his saving message which would spiritually unite in loving service the numerous families of his present day professed followers."[22]

Just as Urantia, which is one of many New Age religions, is trying to convince you of its truth, so do many other religions proclaim that they have the only truth. It never fails—when you, yourself, are familiar with the Bible and its content, it is very easy to spot a counterfeit. As you will find, these false religions fish out different Bible names and attach them to their untrue stories. I will give you some scriptural examples.

The Urantia Book teaches evolution and that angels are subject to the process of evolution. Christians instead believe that angels are beings created by God. We read in Psalm 91:11, "For he shall give his angels charge over thee, to keep thee in all thy ways."

They claim that our ancestral parents were by name Andon and Fonta. We believe, according to the Bible, that they were Adam and Eve.

> And the LORD God planted a garden eastward in Eden; and there he put the man whom he had formed.... And the LORD God took the man, and put him into the garden of Eden to dress it and to keep it.... And the LORD God caused a deep sleep to fall upon Adam, and he slept: and he took one of his ribs, and closed up the flesh instead thereof; And the rib, which the LORD God had taken from man, made he a woman, and brought her unto the man.
>
> —GENESIS 2:8, 15, 21–22

They say in certain words that Rebecca wanted to be the wife of Jesus, yet our Bible states in Genesis 22:20–23:

> And it came to pass after these things, that it was told Abraham, saying, Behold, Milcah, she hath also born children unto thy brother Nahor; Huz his firstborn, and Buz his brother, and Kemuel the father of Aram, And Chesed, and Hazo, and Pildash, and Jidlaph, and Bethuel. And Bethuel begat Rebekah: these eight Milcah did bear to Nahor, Abraham's brother.

Rebekah was the wife of Isaac who became the mother of Jacob and Esau. Can you see this great deception? We are talking of about four thousand years' difference. But if you're not well-versed in the Bible, you can swallow it hook, line, and sinker.

Here is an actual excerpt from "The Bestowal of Michael on Urantia," paper 120 from The Urantia Book, Part IV:

> ...I, the Melchizedek director of the revelatory commission...am authorized to present this narrative of certain events....To live such identical lives as [Michael] imposes upon the intelligent beings of his own creation, thus to bestow himself in the likeness of his various orders of created beings, is a part of the price which every Creator Son must pay for the full and supreme sovereignty of his self-made universe...
>
> ...Michael of Nebadon had bestowed himself six times after the similitude of six differing orders of his diverse creation of intelligent beings. Then he prepared to descend upon Urantia in the likeness of mortal flesh, the lowest order of his intelligent will creatures...to execute the final act in the drama of the acquirement of universe sovereignty...
>
> In the course of each of these preceding bestowals Michael not only acquired the finite experience of one group of his created beings, but he also acquired an essential experience in Paradise co-operation which would, in and of itself, further contribute to constituting him the sovereign of his self-made universe. At any moment throughout all past local universe time, Michael could have asserted personal sovereignty as a Creator Son and as a Creator Son could have ruled his universe after the manner of his own choosing. In such an event, Immanuel and the associated Paradise Sons would have taken leave of the universe. But Michael...desired to ascend through actual experience in co-operative subordination to

> the Paradise Trinity to that high place in universe status where he would become qualified to rule his universe and administer its affairs with that perfection of insight and wisdom of execution which will sometime be characteristic of the exalted rule of the Supreme Being. He aspired not to perfection of rule as a Creator Son but to supremacy of administration...[23]

It all seems to go around in circles. The truth is that you can only get to heaven by accepting Jesus as your Savior.

About Melchizedek, my Bible reads in Genesis 14:18–20: "And Melchizedek king of Salem brought forth bread and wine: and he was the priest of the most high God. And he blessed him, and said, Blessed be Abram of the most high God, possessor of heaven and earth: And blessed be the most high God, which hath delivered thine enemies into thy hand. And he gave him tithes of all."

Many religious teachings lead people straight to hell; judge it for yourself. You can be as sincere as all get out; but unless you have accepted Jesus as Savior and made Him the Lord over your life, it will be impossible for you to enter heaven, because He only comes back for those that look for Him. Jesus Himself said, "No man cometh to the Father, but by Me" (John 14:6). I will list some more of the world's religions. If you compare them with the Bible, you will see without a doubt how they are deceiving their followers.

Buddhism

The Wheel of Dharma

The Sanskrit word *dharma* means "that which is established." It is the way of life a person embraces in order to achieve enlightenment and refers to both doctrine and duty. This belief was founded by Siddhartha Gautama, later to be known as "Buddha" in about 528 B.C. Siddhartha was an Indian *rajah* and head of the *Sakja* warrior caste. Though his family was elite, wealthy, and influential, he found his royal heritage empty and unfulfilling, and so he left in search of enlightenment, adopting the life of a wandering monk. He rejected traditional Hinduism, finding its caste system repellant.

Buddhists are taught to take refuge in "the dharma," which is the teaching of Buddha. Followers of this religion believe that Buddha's instructions to his disciples "set the wheel of dharma in motion." Their eight-spoke symbol represents the Eightfold Path.

Buddhists deny the existence of a personal god or say that God's existence is irrelevant. Christians say that God is personal, omniscient, and omnipotent. Buddhists identify Christ as a good teacher but less important than Buddha. Christians believe that Jesus Christ is the Son of God who died for the sins of all mankind, as described in Matthew 14:33, John 1:34, and Romans 5:6–8.

There are two divisions of Buddhism. Through reincarnation, one's desires or feelings "wander across" to another body, and one then lives another life, making further progress toward absorption into "the Absolute."

Judaism

> This modern term relates to the religious culture of the Jews, those who are identified historically and presently as the remnant of biblical Israel. Though Jews, as God's chosen people, trace their history back to the first man, Adam, their origin is primarily identified with the visitation Abraham

> received from God. At that time Abraham's seed were set apart as a special treasure to God. Moses is one of the most revered prophets in this religion. Through him came the revelation and codification of foundational religious laws of Judaism.[24]

The six-pointed Star of David, which has two inverted triangles, is a symbol for Judaism. It also appears on the Israeli flag. In Hebrew it is called the *magen David*, the Shield of David.

A majority of the Jews in Israel are currently unbelievers. But biblical prophecy indicates that this will change soon.

Jewish family life has always had a rich texture to it, and part of this involved the blessing of children by their parents. The Hebrew patriarchs Abraham, Isaac, and Jacob all blessed their sons. It has continued to the present, and a widely practiced custom today is blessing the children at the Sabbath meal.

The feasts of Jehovah, as given in Leviticus 23, were to be observed every year. Throughout Jewish history there had been two other feast days that they added on their own. Both were to commemorate their deliverance from enemies. You find the Feast of Purim was instituted in Esther 9:20–28, and the Feast of Dedication in 2 Maccabees 10:6–8. This feast, also known as Hanukkah, is the Jewish holiday commemorating the struggle of the Jews against Syria to regain their temple, and for national survival and religious freedom, celebrated on the victory of regaining their temple. The Hanukkah lights became an important part of the festival. The Books of the Maccabees do not report this incident, but it is a big part in the reason for our study. It is reported only by Josephus, the Jewish historian. It is a part of the Jewish tradition of the happenings of the Hanukkah festivities. It is said that when they began to cleanse and rededicate the temple, they found only enough consecrated oil to light the menorah for one day. The menorah is the lampstand of the wilderness tabernacle and the temple, which we can confirm in Exodus 25:31–40; 37:17–24. But at this time a miracle happened, and the oil, enough for just one day, lasted for eight days, allowing the priests to cleanse the temple and sanctify more oil. From this story the nine-branched candelabra arose, and in years to come, the Feast of Dedication also became known as the Feast of Lights, or the Jewish Hanukkah. My Jewish calendar confirms the dates from December 5 through December 12.

Kabbalah (Mystical Judaism)

This is the esoteric offshoot of Judaism. One of its main sacred texts is called the Zohar, which was written in Aramaic and claimed to be a commentary on the Torah. Debates for Kabbalah's origin continue to this day in spite of its growing popularity.

Scientology

I discovered the following report in a July–August 2007 issue of *Lamplighter* magazine:

> Tom Cruise has been declared the new "Christ" of Scientology, according to the leaders of the cultic religion. The movie star has been told that he has been "chosen" to spread the word of his faith throughout the world. David Miscavige, the leader of the religion, says that he believes that in the future, Cruise, age 44, will be worshipped like Jesus for his work to raise awareness of the religion. Jesus said, "Many will come

> in My name, saying, 'I am the Christ,' and will mislead many" [Matt. 24:5]. They have no doctrinal stance on dimensions of existence after death. There is no teaching on Heaven or Hell. Scientology is primarily concerned with the betterment of life here and now, as well as helping to produce a more sane civilization worldwide.[25]

One of my friends attended their meetings for a short time. She told me that the charge for their classes was very steep for the average person.

Many religions are practiced in America. But there is only one truth. Jesus said in John 3:3, "Verily, verily, I say unto thee, Except a man be born again, he cannot see the kingdom of God."

CHAPTER 9

THE ORIGIN OF THE BIBLE

The name "Bible" is derived from the Greek word *biblos*, meaning "book."[1]

The ONLY written revelation of God is found in the Bible. The Bible was completed around A.D. 95 when the Apostle John received the final revelation on the Isle of Patmos.[2]

JESUS SAID IN REVELATION 22:18, "For I testify unto every man that heareth the words of the prophecy of this book, If any man shall add unto these things, God shall add unto him the plagues that are written in this book."

We also read in 2 Timothy 3:16–17, "All scripture is given by inspiration of God, and is profitable for doctrine, for reproof, for correction, for instruction in righteousness: That the man of God may be perfect, thoroughly furnished unto all good works."

The content of the Bible is our manual for living.

> The Bible is made up of 66 different books that were written over 1600 years (from approximately 1500 B.C. to A.D. 100) by more than 40 kings, prophets, leaders, and followers of Jesus. The Old Testament has 39 books (written approximately 1500–400 B.C.). The New Testament has 27 books (written approximately A.D. 45–100). The Hebrew Bible has the same text as the English Bible's Old Testament, but divides and arranges it differently. The New Testament was written in Greek.
>
> The books of the Bible were collected and arranged and recognized as inspired sacred authority by councils of Rabbis as well of councils of Church leaders based on careful guidelines.[3]

The sacred writings of the Jews were divided into three parts:

- *The Law* is made up of the first five books of the Old Testament. They set forth the laws that God gave through Moses;
- *The Prophets* include the four "Former Prophets": Joshua, Judges, Samuel and Kings; and the "Latter Prophets": which consists of Isaiah, Jeremiah, Ezekiel, and the twelve Minor Prophets, twelve brief prophetical books contained in the single scroll. This is why they are looked upon as a single book.
- *The Writings* are divided into four sections: (a) Psalms, Proverbs, Job; (b) Song of Solomon, Ruth, Lamentations, Ecclesiastes, Esther; (c) Daniel; and (d) Ezra, Nehemiah, Chronicles.[4]

The Bible gives a consecutive history of mankind, starting with the story of creation and finishing with the close of history.

In English translations of the Old Testament, the thirty-nine books may be regarded as falling into four categories:

- History, the books from Genesis to Esther, including the Pentateuch;
- Poetry, the books from Job to the Song of Solomon;
- The Major Prophets, the books of Isaiah, Jeremiah, Ezekiel, and Daniel (with Lamentations, a brief poetical book);
- The Minor Prophets, the same brief poetical books spoken of by the Jews as "The Twelve."

The word 'Pentateuch,' derived from the Greek, means 'five books,' and is used to designate the first five books of the Old Testament. This section is also called 'The Law' or 'The Book of Moses,' following the Jewish tradition that these five books were written by Moses.

The twenty-seven New Testament books are also divided into four categories:

- History, including the four Gospels (i.e. books proclaiming the good news) And the book of Acts;
- Paul's Epistles, the books of Romans through Philemon;
- The General Epistles, the books of Hebrew through Jude;
- The Apocalypse, the book of the Revelation.[5]

> Before the printing press was invented, the Bible was very accurately copied by hand, in many cases by special scribes who developed intricate methods of counting words and letters to insure that no errors had been made...
>
> There is much evidence that the Bible we have today is remarkably true to the original writings. Of the thousand of copies made by hand before A.D. 1500, more than 5,300 Greek manuscripts from the New Testament alone still exist today. The text of the Bible is better preserved than the writings of Caesar, Plato, or Aristotle.
>
> The discovery of the Dead Sea Scrolls confirmed the astonishing reliability of some of the copies of the Old Testament made over the years. Although some spelling variations exist, no variation affects basic Bible doctrines.
>
> As the Bible was carried to other countries, it was translated into the common language of the people by scholars who wanted others to know God's Word. Today there are still 2,000 groups with no Bible in their own language. By A.D. 200, the Bible was translated into seven languages; by A.D. 500, 13 languages; by A.D. 900, 17 languages; by A.D. 1400, 28 languages; by 1800, 57 languages; by 1900, 537 languages; by 1980, 1,100 languages.[6]

I already mentioned that the Old Testament was approximately written between 1500–400 B.C. on stone, leather, and clay tablets. The oldest New Testament fragment (from John 18) that we have today was copied in Greek on a papyrus codex around A.D. 110–130. Scrolls of leather, and later of papyrus were used to make copies of the Scriptures. A papyrus codex is a bound volume made from sheets folded and sewn together, sometimes with a cover. They were used more than scrolls after A.D. 1–100. For the next one thousand years, from approximately A.D. 300–1400, fine quality animal skins from calves, antelopes, sheep, and goats provided the necessary materials. Two of the oldest copies (A.D. 325–350) that exist today are the Vatican Codex and the Sinaitic Codex. Wycliffe Bibles were inscribed by hand on vellum in the 1300s–1400s. Some copies took ten months to two years to produce and cost a year's wage.[7]

Now the Bible is printed on paper in many versions and languages. It is also available on tape recordings, compact discs, and computers. Therefore, no one has an excuse for not familiarizing themselves with the Word of God.

Between A.D. 45–100, Matthew, Mark, Luke, John, Paul, James, Peter, and Jude wrote the Gospels, history, letters to other Christians, and the Revelation. These writings, mostly in Greek, were copied and circulated so that by about A.D. 150 they were widely spread. People speak of these texts as the New Testament—the New Covenant. This new covenant that God made with His people was already promised in Jeremiah 31:31 "Behold, the days come, saith the LORD, that I will make a new covenant with the house of Israel, and with the house of Judah." Jesus referred to it in Luke 22:20: "This cup is the new testament in my blood, which is shed for you." Paul wrote about it in 1 Corinthians 12:25: "After the same manner also he took the cup, when he had supped, saying, this cup is the new testament in my blood: this do ye, as oft as ye drink it, in remembrance of me." Hebrews 9:15 also communicates this point: "And for this cause he is the mediator of the new testament, that by means of death, for the redemption of the transgressions that were under the first testament, they which are called might receive the promise of eternal inheritance."

> The church fathers accepted the writings of the Gospels and Paul's letters as canonical. *Canonical* [comes] from a Greek word referring to the rule of faith and truth.[8]

The earliest translations in to Latin; Coptic, which is Egyptian; and Syriac, which is Syrian, are from A.D. 200–300. Martin Luther translated the New Testament into German in 1522. The Matthews Bible, translated by John Rogers under the pen name Thomas Matthew, was the first Bible published with the king of England's permission in 1537. Finally, in 1539, the Great Bible was placed in every church by order of Thomas Cranmer, archbishop under King Henry VIII. It was chained to the church pillars to discourage theft. The King James Version of our day was first printed in 1611. Because the King James Bible was translated from the Greek *Textus Receptus*, we can be sure that it is accurate. Any version of the Bible that does not agree with this Greek version is certain to be founded on corrupted manuscripts.[9]

About sixty years ago as I was growing up in Germany, the Scriptures were still read in Latin by the priest. You can see how boring this was for everyone, and some of the older men fell asleep. I remember later on we heard it in the German language. We have come a long way. Since 1881 over three hundred versions of the Bible have been produced, though some of the later ones are deluded. I will give you different examples of these poor translations so you can see it firsthand.

Inaccuracy of The Living Bible (TLB)

> So the last shall be first, and the first last: for many be called, but few chosen.
>
> —Matthew 20:16, KJV

> And so it is that the last shall be first, and the first, last.
>
> —Matthew 20:16, TLB

"But few chosen," is completely missing from The Living Bible's version of Matthew 20:16! Luke 9:55–56 is also missing text. The words in italics in the King James Scripture below are, as you can see, omitted from The Living Bible.

> But he turned, and rebuked them, *and said, Ye know not what manner of spirit ye are of. For the Son of man is not come to destroy men's lives, but to save them.* And they went to another village.
>
> —Luke 9:55–56, kjv, emphasis added

> But Jesus turned and rebuked them, and they went on to another village.
>
> —Luke 9:55–56, tlb

Notice how the doctrine about salvation ("thou shalt both save thyself, and them that hear thee") is changed in The Living Bible to one of blessing.

> Take heed unto thyself, and unto the doctrine; continue in them: for in doing this thou shalt both save thyself, and them that hear thee.
>
> —1 Timothy 4:16, kjv

> Keep a close watch on all you do and think. Stay true to what is right and God will bless you and use you to help others.
>
> —1 Timothy 4:16, tlb

Inaccuracy of the American Standard Version (asv)

The American Standard Version has removed the word *fasting* from the two following scriptures:

> And Cornelius said, Four days ago I was fasting until this hour; and at the ninth hour I prayed in my house, and, behold, a man stood before me in bright clothing.
>
> —Acts 10:30, kjv

> Cornelius replied, "Four days ago I was praying as usual at this time of the afternoon, when suddenly a man was standing before me clothed in a radiant robe!"
>
> —Acts 10:30, asv

> And he said unto them, This kind can come forth by nothing, but by prayer and fasting.
>
> —Mark 9:29, kjv

> Jesus replied, "Cases like this require prayer."
>
> —Mark 9:29, asv

Luke 4:4 is missing a crucial part of Jesus' instruction to believers about how we are to live as Christians.

> And Jesus answered him, saying, It is written, That man shall not live by bread alone, *but by every word of God.*
>
> —Luke 4:4, kjv, emphasis added

> But Jesus replied, "It is written in the Scriptures, 'Other things in life are much more important than bread!'"
>
> —Luke 4:4, asv

Inaccuracy of the New International Version (niv)

> But go ye and learn what that meaneth, I will have mercy, and not sacrifice: for I am not come to call the righteous, but sinners *to repentance.*
>
> —Matthew 9:13, kjv, emphasis added

> But go and learn what this means: 'I desire mercy, not sacrifice.' For I have not come to call the righteous, but sinners."
>
> —MATTHEW 9:13, NIV

The concept of repentance is left out of the above scripture in the New International Version.

The translator's own agenda is also clear in the following example:

> Wherefore, beloved, seeing that ye look for such things, *be diligent* that ye may be found of him in peace, without spot, and blameless.
>
> —2 PETER 3:14, KJV, EMPHASIS ADDED

> So then, dear friends, since you are looking forward to this, *make every effort* to be found spotless, blameless and at peace with him.
>
> —2 PETER 3:14, NIV, EMPHASIS ADDED

There is a big difference between diligence and making an effort; the former implies tenacity, while "effort" is a more casual attempt.

The New International Version completely omits Matthew 17:21! The King James Version reads, "Howbeit this kind goeth not out but by prayer and fasting." However, in the New International Version, verse 20 is the end of the chapter.

Inaccuracy of the New King James Version (NKJV)

> Yea, and all that will live godly in Christ Jesus shall suffer persecution.
>
> —2 TIMOTHY 3:12, KJV

> Yes, and all who desire to live godly in Christ Jesus will suffer persecution.
>
> —2 TIMOTHY 3:12, NKJV

It is clear from the previous example that the New King James Version makes no distinction between actually living a godly lifestyle and merely desiring to do so. This is misleading.

Even small words can drastically alter the meaning of a sentence. The two-letter change in the following versions of the same scripture is the difference between an instruction about *what* Christians are called to do (the King James) and *how* we are called (the New King James).

> According as his divine power hath given unto us all things that pertain unto life and godliness, through the knowledge of him that hath called us *to* glory and virtue.
>
> —2 PETER 1:3, KJV, EMPHASIS ADDED

> As His divine power has given to us all things that pertain to life and godliness, through the knowledge of Him who called us *by* glory and virtue.
>
> —2 PETER 1:3, NKJV, EMPHASIS ADDED

Chapter 10

Personal Prophecies

It is amazing how the Holy Spirit can reveal to us certain happenings in our life and foretell them years before they take place. He confirmed through prophecy numerous such realities, sometimes precisely for what I was going through right at the time of the prophecy or experiences that were to come in the future. In this chapter, I have transcribed a number of them that came through the mouth of others that were recorded for me on audiotapes. As you continue to read, you will discover that some of these prophecies were specifically for the pastor from the conservative Baptist church, while others were without a doubt for my ministry to the Muslims. One of them confirmed that I was a sent one by the Holy Spirit.

In October 1986, I received my first awesome prophesy from the Seattle prophetess, which was very fitting for me. I wrote it in Chapter 3 of Volume 3, *Is Mohammed Mentioned in the Bible?*

> As time went by I received more: The Lord gives me Ezekiel 33:7: "I made you a watchman for the house of Israel; so hear

the Word I tell you and give them warning from Me" [NIV]. God has made you a watchman. You're as a watchman for the people of God. He gives you words to speak, words of warning. The Lord is encouraging you, that you have been chosen by God to speak the Word of God.

In Ezekiel 37:4–6 [it says], "Prophesy to these bones and say to them, 'Dry bones, hear the word of the LORD! This is what the Sovereign LORD says to these bones: I will make breath enter you, and you will come to life. I will attach tendons to you and make flesh come upon you and cover you with skin; I will put breath in you, and you will come to life. Then you will know that I am the LORD'" [NIV]. The Lord is saying, "Daughter, I made you a mouthpiece for Me; speak forth the Word of God, as you have never spoken it before. And you will see, even as you bring healing to others, I will bring healing to you. I will make tendons come, flesh to come, that which is lacking will come. In the dead churches there will be life." And that is what I see God is using you.

You have brought life in to many, many temples, individual temples, as well as collective churches, collective temples inside a church. In other words, people that are in a church. I see some coming alive in a church and then they bring life to their church. And it is because you prophesied to these dry denominational people, those dry people that have not heard the word of the Lord. You have spoken, you brought breath into them, you brought flesh into them, and they in turn have gone to others and brought life. Thank You, Jesus; thank You, Jesus! There are some places were *Ichabod* was written over the church, but the Lord is saying, "Daughter, you did not fail, for the Lord has given man free will, and if they have rejected My Word, that's their problem, not yours." (*Ichabod* means that there is no anointing present.)

And so the Lord is saying, "You speak, I will water that which you plant, and I will have those come and harvest at the right time." And if there is no harvest, it's like the fig tree, where there was no harvest so the Lord cursed it. The Lord is saying to you, "Don't take the responsibility of the fruit coming forth. You are to plant the seed and leave the results to the Lord and the purposes of God." Thank You, Jesus; thank You, Lord.

Some of the seeds you have sown in the dead churches may not come forth that season, but may spring forth another season. I see some seed dormant; it's like God miraculously kept that seed alive during the winter and the next summer that seed brought forth life. You're going to see life come forth in churches that you have ministered in and people that you have ministered to, but you thought that you failed. And the Lord says, "No, you didn't fail, because you planted My Word and My Word will not return void."

The Lord gives me Hosea 4:6: "My people are destroyed from lack of knowledge" [NIV]. The Lord wants you to know that you're to bring forth knowledge. You have been used by God to bring forth the knowledge that He shows you. I see this as a progressive knowledge. It's like you have some old notes that you have taught before. But the Lord wants you to know that you're going to have new revelation in the days ahead that will delight you. I see, sometimes when you get bogged down, it's like you're thinking, What else is there to say? And you might even get tired of the repetition. The Lord wants you to know as you seek Him and as you're in the flow of what God is saying to the church, you're going to have new revelation and exiting things that will so excite you that as you give it, it will bring new energy to you, a new sense of urgency to get that knowledge to the people of God. It's like a new vaccine that has been discovered, and when it is discovered, the first thing they want to do is get it out to everybody. For instance, if they had an AIDS vaccine, and they knew it, everyone with AIDS would want it yesterday. I see, as God brings revelation, you find an urgency to get that word out to save those who have been inflicted by that bondage or disease.

Father, we just stir up the gifts of the Spirit in Your daughter, according to 2 Timothy 1:6–7, and, Lord, we fan into flame the gifts for Your daughter. We thank You that she has not the spirit of timidity, but of power. And Lord, let that power rise up, the power to heal, the power to discern, the power for the prophetic word to come forth, and the ministry gifts, Lord, now in Jesus' name. And we thank You that she has that love and self discipline now in Jesus' name. Amen.

The Lord gives me Isaiah 26:7: "The way of the just is uprightness: thou, most upright, dost weigh the path of the just."

The Lord is saying, "Daughter, even as you see My hand in judgment coming on the earth, there are many who will not learn righteousness until judgment comes. This can be a personal judgment, this can be the struggles, the pains, the circumstances of a person's life; or it can be even like the earthquake. But you're to encourage people in the time of…personal disaster or worldly disaster, that the people of the world learn righteousness."

And sometimes we look at what's happening in Los Angeles, [the earthquake] and say, "Why, Lord?" They are Christians who are suffering, but [it is so] that the world learns righteousness. What the enemy meant for evil, the Lord will turn for good. The Lord is wanting you to speak His love more and His compassion. Let the compassion of God flow through you. As you give a word to somebody, if it is a hard word, pray until you weep before you give that word, because only then can it come out of a broken heart for that person's correction.

The Lord gives me Lamentations 3:22–24: "Because of the LORD's great love we are not consumed, for his compassions never fail. They are new every morning; great is your faithfulness. I say to myself, 'The LORD is my portion; therefore I will wait for him'" [NIV]. Lord, we just thank You, as Your daughter waits before You, that love that You have for Your people will consume her, and out of that love shall come ministry that shall bear much fruit, much fruit, Lord. We just thank You that You are putting Your love and Your compassion in the body of Christ, that the world will see Your love and be drawn to You through our love. Lord, it's hard to wait; sometimes we get impatient.

> The LORD is good to those whose hope is in him,
> to the one who seeks him; it is good to wait quietly
> for the salvation of the LORD.
>
> —LAMENTATIONS 3: 25–26, NIV

Father we just thank You for patience to wait before You, for Your salvation. I see, Tilly, that you've tried to reach out to those who are not baptized in the Holy Spirit, but the Lord is saying, wait quietly for the salvation of the Lord. Sometimes it takes months and years; just sit there and wait quietly, wait quietly. Lord, give Your daughter grace to wait, and that's hard for a German, right, in Jesus' name. Amen.

The Lord is saying, "Daughter, you've seen the new wave of My Spirit, but you've just seen the tip of the iceberg. You shall see things in your day that you would not believe, even if you were told."

He gives me Haggai 2:9: "'The glory of this present house will be greater than the glory of the former house,' says the

Lord Almighty. 'And in this place I will grant peace,' declares the Lord Almighty'" [NIV]. You are that house. The Lord is saying, "There is going to be greater glory, in other words, greater manifest presence of the living God in you in the latter days than ever in the former days." The Lord is saying, "I'm increasing, and increasing, and increasing My power through the body, through the house of the Lord. With this greater anointing of God upon your life, you will find a greater peace and a greater knowledge of the direction of the Lord that He is directing you. He is going before you, and He is giving you power. He is giving you His authority. He gives me Haggai 2:23: "'And I will make you like my signet ring, for I have chosen you,' declares the LORD Almighty" [NIV]. A signet ring is authority. As you use His ring as a seal of power and authority, the Lord is saying, "I'm giving you that ring, for you have been faithful in the past and I shall pour out My Spirit in these days." It's like you've seen it dripping down, but it's going to come gushing, it's going to come like a river, the power of God.

And He gave me Habakkuk 1:5: "Look at the nations and watch—and be utterly amazed. For I am going to do something in your days that you would not believe, even if you were told" [NIV]. And Habakkuk 2:14: "For the earth will be filled with the knowledge of the glory of the LORD, as the waters cover the sea" [NIV]. The Lord is saying, "Daughter, I'm going to send you to the nations, time after time. There will be doors that open to you, even in your own country in Germany that were never open before, that were closed, but because of My Spirit going before you, there will be doors open that you will walk in." The Lord shows me a red carpet put out before you, which means they are going to receive you as royalty, as from the Lord Himself. Thank you, Jesus.

I sense, some places you've been, the Lord is saying, "You are not to go back; you're not to go back. I'm going to open new doors for you—and doors where the people understand you and you understand them, and they feed from the spiritual food you give them. And I just see, as German food is very different from Chinese food and you can't make Germans eat Chinese food and visa versa, the Lord is saying, "Go and feed My people. Feed My people, for there is a hunger there, but you have to feed the right people, because it will be rejected by those who don't want to receive it but will be received by those who are looking for the good, basic German food." Lord, let Your daughter understand what You are saying here.

There is coming a healing between many of the tragedies that have happened in this world, the tragedies that have happened in Germany, the tragedies that have happened to the Jews, the tragedies between the blacks and the Native Americans here. God is bringing worldwide forgiveness by people repenting. The Lord is saying, "This is opening the way for you to go in." It's something that's happening in the Spirit world all over the nations, all over the world, in many nations. The Lord is saying, "It will open doors for you to go. You're to forget the former things; in other words, forget the former trips God's given you, because He is opening new doors." [Since this word was given, He has closed the doors to Ghana for me, and I have stopped all communication with them.]

He gave me Revelation 3:7–8: "What he opens no one can shut, and what he shuts no one can open. I know your deeds. See, I have placed before you an open door that no one can shut. I know that you have little strength, yet you have kept my word and have not denied my name" [NIV]. Thank You, Jesus. Father, we thank You for that new anointing that is being poured out on the body today. And Lord, You're showing me that it's knee-deep now, but You want it to come way over our heads. You want Your daughter to swim in this new anointing. And Lord, as it comes, it has nothing to do with her, but has all to do with You, Lord. She is going to be right out there knee-deep, and she is saying, "More, Lord; more Lord." I see that anointing rising up, and, "You shall swim in that anointing," saith the Lord. And Father, we thank You. With that anointing there are new doors that You will open for Your people, and we bless Your daughter now in Jesus' name. Amen.

Lord, I thank You for Your Word for her. The Lord gives me Daniel 6:26: "For he is the living God and he endures forever; his kingdom will not be destroyed, his dominion will never end. He rescues and he saves; he performs signs and wonders in the heavens and on the earth. He has rescued Daniel from the power of the lions" [NIV]. I see the Lord rescuing you by giving you a new vision of what He has for this time, for this day. I see you as one to encourage people now. You groomed them, you encouraged them, and now there is going to be an encouragement to release them to minister in a deeper way, in a more fulfilling way. I see this is the day you have been waiting for. It's like you were before your time; you had a vision and you're a "goer." A lot of people need years to get ready to do what the Lord is saying. You heard what He is saying and you went.

It's like the Lord is saying, "You're going to see the masses come up behind you now, and you're not going to be alone." But there are going to be masses coming, and they are going to follow you. It's like you're out leading the parade, but they are going to follow you. And then I see some quite young people coming up, and they are going to pass you up, and you sort of get lost in the center of this parade. But that doesn't stop you. You're still going on. And I see the Lord looking down from heaven and see these young people [who have] come to carry the torch that's in the heart of God, but you're there, too. The Lord looks down and sees you there, and it's like all these young people are going to go fast in the things of God. They are not going to be entangled with a lot of things that the older people—our generation—has had to be entangled with.

The Lord is saying, "Daughter, but you have sent the young ones out. And as you see them go forth, be their audience to cheer them on, because they need it; they are going to need mothering." I see as they go on, some get trampled, and that is why you're back there, further back in the parade, because you see the ones that get trampled on. I see you picking them up and nursing them back to spiritual health that they might go on again. I see the enemy has someone on the rooftop like a sniper; he has a bow and arrow and picks off one here, one there. But because you're back in the parade, you see the ones that are picked off by the enemy and nurse them back to health. Thank You, Jesus.

The enemy would not target someone who is not mightily used by God; he targets those that God has a special calling on their lives. The Lord is saying that you pick up those that have been targeted by the enemy and get them moving. Sometimes they are pastors, sometimes they are leaders. They are not just the average Christian, but they are people that are moving on in God. The Lord says, "As you bring healing to them and encourage them to go on, you shall reap part of their reward of the souls that they bring in." I see them going on and maybe you're already in heaven, yet you're still receiving reward for their souls, because you have encouraged them to go on in the things of God.

The Lord gave me Luke 12:4: "I tell you, my friends, do not be afraid of those who kill the body and after that can do no more" [NIV]. God is going to challenge you to go places where death could come, but the Lord says, "Do not be afraid of those who kill the body and after that can do no more." Lord, we thank You that You're giving Your daughter vision for new doors to open—and dangerous doors, but You will give the grace for her to go wherever You want her to go. In Jesus' name, amen.

JANUARY 5, 1994

The Lord gave me Psalm 119:105: "Your Word is a lamp to my feet and a light for my path" [NIV]. You have loved the Word, and you have believed the Word. You are going to find the Word with a new power in the very words that you speak. Words that you have spoken in the past. The Lord sent that Word—it was to accomplish what was in His plan. You are going to find that in the days ahead you will be using the same Word and yet much more will be accomplished. I see as a farmer plants a field of wheat; and one year there maybe be just a few bushels from that acre, but the next year for no reason that has to do with him, that field produces a hundred-fold over that which it has produced the year before—because God touched it, because God sent the rain at the right time, because God sent the sunshine at the right time. The Lord is saying, "You're going to see a new yield of the wheat coming that the barns will be full." I see many people who will be sent out because you encouraged them and because you discipled them, and you trained them to bring others into the harvest. Thank You, Jesus.

And just as David, as he was anointed, the first thing that he had to deal with after his being anointed in 1 Samuel 16—he met the Goliath. Yet, he had already destroyed the lion and the bear. So, he knew from those smaller beginnings that somehow, some way, God was going to work through him to destroy Goliath. The Lord is saying that you are a David. You have faced the bear, you have faced the lion, and you have faced your Goliath. In this day there is a new touch, a new anointing. As David had three anointings on his life, with each anointing there came a greater measure of responsibility. The Lord is saying...you're going to see that; you're going to know that this year God has done something and that anointing is greater than ever before. Hallelujah.

David was misunderstood. He at times felt like nobody cared and that his life was just going downhill, and yet each time God brought someone into his life and gave him the strength to rise above his circumstance. The Lord is saying, "Daughter, you have risen like David. Every time those circumstances were designed to bring you down." What the enemy meant for evil, the Lord moved in your life. And you cooperated with Him and brought good out of it. I see a strength in you that God has put there through the trials of your life. Hallelujah.

The Lord gives me 1 Samuel 17:47: "All those gathered here will know that it is not by sword or spear that the LORD saves; for the battle is the LORD's, and he will give all of you into our hands" [NIV]. Hallelujah. The Lord is saying that many times this year you will remember this verse. As you will be faced with this, know that the battle is the Lord's. That He will give all of them into your hands. David had to go out and face the giant; that is the hardest part. You can stay in the prayer closet and say, "OK, Lord, take care of the giants." That would be easy, but David had to go out and face the giant, staring face to face in the giant's face is the hard part. The Lord is saying, "People are the giants in your life." I see a confidence coming in you that the Lord will take care of those giants. In fact, it is almost like, "I don't have time to be bothered with those giants." The giants are not going to slow you down like they have in the past, because of your knowing who you are, that you're anointed of the Lord and that you are about your Father's business.

Lord, we thank You for redeeming the time in Your daughter's life. She is going to find more fruit coming forth from her life, because those giants will be destroyed more quickly than ever before, by faith and by her knowledge of Your faithfulness to her. In Jesus' name, amen.

May 6, 1995

The Lord gave me Acts 4:29–31: "'Now, Lord, consider their threats and enable your servants to speak your word with great boldness. Stretch out your hand to heal and perform miraculous signs and wonders through the name of your holy servant Jesus.' After they prayed, the place where they were meeting was shaken. And they were all filled with the Holy Spirit and spoke the word of God boldly" [NIV]. I see you ministering with a plow that you have to hold, and a horse that is not always very active, wanting to work. The Lord says, "Daughter, you have been faithful with that which you had, but I'm giving you new equipment. You no longer will have that horse and that plow, but I'm going to give you a tractor. And you're going to see, it won't have to stop to eat; it won't have to stop to get more water. Yes, you have to give it gas, but it lasts all day long."

The Lord is saying, "You have seen My glory, and you're going to see it more in the days ahead." It's almost like I see you ahead of people, ahead of time, actually; not only ahead of people, but also ahead of your time in that what you have seen and thought what would happen now, is still yet in the future. The Lord is saying, "Just relax, know what you have in your heart is one day coming upon this earth." He gives me Isaiah 43:18–19 "Forget the former things; do not dwell on the past. See, I am doing a new thing! Now it springs up; do you not perceive it? I am making a way in the desert and streams in the wasteland" [NIV]. Father, we just bless Your daughter now, in Jesus' name, amen.

March 16, 1996

The Lord gave me Ezekiel 34:26: "I will bless them and the places surrounding my hill. I will send down showers in season; there will be showers of blessing" [NIV]. The Lord is pouring out His showers of blessing around you. Spiritually, the Lord is saying, "I'm the One that calls for the water." He gives me Amos 9:6: "Who calls for the waters of the sea and pours them out over the face of the land—the Lord is his name" [NIV]. The Lord is saying, "Daughter, you have seen the revival; you have seen the refreshing; you have stood under the refreshing of the Lord. As your praises [have] gone up, down has come the rain." The praise and prayers form the clouds that ascend to heaven, the glory cloud, and then the Lord turns that praise and prayer to the rain that waters you. The rain satisfies your thirst; the rain falls upon you to bless you, to bring refreshing to many.

I see people coming up with their empty cups, and they are saying, "Lord, fill my cup, fill my cup." And out of what God has done in you, you're filling these cups with the fresh rain of the Lord. And with rain, you think of water, but Jesus' first miracle was to turn water into wine. The Lord says, "This rain is the new wine that is being poured out on the body of

Christ to bring the harvest in, in this day." The Lord is saying, "Keep the prayers going; keep doing what you're doing, and you're going to see a tremendous awakening in the body of Christ, especially in ministers, as you have been bold to minister to ministers." The Lord says, "There are some that are quite hard, but they don't know it; they are quite stubborn." He gives me Ezekiel 2:4–8:

> The people to whom I am sending you are obstinate and stubborn. Say to them, "This is what the Sovereign LORD says." And whether they listen or fail to listen—for they are a rebellious house—they will know that a prophet has been among them. And you, son of man, do not be afraid of them or their words...You must speak my words to them, whether they listen or fail to listen, for they are rebellious...open your mouth and eat what I give you. [NIV]

As you have ministered to many different people, you've been able to keep your shield of faith up and ward off the darts. I see some that were rebellious are now praising God for you. And you may not always hear them do that; you may not always get to hear from their lips what is going on in their heart, because they're rebellious, and pride is one of the things that's so difficult. The Lord says, "Come to Me and let Me reassure you, let Me bless you. Don't look for anything from man. If you get something, then you can praise the Lord; but don't expect anything and then you won't be disappointed."

The Lord says, "Keep speaking My Word." He gives me Matthew 7:24–25: "Therefore everyone who hears these words of mine and puts them into practice is like a wise man who built his house on the rock. The rain came down, the streams rose, and the winds blew and beat against that house; yet it did not fall, because it had its foundation on the rock" [NIV]. Lord, we bless Your daughter for enabling many to establish their lives on You, Lord Jesus, the Rock. Lord, give Your daughter even greater anointing in the days ahead, for the work of the gospel for the days ahead.

Some that you have ministered to—I don't know what's happening in the world, but there are some things brewing. The ones you ministered to, they're going to take notice of the things that you've said. It's not going to really take a lot of effect with some of them until what is happening in the world scares them into the kingdom. So keep speaking.

JUNE 4, 1996

The Lord gave me an interesting scripture for you—Ezekiel 9:4: "Go throughout the city of Jerusalem and put a mark on the foreheads of those who grieve and lament over all the detestable things that are done in it" [NIV]. What I see [is that] God sends you to places to destroy the idolatry. Whether it's in Jerusalem or wherever He sends you; to the Muslims, to different places. The Lord says, "As you go through the city, even as you pray or speak, putting a mark on their forehead means changing their thinking, giving them truth, taking out the lie as you see the detestable things that are in the minds of the people." I see you placing God in there, as you speak, as you minister, as you send materials or leave materials behind. It's like you putting a mark on their forehead, and right behind their forehead is their brain. It is marking their understanding of the idolatry. "Thou shall have no other gods before Me." I see you taking away the false gods and putting in the real God. Thank you, Jesus. [This mainly refers to the Muslims. As I speak to them or they read this book, a revelation of who the true God is comes to them. Also in this country, many, including some pastors, will realize that they've only been exposed to a partial gospel, instead of the full gospel's preaching and teaching.]

The Lord says, "Make sure that you are fully armed with the armor of God, because you're on the front lines doing battle and not everybody understands this; not everybody understands the demonic powers that come against you." Yet God has set certain ones around you to pray for you. He gave me Ephesians 6:10–13: "Finally, be strong in the Lord and in his mighty power. Put on the full armor of God so that you can take your stand against the devil's schemes. For our struggle is not against flesh and blood, but against the rulers, against the authorities, against the powers of this dark world and against the spiritual forces of evil in the heavenly realms. Therefore put on the full armor of God" [NIV]. I see you sleeping with your combat boots on. Even in your sleep you're fully armed. But the Lord says, when I send you to other countries there are times when you will meet up with enemies you have not met before. What I'm seeing is that He is saying, "Take special warriors with you, who are intercessors that will dress you with prayer." And I see that their prayers are putting on your armor that you have never had to use before.

But yet, when the enemy comes, you're able to reach for your uniform and pull out that hand grenade or whatever is needed—[like] the knife in your boot, because a bomb will not always do it. Sometimes a knife in your boot will distort the enemy better than a gunshot, which would alert others. The Lord is saying, "I called you as a Green Beret; go in and destroy one-on-one very often the enemy's gun, so that the rest of the people can come in without being shot at."

> Lord, we bless Your daughter, we thank You that You're protecting her, surround her with warriors, even people You wake up in the middle of the night and remind them to pray. That is what I see—you don't even know the ones that are praying for you, Tilly, but God has called forth an army to be around you to pray. Father, bless her. Lord, we thank You that she is strong in the Lord and she is strong in Your mighty power. May she see that mighty power bring forth many souls in the harvest of this day. Lord, may she see herself capturing the enemy and putting a final destruction to the enemy. I don't see you taking them away and putting them in concentration camps. You're doing away with them; you're sending them where the Lord wants them to go. Lord, we thank you that it is a one-way gate. When she uses her authority in the Lord to cast out demons, they are gone, because—I don't know how you pray—but I see them going to await the final day of destruction. It is a one-way gate and they can't get out and get into someone else. Lord, we bless her now in Jesus' name, amen.

All this ammunition she is talking about is strictly spiritual. The one-way gate means that when people read this book, they will get spiritual understanding and will be set free from whatever false denominational and demonic beliefs are controlling them. The demons of all these false religions cannot escape. Once the people read and hear the truth, they await their destruction, since they can't escape through the gate. I had already written the chapter to the Muslims when she gave me this prophetic word. Then a year later I wrote a chapter called "God's Love Letter to the Jews." The Holy Spirit revealed to me that when both groups read these books the scales will fall from their eyes and they will get a revelation of who the real God is. Many other believers—American and foreign—will also have their eyes opened, since a lot of them are indoctrinated by their own religions and are only taught a partial gospel. An awesome revival is just around the corner. Are you ready and as excited as I am to punch the devil's lights out?

All the above were given to me over a period of several years by the same prophetess from Seattle, Washington. Her husband is a retired pastor from a large church in the Seattle area. She was given this prophetic gift from God over thirty years ago, which has allowed her to travel halfway around the world numerous times prophesying in churches and even to high government officials. Each and every person I have talked to over the years told me that she is right on with what she tells a person as she hears it from the Holy Spirit.

The following is from a lady who is the president of one of the Woman's Aglow chapters in Seattle. At the end a Full Gospel Business Men's Fellowship International president finished the prophecy.

May 24, 1997

> I feel led to anoint you with oil. Lord, in the name of Jesus, we lift You, heavenly Father, and praise and magnify Your holy name. You're exalted above the heavens and above everything, every creature, every person. O mighty God, we lift up this servant before you, O God. Lord, in the name of Jesus, she has a heart for the things of God, for the move

of Your Spirit. Lord, her heart is wide open to the things of God. She has facilitated Your program, O God, Your move to bring true revival into this region, into this place, because she has a hunger for the things of God; not church as usual, but a real move of God upon the hearts of men and women to see souls delivered.

Lord, even as we pray, Lord, I lift her up, O God. The enemy has tried to attack her, Lord. He's tried to attack her self-worth; he's tried to attack her physical well-being; he's tried to attack her emotions. But, O God, tonight we form a hedge around her, with prayers to the Most High. He that abides under the shadow of the most high, will dwell under the protection, under the provision and the providence of God. O God, we call it providence for this woman; we call it provision for this woman; we call it protection for this woman. O God, as she has labored, Lord—as Dorcas labored with her hands—to facilitate the gospel, even when she was sick unto dead, and has indeed died, because her work spoke for the things for the kingdom of God. You brought her back from the brink of death, that she might work some more; and now Lord, we pray that those things that the enemy tried to dry up, the things that he tried to cause to die, the things he tried to cause to stop this woman, we bind it in the name of Jesus; and we release the power of the Holy Spirit to move on her behalf. Dispatch heavenly angels, O Lord, to be around her home. Yes, Lord, around her finances, O God. Lord, in the name of Jesus, the very works of her hands—prosper them in the mighty name of Jesus. We pray an anointing upon her, everything she puts her hands to do, O God, in the name of Jesus. Put out a blessing that she is not able to receive, Lord. Let it be pressed down and running over, in the name of Jesus. For You know that she'll give it to the kingdom of God, You know, Lord, that she'll declare Your works. You know, Lord, that she will facilitate the work of God.

O God, today Lord, touch her body, strengthen her while she sleeps. O God, build up the places that are torn down, in Jesus' name. I see (in the spirit) the Lord saying He is making you like a fortified city overcoming the things that used to disturb you. You are a strong woman; it takes a lot to move you. But He says, there have been some things that disturbed you, and He is filling in the breach. He said, that is not going to disturb you, because you have been surrounded by the Holy One. You've been surrounded by the angels God dispatched on your behalf. And the Lord says, "Greater is He that's within you, than he that's in the world." He says, "Don't have any fear, and neither be thou dismayed. Though the wind may blow and the storms may rage like that city built on a rock." He says He has established you and prospered you for the kingdom of God. Thank You, Lord. Hallelujah.

Then he continued with these scriptures in Ezekiel 36:24–27 "For I will take you from among the heathen, and gather you out of all countries, and will bring you into your own land. Then will I sprinkle clean water upon you, and ye shall be clean: from all your filthiness, and from all your idols, will I cleanse you. A new heart also will I give you, and a new spirit will I put within you: and I will take away the stony heart out of your flesh, and I will give you an heart of flesh. And I will put my spirit within you, and cause you to walk in my statutes, and ye shall keep my judgments, and do them."

The Lord is just going to fill you more and more with His love. You're going to glow in the darkness with the love of Jesus. Hallelujah. (Now, that's figuratively.)

Since then I received several more messages from the Seattle prophetess.

JANUARY 7, 1997

Lord, I thank You for Your Word for her. The Lord gave me Acts 28:23–24: "From morning till evening he explained and declared to them the kingdom of God and tried to convince them about Jesus from the Law of Moses and from the Prophets. Some were convinced by what he said, but others would not believe" [NIV]. I see you like Paul was, from morning to night—that is the main thing that is on your heart. How will I go about declaring the kingdom of God? How will I go about it? The Lord says, "Paul could not convince everybody, and Jesus could not convince everybody, so you cannot convince everybody. Just know that you're planting the seed in their lives and someone else will take up from where you left off. It's not a loss. Just like many times Paul was probably touched by things he saw, but it took a Damascus Road experience for him to change." The Lord is saying, "You're preparing some for a Damascus Road experience," and for you to know to keep on doing what you're doing, to know that your life will be from morning to evening.

You're trying to explain to them and declare to them the kingdom of God and trying to convince them about Jesus. The Lord is pleased that it's on your heart, because the Lord put it on your heart. You would not still be motivated to do that if it wasn't the Lord that placed it on your heart, because the warfare is too great. He gave me Acts 4:29–30: "Now, Lord, consider their threats and enable your servants to speak your word with great boldness. Stretch out your hand to heal and perform miraculous signs and wonders through the name of your holy servant Jesus" [NIV]. You're going to see more miracles performed, signs and wonders. In 1997 you're going to begin to see what you declared and wondered why at times it didn't happen, sometimes it did, other times it didn't.

But you're going to see God sovereignly move on the whole body of Christ, and as He does, it is like He is releasing a new power. I used to have a car that had a turbo motor in it, which I understand is an extra little motor that when you need to have power, it kicks in. I see God is putting turbo in the body of Christ for 1997. All you have to do is to step on the gas a little bit and it is there. You don't have to hook up a new engine. You don't have to do anything, it is already there; and God is stepping on the gas for us. He is hooking up that turbo, and you're going to see things happen you have never seen before. Thank You, Lord. I see you returning to pastors and congregations what the enemy had stolen from them. He gave me John 10:10: "The thief comes only to steal and kill and destroy; I have come that they may have life, and have it to the full" [NIV].

And that is what you do. You hate to see pastors ripped off by lack of knowledge or by blindness or by a spirit of religion. The Lord says, "Wear a bulletproof vest, because the policemen and detectives that catch the thief have to be well protected, because they don't know what will happen. Sometimes a thief, when he gets caught, overreacts out of fear. He may not have meant to shoot the policeman, but he did and then he spent his time in prison. Some have shot at you out of fear. They're sorry afterwards, but if you're protected, the bullet flies right off." The Lord has taught you how to wear a bulletproof vest, and I even see a helmet on.

The Lord says, "Be well prepared for the thief to fight back. I'm the good shepherd, the good shepherd lays down his life for the sheep. The hired hand is not the shepherd who owns the sheep. When he sees the wolf coming, he abandons the sheep and runs away. Then the wolf attacks the flock and scatters it. The man runs away because he is a hired hand and cares nothing for the sheep. I'm the good shepherd I know My sheep, and My sheep know Me. I see you coming in when the shepherd has lost the ability to shepherd the sheep. Either they are a hired hand or run out of fear or lack of knowledge. A lot of time it is fear, fear of losing what they have, and by holding on to what they have, they lose it anyway" (John 10:11–14, NIV).

Lord, we ask Your blessing upon Your daughter now. All that has been stolen from the shepherds and the congregations, this woman will return much of the stolen goods. Give her wisdom, Lord, wherever she travels, whether it is to this place or that place. The Lord is not letting you grow moss under your feet. He is going to keep you traveling in different places. He is going to send you to the desert, to hot countries. Lord, bless her in Jesus' name. We thank You for a new anointing in 1997 that You're pouring out on Your body. Even now, Lord, You're pouring it out, and may many come to drink from this woman and the living water that she has to pour out to others in Jesus' name, amen.

MAY 10, 1997

Father, we thank You for Your daughter. I hear the Lord saying that you worked, for the night is coming when man's work will be done. He gave me 1 John 4:4: "You, dear children, are from God and have overcome them, because the one who is in you is greater than the one who is in the world" [NIV]. I see you had many things thrown at you. I see you putting your arm up. Things have been thrown at you, like tin cans and everything. I see you like Stephen saying, "Father, forgive them, for they know not what they do." You have prayed, "Lord, make me like You." The Lord is saying, "You didn't know that in order to be made like Me, you go through the same things that I went through." He went through rejection. He went through false accusations. Yet, because the One who is in you is greater than he who is in the world, you're able to say as Stephen said and as Jesus said, "Father, forgive them, because they know not what they do."

The Lord gave me 2 Timothy 2:15: "Do your best to present yourself to God as one approved, a workman who does not need to be ashamed and who correctly handles the word of truth" [NIV]. I see you with a basket over your arm, and you're feeding the people from the Word of God. You're very selective; you look around in your basket for the right word for the right person, and the Lord wants you to know that this is a blessing to the people, that you're not just feeding them all the same thing. You have prayed and asked the Lord, and He says, "I can trust you to feed My people that which they need that will affect them." The Lord is saying, "Many prophesies have been said over you, and you have wondered, Will they come to pass and when?" The Lord says, "Now is the time. Now is the time that you see many of these words come to pass."

He gave me 1 Timothy 1:18, "Timothy, my son, I give you this instruction in keeping with the prophecies once made about you, so that by following them you may fight the good fight, holding on to faith and a good conscience" [NIV]. Lord, we thank You for revealing to Your daughter these prophetic words that have been said over her. Whether they are on tape or she has written them down or hidden in her heart, Lord, from many different sources, for many different years, I see some of them coming to light in this day. Lord, I pray You give your daughter strength and everything she needs, the

> finances and the strength to go where You want her to go and to do what You want her to do. Amen.

In July 1998 at a Christian conference in Yakima, Washington, I got the following prophecies from a team of five, which they taped for me.

> Oh Tilly, He wants you every morning when you get up, [to] say, "Glory to God, Glory to God! One more day to serve Him; one more day to rejoice in Him. Glory to God!" Let the praises of God just be on your mouth from the moment you wake up in the morning, and let it just fill your day all day long. Hallelujah! The Lord also wants you to know, Tilly, that you have the shoes of the preparation. You are prepared; you go in the preparation of the Most High God. It's no accident that you meet people. It's no accident that you are found here, you're found there, you're found in this part of town, that part of town. You know what it is to be led by God and He just wants to encourage your heart today, "Yes, you are being led by My Spirit. Yes, when I speak to you, I can count on you doing and fulfilling all that I've given you to do. And there is a preparation, the shod with the preparation of the gospel of the Most High God."
>
> And Father, we just thank You for that now. We thank You for this young lady! We thank You, Lord God, that she is a willing worker. She is a willing person that goes and knows what it is to be led by God and also knows how to spent time in Your presence. Lord, she is well acquainted with that. She spent years, Lord, seeking Your face and asking for Your guidance. And Lord, we just know You will bless her openly for her faithfulness, faithfulness, Lord God. Lord, we just thank You

today for her faithfulness to the body of Christ. Wherever she puts her hand, she does it with all her might, with all her might, with all her might.

And Lord, we just say, Oh, thank You, Jesus; thank You, Jesus, for a woman of God. Thank You, Jesus, for a woman of God, a mother of Israel, a mother of Israel that knows what it is to stand in the gap, stand in the gap. Hallelujah. Tilly, in Jesus' name, I ask for new eyes, for a fresh filling of the Spirit, that you're going to see what you have seen in the past with new eyes; that God is going to give you the vision to see His work being done; new ears, in Jesus' name. He is touching your ears; He is giving you new ears to hear Him in a new way.

Lord Jesus, I ask for a fresh filling of Your Spirit upon Tilly, that You begin flowing in her right now, that she would see her circumstances and the people around her in a new way, that You would show her the truth, Lord God, and that she could walk in confidence and in victory, knowing that she hears You, she sees what Your doing. Thank you, Lord Jesus, thank You, Lord!

I see you wearing—it says Woman of the Year—and that is, woman of the year past, but the Lord wants you to know that it is not passed. In fact, your year is coming that He is going to move on you and you're going to bring fire, you're going to bring fire, you're going to bring fire. It is no accident that you wear orange today; it is the color of fire. You're going to bring fire, and where you go, the fire of the Lord will come. And I think it will be in your prayers; you see more results like that. It's going to be a purifying fire, a purifying fire, and a fire of the presence of the Lord. Gold and orange, that was prophetic, just even what your wearing today is prophetic. The gold, the purity and the royalty, the deity, the deity.

God has more for you, and I would urge you, like it was said before, thank you, choose life, choose life. Sometimes you don't want to, but choose life; and as you choose life, life will be released in you and through you. Jesus said, "Blessed are they which do hunger and thirst after righteousness: for they shall be filled" [Matt. 5:6]. I sensed right away when you came up that you have a real hunger for God. There is such a hunger in you. And God is going to fill you, and God is going to meet your needs. God is going to fill you with Himself in such a way that you're going to be immersed, and you'll just be able to relax in God. And you know what? It's going to help you as you minister, because you know you're filled with the very presence of God in your being, even more so than you've ever known; because God is a God of increase, and even those things that He has started in us.

And you say, "Yes, I had that. I had that, but it is a day of increase and it increases as we go." So there is a greater capacity, in that there is a boldness that is going to come upon you in a greater way. It is more of the Holy Spirit—that is what it is. It is He that makes us full as you are filled, and ready to speak out and speak out in His name and minister, because sometimes you feel inadequate, like, "I don't dare, who am I to say...," but God says, "The authority of the name of Jesus is in you, go ahead and speak in His name."

I saw a railroad track, and you know on the railroad track the ties that go along. I see you going very carefully, meticulously going from tie to tie to tie. At the very beginning the Lord kept saying something to me about your knees, but I didn't understand so I waited before the Lord. He says, "Tilly has been afraid to run she walks carefully, calculated, precisely from tie to tie." God says, "Get on the train. He is going to take you for a ride." He says you're going with Him now, at a faster click than you ever have before, but you needed strength to be able to do that with. There has been a draining just recently out of your system, out of your body, so that you didn't have the strength you used to have. It has not only been physical, but there also has been a spiritual significance with that. God wants to strengthen you spiritually and physically today, so we lay hands on your knees.

I'm going to ask God to give you feet to run. Don't be afraid. You walk with those on the railroad ties so carefully, saying, "I know where my next foot is going to be. I can see the next tie, so it is all right. I can put my foot there; it's all right." God says, "I want it to be where you don't know where your foot is going to go, and that you just go with Me;" that your eyes are on Him and not on the next little step that you would take. So we are just going to release your legs, release your knees, release you in the spirit to be able to run with the Lord. Father, thank You that You've released Tilly in Jesus' name from just calculated steps to running with You. You said, Lord God, we would run and not be weary, we would walk and not faint. We would mount up with wings of eagles. Lord, it's those that wait upon the Lord. Tilly has been waiting upon the Lord. And You're saying it's time now to run with the Lord, to run, to go faster than she has ever gone before, to be more adventurous that she has ever been before, to go see the people that she didn't want to see, to talk to that one that she also held back with.

Lord God, I thank You that she is going to run, run. She is going to run, and she has strength for the run. In Jesus' name, Father, infuse her, Father, with the strength for the run. Thank You, Lord God. Thank You, Lord God. And every time she starts to feel the weariness, Lord, she'll wait upon the Lord. Lord, she does not look at the weariness. She is not going to become despondent and discouraged over the weariness. She is going to wait upon the Lord, and new strength will come into her time after time after time. This is not for a one time sprint; this is endurance and this is of those where you're going to go and you get so excited in the going that you'd never want to stop. You just go, go, go.

And God, You're going to take her; she is not going alone. This is Your work; this is Your doing. She is not on her own, Lord God. She is not trying to do something for You; she is doing something with You, and You're the one infusing her. You're the one that set it up before her, Lord God. Some of these other things have been calculatedly set up by her own self to be able to say, "This is a good thing to do"—and it was, it was a good thing to do; but now, Lord, You're going to take her on an adventure that she had never been before, but it is an adventure in You. Lord God, for the glory of the Lord, for the praise of Your honor, Lord God, in Jesus' name. Thank You, Father. Thank You, Father. No fear, no fear, no fear.

I just want to say, the picture of getting on the train is God lifting and carrying you. It's not by your works. It's not something you're going to call up. He is going to carry you; it is in freedom and it is in might and it's in power. You're going to see the power of the living God come into circumstances. Wow! You never expected something like that. And I think you'll find that you'll be looking back all of a sudden and say, "I can't believe that I did that. Wow, it just happened all of a sudden, and I was doing it. I could have not done that before." Because the Lord really is releasing new things in you and through you. He loves you very, very much.

Do you love to worship, Tilly? The Lord keeps bringing back to me the very first word He gave me. He wants you, every morning when you get up, to put your hands into the air and say, "Glory to God. Glory to God." Just worship Him with such boldness and such fervor. It won't matter what everybody else is doing. All that matters is that He'll

> come and fill you. You come back this way; He'll come this way. Pretty soon you won't even know what happened. Your smile is there, not because you tried to; it's because of you worshiping, saying, "Glory to God." And it is going to be such a release to you. Hallelujah.

A different man at this conference told me concerning God, "He really, really loves you." Another time, as I walked past three ladies whom I never seen before, the younger one stopped me and said, "You're a mighty woman of God." I asked her who had told her. She replied that the Lord had just shown it to her as I walked by. You see, when you receive the baptism in the Holy Spirit, these gifts, which are mentioned in 1 Corinthians 12, are available to us from the Holy Spirit. The woman who received from a Lord a vision of me as a mighty woman of God displayed the gift of discernment.

It was obvious that most of the people I met there had a close relationship with the Lord. We read in James 4:8, "Draw nigh to God, and he will draw nigh to you."

FEBRUARY 5, 2000

The following was another prophecy from the prophetess in Seattle.

> The Lord gave me Exodus 3:10: "So now, go. I am sending you to Pharaoh to bring my people the Israelites out of Egypt" [NIV]. I see you've been like a Moses in your life. God continues to send you places to bring people out of Egypt, out of bondage. I believe this is confirmation to you that the

Lord says for you to go. He is sending you, go from your last church to here. He wants you to know that He is sending you. I see you water skiing on a Ski-Doo. The Lord says wherever you go there will be waves, for you to know that He doesn't send you places without causing waves, but that is also your calling, because those waves shake people out of their lethargic situation. I see people on a rubber raft just kind of resting out there in the sun on the lake and your little boat comes along and tips them over, your Ski-Doo. The Lord is wanting you to know you're upsetting a few people wherever He sends you, but that will get them out of just waiting for the Lord to come. What I see is, these people are meditating, they are spiritual, they're looking on to the Son. They are not non-Christians. They are Christians just waiting for Jesus to come, and you're going to stir them up. He is wanting you to know that He is sending you. Thank You, Lord.

The Lord gives me 1 Chronicles 5:20: "Because they cried out to him during the battle. He answered their prayers, because they trusted in him" [NIV]. I hear the Lord saying, "Leave the past behind," because He has heard your cry; He has heard your cry. Thank You, Lord. The water supply—the city of Tacoma has it's own water supply, and that is where you're supposed to get water. But if anything goes wrong with that water supply, then the Lord will rain down on us in the Northwest and we get water. We are not in the desert. The church is supposed to be the water supply; but there are times when the church is not supplying the water, so God brings it through different people not associated with a particular church. I see when you bring other people in, it's that emergency supply. Just like today, there are some in their churches that would not get that supply of water that they are getting here today. God says keep doing what you're doing, because you know where the water is. I see different wells out there. There is a lot of water, but you have to know where to dig the well. The Lord says you have discernment where to dig the well. Lord, we thank You that for many whose water supply has dried up, Your daughter is going to bring that supply, that spiritual nourishment, that they might live and not die of thirst. In Jesus' name.

November 26, 2001

As the granddaughter of a friend of mine was in prayer early that morning, the Lord brought me to her mind. We hardly knew each other. She did not know anything about my situation. After calling her grandmother for my phone number, she contacted me to explain what she had heard from the Holy Spirit: He revealed to her that the ground I touch is mine. The Lord continued, "I know that you have missed the comfort of home, but I want your sight on Me. I want your home to be My temple. My people perish for lack of faith, lack of vision. But I have given health to your bones. For the vision in you is full, and just as a bud cannot hold back from blooming in the sunlight, so you shall bloom in the midst of darkened circumstances. Because My light shines on you, My light gives you growth, My light gives you life. Go into these towns of which I speak to you, be a servant unto the Lord and unto your people. Speak the Word I have given you. Let it be like the lace upon oak tables, fine china upon the lace, because for you I will do My best for these people. You will speak forth the best of My promises. For the Word of God is finer than gold or silver. Make an offer, and I will provide the means. The price will be right and fair to this man."

I was to read the whole chapter of Hebrews 11, especially verses 9–25, which are:

> By faith he sojourned in the land of promise, as in a strange country, dwelling in tabernacles with Isaac and Jacob, the heirs with him of the same promise: For he looked for a city which hath foundations, whose builder and maker is God. Through faith also Sara herself received strength to conceive seed, and was delivered of a child when she was past age, because she judged him faithful who had promised. Therefore sprang there even of one, and him as good as dead, so many as the stars of the sky in multitude, and as the sand which is by the sea shore innumerable. These all died in faith, not having received the promises, but having seen them afar off, and were persuaded of them, and embraced them, and confessed that they were strangers and pilgrims on the earth. For they that say such things declare plainly that they seek a country. And truly, if they had been mindful of that country from whence they came out, they might have had opportunity to have returned. But now they desire a better country, that is, an heavenly: wherefore God is not ashamed to be called their God: for he hath prepared for them a city. By faith Abraham, when he was tried, offered up Isaac: and he that had received the promises offered up his only begotten son, Of whom it was said, That in Isaac shall thy seed be called: Accounting that God was able to raise him up, even from the dead; from whence also he received him in a figure. By faith Isaac blessed Jacob and Esau concerning things to come. By faith Jacob, when he was a dying, blessed both the sons of Joseph; and worshipped, leaning upon the top of his staff. By faith Joseph, when he died, made mention of the

> departing of the children of Israel; and gave commandment concerning his bones. By faith Moses, when he was born, was hid three months of his parents, because they saw he was a proper child; and they were not afraid of the king's commandment. By faith Moses, when he was come to years, refused to be called the son of Pharaoh's daughter; Choosing rather to suffer affliction with the people of God, than to enjoy the pleasures of sin for a season.

Then she asked the Lord if there was anything else He wanted to tell me. He replied, "I brought forth faith with the risen Savior. I gave them the faith to believe. So I provide the faith to accomplish My promises, or how could they be promises? How can you receive if you do not believe? You can believe, because I'm in you and give you the ability to believe. Like all things in Me you can accept it or reject it."

She told me that she often asks the Lord to see His heart when she prays for someone. Then she added that God has great love for me. What the devil meant for evil, God turned to good.

The following is again from the Seattle prophetess.

March 15, 2003

> I see the globe—the world—just like angels flying all around the world. The Lord says, "I'm giving you a worldview of My heart's cry for the world." Even if war is impending, the Lord says He has the whole world in His hands. That song is coming to me more and more: He has the whole wide world

in His hands. The Lord says to occupy until He comes. Don't change your strategy in your work, even though there will be changes. The Lord is saying He is honoring His people who've been faithful through the years. Even as it gets darker and darker, you're going to see brighter and brighter light from what the Lord is doing. I see the word *favor* on His people—favor on the faithful ones, favor on the faithful ones, favor on the faithful ones. And you have been one of those who has been faithful.

You are not to look to the left or the right, behind or before you; just know the Lord is faithful to His faithful ones. He gives me Isaiah 60:1, "Arise, shine; for thy light is come, and the glory of the LORD is risen upon thee." His glory is His presence. I sense that this is a doorway that you choose to enter every day. Choose to enter into the glory, choose to enter into His presence, which is the glory. And in that place you will be shielded physically, emotionally, spiritually. It is like a place of refuge. Like, if it is dark outside and your house is dark, but you come inside and turn the light on, you're in the light because you turn the light on. You could stay in the dark if you didn't turn the light on. The Lord is saying it is by choice in the days ahead for the Christian to turn the light on. As you praise Him, that turns the light on. As you read the Word, that will turn the light on. Even as you listen to Christian music, fellowship with believers, that will turn the light on. The Lord is saying, "Stay in that place of refuge. Stay in that place where the light is. I see you going into places where it is dark, but your presence and the yielding to the Lord in expecting the glory to come will turn the light on.

The Lord has given pieces of truth to His people. No one has the whole answer, but pieces here and there, like pieces to the puzzle. The Lord is saying even as you talk to other people on the Internet, on Christian TV, you're going to see pieces of the puzzle, but no one has the full answer. The Lord says, "I'm giving you a piece of the puzzle, especially for your own personal use, for your own personal knowledge for what is to come." He is going to give it more in the days ahead in dreams and visions. He is saying to you, when you dream, ask the Lord what He means by that dream, because I see Him talking more and more to His people through dreams and visions. He gives me 2 Corinthians 12:1: "It is not expedient for me doubtless to glory. I will come to visions and revelations of the Lord." The Lord is saying you will go on to visions and revelations, especially at night. He is going to speak a lot to you through dreams and visions. As you seek Him, He will give you the interpretation of what He is saying to you. As you know, God is a good God. I see love is poured out on you through the dreams and visions. Not every dream is from the Lord, so if you have a bad dream, and we usually do—some of us—that is not from the Lord, because the enemy is trying to frighten us.

The Lord is saying, put the blood of Jesus over anything that is frightening and does not lead you upward to Him and lead others upward to Him, because His mercy and grace is being poured out on His people. His protection is being poured out on His people. So, expect protection as you drive on the road—protection in your ministry, protection in your business. Lord, we thank You for the angels that are assigned to Tilly. We thank you that she sees more and more angels, that they are assigned to her, and we bless her now in Jesus' name, amen.

April 7, 2007

I get the word *challenge, challenge, challenge.* Then I saw you playing a game, like checkers. It is a challenge to win. God has put within you a competitiveness. You love challenge and you are not afraid to be challenged by what the Lord wants you to do. I see like in every game when you play with someone else, you're not against them, but you want to win. You both want to win. That makes it a challenge.

That makes it fun. God moves, you move, God moves, you move. The Lord says sometimes when you play a game like that with someone you have to wait until they make their decision. Sometimes it gets boring because some people take so long to make their decision. The Lord says He takes His time to make a decision. Your waiting is one of the hardest things that you have to do, yet you don't want to move before God moves.

I see you playing this game and look up and say, Have You moved yet? And the Lord just smiles and says no. And I see the Lord is just happy to play with you, to challenge you. He is not just sitting there wasting your time. He is making each step a challenge to you. This is difficult, the waiting. He does not have to try to figure it out, but He knows that it is good for you to have to wait there until your next move. I believe that has to do with ministry that you are involved in. He is saying be patient. It is all going to come out the way He wants it to. You just have to ask for ability to wait until He moves so that you don't move ahead of Him.

> I will wait for the Lord, who is hiding his face from the house of Jacob. I will put my trust in him.
>
> —Isaiah 8:17, NIV

Sometimes the Lord seems to be hiding His face, but He has His eyes on you. You may not see Him, but He has not lost track of you and is in purpose for this time.

Lord, we thank You for a special anointing in the name of the Father, Son, and Holy Spirit upon Your daughter. Amen.

April 25, 2007

Two pastors and their wives—presbyters of our church—whom our pastor knew for many years came to our church on April 24 to ordain a couple into full-time ministry. They returned for two evenings and prophesied to a number of us. Following is what the four of them individually prophesied over me:

> Surely, the presence of the Lord is in this place. And that is why you're here, right? That's why you're here. Years ago, they used to call ladies' groups "ladies circles," "sewing bees," whatever all they called them. They don't call them by these things anymore, but they still have the same essences—women getting together, doing things together. And I see you as one of those important women of the bee, in the circle. And you love to do a lot of things. You even love to get involved with people's needs and make sure that everything is OK. You love to [say], "O God, if there is a need, please help them. And if they're not saved, Lord get them."
>
> Again, there is another one God wants to commend. He is pleased with you. Keep up the good work, keep up the good deeds, and pray those prayers that come to your heart and your mind. Watch God work, and just say, "Thank You, Lord," when He works, and keep blessing people. God is smiling on you. Just keep it up, OK? Bless you; you're special.

I have a sense in God that there are some loved ones that [have] just broken your heart and [have] not done the right thing for you. And today we're going to commit them to God, who takes care of things really well and knows how to straighten things out. Can we do that? Father, we're believing You. We're trusting You for every one of these situations, every incident, everything, Lord, that You just take it and work it to good for those that love the Lord. And I believe this woman loves You. She is here, Lord, because she loves You. Cause this thing to work for good in the name of Jesus Christ.

And the Spirit of the Lord is going to cause you to rise up high above these circumstances, high above the words that have been spoken in a negative way, the words that have accused you, words that have disrespected you and sometimes destined you. And they're going to turn. I believe that God will raise you up and give you a new sense of confidence in Him and a new sense of His presence to just further establish you in a debt of relationship with Him so that you can come before Him and ask without your heart being bitter or filled with any kind of grief; that you can come before Him and pray without a heart that is hurting; so that you can come as a person that is whole and together and of sound heart and body. For God will come and meet you at that point, and He'll come and draw you closer at that point.

He has not forsaken you, even as others have. He has not—He will not—set you aside as others have. He loves you with an everlasting love. He cares for you and will continue to surround you with His angelic beings. He'll surround you with His presence. He [will] fill you with His love and He [will] shower His mercies on you, says the Lord. Hallelujah, it's done. The scripture I have is "What is bound in heaven is bound in earth, too," OK? [See Matthew 16:19.] And sometimes the earth is not what is in a flowerpot; sometimes the earth is a person, OK? And the mouth of the wicked is going to stop. Amen. Hallelujah. You're too precious. Amen. Hallelujah.

I think that God has a theme here for you tonight. You're real composed on the outside, but the moment you walked up and sat down—I don't know, have you ever seen the video *Shrek*? It is a kid video, like a middle school video. And there is a character, a donkey. You're all composed on the outside, but in this video what I saw—I'm not saying you're a donkey. In this video, Donkey is saying, "Pick me, pick me, pick me." And I just had the sense when you came up and sat down, although you're real proper and composed on the outside, but inside you're saying, "God, pick me, pick me, pick me." And God wants you to know that He has picked you. He has chosen you. And He has a plan and a purpose for your life. Even if it did not unfold the way you thought it should unfold in your earlier years, there are still lots of days ahead for God to fulfill His destiny in you, and He has picked you. You are precious, He has chosen you, He loves you. He thinks you are great and that you're one of the special ones.

Man, I [would] love it if someone told me that. But God has chosen you, and I have a real sense that God wants to use you in the gifts of healing. Gifts of healing, that you would set your heart to study and know the Word of God as it relates to healing. If you would hide His Word deep inside, within your heart...He will make that Word grow, and your faith will increase. And as you pray for people who are sick, as you lift people before the throne of grace at home or in the church, as you hear that someone has a need, if you will bring them before the Lord, He will use you in gifts of healing. As you give yourself to that, then God will work through you in gifts of healing.

And that is a very vital, vital need in our society today. And don't limit your thinking to just the people in the house of God, just believers, just the people in the church. Jesus never healed a single Christian. When He walked the earth He only healed unbelievers. And the healing as you look [at] in the Book of Acts, the gifts of healing that were dispersed through the disciples [were] to unbelievers, and it made believers out of them. Because then they began to understand that this is the God who loves me and cares about me.

So I just want to encourage you that [if] you will set your heart to study, to memorize, to meditate on the Word of God, God will use you in gifts of healing and He will make your faith grow, and He'll make you a mighty woman of faith in the house of the Lord. Hallelujah. Praise God. This is a confirmation to you. Stir up that gift then. Amen.

And you're going to be amazed at your ability to comprehend and to understand the ways of God. You're in a learning mode; always remain in the learning mode. I see you being available for any kind of instruction, whenever you can fit it in to your schedule. Get your notebook and take down anything you can—and take it all up. And then when the opportunity is there, you [will] have a lot to give out. I was just confirming what she was saying.

I saw something else here, and I haven't talked to the pastor about this. I saw—let me back up and say, Indonesia has been a very strong Islamic country. Very, very strong. And after the tsunami hit, Christian people went in there, big time, and they were very, very hostile before to the Christian community. That is changing because the Christians were serving in a practical way. We heard it as a report on the *700 Club*. That's what God is doing. Now I use this as an analogy. I believe and I submit that to the leadership of this house, I believe that God is going to open up many doors for you to serve people all around in practical ways. Even food—I don't know if you do it yet—but food distribution. I see a kitchen were food is being cooked and providing for hungry, needy people. I don't know to what extent this is, but I see you in the middle of all of that. [I have a calling to Egypt and also perceive a feeding program lately. God was giving him wise counsel.] I just sense that I see you in this kind of an arena, cooking and helping and serving with big heart, but it is not just natural food. Because of you submitting yourself to the teaching ministry of the Word, you're going to give out natural food and spiritual food to help the full person, not just to feed their belly but to feed their spirit as well. That is the picture that I had for you. [God will anoint me to lay my hands on their eyes, and He will open their blind eyes in Egypt.]

The circle, the idea of a group I saw when I initially talked with you—I see the importance of you…being linked with others and the strength that there is as you link up with others of like passion, like vision…under the auspices of the local church, whatever you do, wherever you go. But I see you connecting; there is connection where there is strength and fruitfulness.

Father, thank You for precious saints. Thank You for the fact that You choose us, Lord, and You chose that woman as well, to be Your servant, to heal the sick, to touch lives, to affect the lost, that they might come into the kingdom of God. We pray, Lord, that this Word prophesied over her has its full effect, that the Word of God does not fall to the ground without accomplishing its purpose. Let it be done now as it falls on good soil accomplishing Your purpose and bringing forth good fruit—thirty, sixty and a hundredfold; in this case, a hundredfold in the name of Jesus Christ. Bless this woman and the work of her hands, we pray. In Jesus' name. Amen, amen, amen.

OCTOBER 2007

The following prophecy is again from the Seattle prophetess:

> Thank You for Your word for her. I hear the Lord saying, "New things." He is leading you in to new territory that you have not been in before, for you to take these steps and take them slowly. What I see is a big gravel truck going up a hill. And when it goes up a hill, it has to shift down lower. I suppose this is what they call that. My grandson drives one of those trucks and seventeen gears, and they have to know what gear they have to be in depending on where they are going. Shifting gears is what they have to learn, which is the hardest to learn, because you have lots of different roadways, different terrain. I hear the Lord saying, "Daughter, in the next few months you have to use all seventeen gears." Sometimes you [will] be going up the hill and it [will] seem so hard and you [will] think, "I [will] never get to the top going this speed." The Lord is saying, "Shift gears, shift gears."
>
> When people first learn to drive, they drive in first gear for a long, long time until the noise gets so bad that they decide, maybe I was supposed to shift. The more you shift, the more you can hear it when it is time to shift. You just know it. You don't have to look at the speedometer. You go by the ear. And I hear the Lord saying, "Daughter you know Me well enough to know when it is time to shift." Don't stay in the same gear too long. Sometimes you have to shift down. Sometimes you shift up, depending on the terrain.
>
> Lord, I pray that you give Tilly wisdom when to shift. You don't go by sight; you go by hearing. That is when you know when to shift. This is important. A lot of times we look around and shift gears by our circumstances, when the Lord says, "I want [you] to hear Me. I want you to listen for the time to shift." And listening is spirit. We hear by the spirit

within because we have to check with the Scripture. The final result is peace. When you shift, there is peace. The engine quits roaring and there is a peace. If you are in first gear and going downhill, there is a roar. Once you shift, there is peace there; the engine is not roaring. You are the engine, and when you find yourself roaring—in other words circumstances are not working for you and you're not at peace—then shift, shift gears. The Lord says, "You are used to an automatic car." Shifting a big truck is not easy. In the next few months you [will] learn how to hear what the Lord is saying in a new way, because you never had such change as you are going to have in these months.

> Then I said, I will not make mention of him, nor speak any more in his name. But his word was in mine heart as a burning fire shut up in my bones, and I was weary with forbearing, and I could not stay.
>
> —Jeremiah 20:9

The Lord has made you one that you are to speak in His name and mention Him, or you get weary holding it in.

But the Lord is with me as a mighty terrible one: therefore my persecutors shall stumble, and they shall not prevail: they shall be greatly ashamed; for they shall not prosper: their everlasting confusion shall never be forgotten.

—Jeremiah 20:11

Lord, we thank You. You are the mighty warrior in Tilly. Yes, persecution will come, but they will not prevail. So, we anoint her now in the name of the Father, Son, and Holy Spirit. And Lord, we thank You for what You are doing in and through her, and Lord, she is going to be on a road she has never

> driven before. So we thank You that You are in the cockpit, Your in the seat next to her, telling her how to shift and when to shift. In Jesus' name, amen.

February 11, 2008

A friend of mine invited me to a meeting. The speaker, an ordained minister from Puerto Rico whom I knew, shared the Word and then ministered to each of us individually. He ministered in our church before to me, where he prophesied to me that I have the gift of healing and to use my hands. This time he told me:

> Hallelujah, the Lord says the Jews seek for a sign and the Greeks—the heathens—they seek for wisdom. But the Lord has given us Christ. To the Jew a stumbling block, to the Gentiles foolishness, but He has become to us the power of God and the wisdom of God.
>
> The Lord is saying to me, "I have given you much wisdom, My daughter, because My Scripture says, 'In this age My children must be harmless as doves and wise as serpents.'" The Lord is showing me that He has given you wisdom to walk in the middle of a crooked and perverse generation, sowing the Word. The sower sows the seed, and the Lord is saying to me, "You rest, because the harvest is coming," great harvest. And the good thing about you is that you're persistent. And that is patience and endurance, stubbornness [then I said, "A stubborn German for the Lord."] Hallelujah, glory to God. You know that is so true; there are some nations that have a character that is that way. So I would agree 100 percent with you.

> We belong to the nation of heaven. We belong to Christ, and rightfully so. Thank You, Lord, Father God.

After praying a short time in tongues, he continued:

> The Lord is telling me, a relative of yours... went around establishing small churches. Next to a river there is a small church that still caries his fingerprint. The Lord will show you—I don't know how, but if I said it He will—because you come from a backbone heritage that loved Christ, that proclaimed Christ, that prayed over you and over your offspring, over your generation. Thank You, Lord, Father God. Thank you, Jesus. They suffered greatly for their faith, and some of your relatives died because of their faith. Glory be to God forevermore. What I'm saying is that you're an answer to prayer. You just don't come up because your parents got together, because you were born out of the will of God. Thank you, Father. So you come from a generation that is very focused, very determined, a generation that preferred Christ over anything and everything else.
>
> This relative of yours was not married, but my goodness, he was like a flame of fire when he stood in the pulpit and proclaim Christ. He used to walk through villages proclaiming, and the Lord used him a lot in the gifts of the Spirit. It was like in ancient times. When the prophet came to town, people were concerned because he spoke the truth, and they held small meetings in houses. I don't know where, but the Lord will show you eventually who he is so you will understand that you don't just come from nowhere.
>
> Sometimes the Lord will allow me to see things from the past because He wants to do something in the future with you and your linage in the flesh.

The Lord said, "For you shall decree a thing and it shall be established, for such authority have I given to My children, that they can speak even to mountains and they be washed in to the sea," as they believe in their heart; no doubting. Thank You, Lord.

You know they say about you that you're hardheaded, very determined, very stubborn—you know that this is a godly character, godly quality, that the Lord uses to establish His kingdom. The Lord will change your wording and your determination even more so when you pray. The Lord says, "Command ye Me." And He says, "There will arise a boldness within you." My goodness, it might offend others if they hear you speaking. But the Lord said, "It will only offend their lack of faith, not your faith." Thank You, Lord. Amen. God bless you.

CHAPTER 11

THE COST OF BEING SOLD OUT

ON MAY 12, 2001, I attended a powerful Holy Spirit Encounter Conference about forty miles away. I knew with out a doubt that I had to attend and received some good teaching from the father-and-son team. At the end, one of the people of this ministry who recorded the conference handed me a set of the tapes—but who? I was surprised that someone was that generous and blessed me with a set, which ministered to me while I listened to them in my car. I feel led to share part of the last tape with you. It will show you that others, too, who are led by the Holy Spirit call us to repentance and holiness:

> God is about to destroy the kingdoms build by man. And God is going to remove those who are in ministry with a motive for selfish gain, because in this hour…He is saying, "No more."
>
> Church, we are coming to the place of accountability.… When I found out that God began to do the things that came

> out of my mouth, I began to understand the accountability that comes with the call of God....
>
> If you're serious about God, you better start praying for the fear of God in your life. The Laodicean church—listen, we all think, oh, lukewarm; He spews us out of His mouth. But you know, He said, "To him that overcomes...to the person that gets serious about Me, to the person that is sold out and will no longer walk in mediocrity, they're going to sit with Me on My throne and they walk in My authority."...There is a lack of respect and reverence for God...Holy fear is the key to God's sure foundation. Holy fear is the thing that will keep you from sin....
>
> When I was in Korea I asked the believers, What is your opinion of American Christians?...They said, "They are fat and lazy."...You know these people, when they accept Christ, they are 110 percent committed. They get up at four, sometimes three in the morning and go to church to intercede and pray. Guess whom they are praying for? America, thank God!...
>
> Do you want to see your city changed so that the streets flow with salvation, the lame walk, and the beggar on the street is healed and set free; so that there is no more drug addiction, no more prostitution; they can close the prison down...? Then pray for the fear of God. Because when the fear of God comes into you, it's going to affect everyone that is around you.

The Lord tested me and still is, to see how much I am sold out to Him. I told Him many times that I am His battle ax and will do whatever He calls me to do for His kingdom. As soon as I opened my eyes the next morning, I was repeating the words of the song "My Life Is in You, Lord." The things of this world had no longer a hold on me. I was content with the little I had left, which made the total surrender easy. The Holy Spirit has a way of transforming us if we are willing. The many nice things I have meant nothing to me anymore, from the elegant chrome and smoked glass furniture to my yellow porcelain dishes with a butterfly in the center of the plates, accented with numerous different cobalt blue glasses and knickknacks. In the past, everyone had commented on my tastefully decorated home; now I'm ready to give it all up and only want to serve the Lord.

This chapter is not intended to condemn anyone. Rather, it is a wake-up call. It is not to badmouth. Instead, it is an invitation and opportunity from God to look at ourselves. He is giving us a chance to repent so that the Holy Spirit can use us mightily in the days ahead of our great revival, as it will be sweeping throughout the land like never before. He loves you and wants that each one of us has a part in this harvest. When Jesus returns at His second coming, who are the people you think He is talking to when He says, "I never knew you: depart from me" (Matt. 7:23)? They will even try to tell Him that they have driven out demons in His name. What a disappointment on that day when Jesus condemns them into hell. He is not talking to unbelievers; otherwise they would not say to Him that they did works in His name. These are people full of pride and selfish ambition, men and women who think that they are serving God now; otherwise they would not have been ministering in Jesus' name. Their lips speak it, but their heart is corrupt. Here is proof from the Scriptures themselves.

> Wherefore the Lord said, Forasmuch as this people draw near me with their mouth, and with their lips do honour me, but

> have removed their heart far from me, and their fear toward me is taught by the precept of men.
>
> —ISAIAH 29:13

God wants His people to be fully devoted to Him, not to false teaching from men. We cannot fool Him. He knows our hearts and knows whether what we say has integrity.

> For the wrath of God is revealed from heaven against all ungodliness and unrighteousness of men, who hold the truth in unrighteousness; Because that which may be known of God is manifest in them; for God hath shewed it unto them. For the invisible things of him from the creation of the world are clearly seen, being understood by the things that are made, even his eternal power and Godhead; so that they are without excuse.
>
> —ROMANS 1:18–20

I'm sure you don't want to be amongst those that are sent off to hell to burn in the lake of fire forever and ever. As we read in Romans 1:22, "Professing themselves to be wise, they became fools." Some elevated themselves to a position that God never gave them. Jesus said about Himself in John 14:6, "I am the way, the truth, and the life." Yet, there are some that sneak into the fold with wrong motives. Sometimes it takes a long time until God will expose them, but it is always at His proper time. Most pastors are good men, but are they still God-fearing and Christlike, as when they were first called into the ministry, allowing the Holy Spirit to flow through them and humble themselves? Remember God does not override your will and if you disobey you have to face the consequences. He is looking for a broken and contrite heart.

> As many as I love, I rebuke and chasten: be zealous therefore, and repent.... To him that overcometh will I grant to sit with me in my throne, even as I also overcame, and am set down with my Father in his throne. He that hath an ear, let him hear what the Spirit saith unto the churches.
>
> —Revelation 3:19, 21–22

> For the prophecy came not in old time by the will of man: but holy men of God spake as they were moved by the Holy Ghost.
>
> —2 Peter 1:21

> Blessed are they which do hunger and thirst after righteousness: for they shall be filled.
>
> —Matthew 5:6

> That he might present it to himself a glorious church, not having spot, or wrinkle, or any such thing; but that it should be holy and without blemish.
>
> —Ephesians 5:27

Are you a holy man? Will your congregation stand before Jesus one day holy and without blemish? If you're not sure, start with yourself. The flock usually follows its leader.

I'm only obeying His call upon my life. Since I'm no longer a man-pleaser, now I'm a God pleaser! Jesus wasn't always popular, either. Why else would we read in Matthew 7:21–23:

> Not every one that saith unto me, Lord, Lord, shall enter into the kingdom of heaven; but he that doeth the will of my Father which is in heaven. Many will say to me in that day, Lord, Lord, have we not prophesied in thy name? and in thy name have cast out devils? and in thy name done many wonderful

> works? And then will I profess unto them, I never knew you: depart from me, ye that work iniquity.

We also read in Acts 28:25–27:

> And when they agreed not among themselves, they departed, after that Paul had spoken one word, Well spake the Holy Ghost by Esaias the prophet unto our fathers, Saying, Go unto this people, and say, Hearing ye shall hear, and shall not understand; and seeing ye shall see, and not perceive: For the heart of this people is waxed gross, and their ears are dull of hearing, and their eyes have they closed; lest they should see with their eyes, and hear with their ears, and understand with their heart, and should be converted, and I should heal them.

Jesus said in John 14:17, "Even the Spirit of truth; whom the world cannot receive, because it seeth him not, neither knoweth him: but ye know him; for he dwelleth with you, and shall be in you." According to this scripture, Christians should know the Spirit of truth! It is high time that we, especially pastors, get serious with God and use the gift of discernment. Does God allow us certain experiences so that we can sincerely repent?

> And they that are Christ's have crucified the flesh with the affections and lusts. If we live in the Spirit, let us also walk in the Spirit.
>
> —Galatians 5:24–25

It is time that we take the Bible serious, because it is not just a storybook. Everything in it will come to pass, so also the perilous times that are emerging. This is one reason why having proper leadership is extremely important—to teach and prepare congregations of the upcoming hatred towards the true Christians, even from within, in order for them to survive and not compromise. In times to come, the leaders of the world will get together and find schemes to go against God's people.

> Why do the heathen rage, and the people imagine a vain thing? The kings of the earth set themselves, and the rulers take counsel together, against the Lord, and against his anointed.
>
> —Psalm 2:1–2

We will experience persecution like never before. If you're not called by God and divinely ordained to serve Him, you are only a hireling and better quit now, because God is saying in Ezekiel 34:2, "Woe be to the shepherds." You cannot lead your flock into all of God's truth unless you are empowered with the Holy Spirit baptism. You have to listen to the Holy Spirit's guidance, because your orders for direction come from Him, not from what you think or your board decides. Hanging on to your denominational doctrine will have to be a thing of the past if you want to operate under God's divine direction and anointing. There is no corner for the Baptists in heaven and another one for the Pentecostals. Your denomination can't promise you that you will enter heaven. It is up to each individual to search out the Bible for himself or herself and believe and practice all it contains. If you make it up there, then you are a part of the bride of Christ. Why can't we all get along down here on Earth? Have we not all read the same gospel and do we not pray to the same God?

Preachers, you not only need to teach and preach the whole truth of the Bible, but you must also practice it. Listen to what the psalmist David said in 2 Samuel 23:2–3: "The Spirit of the Lord spake by me, and his word was in my tongue. The God of Israel said, the Rock of Israel spake to me, He that ruleth over men must be just, ruling in the fear of God." We will experience signs and wonders from heaven by those who are firmly grounded in the Word and line themselves up with God's timetable. The Word of the living God is coming forth out of our mouth in boldness. Why? Because of what it says in 2 Corinthians 5:7: "For we walk by faith, not by sight," and also Mark 16:20: "And they went forth, and preached every where, the Lord working with them, and confirming the word with signs following." Do you have signs and wonders following each time you preach? The Bible says you should.

If you do not have these signs, then why not? Out of what book are you teaching? Have we relaxed over the years and neglected what the Word of God tells us to do? Have we instead interpreted the Bible to fit our own denominational doctrine, which does not include signs and wonders, instead of His truth, the only truth? Can you say with certainty, "I am God's anointed"? Or are you only playing church and acting as a hireling? The disciples were not deacons in the local organized church. Instead, they were fishermen, anointed and sent to do the work of God amongst the people, with signs and wonders following, as we read in the book of the Acts.

In 1997 a retired pastor and his wife from this area were visiting the church I attended at that time. After our pastor called him to the front, he announced to us that he was a pastor already for ten years prior to him getting saved. One would wonder if it was only a job for him before his salvation. Lord, have mercy! How could his parishioners have ever received anything spiritual from their pastor, be it a sermon or counseling, before he was saved? I'm writing this for you to look at yourself. Who did he worship back then, do you suppose, when they sang hymns like "It Is Well with My Soul" in their service?

> When peace like a river,
> Attendeth my way,
> When sorrows,
> Like sea billows roll;
> Whatever my lot,
> Thou hast taught me to say,
> "It is well,
> It is well, with my soul."

A friend of mine told me that she was very disturbed that her new pastor's wife told the congregation of her unbelief in a literal hell. She should have believed the Word of God while she was alive, because it was not long thereafter that she was struck with cancer and died. We wonder why certain people die at an early age, but we don't know what goes on in their life or from what God spared them in the future.

Jesus told the scribes and Pharisees in Matthew 23:33, "Ye serpents, ye generation of vipers, how can ye escape the damnation of hell?" Yes, God is love, but He is also just. I sometimes wonder if He removes certain people who are a hindrance and are an embarrassment to the furthering of His kingdom.

I give you a few more examples. A number of years ago I met a German lady who was a new Christian. She tried to tell my pastor how to run his church when I invited her. I attended a few of her prayer meetings in her home. If any one of us attending had a prayer request, she would start praying for each situation immediately, not giving anyone else a chance. No question, she was in charge. Amongst some other false imaginations she had, she told us that one time as she was traveling on the freeway, she saw the moon turning red, as described in Revelation 6:12: "And I beheld when he had opened the sixth seal, and, lo, there was a great earthquake; and the sun became black as sackcloth of hair, and the moon became as blood." She was sure that this was the end of the world. She passed away a couple of months later after contracting cancer. Would she have distorted the gospel of Jesus Christ and led many believers astray if she had continued preaching this?

Early one morning, the Lord gave me the following revelation. I was to make it very clear to you, the reader, that He will judge *all* unrighteousness.

> And being made perfect, he became the author of eternal salvation unto all them that obey him.
>
> —HEBREWS 5:9

Does this Scripture then make it clear that if you don't obey Him, you forfeit eternal salvation? Forget about the Baptist slogan, "Once saved, always saved!" You have to live like you are saved in order to stay saved and obey Jesus as your Lord. It is not about you being your own lord! A Christian is one who is living the Christian life and applies Jesus' teaching in his or her daily life. The word

Christian is only mentioned three times in the New Testament, yet *disciple* appears 318 times. Remember His words in Exodus 20:5: "For I the LORD thy God am a jealous God." At the very end of the Bible we read again that there is no private interpretation of the Scriptures.

> For I testify unto every man that heareth the words of the prophecy of this book, If any man shall add unto these things, God shall add unto him the plagues that are written in this book: And if any man shall take away from the words of the book of this prophecy, God shall take away his part out of the book of life, and out of the holy city, and from the things which are written in this book.
>
> —REVELATION 22:18–19

Adding Scriptures to our opinion does not turn it into truth. Throughout the whole Bible, the writers mean exactly what they say. The Word of God is not negotiable. In accordance with the above scripture, a minister should want to make sure that he is conducting himself the way the Bible teaches, leading people in a sinner's prayer, baptizing them by immersion in water, and leading them to the baptism in the Holy Spirit, evidenced by speaking in other tongues.

All too many pastors only preach a social gospel anymore. Many of their Bible translations have the Word of God changed. For instance, where my King James Bible reads "Jesus Christ," some others read "Him" instead. Certain people have been secretly at work to destroy the power of God's Word by deluding the Scriptures in several translations. They have allowed themselves to be used as patsies by Satan. Since man is greedy and forever searching for something new, these people used the excuse that these new versions of the Bible are easier to read. Believe me, it is all a tactic of Satan. By changing the verbiage, it distorts and deludes God's Word as it was originally given to holy men, inspired by the Holy Spirit. It is not your easy-to-read words; rather, it is the Holy Spirit's revelation and understanding of the unchanged Scriptures that translates the Bible codes. Had God wanted different translations, He would have handpicked and anointed certain people, just as He still to this day handpicks and anoints apostles, prophets, evangelists, teachers, and preachers. According to my experience in Africa, the King James Bible is the only version they accept as truth.

The Message Bible perverts God's Holy Word. Its author is not the Holy Spirit; instead, it is a man named Eugene Peterson. Yet, Rick Warren makes eighty-three references of it in his book *The Purpose-Driven Life*, which has been endorsed by many Christian heavyweights. I got two of Rick Warren's books for gifts. The first one I returned; the other includes birthday greetings. I have not opened it because the Holy Spirit prevented me from doing so. Would I otherwise have unknowingly gotten misled? You can see why Jesus, the Light of the World, cannot be portrayed with a false light, a deluded Bible. Here "another Jesus, another spirit, and another gospel" are presented as quoted in 2 Corinthians 11:4, "For if he that cometh preacheth another Jesus, whom we have not preached, or if ye receive another spirit, which ye have not received, or another gospel, which ye have not accepted, ye might well bear with him."

Here are some examples of differences between the King James Version and *The Message*:

> For the preaching of the cross is to them that perish foolishness; but unto us which are saved it is the power of God.
>
> —1 CORINTHIANS 1:18, KJV

> The Message that points to Christ on the Cross seems like sheer silliness to those *hellbent* on destruction, but for those on the way of salvation it makes perfect sense.
>
> —1 CORINTHIANS 1:18, THE MESSAGE, EMPHASIS ADDED

> There is therefore now no condemnation to them which are in Christ Jesus, who walk not after the flesh, but after the Spirit. For the law of the Spirit of life in Christ Jesus hath made me free from the law of sin and death.
>
> —ROMANS 8:1–2, KJV

> With the arrival of Jesus, the Messiah, that fateful dilemma is resolved. Those who enter into Christ's being-here-for-us no longer have to live under a continuous, low-lying black cloud. A new power is in operation. The Spirit of life in Christ, like a strong wind, has magnificently cleared the air, freeing you from a fated lifetime of brutal tyranny at the hands of sin and death. God went for the jugular when he sent his own Son. He didn't deal with the problem as something remote and unimportant. In his Son, Jesus, he personally took on the human condition, entered the disordered mess of struggling humanity in order to set it right once and for all.
>
> —ROMANS 8:1–3, THE MESSAGE

Other Scriptures that are distorted include: 1 Corinthians 1:17; Romans 1:29; 7:22–25; Ezekiel 16:24, 26; 23:21, 49; 24:13;

2 Kings 9:34; 18:27; Hosea 4:2, 10, 12, 19; 11:2; Judges 19:22; Proverbs 1:11; 17:12; Jeremiah 2:23–24; 5:7; 8:14; 18:13; Psalm 68:6; 88:3; Lamentations 3:47, 65; Acts 8:20; Zephaniah 1:9; Numbers 23:7; 1 Chronicles 11:19; and Micah 3:5.

The American Family Association reported the following story:

> The latest fad with some hotels is to replace their Bibles with "intimacy kits." For instance, at New York City's trendy SoHo Grand Hotel guests can enjoy a gourmet mini-bar, an iPod, a flat-screen TV, an intimacy kit, and even the company of a complimentary pet goldfish. But no Bible.
>
> Parent company Accor Hotels decided to replace the Gideon Bibles with "intimacy kits." For Accor, providing travelers with sexual paraphernalia is more important than the Bible....
>
> Since 2001 the number of luxury hotels with Bibles in the rooms has dropped by 18 percent.[1]

Some pastors only preach what the people like to hear, instead of telling them about hellfire and brimstone. Some even get their sermons prewritten on the Internet, by e-mail, or fax. On Sunday, they read it to their congregation, not realizing that God's anointing is absent. Did the Holy Spirit leave them, or was He never present in their life such that they can't hear Him during the week to reveal to them what to preach on Sunday? Some pastors stand in front of their congregation with their hands buried in their pants pockets and preach. They even pray in that position. Where is their reverence for the almighty and holy God?

Pastors, let me tell you, God is building His church and is getting many of you ready for His great outpouring of the Holy Spirit. Make sure you're not left out!

When the Bible is read or the pastor prays out loud, no one should be walking around in church or talking. Parents should train their children so that they respect the house of God at an early age, not running through the sanctuary during the service as if it were a football field. I wouldn't say this if I had I not seen it.

As many young people as are getting saved now, we need to accept them as they are—along with their earrings, wild hairstyles, tattoos, pierced tongues, and body parts. Maybe in time the Holy Spirit will convict them and clean them up, but it is not our job. Let's just love them. I realize that some people never own a suit; they live in blue jeans and sweatshirts. Certain ones who got radically saved out of the drug scene now put the older saints to shame. They are on fire for the Lord and witness where most of us would be afraid to go. We need to love, not judge them, just the way they are, just as Jesus accepted us when we got born again.

If you are a pastor, ask yourself if you are even called by God and anointed by Him to stand in the pulpit.

> But I keep under my body, and bring it into subjection: lest that by any means, when I have preached to others, I myself should be a castaway.
>
> —1 CORINTHIANS 9:27

After five years of marriage to their daughter and after she gave them a cute grandbaby, a pastor and his wife I know still would not accept their son-in-law. They behaved as if he did not exist when he was in their midst and spoke ill of him. Even after they were married, her mother pointed certain men out to her, saying, "How about this one or that one?" She told her that she loved him and no one else. Can you believe that a man of God would hold resentment toward his son-in-law after that many years? Yet, he and his wife were both God-fearing people. How could that happen? Both of them know the Scriptures very well, but they let their own heart be deceived. Does a different set of standards apply in their personal life? I'm sure that they know the following scriptures.

> And as ye would that men should do to you, do ye also to them likewise.... Judge not, and ye shall not be judged: condemn not, and ye shall not be condemned: forgive, and ye shall be forgiven.
>
> —LUKE 6:31, 37

> And when ye stand praying, forgive, if ye have ought against any: that your Father also which is in heaven may forgive you your trespasses. But if ye do not forgive, neither will your Father which is in heaven forgive your trespasses.
>
> —MARK 11:25–26

After the daughter and their son-in-law were married for ten years, I met another member of their family in a grocery store. She told me that the girl's mother had four operations in the previous eighteen months and that the mother and her daughter were estranged. When I spoke to the girl not long after that, she confirmed it and told me that her mother had cancer throughout her whole body. She also told me that she and her husband agreed that, should her mother die, they would not attend her funeral to keep from being subjected to more of their harassment. Did

God send me to speak to her just in time to let her know that she needed to go visit her mother? A couple of weeks later, her mother passed away and she attended the funeral. What will Jesus say to the pastor and his wife when they both stand in front of Him to be judged?

I want my heavenly Father to forgive me when I need it. I told Him to let me know if I need repenting of anything, because I want to have a clean slate before Him. I want to be pure in His sight. What about my pastor friend and his wife? Should they not also have acted in the same manner? You see, after a while when our heart gets hard because we believe that we are all right, we can't even hear the Holy Spirit convict us anymore. For this very reason, many people are not used mightily by God. Do you suppose that pastor's unforgiveness is affecting his anointing as a minister? We read in Romans 8:8, "So then they that are in the flesh cannot please God." Romans 12:1–2 says, "I beseech you therefore, brethren, by the mercies of God, that ye present your bodies a living sacrifice, holy, acceptable unto God, which is your reasonable service. And be not conformed to this world: but be ye transformed by the renewing of your mind, that ye may prove what is that good, and acceptable, and perfect, will of God." Is it not God's will that we forgive? Also, Romans 14:12 tells us that "every one of us shall give account of himself to God." He has it all spelled out for us in the Scriptures!

In the early part of January 1976, I repeated the sinner's prayer with a television evangelist. The Holy Spirit drew me to accept Jesus as my Savior once I realized that I only had religion instead of a born-again experience. I had Jesus in my head only, not in my heart. I asked the pastor of this large local non-denominational church I was attending about being baptized. He told me it was sufficient that I was sprinkled as a baby. However, the Bible says differently. At that time, I was a brand-new Christian and didn't know any better; therefore I believed him. After all, he was my pastor. I assumed he would know and tell me the truth, but he deceived me with his answer. What if I never left this church and never read and applied what the Bible has to say about water baptism? How many others did he deceive? Praise God, five years later the Lord led me to an Assembly of God church. When I inquired about becoming a member, the deacons asked me if I was baptized. The Bible states clearly that after the confession of our faith, we are to be baptized by immersion. I grew a lot spiritually in that church. When the doors were open I was there and became an altar worker, on fire for the Lord.

In 1988 the Holy Spirit called me to attend a different church across town, also an Assembly of God church, which was about ten blocks from the Muslim mosque. God wanted me to start a ministry to the Muslims. When I told the pastor, he threw his hands up into the air in panic. He would not allow it. If someone gave a message in tongues, the pastor would automatically interpret it. He would not wait to see if anyone in the congregation had the gift as well. It always bothered me to see him be that eager. I had to wait two years before the Lord sent me to another church, but all these experiences were training me not to behave like that.

From there, the Lord called me to a small non-denominational church for only six months. I realized later that I was to learn to what degree these pastors served God or self, and to what extent they practiced the truth of the Bible. In this church, they picked up a number of people on Wednesday evening from a nursing home and from the mission where the homeless can stay. They would feed them before the evening service, and some accepted Jesus as their Savior. The only thing wrong was that the pastor said the sinner's prayer for them, instead of having the individual repeat it. The Bible is clear in that it says in Romans 10:9, "That if thou shalt confess with thy mouth the Lord Jesus, and shalt believe in thine heart that God hath raised him from the dead, thou shalt be saved." Someone else's mouth confessing it for you won't do.

About a year before I attended this church, the Lord sent me to minister to this same pastor, though I had not yet met him. We met in the evening in his office after their mid-week service. The Lord had me give him my first book and an audiotape from Anton Sawyer, a South African lady who the Lord sent to prophesy to the American churches, in which she warns pastors to get out of the pulpit if they are only a hireling instead of being called by God. I recorded it from a Christian TV station on June 16, 1989. Afterward I realized why I had to give him this tape. During our conversation, he said that he never wanted to become their pastor, but after his father died they voted him in. He answered the tape ahead of time, before he knew what it contained, so he should not have been surprised once he listened to it. The Holy Spirit knows what we need to hear, even if it seems not right at all in our carnal thinking. When I mentioned that he needed to be empowered by the Holy Spirit, his face turned bright red and he said that he would ask his deacons if they thought he was and call me to let me know. Needless to say, I never heard from him. I don't believe that he was excited to see me attend his church a year later. About five years after I left his church, I attended a function there several days in a row where I heard him give an altar call each evening. I was very pleased that he had the converts now repeat the words after him. In fact, he gave excellent altar calls then.

Afterward, the Lord directed me to a Church of God in Christ church for two years. I attended over a year before He finally revealed to me why I was there. During the membership classes, I was told that they believed like the Assemblies of God denomination, but that was not so. Right in the beginning, the pastor asked me if I expected to be ordained since I told him that I was an evangelist. I told the pastor no, that the Holy Spirit revealed to me that the kind of ministry He wants me to perform has not been done before, therefore He did not want some local church board to tell me that they don't do it that way. I was to get my orders directly from the Holy Spirit. I guess he was relieved with my answer. I had no idea that the Church of God in Christ is against the ordination of women. In fact, one Sunday a pastor from another church of their denomination spent the whole half-hour of his radio program telling why woman should not be ordained. He hammered away at it. Nonetheless, they do have a few women pastors in their denomination. One is the daughter of a bishop, who felt called by the Lord. I also discovered that when women minister in this church they have to use a pulpit that is one level lower than that of the male pastors. Other men are allowed to speak from the upper platform. Is that not discrimination against women's right in the church? Does not the Bible tell us in Galatians 3:28, "There is neither male nor female: for ye are all one in Christ Jesus." This is what God's Word says, but men have perverted it.

Once, another local pastor from their denomination held revival meetings several evenings at this church. He was bald-headed and used a white hand towel to wipe the sweat frequently from his head and face. During the service, he threw his sweat-soaked towel into the audience a couple of times. It was disgusting! He preached that if you wear lipstick, you're not saved. I did not know that he believed that; it was kept from me when I went through their membership classes, although I always wore makeup and lipstick. He looked some of us over who wore lipstick and called a lady up front to minister to her. By doing so, he embarrassed her in front of the whole congregation. I don't believe that the Holy Spirit agreed with his action. People need to know the truth of the Bible themselves to avoid situations like that. Cults get started when people have some truth then add their own doctrine.

I believe that this coming revival is intended by God to get us back to the truth of His Word, not ours. For example, tell me what lipstick has to do with your spirituality. A lady from our church told me when I asked her that a lady wearing lipstick is considered a prostitute. Yet nobody told me of this belief, which is a man-made doctrine anyway. The Lord allows me to experience some of these things firsthand.

That pastor should study how the Jewish girls made themselves up while they were waiting for their future husband to come and get them. He is the one that needed to be ministered to. That is not how a man of God conducts himself. He operated totally in the flesh. During the community revival service one evening, his own congregation presented him with a new robe, making a big show—something that was absolutely out of order and not appropriate to take place in that setting. If they wanted to adore him, let them do it in their own church. He came to hold revival meetings.

Each congregation in the Church of God in Christ honors their pastor yearly, at which time a certain dollar figure per person is suggested to be given him. Around that particular time one year, someone smeared very dark makeup on our pastor's white suit as he hugged us. At our next Bible study—we were only a handful of ladies—the assistant pastor made a big speech about messing up the pastor's suit. Although no name was mentioned, I knew it was meant for me from the way it was presented, because none of the other ladies present wore makeup. I'm sure I was the guilty one in their opinion. However, I don't wear makeup that dark. Another time when we had a big function combined with some of the other churches throughout the state, I was weeping while I shared something with the audience. Afterward I asked the ladies around me for a mirror. I don't know if God allowed this on purpose, because the senior pastor's wife from another church gave me her mirror, which included a used powder cake. If they don't wear any makeup, why did she have a used one in her purse?

Later on, our pastor said from the pulpit that according to the bishop if you don't comply with their rules, you can't be used in ministry. In the past, though, the pastor had me stand up front at certain times with their other missionary ladies dressed in white. He was not man enough to tell me about their rules against wearing makeup in person. After the service in which he explained the bishop's rule against participating in ministry without following their rules about makeup, I told him that I knew that message was meant for me and I would not participate anymore. I did not ask for it in the first place. Some time later at a business meeting, one of the ladies nominated me to be a board member, which I declined. Another time our church mother wrote me a note, which I kept in my Bible, asking me to emcee a revival service with the theme "Back to True Holiness—Do It Now!" The message was to be based on Ephesians 4:23–24: "And be renewed in the spirit of your mind; And that ye put on the new man, which after God is created in righteousness and true holiness." Somehow I was sickened by their church doctrine and declined to do it. Otherwise, I would have been a hypocrite. I would have had to preach the truth and expose certain things.

Some time later, the Lord impressed upon me to teach the young people how to do some fruit canning, crochet, mend, and beginner's sewing. Also how to balance a checkbook and take them shopping and on outings. This was after the pastor's announcement from the pulpit, but I obeyed anyway. I told the pastor's wife and asked her to pray about it, since she was in charge of the young people. She never gave me an answer.

One time the Lord had me minister directly to this pastor. He told me the pastor was to take one day a week off and spend it with his family instead of trying to put one business deal after another together and get donations for their thrift store. When his church needed a new roof, a congregation from a different denomination in another town supplied part of the money and even furnished some of the workers. Later we were invited to fellowship with them in their midweek service. When the pastor made the announcement, he told us to dress down. Why? Because we dressed like millionaires and they were very casual. With financial assistance from state or national government sources, our church directed an alcohol-counseling center, ran a thrift store—which paid the pastor's wife a salary for running it—a day care, and grade school. When he was a guest at a local Christian TV interview, the pastor was asked who was paying for all that. He said that our congregation was financing all these projects, which was not true. The congregation was very small and several of the members were on assistance themselves.

The pastor did not obey what the Lord had me minister to him, and exactly a year later, his whole empire fell apart. Even their church attendance stayed small. After more than thirty years in ministry, one would expect some growth. Instead, the people come and go. Other agencies took over the projects, which shows that our church did not financially support them. That pastor lost all that he was trying to accomplish in the flesh. Did God not bless it, because he did not obey? Is it not time that men start listening to women who are possibly more sensitive to the voice of the Holy Spirit? We need to be very careful that we do not miss what God is trying to tell us. Pray about something before you dismiss it instead of acting so superior. Did God not speak through a donkey in the Old Testament? Perhaps God was trying to teach this pastor that his human efforts were not bringing the results and that instead he needed to trust in Him and turn everything over to the Holy Spirit, asking Him for direction and following it.

It is important to apply the armor of God. Some of you reading this book have no idea what I'm talking about, so I will tell you how Paul describes it in the Word of God.

> Finally, my brethren, be strong in the Lord, and in the power of his might. Put on the whole armour of God, that ye may be able to stand against the wiles of the devil. For we wrestle not against flesh and blood, but against principalities, against powers, against the rulers of the darkness of this world, against spiritual wickedness in high places. Wherefore take unto you the whole armour of God, that ye may be able to withstand in the evil day, and having done all, to stand. Stand therefore, having your loins girt about with truth, and having on the breastplate of righteousness; And your feet shod with the preparation of the gospel of peace; Above all, taking the shield of faith, wherewith ye shall be able to quench all the fiery darts of the wicked. And take the helmet of salvation, and the sword of the Spirit, which is the word of God: Praying always with all prayer and supplication in the Spirit, and watching thereunto with all perseverance and supplication for all saints; And for me, that utterance may be given unto me, that I may open my mouth boldly, to make known the mystery of the gospel.
>
> —Ephesians 6:10–19

My dear people, I hope you understand what I mean. Satan is getting desperate. We Christians know his future. He will end up in the lake of fire and wants as many of us as possible to keep him company.

I finally figured it out. The Lord is training me His own way and is teaching me how to behave once He sends me out on my own. Therefore, He is giving me certain firsthand experiences. Before a pastor becomes a senior pastor, he often starts out as a youth pastor, then moves up to be an associate pastor, and then after he gets a number of years of experience, he finally becomes a senior pastor. All those years he collects experiences that help him to be a leader when he has his own congregation. In my case, God is teaching me Himself through different experiences as He sends me here and there. I had different individuals from other countries, some of whom were pastors, stay in my home. The experiences I obtained through them by far outweigh any Bible school or seminary I could have attended. I learned a lot firsthand in these years of Him training me.

I prayed with a man who was a new Christian who had been heavily involved in pornography and cross-dressing. Had this activity affected his health and put him in a wheelchair? After I prayed with him for deliverance, I told him that we read in the Bible that these kinds of issues only come out by fasting and prayer. I also told him that no sin enters heaven. He moved away, but I heard that he is now out of the wheelchair and walks with a walker. He is very intelligent and has the will to live. May our Lord restore him even more.

I met a pastor who had moved here from out of state. He does not have a church or congregation anymore. He shared with me that the Lord wanted him to hold miracle services and asked me to help him find a building. When I did, he couldn't afford to pay the monthly lease. I told him that when my book was finished I would be teaching different denominations how to receive the baptism in the Holy Spirit and that perhaps he could hold his meetings afterward in their churches. He informed me that instead he would have to be the boss. I was only trying to open the door for him. It showed me how prideful he was and how much work the Lord would have to do in him before He could even use him. In the meantime, he would just have to sit at home and wait, because our Lord will not be embarrassed in the days ahead when He sends us out to represent Him. He is looking for humble servants.

Are we not all part of the family of God? And if "sons of God" according to His Word, should we not also act like it? I can't imagine how disgusted our Lord in heaven must be with all our denominational doctrines. Are we not all serving the same God? Why can't we all just believe what is written in the Bible?

To show you how much in control certain denominations are, I will tell you the experience of a dear saint I met in the early 1980s during our Assemblies of God church conference. David du Plessis was called "Mr. Pentecost" for the impact he made on believers of many denominations. The famous plumber-preacher Smith Wigglesworth prophesied to him in 1936 that the Lord would pour out His Spirit upon the established church and the ensuing revival would eclipse anything the Pentecostals had experienced. He also prophesied that David would be mightily used by God to bring acceptance of the Pentecostal message to the established churches. When I heard him speak, David explained how this extraordinary prophecy was fulfilled in the years that followed.

Living in South Africa, his travels took him to Japan, Canada, America, and several European countries—yes, even to Rome, where he met with three different popes over the years. He told us that one of them said, "We're all pregnant with the Holy Spirit." He was teaching the baptism in the Holy Spirit to many leaders of different denominations and lectured on Pentecostal issues in many well-known schools of theology. In 1955 he was asked to act as their secretary for the next world conference in Toronto in 1958. He reached out to all denominations. During one retreat near Columbus, Ohio, in 1962, he ministered with congregational pastors from the Reformed, Mennonite, Lutheran, Episcopal, Baptist, Methodist, Anglican, Presbyterian, and Pentecostal denominations.

Through the recommendation of the Apostolic Faith Mission of South Africa, he had received his ministerial credentials from the Assemblies of God for his work in the United States. But before the Columbus conference there had been considerable controversy over his activities, even suggestions that he should withdraw from the ministry. Why, one would ask? He did so much good as he was leading all these denominations into a greater understanding of the Bible. Was he not serving God full-time with a very special anointing upon him? Did one organization try to control him as he accomplished more and more for the kingdom of God? When he called her on the last night of the conference, his wife, Anna, was heartbroken as she told him through her tears that they had just received a letter from Springfield, the Assemblies of God headquarters, that they disfellowshiped him. What a shock, since he has been striving for ten years to bring unity among Pentecostals. Was this letter God-ordained or a man-made decision?

Even a couple of years before the letter came, he asked himself, "What happened to our early vision?" as his host country seemed to be fully in charge of each conference. He told us that night that it seemed he was alone. He was sad and discouraged, feeling as though he had wasted ten years of ministry, when he began to hear a whisper in his spirit that said, "Trust in Me and don't despair. Other doors will open. You will see completely unexpected and new things happen." Indeed, other doors opened for him, as he served even without credentials as an unofficial Pentecostal ambassador-at-large from 1962 until 1980, when he was reinstated as an ordained minister. They must have been ashamed of themselves, because God's anointing upon him did not cease, despite of man's control and decision. I'm glad for the outcome, or I would of probably not have met him in my Assembly of God church, where he inspired me greatly. He went to be with the Lord in 1987.

The Holy Spirit had a reason for me to illustrate this dear saint's experience. I'm sure that some of you are to learn from it so you won't be a hindrance and try to block what the Holy Spirit is about to do in our upcoming revival. I believe the reason we don't have more powerful healing evangelists in our day is because people don't want to pay the price required by God. He wants all of you to serve Him with all of your heart. He removes one by one what is undesirable to Him. There is a difference between serving Him and serving Him with all of your heart.

Let's look at some of the healing evangelists from the past, both men and women. Yes, God will use whosoever will make himself available for His service. All of them had to pay a great price in order to be completely sold-out to God and be used mightily. A number of them were afflicted with illnesses or infirmities—just like Moses had stuttered. A few even lay on their deathbed when they were young before God healed them. If it were not for His mercy, they would have died. Knowing that, they owed their life to Him and therefore sold themselves out completely, allowing the Holy Spirit to flow through them in a remarkable way.

We can thank a man from Scotland by the name of John Alexander Dowie for being able to lay hands on people today when we pray for them for healing. When he arrived in Chicago, the law was such that one had to have a medical decree in order to do so. It is sad to say, but he was arrested over hundred times in one year until he finally got the law changed, as large crowds attended his healing meetings.

Maria Woodworth Etter, a Pentecostal pioneer, was one of the most popular healing evangelists in the late 1800s. It was an era in which women were not well received, but the gift always makes room for the person. After all, God is in charge. She was very dramatic and people would fall out or, as we call it now, be slain in the spirit. They would lie on the floor up to a couple of hours, during which time they saw visions of hell or heaven. In one of her meetings, she herself stiffened, standing up for three days. As people came to view her in her "frozen state," they would get saved. When she came to, she continued ministering as if nothing had happened. It is assumed that she was not even aware of the amount of time that had passed. In one of her meetings in San Francisco, a man heckled her. One day she told him that he would get judged that night. His tongue swelled and grew long, hanging out of his mouth, which prevented him from eating. He wrote her notes to remove the curse on him. She replied, "Not until you get saved." God made a believer out of him.

Aimee Semple McPherson had a powerful ministry in the 1920s. Her followers built her the five-thousand-seat Angelus

Temple in Los Angeles. Ambulances loaded with the sick stopped at her back door regularly to be prayed for. Once she made her entrance riding a motorcycle onto the platform. What would our critics say if a lady evangelist would do that today? Would it be called demonic?

Smith Wigglesworth was born in 1859. He was an uneducated plumber from Great Britain whose wife taught him to read at age twenty-three. He had a style all of his own. When he was young, he nearly died of appendicitis. An old woman and a young man came to see him, and as they prayed for him they hit him and he got healed, which became his pattern of ministering to people once the Lord called him into full-time service at age fifty-five. He claimed that he hit the devil and the people would get in the way. He would hit people with back problems and kick them. It is said that he raised nineteen people from death, including his wife. When he did, she asked him what he was doing since she had been conversing with Jesus and asked to be sent back to Him, which he did. He went to be with the Lord in 1946 at the age of eighty-seven. How would people react today to this kind of treatment? People seem to be more concerned with the application rather than the results.

The Jeffrey brothers from England were well-known healing evangelists in the early 1900s. All they would have to say upon entering a building was, "The Master is here," and the people got healed of all kinds of diseases. One of the brothers would literally laugh at people, and they got healed of arthritis. Arms grew out, the lame walked, eyes popped into sockets—you name it.

We, too, will experience these kinds of miracles soon. Either America will repent or we can be sure of God's judgment.

At the Azusa Street revival from 1906–1910, it took an inside job to stop this great move of God. William J. Seymour, who they called "Daddy" and who had attended Charles F. Parham's Bible school in Houston, Texas, was invited to be pastor in Los Angeles. In his first sermon in the spring of 1906, he preached on Acts 2:4 and announced the necessity of speaking in other tongues as evidence of the Pentecostal experience. Because of opposition from another church group, he had to find refuge in the home of Richard Asberry on Bonnie Brae Avenue. After spending several weeks in prayer meetings at the home, he and several others received their sought-after tongues experience, which they attributed to the outbreak of the revival. In the beginning, Pastor Seymour, an African-American minister, held services on the front porch. As the crowd grew, they relocated to 312 Azusa Street, where he preached his first sermon on April 14, 1906. By May, more than a thousand tried to visit the forty-by-sixty-foot mission. Soon they came from all over the nation, including overseas. In October he invited an evangelist friend to come and preach, but he was very much upset by the noisy demonstrations and suspected even demonic activity.[2]

Is it any different in our time? When the Holy Spirit is allowed to move freely—which many have not even known before—it is called demonic because people have not yet had an encounter with the Holy Spirit and therefore they can not discern the source. In the case of the Azusa Street Revival, the end result was that Pastor Seymour was asked to leave by the elders of his own church. You see, his friend saw something he was not familiar with, so right away he concluded it had to be from the devil.

The Bible tells us that rivers of living waters will flow from out of our bellies, but until now many of us have only produced drops. We read in Acts 1:8, "But ye shall receive power, after that the Holy Spirit is come upon you." We will be energized with the power of the Holy Spirit, which we call *dunamis* power (dynamite). People don't behave the same as they were before. The last half of Acts 1:8 says: "And ye shall be witnesses unto me both in Jerusalem, and in all Judaea, and in Samaria, and unto the uttermost part of the earth." How do you think this would be possible without a big dose of the Holy Spirit's power to energize them? Once it happens, the lame duck feeling is gone and you're on fire for the Lord.

I have been for thirty years, ever since I got born again. Now I share the Lord with anyone who will listen. Standing in line to check out at the grocery store or even the post office are good opportunities. I like to witness by telling them what the Lord has done in my life and invite them to a saving experience.

During the Azusa revival, they held three meetings a day, seven days a week, for years with increasing force as people from all nations, races, and culture attended. Blacks and whites worshiped together in harmony. The blood of Jesus washed their prejudice away. It triggered the Pentecostal movement, and missionaries were sent to twenty-five countries, as far as India and China, with this new experience of the baptism in the Holy Spirit, given to them by Jesus Himself and evidenced by speaking in tongues.

Two white ladies who helped with the secretarial aspect of the ministry did not approve of Pastor Seymour's marriage in 1908.

They took the mailing list for his newsletter, which amounted to fifty thousand subscribers. Without it, he could not communicate with the people who depended on his leadership. With the outbreak of World War I, by 1914 a black church arose at Azusa Street. Pastor Seymour became bishop of that church the following year. As segregation was the custom then, a white church movement emerged called the Assemblies of God, and Pastor Seymour ordained a number of their pastors. After his death in 1922, Seymour's wife continued as pastor of the Azusa Mission.

Practically every early Pentecostal movement in the world can trace its origins directly or indirectly to Seymour's Azusa Street Mission. Over 600 million Spirit-filled Christians can claim their roots from the Azusa Street revival.

Kathryn Kuhlman's remarkable ministry lasted for fifty years. During that time, she performed many miracles that millions of people who once thought them impossible came to believe in. She went to be with the Lord in 1976. Her official biography, written by Jamie Buckingham, was eight books of her incredible life and ministry. I have her healing videos, but I won't say anymore about her. I will let you read about her yourself, so I don't spoil your anticipation about perhaps the foremost woman evangelist of our century.

In our era, great deliverances take place. The Toronto Blessing, a revival that started in Canada and has been going on for a number of years, has spread to Great Britain, a few American churches, and by now also to France. Yet certain people condemn it. I even heard a pastor with a large church in Texas voice his disbelief from the pulpit on national Christian TV about the groaning that one pastor in particular displayed. He must have thought that he was right when he condemned it. What if he was wrong? Jesus groaned not one time but two times in the same situation?

> She fell down at his feet, saying unto him, Lord, if thou hadst been here, my brother had not died. When Jesus therefore saw her weeping, and the Jews also weeping which came with her, he *groaned* in the spirit, and was troubled. And said, Where have ye laid him? They said unto him, Lord, come and see. Jesus wept. Then said the Jews, Behold how he loved him! And some of them said, Could not this man, which opened the eyes of the blind, have caused that even this man should not have died? Jesus therefore again *groaning* in himself cometh to the grave. It was a cave, and a stone lay upon it.
>
> —John 11:32–38, emphasis added

Remember, God says, "Vengeance is mine; I will repay" (Rom. 12:19), and He often does so sooner then we realize. I believe that it would be appropriate if that pastor would publicly apologize. The many changed lives should be enough evidence of the revival's legitimacy. Don't judge others with your worldly understanding. Unless you have directly heard from the Lord, you should know not to touch God's anointed. Otherwise, you will lead many other people down the same road of your unbelief.

An Assembly of God church in Pensacola, Florida, began experiencing a mighty revival in 1995, and thousands of people came from all over to take part. Four million people came from around the world within the first five years, where many thousand responded to the altar calls. They were standing in line for twelve to fourteen hours a day, five nights a week just to get a seat. The evangelist that came to preach only a single service on Father's Day stayed five years. They prayed this revival in. God revealed to the pastor to truly make it a house of prayer, which they did for two and one-half years prior.

God moves where and how He chooses! The Community Church in Smithton, Missouri, a small town without even a traffic light and a population of only 549, has been experiencing God's extraordinary grace pouring over this little country church that was built in 1859. Locked up for many years, it finally became alive again in 1996, twelve years after the pastor started it again with thirteen people. God had spoken to him in 1983 that He would bring revival to the local church. Heartbroken, his desperate wife sent him to Florida to check out the Brownsville Revival in Pensacola. As he walked into the church service upon his return to Smithton, the Lord hit him like lightning. His arms shot up in the air as if weights were lifted and he began to jump up and down. It wasn't planned; it just happened. Feeling God's presence, the people rushed forward for prayer. It became a corporate ministry with the whole church participating, including the young people.

God's anointing does not discriminate against age. It is a condition of the heart. Many people who should have been receiving prayer and healing in their own churches were drawn to the revival from all around the globe. Why not? Entire churches have been transformed as thousands of lives have been changed. Here are a few examples.

From Pensacola, the revival spread to Lincoln, Illinois, and on it went as word of mouth testimonies spread. One pastor said that couples from their church that went to Smithton came back with an intense love for Jesus and radically changed marriages. As more people heard about the revival, they, too, then went to check out the revival in Smithton and brought it back home with them to their church.

A local pastor whom I know also went. A ten-year-old child who pointed out some of the pastor's personal defects prayed for him. As the pastor lay on the floor for an extended time, the Holy Spirit revealed to him that if he did not change, his ministry would be over. He shared that he had an awesome experience on the floor. His church, too, has been experiencing a mighty revival fire after his return. They built a large church since. I attended a number of their meetings myself. You see, by now it is too late to harness the Holy Spirit.

Numerous gatherings are taking place now in different places all over the nation. Only if you diligently seek Him, letting go of self, and mean business with the Holy Spirit will revival come to your church. This requires the Holy Spirit baptism, evidenced by speaking in other tongues. Will we have revival in our country, or will we face God's judgment? Revival can only happen if we allow the Holy Spirit to prick and change our hard hearts, as we repent and give Him our all. We read in 2 Chronicles 7:14–15, "If my people, which are called by my name, shall humble themselves, and pray, and seek my face, and turn from their wicked ways; then will I hear from heaven, and will forgive their sin, and will heal their land. Now mine eyes shall be open, and mine ears attend unto the prayer that is made in this place." He calls us His people. His eyes are open and He listens to our prayers. Prepare yourself (your flesh) so that He can pour out His Spirit, as we are told in Joel 2:28: "And it shall come to pass afterward, that I will pour out my spirit upon all flesh; and your sons and your daughters shall prophesy, your old men shall dream dreams, your young men shall see visions;" and 1 Corinthians 2:14: "But the natural man receiveth not the things of the Spirit of God: for they are foolishness unto him: neither can he know them, because they are spiritually discerned."

I wonder through whom Satan is going to rear his ugly neck when our long awaited revival breaks out.

Out of complete obedience to the Lord and without any experience or training, I wrote my first book in 1985. By not having a better vocabulary then, I used *I* a number of times. From 1985 to 1991, He called me out of the very successful real estate career I had since 1971 to serve Him. Remember, obedience is better than sacrifice. God called me to do it, so I had to complete it. If God reveals something for me to do, I will not take no for an answer from any man.

The Lord had me register my ministry in January 1985 when I left the real estate business. A year later He wanted me to start a publishing company. The following day I asked Him what to name it. He replied, "Vision Publishing Company, because I gave it to you in a vision." In 1987 I had another manuscript ready, but the Holy Spirit wanted me to shelve it. He revealed to me that the last chapter had not been written yet. What a disappointment, but I was obedient. It turned out that most of the chapters are contained in this book and the volumes to come. In 1990 I wrote my second book, which was quite an improvement in my vocabulary. The Lord had me expose a self-proclaimed prophet. Now I realize He had me register the publishing company so I could write what the Holy Spirit dictated me, because my books are very controversial. (This book was much too large of a project for me to handle by myself.)

God allows me several years of experiences, directed by Him, and then has me write them down. Some of these episodes were very painful, but I'm doing it to bring glory to God, to equip me for my calling, and to minister to you, the reader. My life is no longer my own. I completely sold out to Him a number of years ago.

From 1985 to 1991 I made three trips to Ghana, West Africa; two to Egypt; two to Israel and the West Bank; and one to Germany. I also hosted several people from Ghana in my home during this time, most of them pastors.

The Lord wants you to know what most people in this country have no idea of—how tricky and mean Satan works. A lot of people don't know what the spirit of deviation and many other spirits are like. God allowed me firsthand experiences that would open my eyes and prepare me for my calling overseas to the Muslims in Egypt and wherever else He sends me to minister. While I was attending a Full Gospel Business Men's Fellowship International meeting in Ghana, I was led by the Holy Spirit to buy a small book called *Delivered from the Powers of Darkness*, written Emmanuel Eni from Nigeria. It is said that one out of every four black persons in the world has his or her roots from Nigeria. God wants you to get a glimpse of that man's awesome testimony. It is gross, and hopefully gives you some insight into the spirit world, of which most of us in this country have little knowledge.

The tragic experience he describes took place over sixty years ago in a small village in Nigeria before most of us had even heard of demons, let alone experienced any; if we did, we did not recognize it as such. This young man was one of four children. His father inherited a large tract of land from his father. Although it was supposed to bring happiness to the family, instead, it brought tragedy, one after another. First, his mother died, then four years later his father died—both victims of witchcraft. Since more problems occurred, I believe that it was an ancestral curse, which can only be broken by the power of God after it is recognized as such. Two years later, his oldest sister disappeared mysteriously, than the sister next to her became mentally ill. He and his youngest sister were sent to his grandparents, but after a few years they also died. The sister went to other relatives, and he never heard from her again. He was forced to return to his father's house at the age of thirteen to live amongst his father's enemies, who became his enemies also. It must have been their jealousy because the father inherited the land. The parents of a friend he knew from school took him in, and he lived carefree for two years with his new parents until all three of them got killed in a car accident on vacation. With no place else to go, he returned home again and did menial jobs in order to eat.

After all of these hardships, a girl he once attended school with appeared. Although she was five years older than he, when he was only eleven and still in school she had told him that she would marry him some day. This time when they met she was twenty; he, fifteen. She had moved to the city were she worked as an accountant for a large bank. Knowing his plight, she took advantage of him by giving him her address and more money than he would normally earn in a month. He thought moving to the big city and earning big money was his escape to freedom.

She insisted that he live with her instead of her parents, since they were getting married. She told him that she would make him rich. He never knew that such a lifestyle could be possible—a beautiful wife, a well-furnished apartment, gifts, new clothing, money, and her love. But we read in John 10:10, "The thief comet not, but for to steal, and to kill, and to destroy." He soon found out that the devil gives no free gifts. Whatever he gives you is in exchange of your soul. After three months of living with her, strange things started to happen. As he awoke one night, a boa constrictor was lying beside him in bed. His wife turned into one. He wanted to scream but couldn't. Some other nights he would see her body looking as transparent as a cellophane bag. Other nights she would disappear and reappear. Some nights he would hear strange noises or dancing in the living room. He could no longer take these fearful happenings and asked her what was going on. She reacted violently and seriously warned him not to ask these questions again—or else. He knew that his life was in danger. Her parents had no idea that their pretty daughter with a good job was deeply involved in the occult and spiritism. She looked harmless but she was the devil's agent. The writer warns that there are many more like her out there in the world.

She had four refrigerators in the apartment where she kept parts of human bodies she used during different rituals. He knew that she could discern in her office what he did at home and saw himself as a dead man if he did not cooperate and keep his mouth shut. The following day she asked him to come along to a meeting. The very large building in which she worked on the outskirts of the city had an underground conference room, which they entered backwards. About five hundred young men and women who were students, graduates, and teachers sat around in a circle. Seated above them was the leader, but only his head and not his body were visible. As his wife pressed a button on the wall, a seat appeared from underground. She introduced the young man as a new member to the congregation, and they applauded and welcomed him, which prompted her to get promoted. He could not understand what they talked about but was asked to come back alone the next day by the leader, where he got initiated with nine others. I prefer not to describe the process. She woke him up that night at two o'clock, which is the usual hour of meetings and dangerous operations of all the forces of darkness and their agents. She admitted to him that she was not any ordinary human being, rather half-human and half spirit. She said, "What you see in my room is what I use every morning during my prayers, so that the spirits will guide me through the day. I will tell you later about the skeletons."

She had great power over him. He explained that after the command by Lucifer to fight the Christians, they then sat and mapped out ways of fighting them as follows:

1. Causing sickness
2. Causing barrenness
3. Causing slumber in the church
4. Causing confusion in the church

5. Causing lukewarmness in the church
6. Making them ignorant of the Word of God
7. Fashion and emulation
8. Fighting them physically

He continued, "I would see the born-again Christians through a TV. We do not fight hypocrites because they belong to us already. We would send our girls first to the big churches, where they would do anything to distract the people from hearing the Word of God or cause them to fall asleep as the Word was preached." He described many more situations, but let me open your eyes with this testimony he gives about a minister.

> In the evil spirit world he is known as a man of God. When he went on his knees there would be confusion among us. So we sent some girls to him to entice him. Instead he fed them. They did all they could, but never succeeded. As a result they were killed for failing. I myself then changed into a woman and went to see him. I tried to entice him with words and actions, but he was adamant. This was too much for me, so I decided to kill him physically. One day, this minister went to a market in another town. I watched him and as he bent down to check the prices I instantly had a trailer loaded with oil drums run into the market were he was. The trailer struck the high-tension pole and fell unto the people in the market, leaving many dead, but the minister escaped, which was a miracle. Another time I saw him going to town on foot; this time I decided on an oncoming truck loaded with potatoes to kill him. Many got killed that day, but the minister escaped again. After this second attempt we gave up and the minister is still alive.

> Because of a single Christian, the Devil may decide to destroy many people, thinking he could kill that particular person, but he always fails. These incidents have happened to many Christians unknown, but God always delivered them. The trouble is, the Devil does not give up. He thinks, maybe next time. As long as the Christian walks with God's love and remains in Him and does not get entangled with the affairs of this life, the Devil can never succeed, no matter how hard he tries. Only the unbeliever is at his disposal.
>
> Jesus gave the great commission in Mark 16:15, "Go ye into all the world, and preach the gospel to every creature." Yet while some Christians are still waiting for a more convenient time to obey, the Devil has also given his command to his agents. The difference is that the Devil's agents are more serious in winning souls than the Christians.[3]

If this was already the case many years ago, can you imagine how much more aggressive Satan is now? It should be clarified that Satan does not force anyone; he only attracts and makes you come willingly. The gangs, random shootings, and narcotics are demonic. These people need to accept Jesus and be delivered from those evil spirits. Prison terms won't set them free; it is a spiritual matter. That is why the Bible says in James 4:7, "Resist the devil, and he will flee from you." The Nigerian man proceeds to share in his book that the born-again Christian is not known by the Bible he or she carries to church. Rather, they are known in the spirit world by the light that shines continuously like a very bright candle in their heart or a circle of light around the head (a halo) or a wall of fire around them. He says:

> When they walk, we see angels walking along with them, one on the right side, one on the left, and one behind. This makes it impossible for us to come near them. The only way we succeed is by making the Christian sin, thereby giving us a loophole to come in. When a Christian is driving a car and we want to harm him, we find that they are never alone; an angel is always by their side. If a Christian only knew what all God has for him or her, they would not sin or live carelessly.[4]

Is this enough reason for us to spend some time in prayer with our heavenly Father in the morning before we start our day?

After she was sure that he was fully involved in the occult, the woman sat him up in his own apartment and divorced him. Is that not just like the devil? When he is through with you, he discards you. This is the reason so many young people commit suicide. His experiences get much, much deeper and most people would not believe it, even if I described them. He shared that he could travel at will to any part in the world and also talked about their demonic activity under the sea. By making certain incantations, he would disappear. I want you to get the idea what is going on in the demonic world. Through different circumstances, Jesus appeared to him and he finally got set free. Remember, at the mention of Jesus' name and through the shedding of His blood, every knee will bow sooner or later. Before that man made a total commitment to the Lord as an adult, Jesus appeared to him numerous times. The man knew Jesus when he was a child, but this time Jesus took him to see hell, which he describes as a whole city being on fire. You see, someone involved that deep with the demonic world needs more than just a prayer to be delivered and set free.

It took Jesus appearing to him and showing him hell and heaven to convince him.

So also is it with a person that has a great calling from the Lord. A prophetic message sometimes is assurance that the person hears correctly from the Lord himself. Prophecy is confirmation from God. Usually God has already told the person His calling upon his or her life. Discussing a word of prophecy with others less spiritual or those that are not even Spirit-filled could cause worldly wisdom to creep in, which I experienced several times with a friend and even a couple of pastors. They may even try to talk you out of it, suggesting that you are acting in the flesh, and laugh at you. A pew-sitter who does nothing for the Lord doesn't need a prophecy and often does not even understand the enormous calling bestowed upon other individuals. You must be sure that you heard from the Lord and then stand your ground, because it can take many years sometimes before it comes to pass. They even tried to disqualify Jesus by saying, "Can there any good thing come out of Nazareth?" (John 1:46).

Some people see things in the spirit realm. During one of our prayer meetings in my home, one of the intercessors saw a demon with long, skinny fingers walk down the stairs. Did my houseguest from Ghana bring him with him? When he reached the hardwood floor at the entry, he disintegrated.

God has allowed me all sorts of experiences so when He sends me out I will be prepared to handle them and won't panic. On a certain Sunday morning in November, 1997, about eight o'clock in the morning, my Spirit-filled pastor friend called me. He told me that the Lord wanted me to know that my book will be used to teach and enlighten the world about false religions. Some time later when I saw him, I asked if he was serious about what he told me that morning on the phone. He assured me that he would have never called me if it were not so.

Now that I'm coming to the end of this book several years later, I can see that God will use the young people mightily in our revival. I'm sure that many have never heard about Jesus from their parents. Is this the reason why I include so many Bible verses? You see, God can speak through us as well as through the Bible.

The Lord had that pastor give me an encouraging message. We read in Scriptures over and over again that when the people called on God, He sent them someone to deliver them. I believe my pastor friend was to give me a spiritual lift that day, and later he wrote me the foreword to my book. God is asking, "Would you be so one with Me that I might do just as I will to make you life and light and love—My Word fulfilled?" You see the work He has to do in us to make it a reality? "Oh, will you turn loose?" He asks. "Will you let go? Will you let Me be the purger in thee?"

Had I done that yet all the way when He stripped me completely of my finances? No! He had to do it in order to make me pliable in ways that it hurt to get my complete attention. The pruning process is usually painful, but the fruit thereafter is much greater. I'm a different person now, having more love and compassion towards others, having allowed some of my sap to bleed out of me. We read in Matthew 16:24, "Then said Jesus unto his disciples, If any man will come after me, let him deny himself, and take up his cross, and follow me." At this time we don't know what our cross-bearing will pertain, but we also read in the Scriptures that He will not put more on us than we can handle.

What hardship does He have to allow in your life in order to get you to listen to Him so that He can say afterward, "You have suffered to the measure you have ceased to sin. Your blood has been made pure, and My blood has flowed through thy veins till it is My blood that has poured from thee and not thy own, till it is holiness and purity, till it's royalty that flows from thy veins"? I did not let Him flow through Me to this extent before. I tried to do much of it in my own wisdom until I was forced to cry out to Him. Why is it so hard to let completely go of self and give the Holy Spirit complete reign in our life, to the extent that we need to endure in order to serve Him completely? I am growing, and believe me, each day I die more and more to my flesh.

I can see now as I recall the past several years that in order to be of service in all aspects of the calling God had for me I needed to be available. Had I kept my two apartment houses I could not be able to leave them for an extended time when God calls me to Egypt. They would have been paid for by now and worth several million dollars, but God wanted me. Now instead of dollar bills, in my spirit I see souls looking out of the windows when I drive by a certain condominium complex under construction. Would I have been willing to go through all the hardships I endured if I knew in advance? Would I even been willing to leave my successful real estate career, which started my financial collapse? Many years later I realized that God had it purposed for me to be completely broke in order to use me wherever He wanted me and with whom.

Not knowing the depth of what I was saying, I remember making the Lord my partner in the early eighties. He figured out how to get rid of my money. I have been confronted by demons and was once told by one of them up-close to my face, "I'm going to kill you." Maybe I should have panicked, but instead I carried on as if nothing happened.

A lady I once knew was unable to forgive a family member who had hurt her when she was a child. We read in Matthew 6:14–15, "For if ye forgive men their trespasses, your heavenly Father will also forgive you: But if ye forgive not men their trespasses, neither will your Father forgive your trespasses." This tells us that if we hang on to unforgiveness, we will not be able to enter heaven. I tried to tell her a few times that she needed to repent and be delivered, but every time she told me off, telling me that she would never have me pray for her. Jesus said in Luke 4:18 that He came "to preach deliverance to the captives;" since that was His mission, it should be ours as well. Yes, she was captured by those demons. They felt comfortable in her body for so many years and had no intention of leaving, even though she participated in church activities. However, since no one in her congregation or church leadership believed in the baptism in the Holy Spirit, no one could discern that demons were tormenting her.

I have known her almost forty years and really love her. Several weeks ago, I gave her a Christian book about hell for her birthday, not realizing that the demons don't want her to read it. She gave it back to me, saying that she did not read that kind of material. Then a demon spoke through her, accusing me of all sorts of lies on the phone. On another occasion, she told me that she tried to witness to her Catholic neighbor by mentioning God to him. I told her to say "Holy Spirit" instead. It made her furious, and she gave me a look that could kill. I'm willing to stick my neck out to keep her and hopefully many others from going to hell.

There was going to be a healing crusade in our area, at which I expected to receive my healing for physical problems from a work-related accident. I had an unsatisfactory MRI already on my right knee. At my appointment three days after the crusade, I wanted to be able to tell the doctor and many others that I was healed, instead of making an appointment for the surgery. In faith I believed and claimed it, even prior to the crusade.

In the meantime, on August 19, I totaled my car. A few weeks before as I looked at my speedometer with 104,000 miles showing, I asked the Lord, "When it is time for me to have another car? You know and will provide one for me." Less than a mile from my home as I went around a curve, I collided with a red pickup truck. I bent his fender, but the frame of my car was bent to the extent that I could not open the passenger door properly. A warning: be careful what you say to God; He might answer you immediately.

On my way to the crusade in a rental car on Friday, August 22, in Seattle—about twenty-five miles away—I talked to the Lord and prayed that He would heal me. I was desperate and told Him so. I pleaded with Him to fix my knees. I absolutely did not want to have an operation because I could not afford financially to recuperate for some time before I could drive again. Praise God, I got healed and did not need the operation. At pool therapy on the day before the crusade, I told the attendant that I was going to the crusade the next day and expected to be healed. She laughed in total disbelief when I told her.

As I was driving along, I remembered a song I learned in a church in Ghana, where I ministered several years prior. It declares that God is a prayer-answering God. I started to sing it several times in all sincerity. As the pastor at the crusade preached that night, he called out different sicknesses and diseases and said to step out in the aisle in faith. I was fourteen rows up and obeyed by stepping out in faith. The anointing was very strong and my faith so great that I received my healing instantaneously. Jesus said in Matthew 9:22, "Daughter, be of good comfort; thy faith hath made thee whole. And the woman was made whole from that hour." All my pain was gone. I was healed and able to run up the stairs to my seat. We need to make the first step in pure faith, as we read in Matthew 12:13: "Then saith he to the man, Stretch forth thine hand. And he stretched it forth; and it was restored whole, like as the other." I was able to share my healing testimony and gave God all the glory for it. Let me tell you, I was on a spiritual high all day and couldn't stop singing about how He is a prayer-answering God.

Now, though, I still need to protect my healing from Satan, as Jesus Himself said in John 10:10, "The thief cometh not, but for to steal, and to kill, and to destroy."

I kept my 8:30 A.M. pool therapy appointment on Monday to share my healing with the unbelieving physical therapist. Afterward I went to see the doctor and asked him for an X-ray. He told me that it would only show on an MRI. I realized that this would be too expensive just to prove my point, as the cost was then around $1,400. He said that he would record it in the file and close my case. He was happy for me. Some people think I'm crazy. If they are not familiar with the supernatural power of God, they don't know the joy of the Lord I'm experiencing!

I even called the State Department in Olympia, because it was a labor and industry case and a work-related accident. I talked to a lady there, but when I signed the closing papers for the sale of my home to record them in to the purchaser's name, one thousand dollars of so-called overpayment was recorded against my title. There was no time to contest and dispute it, and I had to pay it. In other words, they reclaimed the amount I collected for being out of work, because they did not believe that I was telling the truth about my healing. When I told my lawyer years later that I was healed, he told me that I couldn't say that in court; no one would believe me. They make you swear to tell the truth, but when it comes to God, they don't want to hear it because of their unbelief in Jesus Christ. What a shame that it has come to that.

God continued to allow my finances to deteriorate so that I had to trust Him for every dollar. Have you ever asked what His purpose is for your life? How much are you willing to endure for the sake of the cross? Does your life show that He is your everything, your reason for living?

Hopefully my prophesied training for my calling (see Chapter 10) from the Lord to pour out gold is soon coming to an end as I complete graduating from the Holy Spirit's training school. I turned it all over to God and wait now for His direction and the time for the publishing of my book. One of the prophesies given to me years ago told me, "You shall see things in your day that you would not believe, even if you were told." I'm amazed that the revival the Lord told me about in 1991, the one that this book would cause, is turning out this way. Is this the unexpected path that He is leading me down?

I will give you an example of some of the hardships I had to experience. They are situations the Lord allowed me to endure in order to bring me to this situation. My financial downfall began in 1985 when He called me out of my successful real estate career to serve Him. I did not know it then, but He had it purposed to bring me all the way down financially by drying up my funds. In the past I could rely on my checkbook. In 1978, according to my broker, I was the first real estate agent in our state to earn over $100,000 in commissions. In fact my W-2 form for that year showed that I earned $138,687. Only God knew what He would have me spend the money on later. My investments included a new 18-unit stucco apartment complex build in 1976. In 1982, I helped somewhat with the design of a 19-unit complex with my own townhouse and a swimming pool in my backyard. Including my savings, I was set up for a comfortable retirement. Then the Lord impressed upon me to sell them both and use the money for His work.

After five and one-half years of ministering at my own expense, including several trips overseas to Israel, Egypt, and Ghana, my money was soon coming to an end. As I waited on the Lord for direction, a real estate lady who was baptized with the Holy Spirit baptism from the church I was attending then came to visit me at my home. She informed me that the Holy Spirit revealed to her to tell me that I was to go back into real estate. He also told her to pay for my schooling, since I had turned my real estate license in when the Lord called me to serve Him. Afterward, as I was waiting for the Lord to tell me what real estate company I was to work for, while I was planting geraniums in my flower boxes on my deck, He showed me in a vision the face of the Christian broker in one of the branch offices I had left five and one-half years before. A Christian realtor who attended the class with me to obtain his broker's license was prompted by the Holy Spirit to pay for my license.

Somehow the Lord never allowed me to get in full swing again financially. I committed to serve Him instead of my bank account. Yes, I had to depend on Him for every dollar, which deepened my faith too greatly to describe. Looking back now, I can plainly see that God wanted me to be completely broke in order to get close to Him and He to me. He stripped me of all my financial security in order to teach me the debt I now have in Him.

I spent a lot of money on my Ghanaian visitors. To a Methodist pastor, I sent over one hundred thousand dollars to help build a school for children with mental and physical defects. When I was in Ghana on one of my trips, it touched my heart to see a young man spoon dirty liquid out of a ditch on the side of the road with his hands and eat it as if it were chocolate. I'm sorry to say, but instead this pastor used my money to buy himself a new home with a store attached on the end of it, which his wife manages. To another visitor I gave twenty thousand dollars so he and a friend back home could import rice from China and buy himself a nice car. He never purchased the rice, and when he got home he wrecked the car right away. For another one I bought a large suitcase because I sent many gifts home with him—the communion emblems for both of his churches, one in Great Britain and the other in Ghana; a satin robe for his wife; and money to purchase a refrigerator when he got back home.

Then in 1999 I invested heavily in a company from Dallas, Texas, which closed its doors unexpectedly. I put most of the amount on two credit cards. All of us investors were dealing with a crook. The Lord prompted me to file for bankruptcy to get rid of the two credit card debts. No way was I considering doing that. As a German, I had character and integrity. I was going to pay the money back on my own, ignoring the prompting of the Lord to do it. Since I refused, I experienced strong chest pains on a Sunday evening. When I called the hospital, they recommended that I dial 911. Two attendants came with an ambulance. One of them put a few drops of nitroglycerin under my tongue, which lifted the pain immediately off my chest. Then they insisted to take me to the hospital for observation. The nurse told me that they had to take blood every four hours. If I had a heart attack something would have shown up in the blood each time. Thank goodness I did not have one. Was this a scare tactic from the Lord for not obeying because He knew I would never earn that much money? After I returned home from the hospital, two days later I promptly filed.

Also in 1999, I signed up for a high-performance realtor coaching program and paid $295 to start it. My heart gave me problems again, so I had to cancel the program; but it felt fine afterward.

Another time I paid a large sum of money to an organization to have the servicemen e-mail me that were going to be transferred to a nearby military base. I received more then one hundred e-mails during the year as they were requesting information on our housing availability and the prices of the homes, but I never met one once they arrived here and didn't make one sale.

In 1990, I had to take out a mortgage for my home, which was once paid for, in order to be able to send the large amount to Ghana. In 2000, my finances dried up even more. I could not understand why I was experiencing such a slump. I lost two commercial sales, one in 2000, and the other one in 2001, which were to pay me over $60,000 each in commissions. This brought my finances to an all-time low. In July 2000, I got a foreclosure notice. I got behind in my mortgage payment and was informed that my home would be sold at public auction on November 3. I panicked and questioned the Lord about it. He comforted me by revealing to me that the Levites did not own any property either; they were supported by the people. As I was lying in bed that morning praying at seven o'clock, I told the Lord that if I was to sell my home He would have to show me where to move. Within three and one-half hours I knew were I was moving. The Holy Spirit directed me to this very nice three-bedroom duplex with a two-car garage. The owner lived at another place. When I drove by, I met the tenant next door, who allowed me to look through his unit. Evidently I made a good impression; he was also a Christian and spoke highly of me to the landlord, so I did not have to supply a credit report—which I would have flunked.

Then the Lord revealed to me that the first couple that would look at my home would be purchasing it. This is exactly what happened. Within three weeks my home sold and closed. After I lived in the duplex for thirteen months, I had to move again because I was already one month behind in my rent. A friend told me some time before that when I was to go to Egypt, I could store some of my things at her house. But as life would have it, she offered for me to move into the five hundred square foot loft of her very nice A-frame log house by the end of August 2001. I had a large open bedroom with cathedral ceiling and skylights, a small sitting room, and my own bathroom. It must have been God's will for me to end up in her home. It was very tiny with my many boxes of books, ministry, and witnessing materials stacked up behind my furniture, but I was content and praised the Lord that He kept me from living out of my car or under an overpass. I conducted a moving sale and parted from many of my nice belongings, including most of my furniture. I had no problem detaching myself from all of it. They were no longer dear to me.

The Lord was practically stripping me of everything. I was only interested anymore in serving Him and Him alone. He had it all figured out way in advance and implemented step by step what His will was for my life. My friends could not understand my calling. I was on assignment from the Lord. Most of them talked to me in the same manner as Job's friends did when he was covered with boils from head to toe, which God allowed Satan to inflict him.

> And the Lord said unto Satan, Hast thou considered my servant Job, that there is none like him in the earth, a perfect and an upright man, one that feareth God, and escheweth evil? and still he holdeth fast his integrity, although thou movedst me against him, to destroy him without cause.
>
> —Job 2:3

Even his own wife questioned him, as we read in Job 2:9: "Dost thou still retain thine integrity? curse God, and die." Then Job's three friends came to visit him with their wisdom. Eliphaz rebukes Job saying, in effect, "Innocent people aren't punished." He advises Job to seek God and confess his sins. Job reproved his friends in Job 6:14: "To him that is afflicted pity should be shewed from his friend."

You see, nothing has changed in all these years. People still rely on head knowledge instead of searching their spirit for the correct answer before they open their mouth. Two Christians told me several years ago that I was cursed because my finances did not improve. When I told my long-time, German friend and her husband about my move, they could not believe it. As I was leaving their home that evening, she explained to me that they could not help me financially, that they needed to keep their money in reserve for their son. She told me later that she couldn't sleep that night. It was not the will of the Lord for me to depend on them financially. However, when it comes to money, what a person is made of surfaces.

My Christian chiropractor prophesied to me that God allowed my financial destruction in order to get me to move across the Narrows Bridge, where I had some unexpected experiences.

Since the pastor from the conservative Baptist church would not receive the baptism in the Holy Spirit, the Lord picked another church for me. As time went on there was no doubt about it—my experiences with this pastor and certain people from the congregation were no different and perhaps even worse than at my former church. Their doctrine was the same. Only the power of the Holy Spirit can open their spiritual eyes.

I met with the pastor three different times in the beginning. The Sunday following our first meeting he stood in the foyer, greeting me with a handshake. He said that he was delighted with our meeting, at which time I left him my first book and information from the prophetess. He told one of the ladies from the church that he liked my enthusiasm for the Lord. But only a few days later he called me to say that I heard from Satan and forbade me as my pastor to attend any more meetings with the prophetess until I went to her home and checked it out. I have no idea what I was supposed to find there. Her husband is a retired counseling pastor from a very large church in the Seattle area. She has ministered half around the world and is very well received in Pentecostal churches and by the Full Gospel Business Men's Fellowship International. The pastor expressed that he did not believe in any of the prophecies she had given me, and he said they were all coincidental happenings. He told my friend where I was staying that my calling to Egypt is something I myself desire and therefore believe.

Since I had no tithe money in the beginning, I donated about 140 Christian books to the church, which I delivered to the pastor and asked him to check over. At our final meeting, he made fun of one of the books that talked about prophecy, which according to him is not practiced in our time. When I told him that Paul was slain in the spirit on his journey, he replied, "But Paul is dead now." I would like to know if the Holy Spirit died then, too? Evidently he believes so because of how unfamiliar the pastor was with Him. The Holy Spirit was not allowed to function in that church. If we have fellowship with the Holy Spirit, we also need to speak His language, which is speaking in other tongues.

This pastor, too, recommended that I leave his church. He suggested that I attend an Assembly of God church where they believe like I do. He told me that the pastor was a friend of his. I said to him that since I turned my life completely over to the Lord, I have to hear from Him if He wants me to leave and where to go. This upset him, and he asked me if I had to hear from God first before I got out of bed in the morning. He said that God gave us a brain and the written Word—the Bible. The Bible, though, is the *logos* word, and I could see that he didn't know a thing about the *rhema* word, which is supernatural. Since he only relied on his head knowledge, he believed in only part of the Bible. He tried to convince me that I had false teaching like the Pentecostals and offered to deprogram me. "Sorry," I told him. I came too far to go backward again.

What a shame. It showed me how desperate we should be to establish the true body of Christ, one that believes in the whole Bible. By denying part of the Bible, will they even be candidates for the Rapture?

I asked the pastor in the beginning if he could recommend someone to read and check some of the chapters in this book. He gave me the name of two ladies from the congregation. One of them returned the chapters shortly thereafter, saying that she would not have time. The other one, too, gave them back to me after a while also with a card saying, "I want you to know I enjoyed reading of your travels and your ministry to the Muslims, but I have a hard time with all the prophecies and loftiness of them.

I feel the Lord is already using you just as you are in praying for others and telling them about Him. I truly believe He works more practically on a daily basis of our obedience than just choosing a few to do huge things, and He cares more about our hearts than what we accomplish for Him." It showed me clearly that their belief does not stretch enough; rather, they expect me to be disobedient to God's anointing and calling upon my life. I'm His humble handmaiden, who follows and obeys the voice of the Holy Spirit.

One year on Resurrection Sunday, one of our elders preached in the pastor's absence. We had two unsaved visitors with us, but he did not give an altar call. Afterward, I complained to another pastor. The Holy Spirit showed him to me as a mechanical bull, hollow, without any flesh, having an empty ribcage only. He had told my friend that I write nothing but a bunch of garbage. Later he asked her if I was still trying to peddle my book. When he volunteered to fix a short in her two-way light, I helped him by handing him certain tools. While we were alone, he informed me that I should get an apartment by myself. Was this any of his business? He did not know that she needed me, too. Many times, she was not even able to drive. We had already known each other for over thirty-five years. What would he have said if I told him that I had married her and her husband about fifteen years earlier? I should have lost my desire to return to the church after hearing a certain healing minister being torn to shreds by a member of our congregation who was studying for the ministry. All this demonstrated their refusal to accept the Holy Spirit's power. I knew that the Lord wanted me there to observe what was going on.

The morning after my second meeting with the pastor, the Holy Spirit reminded me, "'It is not by might, nor by power, but by My Spirit,' says the Lord." (See Zechariah 4:6.) I don't think that Satan wanted me to keep my third appointment with the pastor, because first I spilled coffee on the white collar of my dress at the office, then I locked my keys in the car. When these tricks did not work, I choked very badly on my own saliva while I was previewing a vacant home in an unfamiliar neighborhood with no one in sight. None of Satan's tactics worked, and I was able to arrive on time.

My friend and a few church members all wanted me to get a paying job and condemned the few chapters I showed them. I already had a job, and although it did not pay any money then, it would yield souls in the future. God set me aside to work for Him. He wanted me to finish this book as soon as possible, which also required a lot of studying, sometimes until late in the night, just to write a few lines, although He allowed me a few real estate sales. Two couples from our Bible study had already given me one hundred dollars each. The pastor, too, pulled forty dollars out of his billfold when I told him that I didn't have any money for my medicine. I was able to pay them back at a later date. Two other churches helped me occasionally, each with half of my car payment.

Not having enough money to pay my bills on time month after month caused me to come down with shingles two different times. My flesh got in the way, instead of me completely turning it over to the Lord, which is a learning experience. It is easier said than done. These sure were humbling experiences. To commit suicide would have been a relief. Believe me, it entered my mind numerous times, but I'm too grounded in the Word of God to consider it an option.

As I was praying in the spirit (in tongues) at an intercessors meeting, the Holy Spirit reminded me of the following song: "Trust and obey, For there's no other way, To be happy in Jesus, But to trust and obey." I experienced a comforting peace as I sang this song numerous times quietly to myself.

I made very few sales during that time, and until I received Social Security several months later, things were very tight for me. Afterward, my friend and I shared the expenses for food and utilities. Eventually she was ready for me to leave, but I had no money for the first and last month's rent plus a deposit, which were necessary to be able to get an apartment. She told me in front of her daughter, who was waiting to move in, that she was putting me out on the street. I replied that if she were, God would deal with her. She accused me of threatening her with this statement, which I wasn't, and she made an appointment with the pastor.

I had no idea for what reason he called to see me. As I waited for him, the Holy Spirit revealed to me that just as they lead Jesus to the slaughter and He said not a word, in the same way was I to conduct myself. To my surprise, my friend showed up, too. Unexpectedly, I was asked by the pastor that day to move out of her house within thirty days. I was shocked because I had no money. After the pastor's announcement to me, she left again. I told the pastor that the Bible tells us that He never leaves us, nor forsake us. He asked me if I thought I could make it. I asked him, "Make what?" He replied, "In this church," and then spoke some unkind words to me. Finally, he was able to get rid of me. Jesus said in John 16:1–2, "These things have I spoken unto you, that ye should not be offended. They shall put you out of the synagogues: yea, the time cometh, that whosoever killeth you will think that he doeth God service."

On my way home I told the Lord that I needed to feel His arms around me because I did not know for a couple of weeks yet if the buyer's financing on one of my real estate sales would go through. My meeting with the pastor was on a Friday. On the following Monday, without much effort on my part, the Lord provided me with an older, small, two-bedroom duplex with a 2-car garage—exactly what I would have liked to have and needed. Yes, He gives us the desires of our heart. I moved two miles from my office and the same distance from my new church.

Here are some excerpts from a Bible study I did about speaking in tongues.

In order for us to have fellowship with the Holy Spirit, we also need to speak His language—which is tongues. If we only rely on the written Word—the Bible—we will miss out on other important messages from God.

> For by one Spirit are we all baptized into one body, whether we be Jews or Gentiles, whether we be bond or free; and have been all made to drink into one Spirit.
>
> —1 Corinthians 12:13

This Scripture tells us that we are by one Spirit, the Holy Spirit, baptized into one body—the body of Christ. It does not say anywhere that this occurs by only one baptism! You see how Satan has fed many a lie. The Bible also tells us of other baptisms, such as the baptism with the Holy Spirit. The primary purpose of Spirit baptism, according to the book of Acts, is power. The biblical term is dunumis, which means "power, strength, force," and represents an endowment of spiritual power. Jesus Himself told His disciples in Luke 24:49, "And, behold, I send the promise of my Father upon you: but tarry ye in the city of Jerusalem, until ye be endued with power from on high."

Again Jesus said in John 7:38, "He that believeth on me, as the scripture hath said, out of his belly shall flow rivers of living water." We should have rivers of living water flowing out of us. We continue to read in verses 39–43:

> (But this spake he of the Spirit, which they that believe on him should receive: for the Holy Ghost was not yet given; because that Jesus was not yet glorified.) Many of the people therefore, when they heard this saying, said, Of a truth this is the Prophet. Others said, This is the Christ. But some said, Shall Christ come out of Galilee? Hath not the scripture said, That Christ cometh of the seed of David, and out of the town of Bethlehem, where David was? So there was a division among the people because of him.

It is easy to see that there are two parts to their experience—first they believed and then they waited on the Holy Spirit. In the meantime, they reasoned with their intellect, because the Holy Spirit was not yet given. But today we have no excuse. The Trinity consists of Father, Son and Holy Spirit. Many people absolutely will not accept the Holy Spirit as the third one in the Trinity. If you were speaking in tongues, you can shut Satan out, because he does not understand what you are praying.

We read that those that believe on Him shall receive. Second Peter 1:20 tells us, "Knowing this first, that no prophecy of the scripture is of any private interpretation." Therefore, certain denominational doctrine is a deception from Satan, though the people have no idea that they are led astray.

Since we are told in Revelation what is yet to come in the future, the writers of the Bible would have let us know if and when the gifts were no longer needed! Jesus Himself tells us in Acts 1:5, 8, "For John truly baptized with water; but ye shall be baptized with the Holy Ghost not many days hence.... But ye shall receive power, after that the Holy Ghost is come upon you: and ye shall be witnesses unto me both in Jerusalem, and in all Judaea, and in Samaria, and unto the uttermost part of the earth." I experience His power when I minister to people on a daily basis. We simply can't dictate to God; when He speaks, He means it. He does not tolerate our stubbornness.

> But the anointing which ye have received of him abideth in you, and ye need not that any man teach you: but as the same anointing teacheth you of all things, and is truth, and is no lie, and even as it hath taught you, ye shall abide in him.
>
> —1 John 2:27

> But as it is written, Eye hath not seen, nor ear heard, neither have entered into the heart of man, the things which God hath prepared for them that love him. But God hath revealed them unto us by his Spirit: for the Spirit searcheth all things, yea, the deep things of God. For what man knoweth the

> things of a man, save the spirit of man which is in him? even so the things of God knoweth no man, but the Spirit of God. Now we have received, not the spirit of the world, but the spirit which is of God; that we might know the things that are freely given to us of God. Which things also we speak, not in the words which man's wisdom teacheth, but which the Holy Ghost teacheth; comparing spiritual things with spiritual. But the natural man receiveth not the things of the Spirit of God: for they are foolishness unto him: neither can he know them, because they are spiritually discerned. But he that is spiritual judgeth all things, yet he himself is judged of no man. For who hath known the mind of the Lord, that he may instruct him? but we have the mind of Christ.
>
> —1 CORINTHIANS 2:9–16

John the Baptist even told us of the baptism with fire.

> I indeed baptize you with water unto repentance. but he that cometh after me is mightier than I, whose shoes I am not worthy to bear: he shall baptize you with the Holy Ghost, and with fire: Whose fan is in his hand, and he will thoroughly purge his floor, and gather his wheat into the garner; but he will burn up the chaff with unquenchable fire.
>
> —MATTHEW 3:11–12

Jesus explained to us the baptism of suffering.

> But Jesus said unto them, Ye know not what ye ask: can ye drink of the cup that I drink of? and be baptized with the baptism that I am baptized with? And they said unto him, We can. And Jesus said unto them, Ye shall indeed drink of the cup that I drink of; and with the baptism that I am baptized withal shall ye be baptized.
>
> —MARK 10:38–39

You can see that there are several other baptisms. Satan has you off track if you believe in only one baptism.

The Charismatics and Pentecostals have no problem laying hands on people and seeing them healed and even delivered from evil spirits. It is only possible by the power of the Holy Spirit, who sets the captives free, but the Devil wants you to do nothing and remain dormant in your churches. We read in Romans 8:11, "But if the Spirit of him that raised up Jesus from the dead dwell in you, he that raised up Christ from the dead shall also quicken your mortal bodies by his Spirit that dwelleth in you." Shouldn't we also be ministering in the Holy Spirit's power, which Jesus described Luke 4:18?

> The Spirit of the Lord is upon me, because he hath anointed me to preach the gospel to the poor; he hath sent me to heal the brokenhearted, to preach deliverance to the captives, and recovering of sight to the blind, to set at liberty them that are bruised.

Are you allowing the Lord to use you to heal the broken-hearted, deliver the captives, recover the sight of the blind, and set at liberty the bruised? Since the Holy Spirit has been run out of many churches, few get healed when they pray, or are prayed for.

The pastor also told me several months before I left that I could only stay in that church if it was all right with me that neither he nor the congregation was speaking in other tongues. He has to stand before Jesus one day and give an account of himself.

When the pastor called to inquire if I found a place, I told him that the coming Sunday was to be my last time in church. He must have been relieved to finally get rid of me after trying numerous times before. As I walked to the front of the church after the Sunday service to tell him good-bye and that I was sore from moving a lot of boxes, he turned around and walked out the side door. He saw me coming but chose not to say good-bye, God bless you, or anything else. Is there any wonder that some people no longer attend church because they get hurt over and over again by these kinds of treatments, yes, even from pastors?

About eight months before I moved, I met a lady and her children while I was out shopping. As we carried on a conversation, she invited me to her church. At that time, I still lived over thirty miles away. After I moved and entered the sanctuary the first Sunday morning on June 13, 2004, I had the feeling that I was coming home. The people were all very friendly. It is an independent full gospel, non-denominational church. It is charismatic in its practice of the manifestation of the Holy Spirit gifts given to build and strengthen the body of believers in the local church.

Their mission statement is to build a new-testament, local church and proclaim the good news about Jesus Christ to young and old, rich and poor, and all ethnic groups in order to build people, leaders, and families; first in our city, then in the surrounding area, and in the ends of the earth.

In November 2006, the pastor announced to us from the pulpit that he had a hard week. The leader of the organization of thirty-thousand plus evangelicals of which our church was a part admitted that he had homosexual problems. He had a congregation of fourteen thousand, which removed him immediately once his sin was exposed and he admitted it. The Scripture tells us in 1 Peter 5:8, "Be sober, be vigilant; because your adversary the devil, as a roaring lion, walketh about, seeking whom he may devour." You see, Satan is not in hell now. That is where he will end up someday, but now he is roaming the earth to see who he can lead astray and tempt to sin. We also read in Numbers 32:23, "Be sure your sin will find you out."

In one of our Monday evening ladies' meetings, the pastor's wife asked us to pray and seek the Lord for an answer about why so many people in our church were sick and had numerous other problems. The Holy Spirit quickened the answer immediately to my spirit. I told the ladies that I knew but had to tell the pastor first. When I met with him, I told him that the Lord wanted him to preach from the King James Bible and that I was to donate two hundred dollars toward the purchase of King James Bibles for the pews. But nothing ever became of it. He was not receptive to it. Instead, he told me that he preached from the New King James Bible. After a few more meetings, I learned quickly that he did not respond to anything God wanted me to relate to him. So I told the Lord that He would have to deal with him His own way. Having traveled two times to Israel, I had many slides of the sights I visited and have them backed up with the appropriate Scriptures. It would give many in the congregation quite an understanding of Israel. But no one, including the church leaders who have never been there, ever requested for me to present them.

The Lord has sent me to several other churches in the last twenty years. Were all those pastors too much into themselves?

Could we have been experiencing our revival already years earlier? Instead, God had to eliminate one pastor after another and then direct me to the next church He would point out to me. Did each one of them tell God to get off His throne while they occupied it themselves in their pride and unbelief in the printed Word, the Bible? We read in James 4:10, "Humble yourselves in the sight of the Lord, and he shall lift you up."

The books that I'm writing will reflect God's anointing upon me, and my waiting for His calling to be completed is proof of my loyalty to Him. Jesus says in John 15:16, "Ye have not chosen me, but I have chosen you, and ordained you, that ye should go and bring forth fruit, and that your fruit should remain: that whatsoever ye shall ask of the Father in my name, he may give it you." Now that I'm sure of my calling, it does not matter what anyone says to discourage me and put me down. Jesus said in John 15:5, "He that abideth in me, and I in him, the same bringeth forth much fruit: for without me ye can do nothing." It also says in Matthew 6:9–10, "After this manner therefore pray ye: Our Father which art in heaven, Hallowed be thy name. Thy kingdom come, Thy will be done in earth, as it is in heaven."

One pastor told me, "If you hear from God but it does not come to pass after a certain time, move on." It wouldn't be moving on with God if He has not had me accomplish the first task and has not given me a second one. So then, it seems that if to move on in the flesh would mean I was totally out of the will of God. It took many years for this revelation from the Lord about my calling to unfold. Had I not waited on Him and instead moved on in the flesh, I would have missed God's plan, which includes the start of this revival. Moses had to wait forty years in the wilderness.

He also told me that I was full of pride. I used to be very outgoing since I had traveled to many places and had been ministering for many years. I thought I had a lot to contribute, but since that meeting I do not have much to say anymore.

In 1988 when I returned from a visit to Germany, the Holy Spirit gave me certain revelations while flying in the airplane and asked me to share it with the congregation of the Assembly of God church I was attending at that time. It was on Pentecost Sunday evening that the pastor allowed me to preach, and at the end I gave the invitation for the people to come forward to receive the baptism in the Holy Spirit. A friend of mine came with his ten-year-old son, who was the first one to receive it. They recorded the service and gave me a copy of the tape, which I only recently discovered. You see, I have already been anointed for thirty years and had meetings in my home were people were lying on my living room floor slain in the Spirit after I laid hands on them and prayed. I registered my ministry in 1985 at the time the Lord called me out of real estate to serve Him.

On September 19, 2004, I was prophesied over by a gifted visiting pastor who was standing next to our senior pastor when he said that I have the gift of healing and I should use my hands. One Sunday, one of our ordained children's pastors waited for me to arrive at the church. She had me pray for one of her students for healing of pinkeye.

That same night in September 2004, the senior pastor himself prophesied the following to me:

> The things that the Lord has really impressed upon you, is concerning the things that God has given you, direction and things for you to do. He wants you to know that He doesn't want you to do it in your power. He wants to do it in His power, His anointing. "So daughter, as you yield yourself to Me," says the Lord, "you allow My Spirit to work in you. As you yield in those desires of your heart that I have placed there," says the Lord, "I have placed those desires there. I have given you a promise," says the Lord, "that as you yield to those things, you can not do it on your own. And He wants you to know that He will accomplish those things that He has spoken to you in His time and in His power, that He will do it. Thank you, Lord.

The following is another prophecy given to me that evening by an ordained minister. It speaks of telling people what I hear from the Lord. He said, "The Lord has given this person [me] 'immunity' for Me." My dictionary explains *immunity* as exemption from something burdensome, as a legal obligation. *Immune* means, "Having a special capacity for resistance or exempt from or protected against something disagreeable or harmful." He continued, saying that God is fine-tuning me and that a lot of what I know and what I have experienced is all in place. He explained that I was looking for the final pieces of the puzzle to compliment the full vision that God had given me. He told me:

> God said, "If you just wait on Me—because I don't want you getting ahead of someone else—He wants that body to come together and be perfected together." The Lord would speak to you in the place that He called you to be. It is very important that you walk with one foot at a time as He leads, because God is going to show you, in fact He probably has already at times

shown you, the area of the body where the immune system has become nonfunctional. And you see things happen, and you say, you know this has to be attended to, and this has to be taken care of...The progression of the spiritual immune systems will come to the point where they are supposed to be, and it is the immune system that removes the toxicity from the natural body. And so, there are spiritual immune systems that need to be touched, and God is well aware of what He is doing.

...Jesus said in Matthew 16:18, "I will build my church." The head will build His church, and then He comes down to each individual, including you, to bring about the necessary changes, because that spiritual immune system must be touched to remove the toxicity out of the body of Christ so that it can begin to function. A leg that's bad and can't walk, as the immune system is touched, that will be all cleared out and He will use you to help do that. That is why He talks to you about the puzzle and not getting ahead of what God is doing in your life. He progressed you to a point; you're more mature than a lot of people, but don't forget that we must humble ourselves daily. And I know you're a humble woman; I'm not saying that you're not humble...That is what He is saying to you tonight. He is for you; He is very happy, He is very satisfied with what you have done to this point and that you are an important cog in the body of Christ. [According to the dictionary, a cog is one of the teeth on the rim of a cogwheel.]

...He is speaking to me tonight, "Move on, sister in the Lord; move on in the things of the Lord."...Lord, bless her continually. Let her continue to hear, "Thus sayeth the Lord," not only in her own individual life, but let her know that she is a part of what You're doing in this hour to perfect Your church, to bring it to perfection, and to bring it to a place

> where it will truly be a place in the earth as You have designed for it to be. We charge her with this and we commend her, Lord, to the work that You called her to do with the leadership in this house. In Jesus' name, amen.

Jesus will not reign where sin is in control. He is too holy to enter where the flesh reigns. As the prophecy said, He has to remove the toxicity out of the body of Christ so that it can begin to function. This toxicity is spiritual.

How much longer must God wait before He finds a humble pastor with a repentant heart? Let me make a bold statement, by saying that we will have revival starting out of this church. There are other indications that have been prophesied to certain people who are getting stirred by the Holy Spirit to a calling that would require a large congregation to support it.

We read in 1 Samuel 15:22–23:

> And Samuel said, Hath the LORD as great delight in burnt offerings and sacrifices, as in obeying the voice of the LORD? Behold, to obey is better than sacrifice, and to hearken than the fat of rams. For rebellion is as the sin of witchcraft, and stubbornness is as iniquity and idolatry. Because thou hast rejected the word of the LORD, he hath also rejected thee from being king.

You see, it is God that promotes us or strips us down. I have nothing to do with it. I obey what the Lord asks me to do.

This is why the last sin to die is often the fear of man, as we read in Proverbs 29:25: "The fear of man bringeth a snare: but whoso putteth his trust in the LORD shall be safe." Second Timothy 1:7

confirms, "For God hath not given us the spirit of fear; but of power, and of love, and of a sound mind."

When Haman sent out the order for the Jews to be killed, Mordecai told Esther that if she kept quiet and did not intercede for her people, deliverance to the Jews would come from another place, but she and what was left of her family would be destroyed: He said, "And who knoweth whether thou art come to the kingdom for such a time as this?" (Esther 4:14). This Scripture applies to me as well. Remember, way back in 1987 at an intercessory prayer meeting in my home, it was prophesied to me that I would establish the body of Christ. Therefore, I never got discouraged or depressed through all I had to experience, because I knew that one day it would all end. The Holy Spirit anointed me for this task and has given me the boldness that it will take to accomplish it in spite of discouragement over the years. My calling is a gift from God and cannot be controlled by others or circumstances.

I have been struggling with my finances and have had to go several times to the local food bank and the one at our church. On Thanksgiving in 2007 I got a turkey from my church and a good-sized gift certificate for the Safeway supermarket. In the meantime, the bottom has fallen out of the real estate market even more. I had to wait ten months for my next commission check. Did God allow me this extra time to finish the manuscript? In January 2008, I finally settled with the insurance company concerning my November 2004 car accident. They paid me a fraction of my expenses.

Consider Hebrews 12:1–2: "Let us run with patience the race that is set before us, Looking unto Jesus the author and finisher of our faith." I read in Psalm 4:3, "But know that the Lord hath set apart him that is godly for himself: the Lord will hear when I call unto him." Jesus said in Matthew 16:18, "Upon this rock I will build my church; and the gates of hell shall not prevail against it."

Chapter 12

God Bless America

On July 4, 2001, Independence Day, America celebrated its two hundred and twenty-fifth birthday. I heard on the news that in Seattle alone over five hundred people from seventy countries became American citizens. This is only possible in this country. You cannot go to Russia and become a Russian that easily, nor a Chinese citizen in China, nor whatever other country you try. In fact, certain countries won't even allow ownership of property. Thirteen months after that celebration I read in the newspaper that immigration to the United States from the Middle East alone has grown from fewer than 200,000 in 1970 to almost 1.5 million in 2000. The 15 percent Muslim portion in 1970 jumped to 73 percent in 2000.[1]

According to a Christian newsletter from March 2008, the number of Muslim immigrants to the United States has increased dramatically in recent decades. The number of mosques has also risen significantly to keep up with the population. Why do so many radical Muslims call America "the Great Satan" if they are so eager to live here? Is their real motive to set up a system of world domination?

When I was seeking an answer from the Lord, He did not respond to me as quickly as I expected. Finally, I asked my friend to pray for an answer for me since He usually answers her promptly. A few days later, on December 5, 2007, she heard Him say, "I know you want me to tell you what Tilly is to do. Tilly is doing what I want her to do. I am still on the throne. I am never too late or too early. Tell her to rest in Me. I know you get discouraged once in a while. I understand. I will never leave you or abandon you. I am your husband, your friend, your confidant, a close, trusted friend. I love you *so* much. You are My faithful servant. I am pleased with your exuberance. You're blessed beyond measure. You may not have earthly wealth, but you have great spiritual wealth. You are rich in spiritual matters. My peace I give you. Take hold and rest in Me. Love, your Father."

On January 30, 2008, after asking her again, the Lord responded. He had her tell me, "You are where I want you to be. Stay where you are. I know it looks like I'm not doing anything, but I am working on your behalf. Don't give up." A few days later, several loose ends smoothly came together.

Without asking her again, on March 23, 2008, she got another message for me at 3:30 a.m. The Lord said, "A few Muslims will be saved, not many. But He says He always gives a warning before destroying a people or a nation. They deserve at least that. You are the one to do it. The Lord said signs and wonders will follow you to show them that your God sent you. He said that you will be martyred for this, but not until your work for the Lord is done.

You will be the evangelist to the Muslims in Egypt. The Lord says you have the gift of faith and healing."

While I was waiting, because I had no idea how this was going to take place, the Holy Spirit revealed to me two months later that God was giving them another chance to decide were they will spend eternity—in heaven or in hell. I was to give them the warning by printing all the verses in the last four chapters of the New Testament, which are Revelation 19–22. (These will appear in the third volume of this series, *Is Mohammed Mentioned in the Bible?*)

Revelation 19:11 says, "And I saw heaven opened, and behold a white horse; and he that sat upon him was called Faithful and True, and in righteousness he doth judge and make war." It records the final prophetic hour regarding the Second Coming, in which our Savior, Jesus Christ, arrives. Yet, I heard the Iranian president say on TV that their last *imam*, or leader, will come on a white horse. In order to be informed about the subject, I stopped at our local mosque to have the *imam* there give me an explanation, but he didn't know anything about that. They are Sunni Muslims who speak Arabic and don't believe like that at all. I was told that the Iranian president was a Shiite Muslim and that the Shiites and Sunni's have two completely different sets of beliefs. The Shiites are amongst the 110 million Farsi-speaking people in the Middle East.[2]

I am very patriotic because I have a lot to be thankful for. Were it not for me coming to this country, I most likely would not have come to know Jesus as my Savior. Each year I fill my flower-boxes with red geraniums, white petunias, and blue lobelias—red, white and blue. I also dress in red, white, and blue to go to church each Fourth of July. Being born in another country—although by now I've already been here for forty-six years and have been an American citizen for many years—it is always a very special day for me and has absolutely nothing to do with politics. I communicate with God during the day, reflecting back and thanking Him that He allowed me to come to the USA, receive Him as my personal Savior, and gradually make Him the Lord over my life.

Our forefathers came here to find three unalienable rights: life, liberty, and the pursuit of happiness. I remember one particular Fourth of July in which I spent the day picking raspberries, currants, and dark Bing cherries in my backyard. As I reminisced about my childhood days in Germany, I recalled when I, together with my father and younger sister, went up to my uncle's property, which had on it an enormous old cherry tree. We used to hang two cherries with attached stems over our ears as earrings.

Later that day as I changed the channel on the TV, I discovered a soccer game in progress. Croatia was playing another country for the championship qualification. They played just as exciting as the German team did over fifty-five years ago when they won the World Cup. I was sixteen years old at that time. The German people were crazy with excitement, and some even took time off from work in order not to miss the championship game. I was in their midst in a side room at a restaurant. Remember, there were no TVs available in private homes then. Several young men a few years older than me threw me up in the air in their excitement when Fritz Walter shot the winning goal. I remember it to this very day. Soccer was the only sport we knew growing up during and after the war. After the Sunday afternoon church service and some quick coffee and cake, off we went to the *sportplatz*—the playing field. My father was the first aid man for the volunteer fire department. He faithfully carried his first aid kit to the games in case a player would get injured.

As I was reminiscing about the past, I could not get the preaching I heard earlier that day out of my mind. A very popular and godly black minister, Dr. E. V. Hill, who has since gone to heaven, told of the slave trade many years ago. He also mentioned that at the end of the emancipation, the former slaves were promised a mule and forty acres of land, which they never received. My ears perked. I remembered seeing the slave castles on the Ghanaian coast on TV before, but the three times I was over there, no one brought up the subject, so I wouldn't either. Nonetheless, I was still fascinated to learn more about slavery and the number of lives it impacted, as well as the promise to provide a mule and land.

> On January 12, 1865, in the midst of his "March to the Sea" during the Civil War, General William T. Sherman and Secretary of War Edwin M. Stanton met with 20 Black community leaders of Savannah, Georgia. Based in part of their input, Gen. Sherman issued Special Field Order #15 on January 16, 1865, setting aside the Sea Islands and a 30 mile inland tract of land along the southern coast of Charleston for the exclusive settlement of Blacks. Each family would receive 40 acres of land and an army mule to work the land, thus 'forty acres and a mule.' Gen. Rufus Saxton was assigned by Sherman to implement the Order.
>
> On a national level, this and other land, confiscated and abandoned, became the jurisdiction of the Freedman's Bureau, which was headed by Gen. Oliver Otis Howard

> (Howard University). In his words he wanted to "…give the freedmen protection, land and schools as far and as fast as he can." However, during the summer and fall of 1865, President Johnson issued special pardons, returning the property to the ex-Confederates. Howard issued Circular 13, giving 40 acres as quickly as possible. Upon his knowledge, Johnson ordered Howard to issue Circular 15, returning the land to the ex-Confederates.[3]

Therefore, the black people never received the land General Sherman promised them, and to this very day some of the older people have not forgotten it. This should be a valuable lesson to us: don't promise something you cannot fulfill. It causes hard feelings. Over the years many black people became successful and respected businessmen and women; others, preachers and educators; besides the large number of great athletes, of which many are outstanding Christians and openly proclaim their faith in Jesus Christ.

Around 12 million men, women, and children were brought from Africa to North America as slaves. Some researchers believe that there is evidence that the slave trade began as early as the mid-sixteenth century.[4]

> In 1782, the United States Congress voted this resolution: "The Congress of the United States recommends and approves the Holy Bible for use in all schools."
>
> …Of the first 108 universities founded in America, 106 were distinctly Christian, including the first, Harvard University, chartered in 1636. In the original Harvard

> Student Handbook, rule number 1 was that students seeking entrance must know Latin and Greek so that they could study the scriptures: "Let every student be plainly instructed and earnestly pressed to consider well, the main end of his life and studies is, to know God and Jesus Christ, which is eternal life, John 17:3; and therefore to lay Jesus Christ as the only foundation for our children to follow the moral principles of the Ten Commandments.[5]

Jesus said in John 17:3 "And this is life eternal, that they might know thee the only true God, and Jesus Christ, whom thou hast sent."

It is impossible to deny that America is a Christian nation. The separation of church and state is not found in our constitution. The pilgrims left Europe to establish a godly country here. John Adams, one of our nation's founding fathers, declared, "The general principles upon which the Fathers achieved independence were the general principals of Christianity…I will avow that I believed and now believe that those general principles of Christianity are as eternal and immutable as the existence and attributes of God."[6] Therefore, we never had a secular government. Who started this lie? Everyone spoke freely about our Lord if they so desired.

Our first president George Washington bent down to kiss the Bible. Patrick Henry said, "It cannot be emphasized too strongly or too often that this great nation was founded, not by religionists but by Christians, not on religions, but on the gospel of Jesus Christ."[7] Does not to this day each new elected president place his hand on the Bible when he takes the oath of office?

The psalmist wrote in Psalm 33:12, "Blessed is the nation whose God is the Lord."

> William Holmes McGuffey is the author of the McGuffey Reader, which was used for over 100 years in our public schools with over 125 million copies sold until it was stopped in 1963. President Lincoln called him the "Schoolmaster of the Nation." Listen to these words of Mr. McGuffey: "The Christian religion is the religion of our country. From it are derived our nation on the character of God, on the great moral Governor of the universe. On its doctrines are founded the peculiarities of our free Institutions. From no source has the author drawn more conspicuously than from the sacred Scriptures. From all these extracts from the Bible, I make no apology."[8]

I would say that we desperately need to turn back to our Christian roots and repent of all our sins in order to escape God's judgment and receive His blessings. How can He bless us as a nation when we have departed so far from Him?

Our first chief justice of the Supreme Court, John Jay, who was appointed by President Washington, said that the people should select Christians for their rulers, because we are a Christian nation. Even after thorough examination the Supreme Court in 1892 confirmed that the USA was a Christian nation, though for many years now we have heard the phrase "the separation of church and state."[9] It is intended to chip away at our religious freedom. Do many of our lawyers and judges today even know the First Amendment to our Constitution? Our founding fathers intended it differently.

George Washington (1732–1799) was the first president of the United States and commander-in-chief of the Continental Army during the Revolutionary War. During that war, many of our soldiers' feet and legs froze, which often required amputation. They suffered, bled, and died in the snows of Valley Forge in order for us to enjoy our freedom today. General Washington was seen on his knees praying to God and heard interceding for his beloved country.[10] God heard his unshakable faith.

On June 1, 1774, as the colonies were seeking God's will as to whether they should break ties with England, George Washington made this entry in his diary: "Went to church and fasted all day."[11]

On July 4, 1775, in his orders from the headquarters at Cambridge, General George Washington gave the order, "The General most earnestly requires, and expects, a due observance of those articles of war, established for the Government of the army, which forbid profane cursing, swearing and drunkenness; And in like manner requires and expects, of all Officers, and Soldiers, not engaged on actual duty, a punctual attendance on divine Service, to implore the blessings of heaven upon the means used for our safety and defense."[12]

The Navy cruisers flew as their ensign a white flag with a green pine tree and the inscription "An Appeal to Heaven."[13]

In 1776, chaplains were appointed for the troops. General Washington issued this order to his troops: "The General hopes and trusts that every officer and man will endeavor so to live, and act, as becomes a Christian Soldier defending the dearest Rights and Liberties of his country."[14]

In August 1776, the British General Howe had trapped General Washington and his 8,000 troops in Long Island. He intended to overrun them the next day. Desperate to escape, General Washington ferried his army all night long across the Delaware

River. By morning there were still a large number of very concerned soldiers exposed to the British. But as God would have it, the river was covered with dense fog, which did not lift until the whole army had made it across. Do we call that a divine intervention from God which allowed them to escape and cancelled the chance for the British to win the war? Remember prayer does wonders![15]

On April 30, 1789, as the first president of the United States of America, George Washington took the oath of office on the balcony of the Federal Hall in New York City, with his hand on an open Bible.[16] Although it is lengthy, I'm led to print it for you, because many have never heard it. Here is what our first president proclaimed in his inaugural speech:

> Such being the impressions under which I have, in obedience to the public summons, repaired to the present station, it would be peculiarly improper to omit in this first official act my fervent supplications to that Almighty Being who rules over the universe, who presides in the councils of nations, and whose providential aids can supply every human defect, that His benediction may consecrate to the liberties and happiness of the people of the United States a Government instituted by themselves for these essential purposes, and may enable every instrument employed in its administration to execute with success the functions allotted to his charge. In tendering this homage to the Great Author of every public and private good, I assure myself that it expresses your sentiments not less than my own, nor those of my fellow- citizens at large less than either. No people can be bound to acknowledge and adore the Invisible Hand which conducts the affairs of men more than those of the United States. Every step by which they have advanced to the character of an independent

nation seems to have been distinguished by some token of providential agency; and in the important revolution just accomplished in the system of their united government the tranquil deliberations and voluntary consent of so many distinct communities from which the event has resulted can not be compared with the means by which most governments have been established without some return of pious gratitude, along with an humble anticipation of the future blessings which the past seem to presage. These reflections, arising out of the present crisis, have forced themselves too strongly on my mind to be suppressed. You will join with me, I trust, in thinking that there are none under the influence of which the proceedings of a new and free government can more auspiciously commence.

We ought to be no less persuaded that the propitious smiles of Heaven can never be expected on a nation that disregards the eternal rules of order and right which Heaven itself has ordained; and since the preservation of the sacred fire of liberty and the destiny of the republican model of government are justly considered, perhaps, as deeply, as finally, staked on the experiment entrusted to the hands of the American people…

…I shall take my present leave; but not without resorting once more to the benign Parent of the Human Race in humble supplication that, since He has been pleased to favor the American people with opportunities for deliberating in perfect tranquility, and dispositions for deciding with unparalleled unanimity on a form of government for the security of their union and the advancement of their happiness, so His divine blessing may be equally conspicuous in the enlarged views, the temperate consultations, and the wise measures on which the success of this Government must depend.[17]

Six months later, on October 3, 1789, the president issued a National Day of Thanksgiving Proclamation. He states:

> Whereas it is the duty of all nations to acknowledge the providence of Almighty God, to obey His will, to be grateful for His benefits, and humbly to implore His protection and favor…
>
> Now, therefore, I do recommend and assign Thursday, the 26th day of November next, to be devoted by the people of these States to the service of that great and glorious Being who is the beneficent author of all the good that was, that is, or that will be; that we may then all unite in rendering unto Him our sincere and humble thanks for His kind care and protection of the people of this country previous to their becoming a nation; for the signal and manifold mercies and the favorable interpositions of His providence in the course and conclusion of the late war; for the great degree of tranquillity, union, and plenty which we have since enjoyed; for the peaceable and rational manner in which we have been enabled to establish constitutions of government for our safety and happiness, and particularly the national one now lately instituted; for the civil and religious liberty with which we are blessed…
>
> And also that we may then unite in most humbly offering our prayers and supplications to the great Lord and Ruler of Nations, and beseech Him to pardon our national and other transgressions; to enable us all, whether in public or private stations, to perform our several and relative duties properly and punctually; to render our National Government a blessing to all the people by constantly being a Government of wise, just, and constitutional laws, discreetly and faithfully executed and obeyed; to protect and guide all sovereigns and nations (especially such as have shown kindness to us), and

> to bless them with good governments, peace, and concord; to promote the knowledge and practice of true religion and virtue, and the increase of science among them and us; and, generally, to grant unto all mankind such a degree of temporal prosperity as He alone knows to be best.[18]

John Adams (1735–1826) was the second president of the United States of America. Before his election, he served eight years as vice-president. Just prior to the start of the Revolutionary War, he boldly declared of the colonists, "We recognize no sovereign but God, and no King but Jesus!"[19]

John Quincy Adams (1767–1848), the son of John Adams, was the sixth president of the United States. He once said:

> It is no slight testimonial, both to the merit and worth of Christianity, that in all ages since its promulgation the great mass of those who have risen to eminence by their profound wisdom and integrity have recognized and reverenced Jesus of Nazareth as the Son of the living God.[20]

He also wrote, "So great is my veneration for the Bible, that the earlier my children begin to read, the more confident my hope, that they will prove useful citizens of their country and respectable members of society. I have for many years made it a practice to read the Bible through once every year."[21]

Abraham Lincoln (1809–1865) was the sixteenth president of the United States of America. He said, "I believe the Bible is the best gift God has ever given to man."[22] In his Thanksgiving Proclamation in 1863 he said, "It is the duty of nations as well as of men, to own their dependence upon the overruling power of

God, to confess their sins and transgressions in humble sorrow, yet with assured hope that genuine repentance will lead to mercy and pardon."[23]

Patrick Henry (1736–1799) was the American Revolutionary leader and orator who spoke the now-famous phrase, "Give me liberty or give me death!" He was five times elected governor of the state of Virginia and was instrumental in writing the Constitution of Virginia. While he was dying, he said, "Doctor, I wish you to observe how real and beneficial the religion of Christ is to a man about to die."[24]

Even in our time, many years after the founding of this country, President Ronald Reagan declared, "Within the covers of the Bible are all the answers for all the problems men face. The Bible can touch hearts, order minds, and refresh souls."[25] President George W. Bush declares his faith openly.

On February 22, 2002, I was invited to a weekly intercessors prayer meeting. First, I would like to say that it was a very powerful meeting with the awesome presence of the Holy Spirit, who spoke through a number of us. Secondly, there were people in attendance from several foreign countries, like Uganda, Ghana, Zambia, Panama, Trinidad, Japan, the Ukraine, as well as numerous Americans. I was surprised how they all found their way to this home where strong Christians were praying heaven down. Yes, America is a melting pot for all nationalities.

For the many people who live here, especially foreigners who have not had the opportunity to study it, I would like you to read the following.

THE DECLARATION OF INDEPENDENCE, JULY 4, 1776

When in the course of human events, it becomes necessary for one people to dissolve the political bands which have connected them with another, and to assume among the powers of the earth, the separate and equal station to which the laws of nature and of nature's God entitle them, a decent respect to the opinions of mankind requires that they should declare the causes which impel them to the separation.

We hold these truths to be self-evident: That all men are created equal; that they are endowed by their Creator with certain unalienable rights; that among these are life, liberty, and the pursuit of happiness; that, to secure these rights, governments are instituted among men, deriving their just powers from the consent of the governed; that whenever any form of government becomes destructive of these ends, it is the right of the people to alter or to abolish it, and to institute new government, laying its foundation on such principles, and organizing its powers in such form, as to them shall seem most likely to effect their safety and happiness. Prudence, indeed, will dictate that governments long established should not be changed for light and transient causes; and accordingly all experience hath shown that mankind are more disposed to suffer, while evils are sufferable than to right themselves by abolishing the forms to which they are accustomed. But when a long train of abuses and usurpations, pursuing invariably the same object, evinces a design to reduce them under absolute despotism, it is their right, it is their duty, to throw off such government, and to provide new guards for their future security. Such has been the patient sufferance of these colonies; and such is now the necessity which constrains them to alter their former systems of government. The history of the present King of Great Britain is a history of repeated injuries and usurpations, all having in direct object the establishment of an absolute tyranny over these states. To prove this, let facts be submitted to a candid world.

He has refused his assent to laws, the most wholesome and necessary for the public good.

He has forbidden his governors to pass laws of immediate and pressing importance, unless suspended in their operation till his assent should be obtained; and, when so suspended, he has utterly neglected to attend to them.

He has refused to pass other laws for the accommodation of large districts of people, unless those people would relinquish the right of representation in the legislature, a right inestimable to them, and formidable to tyrants only.

He has called together legislative bodies at places unusual uncomfortable, and distant from the depository of their public records, for the sole purpose of fatiguing them into compliance with his measures.

He has dissolved representative houses repeatedly, for opposing, with manly firmness, his invasions on the rights of the people.

He has refused for a long time, after such dissolutions, to cause others to be elected; whereby the legislative powers, incapable of annihilation, have returned to the people at large for their exercise; the state remaining, in the mean time, exposed to all the dangers of invasions from without and convulsions within.

He has endeavored to prevent the population of these states; for that purpose obstructing the laws for naturalization of foreigners; refusing to pass others to encourage their migration hither, and raising the conditions of new appropriations of lands.

He has obstructed the administration of justice, by refusing his assent to laws for establishing judiciary powers.

He has made judges dependent on his will alone, for the tenure of their offices, and the amount and payment of their salaries.

He has erected a multitude of new offices, and sent hither swarms of officers to harass our people and eat out their substance.

He has kept among us, in times of peace, standing armies, without the consent of our legislatures.

He has affected to render the military independent of, and superior to, the civil power.

He has combined with others to subject us to a jurisdiction foreign to our Constitution and unacknowledged by our laws, giving his assent to their acts of pretended legislation:

For quartering large bodies of armed troops among us;

For protecting them, by a mock trial, from punishment for any murders which they should commit on the inhabitants of these states;

For cutting off our trade with all parts of the world;

For imposing taxes on us without our consent;

For depriving us, in many cases, of the benefits of trial by jury;

For transporting us beyond seas, to be tried for pretended offenses;

For abolishing the free system of English laws in a neighboring province, establishing therein an arbitrary government, and enlarging its boundaries, so as to render it at once an example and fit instrument for introducing the same absolute rule into these colonies;

For taking away our charters, abolishing our most valuable laws, and altering fundamentally the forms of our governments;

For suspending our own legislatures, and declaring themselves invested with power to legislate for us in all cases whatsoever.

He has abdicated government here, by declaring us out of his protection and waging war against us.

He has plundered our seas, ravaged our coasts, burned our towns, and destroyed the lives of our people.

He is at this time transporting large armies of foreign mercenaries to complete the works of death, desolation, and tyranny already begun with circumstances of cruelty and perfidy scarcely paralleled in the most barbarous ages, and totally unworthy the head of a civilized nation.

He has constrained our fellow-citizens, taken captive on the high seas, to bear arms against their country, to become the executioners of their friends and brethren, or to fall themselves by their hands.

He has excited domestic insurrection among us, and has endeavored to bring on the inhabitants of our frontiers the merciless Indian savages, whose known rule of warfare is an undistinguished destruction of all ages, sexes, and conditions.

In every stage of these oppressions we have petitioned for redress in the most humble terms; our repeated petitions have been answered only by repeated injury. A prince, whose character is thus marked by every act which may define a tyrant, is unfit to be the ruler of a free people.

Nor have we been wanting in our attentions to our British brethren. We have warned them, from time to time, of attempts by their legislature to extend an unwarrantable jurisdiction over us. We have reminded them of the circumstances of our emigration and settlement here. We have appealed to their native justice and magnanimity; and we have conjured them, by the ties of our common kindred, to disavow these usurpations which would inevitably interrupt our connections and correspondence. They too, have been deaf to the voice of justice and of consanguinity. We must, therefore, acquiesce in the necessity which denounces our separation, and hold them as we hold the rest of mankind, enemies in war, in peace friends.

We, therefore, the representatives of the United States of America, in General Congress assembled, appealing to the Supreme Judge of the world for the rectitude of our intentions, do, in the name and by the authority of the good people of these colonies solemnly publish and declare, That these United Colonies are, and of right ought to be, free and independent states; that they are absolved from all allegiance to the British crown and that all political connection between them and the state of Great Britain is, and ought to be, totally dissolved; and that, as free and independent states, they have full power to levy war, conclude peace, contract alliances, establish commerce, and do all other acts and things which independent states may of right do. And for the support of this declaration, with a firm reliance on the protection of Divine Providence, we mutually pledge to each other our lives, our fortunes, and our sacred honor.

—John Hancock, President

New Hampshire: Josiah Bartlett, William Whipple, Matthew Thornton

Massachusetts Bay: Samuel Adams, John Adams, Robert Treat Paine, Elbridge Gerry

Rhode island: Stephen Hopkins, William Ellery

Connecticut: Roger Sherman, Samuel Huntington, Oliver Wolcott; William williams

New York: William Floyd, Philip Livingston, Francis Lewis, Lewis Morris

New Jersey: Richard Stockton, John Witherspoon, Francis Hopkinson, John Hart, Abraham Clark
Pennsylvania: Robert Morris, Benjamin Rush, Benjamin Franklin, John Morton, George Clymer, James Smith, George Taylor, James Wilson, George Ross
Delaware: Caesar Rodney, George Read, Thomas McKean
Maryland: Samuel Chase, William Paca, Thomas Stone, Charles Carroll of Carrollton
Virginia: Gorge Wythe, Richard Henry Lee, Thomas Jefferson, Benjamin Harrison, Thomas Nelson, Jr., Francis Lightfoot Lee, Carter Braxton
North Carolina: William Hooper, Joseph Hewes, John Penn
South Carolina: Edward Rutledge, Thomas Heyward, Jr., Thomas Lynch, Jr., Arthur Middleton
Georgia: Button Gwinnett, Lyman Hall, George Walton[26]

These names of the fifty-six men who signed the Declaration of Independence are listed under the name of the states they represented. John Hancock, then president of the Congress, signed on July 4. Most of the others signed on August 2.[27]

> Did you know that 52 of the 56 signers of The Declaration of Independence were orthodox, deeply committed Christians? The other four all believed in the Bible as the divine truth, the God of scripture, and His personal intervention. Immediately after creating the Declaration of Independence, the Continental Congress voted to purchase and import 20,000 copies of scripture for the people of this nation.[28]

Most of this information was not taught after the early 60s. Our courts have seen to that.

Thomas Jefferson, the chairman of the American Bible Society wrote in the front of his Bible, "I am a Christian, that is to say a disciple of the doctrines of Jesus."

> James Madison, the primary author of the Constitution of the United States, said this: "We have staked the whole future of our new nation, not upon the power of government; far from it. We have staked the future of all our political constitutions upon the capacity of each of ourselves to govern ourselves according to the moral principles of the Ten Commandments."[29]

It is too bad that the Ten Commandments are now ordered to be removed from court. We have slipped a long way!

> Calvin Coolidge, our 30th President of the United States reaffirmed this truth when he wrote, "The foundations of our society and our government rest so much on the teachings of the Bible that it would be difficult to support them if faith in these teachings would cease to be practically universal in our country."[30]

Let us examine on what principal the government systems of certain modern countries were founded:

1. *America* was founded on the gospel of Jesus Christ—one nation under God. The gospel is the good news of the Bible. When the Pilgrims who experienced great hardships arrived here, their most precious possession was their Geneva

Bible. They had a bright hope for the future and a consuming passion to advance the kingdom of Christ. This is the reason they came here, to worship the Lord.

2. *Israel* was founded on Judaism, a religion developed among the ancient Hebrews and marked by belief in one God who is Creator, Ruler, and Redeemer of the universe. It is based in the moral and ceremonial laws of the Old Testament and the rabbinic tradition.
3. *China* was founded on Confucianism. It explains the reason for the Chinese zodiac.

> The Chinese Zodiac is based on a twelve year cycle—each year being represented by an animal that imparts distinct characteristics to its year. Many Chinese believe that the year of a person's birth is the primary factor in determining that person's personality traits, physical and mental attributes and degree of success and happiness throughout his lifetime.[31]

4. *South Arabia* was founded on Islam, the faith of Muslims.
5. *Russia* was founded on atheism, a belief that there is no God.
6. *Haiti*: Haiti was dedicated to Satan in 1791 in exchange for his help in gaining the people's independence from the French. President Aristide renewed this dedication in 1991.[32]

Can you see the contrast in these countries and the shape they have turned out to be in spiritually?

If you're still in doubt, then visit Washington D.C. and examine it for yourself. The displays edged in the walls many years ago and life-sized statutes are a reminder of our Christian heritage. The Washington Monument for example has many descriptions, such as 'Search the scriptures' including a scripture out of Proverbs 22:6, "Train up a child in the way he should go: and when he is old, he will not depart from it." Need I say any more?

The American Flag

Do You Know the History of the Early American Flag?

America had a flag—the Continental Colors—even before the Declaration of Independence in 1775. It included red and white stripes, but instead of stars it retained the British Flag in the upper left corner.

After American gained its independence, the Continental Congress removed the British flag from the corner and replaced it with thirteen stars on a blue field. There was no official arrangement for the stars. In fact, the famous "Betsy Ross" arrangement of thirteen stars in a circle was rarely used. The most popular style had alternating rows of three, two, three, two, and three stars.

After Vermont and Kentucky became states in 1791 and 1792, two additional stars were added to the blue field. By 1818, after five more states had joined the Union, a new flag law established that with the admittance of each state, one star would be added to the blue field, effective on the upcoming Fourth of July. The longest time the flag was without a change was between 1912 and 1959, with forty-eight stars for a period of forty-seven years.

Alaska gained statehood in 1959, and the last star was added to the flag on July 4, 1960, when Hawaii became the fiftieth state. As a guide for the proper use and display of the flag, a code was drawn up at the National Flag Conference in Washington, D.C., in 1923. That code later became law. The code specifies, "It is the universal custom to display the flag only from sunrise to sunset…However, when a patriotic effect is desired, the flag may be displayed twenty-four hours a day if properly illuminated during the hours of darkness."[33] June 14 is America's Flag Day.

THE MEANING OF A FLAG-DRAPED COFFIN

…The honor guard pays meticulous attention to correctly fold the United States of America's Flag 13 times…

The 1st fold of the flag is a symbol of life.

The 2nd fold is a symbol of the belief in eternal life.

The 3rd fold is made in honor and remembrance of the veterans departing the ranks who gave a portion of their lives for the defense of the country…

The 4th fold represents the weaker nature, for as American citizens trusting in God, it is to Him we turn in times of peace as well as in time of war…

The 5th fold is a tribute to the country…

The 6th fold is for where people's hearts lie. It is with their heart that they pledge allegiance to the flag of the United States of America…

The 7th fold is a tribute to its armed forces…

The 8th fold is a tribute to the one who entered into the valley of the shadow of death, that we might see the light of day.

The 9th fold is a tribute to womanhood, and mothers…

The 10th fold is a tribute to the father, for he, too, has given his sons and daughters for the defense of their country…

The 11th fold represents the lower portion of the seal of King David and King Solomon…

The 12th fold represents an emblem of eternity and glorifies, in the Christian's eyes, God the father, the Son and the Holy Spirit.

The 13th fold, or when the flag is completely folded, the stars are uppermost reminding them of their nation's motto, "In God We Trust."

After the flag is completely folded and tucked in, it takes on the appearance of a cocked hat, ever reminding us of the soldiers who served under General George Washington…[34]

Have You Ever Examined a Dollar Bill?

…This one-dollar bill you're looking at first came off the press in 1957 in its present design.

This so-called paper money is in fact a cotton and linen blend, with red and blue minute silk fibers running through it. It is actually material. We've all washed it without it falling apart. A special blend of ink is used…It is overprinted with symbols and then it is starched to make it water resistant and pressed to give it that nice crisp look.

If you look on the front of the bill, you will see the United States Treasury Seal.…If you turn the bill over, you will see two circles. Both circles, together, comprise the great Seal of the United States. The First Continental Congress requested

> that Benjamin Franklin and a group of men come up with the Seal. It took them four years to accomplish this task and another two years to get it approved. If you look at the left hand circle, you will see a Pyramid.... "In God We Trust" is on this currency. The Latin above the Pyramid, *Annuit Coeptis,* means, "God has favored our undertaking." The Latin below the Pyramid, *Novus Ordo Seclorum,* means "a new order has begun." At the base of the Pyramid is the Roman numeral for 1776....
>
> The Bald Eagle was selected as a symbol for victory for two reasons: first, she is not afraid of a storm; she is strong and she is smart enough to soar above it. Secondly, she wears no material crown. We had just broken from the King of England....
>
> In the Eagle's beak you will read, *E Pluribus Unum,* meaning "one nation from many people" or "from many, one"....[35]

Our churches were filled for a short period after the September 11, 2001, terrorist attacks and the people became very patriotic, displaying all kinds of flags and stickers on their cars and homes. But God wants our whole nation to repent from the debt of our hearts for the sins we had committed prior to that event and are still continuing to commit. If God created the world in six days, He also controls it.

We read in the Bible that the shedding of innocent blood will put a curse on the land. Genesis 9:6 says, "Whoso sheddeth man's blood, by man shall his blood be shed: for in the image of God made he man." Are earthquakes, hurricanes, tornados, and fires, all of which have our food supply way down, the result of our sin?

I'm not telling anyone how to live, because each one of us will have to give an answer one day when we stand before God. He tells us in Genesis 9:7, "And you, be ye fruitful, and multiply; bring forth abundantly in the earth, and multiply therein." Some people have no idea what the Bible clearly tells us in Romans 1:17–32:

> For therein is the righteousness of God revealed from faith to faith: as it is written, The just shall live by faith. For the wrath of God is revealed from heaven against all ungodliness and unrighteousness of men, who hold the truth in unrighteousness; Because that which may be known of God is manifest in them; for God hath shewed it unto them. For the invisible things of him from the creation of the world are clearly seen, being understood by the things that are made, even his eternal power and Godhead; so that they are without excuse: Because that, when they knew God, they glorified him not as God, neither were thankful; but became vain in their imaginations, and their foolish heart was darkened. Professing themselves to be wise, they became fools, And changed the glory of the uncorruptible God into an image made like to corruptible man, and to birds, and fourfooted beasts, and creeping things. Wherefore God also gave them up to uncleanness through the lusts of their own hearts, to dishonour their own bodies between themselves: Who changed the truth of God into a lie, and worshipped and served the creature more than the Creator, who is blessed for ever. Amen. For this cause God gave them up unto vile affections: for even their women did change the natural use into that which is against nature: And likewise also the men, leaving the natural use of the woman, burned in their lust one toward another; men with men working that which is unseemly, and receiving in themselves that recompence of their error which was meet. And even as they did not like to retain God in their knowledge, God gave

> them over to a reprobate mind, to do those things which are not convenient; Being filled with all unrighteousness, fornication, wickedness, covetousness, maliciousness; full of envy, murder, debate, deceit, malignity; whisperers, Backbiters, haters of God, despiteful, proud, boasters, inventors of evil things, disobedient to parents, Without understanding, covenantbreakers, without natural affection, implacable, unmerciful: Who knowing the judgment of God, that they which commit such things are worthy of death, not only do the same, but have pleasure in them that do them.

The tsunami catastrophe on the December 26, 2004—a huge sea wave caused by an undersea earthquake—showed the whole world the willingness of the American people to help. The American public contributed billions of dollars to relief efforts, besides Christian ministries' and the government's contribution. Signs were posted everywhere requesting donations for the victims from eleven different countries—of which many were vacationing there when the tsunami hit. Other countries sent volunteers and money. American airplanes, helicopters, and military personnel were volunteered, no questions asked. The need was great, so the mentality was, "Let's pitch in and provide the needed aid."

This is the American spirit. Why, then, are we hated by so many? I believe that it is mainly a spiritual matter. They hate the God we serve.

Many of those who died in the tsunami were children. We also know, according to the Bible, that if the children are not yet of the age of accountability, they automatically go to heaven. If you have lost loved ones under this age, you could see them again and be reunited with them when you die if you have made heaven your home. We read in Psalm 127:3, "Lo, children are an heritage of the Lord: and the fruit of the womb is his reward."

Our God is an all-powerful God. Why don't you ask Him to answer your prayers? We read in 2 Corinthians 4:3–7:

> But if our gospel be hid, it is hid to them that are lost: In whom the god of this world hath blinded the minds of them which believe not, lest the light of the glorious gospel of Christ, who is the image of God, should shine unto them. For we preach not ourselves, but Christ Jesus the Lord; and ourselves your servants for Jesus' sake. For God, who commanded the light to shine out of darkness, hath shined in our hearts, to give the light of the knowledge of the glory of God in the face of Jesus Christ. But we have this treasure in earthen vessels, that the excellency of the power may be of God, and not of us.

Psalm 46:8, 10 tells us, "Come, behold the works of the Lord, what desolations he hath made in the earth.... Be still, and know that I am God: I will be exalted among the heathen, I will be exalted in the earth."

This is the reason we need to repent of our sins and follow the true God. Let me explain it to you with Scriptures.

> Now while Paul waited for them [Silas and Timotheus] at Athens, his spirit was stirred in him, when he saw the city wholly given to idolatry.....And they took him, and brought him unto Areopagus, saying, May we know what this new doctrine, whereof thou speakest, is? For thou bringest certain strange things to our ears: we would know therefore what these things mean.... Then Paul stood in the midst of Mars' hill, and said, Ye men of Athens, I perceive that in all things ye are too superstitious. For as I passed by, and beheld your devotions,

> I found an altar with this inscription, TO THE UNKNOWN GOD. Whom therefore ye ignorantly worship, him declare I unto you. God that made the world and all things therein, seeing that he is Lord of heaven and earth, dwelleth not in temples made with hands; Neither is worshipped with men's hands, as though he needed any thing, seeing he giveth to all life, and breath, and all things; And hath made of one blood all nations of men for to dwell on all the face of the earth, and hath determined the times before appointed, and the bounds of their habitation; That they should seek the Lord, if haply they might feel after him, and find him, though he be not far from every one of us: For in him we live, and move, and have our being; as certain also of your own poets have said, For we are also his offspring. Forasmuch then as we are the offspring of God, we ought not to think that the Godhead is like unto gold, or silver, or stone, graven by art and man's device. And the times of this ignorance God winked at; but now commandeth all men every where to repent: Because he hath appointed a day, in the which he will judge the world in righteousness by that man whom he hath ordained; whereof he hath given assurance unto all men, in that he hath raised him from the dead. And when they heard of the resurrection of the dead, some mocked: and others said, We will hear thee again of this matter.
>
> —Acts 17:16, 19–20, 22–32

The Apostle Paul declared in Romans 1:16, "For I am not ashamed of the gospel of Christ: for it is the power of God unto salvation to every one that believeth; to the Jew first, and also to the Greek."

Our country has been spared from many large-scale natural disasters, except for several earthquakes and fires in California, but are government officials in certain countries messing with nature by having a one- or two-child per family policy? Do all the baby girls get aborted? Is the young man later responsible to take care of his aging parents after first serving in the military? Who are their men going to marry in times to come if they abort all the baby girls? Do they have to import wives for them then? Is God's judgment imminent?

> Whose voice then shook the earth: but now he hath promised, saying, Yet once more I shake not the earth only, but also heaven.
>
> —Hebrews 12:26

> Thus saith the Lord of hosts, Behold, evil shall go forth from nation to nation, and a great whirlwind shall be raised up from the coasts of the earth.
>
> —Jeremiah 25:32

> For I bear them record that they have a zeal of God, but not according to knowledge. For they being ignorant of God's righteousness, and going about to establish their own righteousness, have not submitted themselves unto the righteousness of God. For Christ is the end of the law for righteousness to every one that believeth.... That if thou shalt confess with thy mouth the Lord Jesus, and shalt believe in thine heart that God hath raised him from the dead, thou shalt be saved. For with the heart man believeth unto righteousness; and with the mouth confession is made unto salvation. For the scripture saith, Whosoever believeth on him shall not be ashamed.... So then faith cometh by hearing, and hearing by the word of God.
>
> —Romans 10:2–4, 9–11, 17

> For who hath known the mind of the Lord? or who hath been his counsellor?
>
> —Romans 11:34

> I am sought of them that asked not for me; I am found of them that sought me not: I said, Behold me, behold me, unto a nation that was not called by my name.
>
> —Isaiah 65:1

> Ask of me, and I shall give thee the heathen for thine inheritance, and the uttermost parts of the earth for thy possession.
>
> —Psalm 2:8

Jesus Himself tells us in Luke 21:25–26, 31–33, 35–36:

> And there shall be signs in the sun, and in the moon, and in the stars; and upon the earth distress of nations, with perplexity; the sea and the waves roaring; Men's hearts failing them for fear, and for looking after those things which are coming on the earth: for the powers of heaven shall be shaken.... So likewise ye, when ye see these things come to pass, know ye that the kingdom of God is nigh at hand. Verily I say unto you, This generation shall not pass away, till all be fulfilled. Heaven and earth shall pass away: but my words shall not pass away.... For as a snare shall it come on all them that dwell on the face of the whole earth. Watch ye therefore, and pray always, that ye may be accounted worthy to escape all these things that shall come to pass, and to stand before the Son of man.

Number of Earthquakes Worldwide and Mortality Figures for 1987–September 2004[36]

Magnitude	1987	1988	1989	1990	1991	1992	1993	1994	1995	1996	1997	1998	1999	2000	2001	2002	2003	2004
8.0–9.9	0	0	1	0	0	0	1	2	3	1	0	1	0	1	1	0	1	2
7.0–7.9	11	8	6	12	11	23	15	13	22	21	20	11	18	14	15	13	14	13
6.0–6.9	112	93	79	115	105	104	141	161	185	160	125	117	128	158	126	132	140	128
5.0–5.9	1437	1485	1444	1635	1469	1541	1449	1542	1327	1223	1118	979	1106	1345	1243	1183	1203	1180
4.0–4.9	4146	4018	4090	4493	4372	5196	5034	4544	8140	8794	7938	7303	7042	8045	8084	8620	8462	10008
3.0–3.9	1806	1932	2452	2457	2952	4643	4263	5000	5002	4869	4467	5945	5521	4784	6151	7006	7624	7093
2.0–2.9	1037	1479	1906	2364	2927	3068	5390	5369	3838	2388	2397	4091	4201	3758	4162	6420	7727	6037
1.0–1.9	102	118	418	474	801	887	1177	779	645	295	388	805	715	1026	944	1137	2506	1336
.1–.9	0	3	0	0	1	2	9	17	19	1	4	10	5	5	1	10	134	103
No mag.	2639	3575	4189	5062	3878	4084	3997	1944	1826	2186	3415	2426	2096	3120	2807	2935	3608	3292
Total	11290	12711	14585	16612	16516	19548	21476	19371	21007	19938	19872	21688	20832	22256	23534	27456	31419	29189
Deaths	1080	26552	617	51916	2326	3814	10036	1038	7949	419	2907	9430	22662	231	21357	1712	33819	22908

Numerous Earthquakes Are Mentioned in the Bible

The end of this age connects the judgments of God with signs and wonders, including earthquakes. I will give you Scripture references from the Old and New Testament that prophesy about the increase in earthquakes on the earth before Jesus' return, called the second coming of our Lord Jesus Christ. In spite of all the examples of earthquakes through the centuries, we have seen nothing yet compared to the last one to come.

At Sinai, before the giving of the Ten Commandments

> And mount Sinai was altogether on a smoke, because the Lord descended upon it in fire: and the smoke thereof ascended as the smoke of a furnace, and the whole mount quaked greatly.
>
> —Exodus 19:18

At the rebellion of Korah

> And the earth opened her mouth, and swallowed them up, and their houses, and all the men that appertained unto Korah, and all their goods.
>
> —Numbers 16:32

At Jonathan's defeat of the Philistines

> And there was trembling in the host, in the field, and among all the people: the garrison, and the spoilers, they also trembled, and the earth quaked: so it was a very great trembling.
>
> —1 Samuel 14:15

Releasing Paul from prison at Philippi

And suddenly there was a great earthquake, so that the foundations of the prison were shaken: and immediately all the doors were opened, and every one's bands were loosed.

—ACTS 16:26

As a revelation of God's power

And he said, Go forth, and stand upon the mount before the LORD. And, behold, the LORD passed by, and a great and strong wind rent the mountains, and brake in pieces the rocks before the LORD; but the LORD was not in the wind: and after the wind an earthquake; but the LORD was not in the earthquake.

—1 KINGS 19:11

As a natural calamity

Though the waters thereof roar and be troubled, though the mountains shake with the swelling thereof. Selah.

—PSALM 46:3

As a sign of God's power

He looketh on the earth, and it trembleth: he toucheth the hills, and they smoke.

—PSALM 104:32

At the death of Jesus Christ

> And, behold, the veil of the temple was rent in twain from the top to the bottom; and the earth did quake, and the rocks rent....Now when the centurion, and they that were with him, watching Jesus, saw the earthquake, and those things that were done, they feared greatly, saying, Truly this was the Son of God.
>
> —Mathew 27:51, 54

Earthquakes Prophesied for the Final Days

Speaking of God's future power

> Therefore I will shake the heavens, and the earth shall remove out of her place, in the wrath of the Lord of hosts, and in the day of his fierce anger.
>
> —Isaiah 13:13

Of the Lord's future judgments

> The earth shall reel to and fro like a drunkard, and shall be removed like a cottage; and the transgression thereof shall be heavy upon it; and it shall fall, and not rise again.
>
> —Isaiah 24:20

A sign of coming judgment

> The words of Amos, who was among the herdmen of Tekoa, which he saw concerning Israel in the days of Uzziah king of Judah, and in the days of Jeroboam the son of Joash king of Israel, two years before the earthquake.
>
> —Amos 1:1

As a sign of God's power

The mountains quake at him, and the hills melt, and the earth is burned at his presence, yea, the world, and all that dwell therein.

—Nahum 1:5

Speaking of God's power

For thus saith the Lord of hosts; Yet once, it is a little while, and I will shake the heavens, and the earth, and the sea, and the dry land.

—Haggai 2:6

Whose voice then shook the earth: but now he hath promised, saying, Yet once more I shake not the earth only, but also heaven.

—Hebrews 12:26

At the Messiah's return upon the Mt. of Olives

And ye shall flee to the valley of the mountains; for the valley of the mountains shall reach unto Azal: yea, ye shall flee, like as ye fled from before the earthquake in the days of Uzziah king of Judah: and the Lord my God shall come, and all the saints with thee.

—Zechariah 14:5

Christ speaking of the end of this age

For nation shall rise against nation, and kingdom against kingdom: and there shall be famines, and pestilences, and earthquakes, in divers [various] places.

—Matthew 24:7

> For nation shall rise against nation, and kingdom against kingdom: and there shall be earthquakes in divers places, and there shall be famines and troubles: these are the beginnings of sorrows.
>
> —Mark 13:8

> And great earthquakes shall be in divers places, and famines, and pestilences; and fearful sights and great signs shall there be from heaven.
>
> —Luke 21:11

End-time judgment of modern Babylon

> And there were voices, and thunders, and lightnings; and there was a great earthquake, such as was not since men were upon the earth, so mighty an earthquake, and so great.... And every island fled away, and the mountains were not found.
>
> —Revelation 16:18, 20

Prophesied End-Time Floods

> Thou carriest them away as with a flood.
>
> —Psalm 90:5

Are we witnessing the fulfillment of the prophesies leading up to the beginning of the Tribulation period?

Here is a partial list of floods since 1992:

- August 24, 1992—Hurricane Andrew slammed across Florida.

- March 12–15, 1993—Upwards of fifty inches of snow covered the Eastern Seaboard of North America from Cuba to Canada.
- June 27, 1993—The upper Mississippi and Missouri Rivers overflowed, creating a temporary great lake.
- August 1–10, 1993—Two typhoons and a tidal wave swept over Japan.
- August 1993—Tropical storm Bret flooded Caracas, Venezuela.
- August 21, 1993—Flooding in Nepal, Malaysia, Bangladesh, and China. Floods covered over half of the landmass of the Himalayan kingdom of Nepal. Over 1,100 were drowned. China coined a new phrase to describe flooding—"black rain."
- October 1993—Europe suffered spectacular flooding through the entire month.
- December 25, 1993—The second time around Europe; over 50,000 were left homeless.
- December 26, 1993—Algiers, Algeria, suffered rain-soaked mudslides; twelve killed, forty-six injured.
- January–March 1994—Several snow and ice storms destroyed millions of trees across the United States from Arkansas to the East Coast.
- March 27, 1994—Devastating tornadoes hit Alabama and adjoining states.

- July 6, 1994—Tropical storm Alberto dumped twenty-one inches of rain in Georgia. It was the worst flooding in one hundred years.
- October 15, 1994—North Houston, Texas, was under as much as fifteen feet of water.
- October 15, 1994—Greece flooded.
- October 16, 1994—A typhoon swept across Indonesia.
- November 1–15, 1994—Egypt flooded for the first time since Noah's flood.
- November 8–11, 1994—France and Italy suffered intense flooding again.
- November 8–21, 1994—Hurricane Gordon killed 829 people in Haiti, Jamaica, Cuba, and Florida.

This is just a partial listing of devastating floods throughout the world.

> The floods have lifted up, O Lord, the floods have lifted up their voice; the floods lift up their waves.
>
> —Psalm 93:3

From what I understand, the Katrina incident was the cause of faulty construction.

This U. S. Geological Survey is from the National Earthquake Information Center. Following are thirty-five earthquakes listed in *The World Almanac and Book of Facts 2008*.

- 1998
  May 30—Northeast Afghanistan
  June 27—Adana, Turkey

- 1999

  January 25—Armenia, Columbia
  August 17—Western Turkey
  September 7—Athens, Greece
  September 21—Taichung, Taiwan
  November 12—Duzce, Turkey

- 2000

  June 4—Sumatra, Indonesia

- 2001

  January 13—San Vicente, El Salvador
  January 26—Gujarat, India
  February 13—San Vicente, El Salvador
  June 23—Arequipa, Peru

- 2002

  February 3—Central Turkey
  March 3—North Afghanistan
  March 25–26—Nahrin, north Afghanistan
  April 12—Hindu Kush, Afghanistan
  June 22—West Iran

- 2003

  January 22—Colima, Mexico
  February 24—South Xinjiang Province, China
  May 1—East Turkey
  May 21—North Algeria
  December 26—Bam, southeast Iran

- 2004
  February 04—Papua, Indonesia
  February 24—Al Hozeima, northeast Morocco
  May 28—North Iran
  December 26—North Sumatra, Indonesia

- 2005
  February 22—Central Iran
  March 28—Islands off Sumatra, Indonesia
  October 8—Kashmir, Pakistan, India

- 2006
  March 31—West Iran
  May 27—Java, Indonesia
  July 17—south of Java, Indonesia

- 2007
  March 6—South Sumatra, Indonesia
  August 15—North coast of central Peru[37]

Our Savior Jesus Christ spoke of the future Tribulation period

> But as the days of Noah were, so shall also the coming of the Son of man be. For as in the days that were before the flood they were eating and drinking, marrying and giving in marriage, until the day that Noe entered into the ark, And knew not until the flood came, and took them all away; so shall also the coming of the Son of man be.
>
> —Matthew 24:37–39

Let's each and every one of us make an effort to return this great country of America, which is made up of people from many nations, to what our forefathers intended it to be.

BIBLIOGRAPHY

Guilttner, Jerry. "Mormons to Celebrate Joseph Smith's Birth." *Bible in the News*. March 2005. N–169.

Kuske, David P. *Luther's Catechism.* The Board for Parish Education.

Luther, Martin. *Basic Luther.* Springfield, IL: Templegate Publishers, 1994.

Makrakis, Apostolos. *Divine and Sacred Catechism.* Chicago: Hellenic Christian Society, 1946.

O'Neill, Judith. *Martin Luther.* Cambridge University Press, 1975.

Pringle, Ray S., Sr. *Per-versions of the Bible.* Jacksonville, FL: Word of Prophecy Fellowship, 1999.

Reidt, Wilford. *John G. Lake: A Man Without Compromise.* Tulsa, OK: Harrison House, 1989.

Riplinger, G. A. *New Age Versions.* Ararat, VA: A. V. Publications Corporation, 1997.

Notes

Chapter 1
Facing the Facts

1. Jim Pye, "B.C.P.Trinity 8 Matthew 7:15–21 10/8/03," Sermon's Plus,http://www.sermonsplus.co.uk/Matthew%207.15-21.htm(accessed October 29, 2008).

2. "Report 1: Religious Affiliation," *U.S. Religious Landscape Survey*, The Pew Forum on Religion and Public Life, http://religions.pewforum.org/reports# (accessed October 29, 2008).

3. "Revival or Apostasy?" The Jeremiah Project, http://www.jeremiahproject.com/prophecy/revival.html (accessed October 29, 2008).

4. "Religious Beliefs Remain Constant but Subgroups Are Quite Different," The Barna Group, March 19, 2004, http://www.barna.org/FlexPage.aspx?Page=BarnaUpdate&BarnaUpdateID=160 (accessed October 29, 2008).

5. "Evangelism Is Most Effective Among Kids," The Barna Group, October 11, 2004, http://www.barna.org/FlexPage.aspx?Page=BarnaUpdate&BarnaUpdateID=172 (accessed October 29, 2008).

6. John MacArthur, "Understanding the Issues," Bible Bulletin Board, http://www.biblebb.com/files/MAC/sg1948.htm (accessed October 29, 2008).

7. "Partial Birth Abortion: D & X," Pro-Life SA; http://www.lifesa.asn.au/01_22_partial.htm (accessed October 10, 2008).

8. Tanya LeBlanc, "The Baby's Cry," http://smiley00.tripod.com/poem331.html (accessed October 10, 2008).

9. "Abortion and the African-American Community," New York State Right to Life Committee, Inc., http://www.nysrighttolife.org/Education/Abortion%20&%20the%20African-American%20Community.htm (accessed October 29, 2008).

10. "Beliefs About Jesus' Resurrection Among Christian Laity and Clergy," *Religious Tolerance*, Ontario Consultants on Religious Tolerance, http://www.religioustolerance.org/resurrec8.htm (accessed October 29, 2008).

11. *Strong's Exhaustive Concordance of the Bible* (Nashville, TN: Royal Publishers, Inc., 1979), s.v. "glory."

Chapter 2
Is It Revival?

1. "Evangelist Reinhard Bonnke: A Biography," Christ for all Nations, http://us.cfan.org/Reinhard-Bonnke-Biography.aspx (accessed October 29, 2008).

2. "John G. Lake: A Man of Faith and Works," Christian Assemblies International, http://www.cai.org/bible-studies/john-g-lake-man-faith-and-works (accessed October 30, 2008).

Chapter 3
When Will He Return?

1. Henry Crocker, "Evangelize," CrossGlobal Link, http://www.crossgloballink.org/Spring_2007 (accessed October 10, 2008).

Chapter 7
Different Holidays

1. "What Does Kwansaa Mean?" WikiAnswers.com, http://wiki.answers.com/Q/What_does_Kwansaa_mean (accessed October 9, 2008).

2. "Kwanzaa," Wikipedia.com, http://en.wikipedia.org/wiki/Kwanzaa (accessed October 9, 2008).

3. Ibid.

4. "Should Christians Observe Thanksgiving?" Hope of Israel Ministries Online, http://www.hope-of-israel.org/thankgiv.htm (accessed October 10, 2008).

5. "Pagan Origins of Easter," Right Division, http://www.rightdivision.com/html/easter_pagan_influences.html (accessed October 10, 2008).

6. Ibid.

7. Lorraine Day, MD, "Christmas: Is It 'Christian' or Pagan?" http://www.goodnewsaboutgod.com/studies/holidays2.htm (accessed October 30, 2008).

8. Ibid.

9. Ibid.

10. "Easter," Catholic Encyclopedia.

11. Niall Kilkenny, "The Vatican and Islam," Reformation.org, http://www.reformation.org/vatican-and-islam.html (accessed October 10, 2008).

12. Ibid.

13. Ibid.

14. Dr. D. A. Waite, "Halloween: The Devil's Birthday," The Flaming Torch, http://www.theflamingtorch.org/archives/2006/halloween-the-devils-birthday.htm (accessed October 10, 2008).

15. "Halloween: Trick or Treat," Gospel Center Church, http://www.gospelcenterchurch.org/halloween.html (accessed October 9, 2008).

16. Marc White, "Oh, It's Not So Bad," *Walk Worthy*, July 14, 2005, http://walkworthy.org/index.php?Itemid=5&id=37&option=com_content&task=view (accessed October 30, 2008).

17. "Halloween: The History of Halloween," Believers Web, http://www.believersweb.org/view.cfm?id=611&rc=1&list=multi (accessed October 30, 2008).

18. "The Truth About Halloween," *Walk Worthy* at InJesus.com, October 15, 2008, http://www.injesus.com/index.php?module=message&task=view&MID=GB007FCI&GroupID=PB0070XJ (accessed October 30, 2008).

19. Barry A. Kosmin, Egon Mayer, and Ariela Keysar, "American Religious Identification Survey 2001," http://www.gc.cuny.edu/faculty/research_briefs/aris.pdf (accessed October 30, 2008).

Chapter 8
Religious Versions—What Is the Truth?

1 "Pope: Other Christians Not True Churches," http://www.christianlifeandliberty.net/CATHOLIC-07-01.DOC (accessed October 9, 2008).

2. "Homily of the Holy Father John Paul II," http://www.vatican.va/holy_father/john_paul_ii/homilies/2002/documents/hf_jp-ii_hom_20020818_beatification-krakow_en.html (accessed October 9, 2008).

3. *Time Webster's New Ideal Dictionary* (G & C Merriam Co., 1978), s.v. "sorcery."

4. Helen L. Owen, "When Did the Catholic Church Decide Priests Should Be Celibate" *History News Network*, George Mason University, April 30, 2002, http://hnn.us/articles/696.html (accessed October 31, 2008).

5. Mark Jenkins and Carol Hilliker, "Why Christmas Is So Important to God," TheTrumpet.com, http://www.thetrumpet.com/index.php?q=2024.2860.0.0 (accessed October 10, 2008).

6. Peter Gasparri, *Catholic Catechism* (New Providence, NJ: P. J. Kenedy and Sons, 1932).

7. Martin Luther, "Disputation of Doctor Martin Luther on the Power and Efficacy of Indulgences," Project Wittenberg, http://www.iclnet.org/pub/resources/text/wittenberg/luther/web/ninetyfive.html (accessed October 10, 2008).

8. "IV: Conventions, Conferences, and Debates," *Martin Luther, a Unique Vessel,* http://www.mluther.org/vessel/4.html (accessed November 3, 2008).

9. Luther at the Imperial Diet of Worms," CDG Wittenberg, http://www.luther.de/en/worms.htm (accessed October 10, 2008).

10. Martin Luther, "Martin Luther's 95 Theses," Project Gutenberg, http://www.gutenberg.org/catalog/world/readfile?fk_files=773195&pageno=1 (accessed October 10, 2008).

11. Charles R. Biggs, "The Story of Martin Luther," Reformation Theology, http://www.reformationtheology.com/2007/10/the_story_of_martin_luther_the.php (accessed October 10, 2008).

12. Martin Luther, "Concerning Christian Liberty," Bartleby.com, http://www.bartleby.com/36/6/2.html (accessed October 10, 2008).

13. Dr. David R. Reagan, "The Legacy of Pope John Paul II," *Lamplighter,* Lamb and Lion Ministries, July–August 2005, pp. 7–9.

14. Source unavailable.

15. "Russell, Charles Taze," The Pennsylvania Center for the Book, http://www.pabook.libraries.psu.edu/palitmap/bios/Russell__Charles_Taze.html (accessed November 3, 2008).

16. "The Failed Prophecies of the Watchtower Bible and Tract Society," TowerWatch Ministries, http://www.towerwatch.com/Witnesses/Prophecies/failed_prophecies.htm (accessed November 3, 2008).

17. "General Information FAQ," Utah Lighthouse Ministry, http://www.utlm.org/faqs/faqgeneral.htm#2 (accessed November 3, 2008).

18. "What About the Mormons or the Church of Jesus Christ of Latter-day Saints?" *True Light Educational Ministry,* http://www.tlem.net/mormons.htm (accessed November 3, 2008).

19. Bill McKeever, "As God Is, Man May Become?" Mormonism Research Ministry, http://www.mrm.org/topics/salvation/god-man-may-become (accessed November 3, 2008).

20. Milton R. Hunter, *The Gospel Through the Ages* (Salt Lake City, UT: Deseret Book Co., 1945), 15.

21. Selwyn Stevens, "Masonic Prayer," Proclaiming His Word Ministries, http://www.healinghouse.org/pubdownloads/MasonicPrayer.ppt (accessed October 10, 2008).

22. "Detailed Description of *The Urantia Book*," Urantia Foundation, http://www.urantia.org/detail.html (accessed November 3, 2008).

23. "Part IV," *The Urantia Book*, http://www.urantia.org/papers/paper120.html (accessed October 10, 2008).

24. Mike Shreve, "Judaism," In Search of the True Light, http://www.thetruelight.net/religions/judaism.htm (accessed October 10, 2008).

25. "False Christs," *Lamplighter*, Lamb and Lion Ministries, July–August 2007, p. 13, http://www.lamblion.com/files/publications/magazines/Lamplighter_JulAug07_Angels.pdf (accessed November 3, 2008).

Chapter 9
The Origin of the Bible

1. Kraig Josiah Rice, "How Do We Know That the Bible Is God's Word and That It Is True?" Bread on the Waters Ministry, http://www.breadonthewaters.com/0062_authenticity_of_bible.html (accessed October 10, 2008).

2. Niall Kilkenny, "The Vatican and Islam," The Reformation Online, http://www.reformation.org/vatican-and-islam.html (accessed October 10, 2008).

3. "How We Got the Bible," http://msandchrist.tripod.com/symbolisminthebible/id6.html (accessed October 10, 2008).

4. Rice.

5. Ibid.

6. "How We Got the Bible."

7. Ibid.

8. Jim Lay, "New Testament Survey Class," http://www.jmlay.com/Special%20Lessons/NT%20Survey%20Part%20One-%20Notes.pdf (accessed October 10, 2008).

9. Ray S. Pringle, Sr., *Per-versions of the Bible, 7th edition* (Word of Prophecy Fellowship, 1999).

CHAPTER 11
THE COST OF BEING SOLD OUT

1. "Hotels Replace Gideon Bibles with 'Sex Kits,'" American Family Association Action Alert, http://www.afa.net/emails/transform.asp?x=hotels_111407&m=11&y=2007&s=browser (accessed October 10, 2008).

2. Frank Bartleman, *Azusa Street* (Orlando, FL: Bridge-Logos Publishers, 1980).

3. Emmanuel Eni, *Delivered from the Powers of Darkness* (Ibadan, Nigeria: Scripture Union Press and Books, 1987).

4. Ibid., 29.

CHAPTER 12
GOD BLESS AMERICA!

1. "Mideast Immigration to US Growing Fast," Center for Immigration Studies, August 14, 2002, http://www.cis.org/articles/2002/mideastcoverage.html (accessed October 10, 2008).

2. "Overview of the Farsi Language," *Transparent Language,* http://www.transparent.com/languagepages/Farsi/overview.htm (accessed November 3, 2008).

3. "On this day in 1865, Forty Acres and a Mule was inacted [sic]," The African American Registry, http://www.aaregistry.com/detail.php?id=705 (accessed October 10, 2008).

4. "Archaeologists Find Evidence of Earliest African Slaves Brought to New World," *Science Daily,* February 1, 2006, http://www.sciencedaily.com/releases/2006/02/060201185928.htm (accessed November 3, 2008).

5. "America Is Rooted in the Christian Faith," Race Matters, http://www.racematters.org/americarootedinchristianity.htm (accessed October 10, 2008).

6. "Founding Fathers Quotes," Eads Home Ministries, http://www.eadshome.com/QuotesoftheFounders.htm (accessed November 3, 2008).

7. "America Is Rooted in the Christian Faith."

8. Mary Jones, "Forsaken Roots," The WTV-Zone, http://www.wtv-zone.com/Mary/forsakenroots.html (accessed October 10, 2008).

9. "America: A Christian Nation," TruthMatters.info, http://truthmatters.info/america-a-christian-nation/ (accessed November 3, 2008).

10. "The Prayer at Valley Forge," *The Prayer at Valley Forge*, http://www.prayer-at-valley-forge.com/ (accessed November 3, 2008).

11. "Today in History: November 25," *Library of Congress*, http://lcweb2.loc.gov/ammem/today/nov25.html (accessed November 3, 2008).

12. Peter J. Marshall, "Was George Washington a Christian, Part 2," April 17, 2008, http://petermarshallministries.com/commentary.cfm?commentary=156 (accessed October 10, 2008).

13. "Massachusetts," *Merriam-Webster's Atlas*, http://www.merriam-webster.com/cgi-bin/mwmapsstu.pl?Massachusetts (accessed November 3, 2008).

14. "General Order Respecting the Observance of the Sabbath," Wallbuilders, http://www.wallbuilders.com/LIBissuesArticles.asp?id=51 (accessed November 3, 2008).

15. "The American Revolution: First War for Independence," GlobalSecurity.org, http://www.globalsecurity.org/military/ops/revolution.htm (accessed November 3, 2008).

16. "Federal Hall, New York," The Constitution Society, http://www.constitution.org/img/fed-hall.htm (accessed November 3, 2008).

17. George Washington, "First Inaugural Address of George Washington," The Avalon Project at Yale Law School, http://www.yale.edu/lawweb/avalon/presiden/inaug/wash1.htm (accessed October 10, 2008).

18. George Washington, "George Washington: Proclamation, A National Thanksgiving," BeliefNet, http://www.beliefnet.com/resourcelib/docs/49/George_Washington_Proclamation_A_National_Thanksgiving_1.html (accessed October 10, 2008).

19. "John Adams," Eads Home Ministries, http://www.eadshome.com/JohnAdams.htm (accessed November 3, 2008).

20. "Other Founding Fathers," America's Christian Heritage, http://www.whateveristrue.com/heritage/ofathers.htm (accessed October 10, 2008).

21. "John Quincy Adams," Eads Home Ministries, http://www.eadshome.com/JohnQuincyAdams.htm (accessed November 3, 2008).

22. "Marvelous Bible Quotes," Bibleresources, http://bibleresources.bible.com/Bquotes.php (accessed October 10, 2008).

23. "Thoughts and Quotations About Thanksgiving," *GodWeb*, http://www.godweb.org/thanksgivingquotes.htm (accessed November 3, 2008).

24. "Last Words of Famous People," *Answers from The Evidence Bible*, http://www.livingwaters.com/witnessingtool/lastwords.shtml (accessed November 3, 2008).

25. "Ronald Reagan," Eads Home Ministries, http://www.eadshome.com/Reagan.htm (accessed November 3, 2008).

26. "The Declaration of Independence," The Avalon Project at Yale Law School, http://www.yale.edu/lawweb/avalon/declare.htm (accessed October 10, 2008).

27. John Dunlap, "The Declaration of Independence," http://www.williams.edu/resources/chapin/exhibits/founding.html#declaration (accessed October 10, 2008).

28. Mary Jones, "Forsaken Roots."

29. Ibid.

30. Ibid.

31. "Chinese Zodiac and Calendar," China Style, http://library.thinkquest.org/05aug/01780/chinese-zodiac-calendar/index.htm (accessed October 10, 2008).

32. Tom Barrett, "Government of the Devil, by the Devil, and for the Devil," *American Daily*, March 11, 2004, http://www.americandaily.com/article/95 (accessed November 3, 2008).

33. "Flag Code," Betsy Ross Homepage, the Independence Hall Association, http://www.ushistory.org/betsy/flagcode.htm (accessed October 10, 2008).

34. "Flag-Draped Coffin," Vandemonium's Weblog, http://vandamonium.wordpress.com/2008/07/17/flag-draped-coffin/#more-437 or http://www.usflag.org/foldflag.html (accessed October 10, 2008).

35. "Understanding the Design and Symbolism of the U.S. One-Dollar Bill," National Institute of Environmental Health Sciences Kids Pages, http://kids.niehs.nih.gov/triviadollar.htm (accessed October 10, 2008).

36. Noah W. Hutchings, "The Christmas Earthquake of 2004: Its Prophetic Relevance," *Prophetic Observer*, January 2005, Vol. 12, No. 1, pp. 2–3.

37. C. Alan Joyce, ed., *The World Almanac and Book of Facts 2008, 1st ed.* (New York City, NY: World Almanac Books, 2007).

To Contact the Author

Tilly Steward
P.O. Box 44158
Tacoma, WA 98448